Hoop Lore

Hoop Lore

A History of the
National Basketball Association

CONNIE KIRCHBERG

Foreword by JIM BARNETT

McFarland & Company, Inc., Publishers

Jefferson, North Carolina, and London

Connie Kirchberg and coauthor Marc Hendrickx are the
authors of *Elvis Presley, Richard Nixon, and the American Dream*
(McFarland, 1999)

LIBRARY OF CONGRESS CATALOGUING-IN-PUBLICATION DATA

Kirchberg, Connie, 1956–
    Hoop lore : a history of the National Basketball Association /
Connie Kirchberg ; foreword by Jim Barnett.
        p.   cm.
    Includes bibliographical references and index.

    ISBN-13: 978-0-7864-2673-7
    ISBN-10: 0-7864-2673-X
    (softcover : 50# alkaline paper) ∞

    1. National Basketball Association — History.   I. Title.
    GV885.515.N37K57   2007
    796.323'64 — dc22   2006036268

British Library cataloguing data are available

Cover photograph © 2007 PhotoSpin

Manufactured in the United States of America

McFarland & Company, Inc., Publishers
  Box 611, Jefferson, North Carolina 28640
  www.mcfarlandpub.com

To everyone who has ever played
the game of basketball:
thank you for making it
the greatest spectator sport in the world

ACKNOWLEDGMENTS

My grateful appreciation to the following who helped make the concept of this book a reality: my good friend and editorial consultant, Lesley Kellas Payne: I couldn't have done it without you; Jim Barnett: your insightful commentary on the game continues to amaze me; Matt Zeysing: your support and competence rises above the call to duty; Steve Lipofsky and Dick Raphael: thanks for sharing your fantastic photos with my readers. Thanks also to Robert Bradley at the Association for Professional Basketball Research, Craig Miller from USA Basketball, Dagmar Getz and Jennifer Claybourne-Torkelson at the University of Minnesota, and Mary Stobbe of YMCA Canada.

TABLE OF CONTENTS

FOREWORD

BY JIM BARNETT

Have you ever wondered how professional sports came to be so powerful and influential in our daily lives?

Are you amazed at the immense salaries professional athletes command today?

What is the reason for the popularity of the athletes and the fierce competition they between them?

If you are specifically interested in basketball, and particularly the NBA, Connie Kirchberg's *Hoop Lore: A History of the NBA* is a must-read. It is the most comprehensive I have seen in all of my travels throughout the basketball world; it is an informative, moving history lesson for all basketball fans. The pages take you from the YMCA with Dr. James Naismith in 1891 and weave you through more than a century of basketball growth. You read about the Buffalo Germans in the early 1900s, the barnstorming Harlem "Rens" and the Original Celtics with Joe Lapchick in the Roaring '20s. I learned how basketball became an Olympic sport in 1936 in Berlin, as James Naismith watched at the age of 74. This spawned his idea to start a national collegiate tournament which formed the basis of the NCAA tournament today.

This is a book about people with dreams and a passion for the sport of basketball. It includes the players of the early NBA as well as those through the 2004-2005 season. It chronicles the struggles and failings of the early organizations: the NBL, BAA, ABL, and the ABA to name just a few. How interesting to learn that George Steinbrenner owned the Cleveland Pipers in the ABL in 1960 and hired the first black professional coach in any sport. How enjoyable to read of the Celtics' dynasty and the battles between Russell and Chamberlain, the heroics of Baylor and West, and the dominance of Oscar Robertson.

Kirchberg writes in vivid detail of the Magic Johnson–Larry Bird era and the transition to superstar Michael Jordan. She brings to light the importance of Commissioner David Stern, who oversees the NBA and has been the most influential marketer of the league. In short, everything is covered in its entirety in an easy, fun-filled read.

Hoop Lore is a history lesson, a compelling story, and a walk down memory lane told with accuracy and social conscience. It is a must read for all basketball fans, particularly those of us who "think" we know the game.

Jim Barnett began his NBA career in Boston as the eighth overall pick in the 1966 draft and went on to play with some of the game's top talents. During his 11 years in the league, Jim posted averages of 11.7 points, 3.1 rebounds, and 3 assists. He is a broadcasting analyst and color commentator for the Golden State Warriors.

PREFACE

The idea for *Hoop Lore* began some five years ago when I realized that very few titles dealing with the actual history of the National Basketball Association exist. Some excellent books have been published over the years, among them *The Basketball Man* by Bernice Larson Webb, an account of Dr. James Naismith's life. Books such as Jerry West's *Mr. Clutch* and *My Life* by Magic Johnson give first-person accounts of the game while providing insight into the players. Robert Peterson's *Cages to Jump Shots* is a fascinating account of pro basketball's pre–NBA days. Racial struggles are bluntly documented in *They Cleared the Lane: The NBA's Black Pioneers* by Ron Thompson. Equally important from a cultural aspect is Nelson George's *Elevating the Game: The History and Aesthetics of Black Men in Basketball.* Nowhere, however, was I able to locate a book that purports to cover the entire history of the NBA.

Once I began the daunting task of outlining such a book, I began to understand why. Basketball has undergone more changes and revisions than any other professional sport, and it continues to evolve. Since the media did not originally consider pro basketball a "real" sport, little written documentation of its early years exists.

This book — which covers 115 years — was conceived to fill the need for an NBA history. Readers will get a detailed look at how the NBA was able to overcome so many of the obstacles that crushed its predecessors to become the most successfully marketed league in professional sports. Profiled are individuals instrumental in that success—from the game's inventor, James Naismith, to the owners and commissioners, coaches, players, and fans. While this work is not meant to be a social commentary, it is impossible not to explore the profound effect that the rise and continued growth of the NBA has had on our modern-day culture.

I have followed the NBA for nearly 40 years, during which time I've had the pleasure to watch remarkable athletes perform amazing feats that oftentimes defy gravity. Whether my team wins or loses, I know I will always experience 48 minutes of pulsing, nonstop action. And that's what watching sports *should* be all about: the ride. Mine began in 1970, when I turned on the radio for the weekly Top 40 countdown and got Eddie Doucette's play-by-play of a Milwaukee Bucks overtime game instead. I went to school the next morning without knowing what song was number one — a cardinal sin for a 13-year-old girl. Worse, all I really wanted to know was when the next Bucks game would be on. About all that has changed since then is my team allegiance, which varies depending on where I call home.

Welcome to the passion that is the NBA.

But why basketball? What sets it apart from its major rivals? Why is it fast becoming *the* most popular sport on the globe? Those questions are answered in the pages of this book.

Three years of meticulous research went into the writing of this book. In addition to the titles listed in my bibliography, I relied heavily on newspaper articles of the day. For the modern era (post–1946), I found countless Web sites that provided a wealth of data and statistics. The most notable of these are the Basketball Hall of Fame, NBA.com/history, the Association for Professional Basketball Research, and databaseBasketball.com. In all, I visited hundreds of sites, both commercial and fan-based. All stats and data used in this book have been verified by at least three differ ent sources to ensure accuracy. Information that could not be verified by at least three sources was omitted. Several people in the basketball world reviewed the text. What you now hold in your hands is, to my knowledge, the most comprehensive work ever written on the NBA. I hope you enjoy reading it as much as I did putting it all together.

Because the scope of this project covers such a vast period of time, beginning with a short biography of Dr. Naismith and ending with the 2005 playoffs, it was impossible to mention every noteworthy person and/or event that occurred during that timeframe. The omission of any such persons or events is not meant to diminish their importance in any way.

The majority of statistics that appear in *Hoop Lore* are readily available on numerous Web sites, and thus are not individually cited via endnotes. In the case when data was not so easily obtainable, I opted to list the source, though doing so in no way suggests that source is all-inclusive.

Stats involving active players often changed as I wrote. This in turn affected stats on retired players. Stats in this book were current as of spring 2005. It must be noted that the method for compiling statistics tends to vary with the source. For details and up-to-the-minute stats, visit Robert Bradley's excellent website, the Association for Professional Basketball Research (http://www.apbr. org.), Justin Kubatko's basketballreference.com (http://basketball-reference. com), and the folks at databaseBasketball.com (http://basketballreference.com/ index.htm).

INTRODUCTION

Imagine a professional basketball league dominated by stationary, two-handed set shots and player salaries of $5,000 a year. Now fast-forward to today's NBA, where slam dunks are routine and a teenager can collect endorsement fees of $90 million without setting foot on a professional court. *Hoop Lore* is the story of how we got from there to here.

Although current NBA players are among the most recognizable and wealthy athletes in the world, few people, including the majority of the players themselves, are aware of how it all came to be. In truth, establishing professional basketball was a war, a battle for survival. Only the strong survived, and it took players, owners, coaches, and fans decades of hard work, personal sacrifices, and astute vision to bring it all together. This book explores that struggle, taking the reader on a thorough but fast-paced journey through the history of professional hoops where the sky is — amazingly — no longer the limit.

To suggest the game has evolved since its creation in 1891 would be the equivalent of comparing a 1950s television to today's high-definition plasma or LCD sets; there really is no comparison, either in programming or picture quality. Still, as with basketball, the basic idea existed to be built on, improved, changed, and rearranged. When all is said and done, television is still about watching stories unfold on a screen, be they in grainy black and white or glorious, razor-sharp color. And basketball is still about putting a ball through a net.

Some would argue that today's rugged high-wire act that is the NBA bears little resemblance to the early days. They are wrong. Many similarities remain, both in substance and style. Whether or not evolution has improved the game is another question. The answer depends on who you ask, but few would dispute the bottom line: Basketball, be it nineteenth- or twenty-first-century style, remains a passionate game of *attitude* to all whom embrace it.

Ask a pre–NBA player who drove himself to games in a beat-up jalopy for little more than gas money what he has in common with today's world-renowned stars. Ask a kid playing hoops at a local playground what he has in common with the average NBA player making $5 million a year. Ask his little brother or his girlfriend what they have in common with celebrities sitting courtside at today's multimillion-dollar arenas. All will probably react with a shrug or quizzical look. But give them a minute and they'll tell you: a racing pulse, sweaty palms ... and an indescribable feeling deep in their gut.

It's basketball, and yes, they really *do* love this game!

PEACH FUZZ

By most accounts, the first game of basketball, then referred to in print as Basket Ball, was played on or around December 21, 1891, at the YMCA (Young Men's Christian Association) training school in Springfield, Massachusetts. The game was the brainchild of James Naismith, a Canadian theology student who believed the key to building strong moral character lay in the rigorous competition of sports.

Naismith underwent plenty of character-building early in life. He was only nine when his parents, John and Margaret, died of typhoid fever. Jim's grandmother took care of him and his two younger siblings, Robbie and Annie, until she passed away in 1872. The orphaned trio then went to live with their mother's brother, Peter Young, a devout Christian who owned a farm on the outskirts of Quebec. Uncle Peter expected the Naismith children to work for their keep, a situation that forced Jim to drop out of high school at age 15 so he could work full-time at a nearby lumberyard.

Thankfully for basketball fans, five years of manual labor taught Naismith the importance of getting an education. Over his uncle's objection, he returned to high school in 1881, got his degree in two short years, and applied to McGill University in Montreal, a school renowned for its students of exceptional academic abilities. Basketball's future inventor, now a confident 22-year-old man, was accepted at McGill (otherwise known as the Harvard of the North[1]) on full scholarship. A grateful Jim excelled in his studies, but found it impossible to abandon the active lifestyle he'd grown accustomed to since his boyhood days on Uncle Peter's farm. In addition to his daily chores, young Naismith had regularly engaged in swimming, canoeing, and camping during his off hours. Convinced such activities contributed to a healthy mental state, he was determined to continue the trend during his stay at the college.

University sports programs left much to be desired at the time, but McGill did have an excellent gymnasium with equipment ranging from ladders, bars, and dumbbells to rings and trapezes. It wasn't long before Jim became an expert on all of the equipment. Along the way, he developed a love for rugby football, which he played competitively from 1884 to 1891.[2]

After Naismith received his B.A. in philosophy and Hebrew from McGill in 1887, he enrolled at Presbyterian College, one of four theological schools affiliated with McGill. To help pay the bills, he took a part-time teaching position at McGill, where he quickly became one of the school's most popular athletic instructors. But not everyone was taken with Naismith's determination to blend his love for sports with theology. Many of his professors at Presbyterian harshly disapproved of athletics in general, especially rugby, which they referred to as the "tool of the devil."[3] Regardless, Jim's notion that sports helped feed intellect proved true in his own case, as he remained among the top students in the seminary.

During Jim's second year at Presbyterian, his mentor at McGill, Frederick Barnjum, passed away. Shortly thereafter, the school offered Barnjum's former position as directory of gymnastic activities to Naismith. The move was no small gesture, given that Barnjum had been considered the top PE teacher in Canada. Naismith discarded concerns by friends and family that accepting the job would interfere with his religious studies. And of course they need not have worried. True to form, Jim worked so hard the rest of the year that he finished second in his class—an honor which netted him a $50 scholarship.[4]

Nonetheless, seeds planted by his late mentor began to poke through the ground. Although Naismith continued to believe ministry served an important role in civilized culture, he began to wonder whether athletics might not offer a better way to reach society's youth. He knew Uncle Peter would be disappointed if he opted out of his theology major. Likewise his sister, Annie, who shared his professors' distain for sports. Yet the more he debated the issue, the clearer the answer became. During his senior year, he formally switched his major from theology to physical education.

His professors were stunned. Most everyone who had his so-called best interests at heart begged him to reconsider, to stay the course at least until he had finished the seminary program. But Naismith's mind was made up. He was going to make a difference his way, by teaching other young people how to live respectable, productive lives, through the vigorous world of athletics.

By this point, Jim was a regular at the nearby YMCA in Montreal, where he had come to know the Y's secretary, D. A. Budge, quite well. Budge understood Naismith's dream completely and did all he could to support his determined friend. Budge's major contribution was a tip concerning a private school he had recently heard about in Springfield, Massachusetts. Budge thought the nonsectarian school's objective — to instruct laymen how to perform Christian work with young people, in churches and other volunteer organizations — fit in nicely with Jim's personal goal. Naismith couldn't have agreed more, especially when he learned about the school's full-time physical training department and its motto: "A strong mind is a strong body."[5]

Naismith finished his senior year at Presbyterian College and left without becoming ordained, a decision that left his professors and fellow classmates diligently praying for his soul. Undaunted, the 29-year-old packed his bags and headed south to Springfield, where he enrolled in the School for Christian Workers (later renamed the International Young Men's Training School). The facility was peppered by out-of-the-box thinkers, men like Alonzo "Lonnie" Stagg, another seminary dropout who had abandoned the ministry in favor of working in athletics, and the school's superintendent of physical education, Dr. Gulick, the son of missionary parents. Like Jim, they believed in a similar goal: putting their religious beliefs to use toward the betterment of society via nontraditional methods.

Prior to Naismith's arrival, the school's PE program had consisted mainly of gymnastics and calisthenics—activities that could be performed indoors in limited space. But things changed quickly when football was added to the slate that fall. Stagg, a former All American in his years at Yale, was appointed coach. Naismith joined the 13-man squad at center. Dubbed "Stagg's stubby Christians,"[6] the group of undersized, inexperienced men in their mid- to late twenties proceeded to tear up the circuit in their surprising debut, posting numerous victories against such powerhouses as Yale and Harvard.

The team's success would prove just the beginning for Stagg, who went on to become one of the most successful football coaches in history. Naismith's contribution also went beyond playing time and competitive spirit. The following year, probably in response to the increasing roughness of the game and his own light weight (160 pounds), he invented the football helmet.

Once the inaugural football season ended, the Springfield students had to resort to keeping fit in the stuffy gymnasium, doing boring exercises they quickly grew to despise. With nothing on the horizon until spring, when baseball and track would begin, it became a challenge for Dr. Gulick to keep students motivated. To solve the dilemma, he turned to the trainees themselves for suggestions. The general consensus was they needed an enjoyable indoor activity to engage body and mind. Naismith, who by now had been put on staff and assigned a class of his own, offered several ideas for combining elements of other games. Jim's proposals must have impressed, as Dr. Gulick assigned him the task of inventing the activity and told him to have it ready in no more than two weeks.

Naismith experimented with indoor variations on several existing games, including football, soccer, cricket, and baseball. But all proved too rough for the confines of a gym, as numerous injuries were sustained. With the deadline fast approaching, he sat down at his desk and concentrated on what he considered the major criteria: A ball is essential for any team sport, and the size of the ball determines the difficulty level of the game. Given how small balls required additional equipment, such as a bat or stick, Jim reasoned that using a large ball would simplify the game because the ball itself would be the object of the competition.[7]

Once he had decided on the size of the ball, Naismith set about devising the actual rules that would make up his game. Due to the limited space in the gym and its hard wooden floor, the participants would not be able to tackle others as in football, or serious injuries would result. Additionally, running would have to be kept to a minimum. Given those restrictions, Jim decided players would advance the ball by passing it to each other from stationary positions on the floor.

With the basic elements of the game in place, all that remained was to determine how points would be scored. For that stroke of genius, Jim turned to a game he had played as a child called Duck on the Rock. The "rock" was a boulder about three feet tall which served as a platform for a smaller rock called the "duck." A player who was deemed "it" was assigned to guard the duck, which was set atop the platform. The other children stood in line at a base situated about 20 feet away from the duck and took turns attempting to knock it to the ground by hurling pebbles. Regardless of whether the thrower was successful or not, he had to run to the bolder to retrieve his pebble, then hurry back to the throwing base before the guard could retrieve the fallen duck and tag him with it. If a player was tagged prior to reaching base, he would take the duck guard's "it" spot at the boulder.

The best players lobbed their pebble at the target, tossing it up with a gentle arch so it landed fairly close to the boulder. Throwing hard and straight sent the pebble hurling past the platform like a wild pitch, making it nearly impossible for the thrower to retrieve his pebble *and* make it back to base prior to getting tagged. The lesson was that precision, not power, ruled the game, an observation that fit in nicely with Dr. Gulick's main criteria: that the game be easy to learn and equally accessible to all players, regardless of height or weight.

According to several written accounts, the inspiration to use baskets as goals originated during Jim's days at McGill, where he was said to have organized competitive throwing teams made up of off-season rugby players. The object was for players to score points by throwing balls into empty boxes placed on the floor across the gym. The trouble was, the defensive players were allowed to do just about anything to stop a score, including sitting inside the box. Suffice it to say, the game did not catch on.[8]

Jim had boxes on his mind in Springfield, but with a new twist: the goals would be mounted on poles above players' heads. In that way, scoring and defense would be far more challenging.

That dilemma solved, Jim had the fundamental rules of his new game in place:

1. No running with the ball.
2. No tackling or other rough body contact.
3. A horizontal goal above the players' heads.
4. Freedom of any player (while adhering to the no-contact rule) to obtain the ball and score at any time.[9]

Dr. James Naismith examines the tools of his invention (Basketball Hall of Fame, Springfield, Massachusetts).

It was Deadline Eve. Naismith jotted down the above and headed home. His game was almost ready. A few more details to work out and he could present it to his class. He was confident they were going to like it. They *had* to, or he would suffer the ultimate disgrace: failing his good friend and mentor, Dr. Gulick.

PLAY BALL

The next morning, Naismith tracked down the school janitor, Mr. Stebbins, and asked for a couple of boxes about 18 inches square. There were no boxes that size as it turned out, though Stebbins did have a couple of old peach baskets sitting around in the back of the storeroom. Naismith took a look. The would-be goals measured about 15 inches across the top, and tapered down slightly toward the bottom. Deciding they would suffice, Jim nailed the peach baskets to rails protruding from opposite ends of the gymnasium court via the balcony above. The vertical distance from floor to goal measured about what he had had in mind: 10 feet.

He returned to his office to finalize the rules, which had expanded substantially since the night before. When complete, he had a list of 13 do's and don'ts.

1. The ball may be thrown in any direction with one or both hands.

2. The ball may be batted in any direction with one or both hands (but never a fist).

3. A player cannot run with the ball. The player must throw it from the spot on which he catches it, allowances to be made for a man who catches the ball when running at a good speed, if he tries to stop.

4. The ball must be held in or between the hands; the arms or the body must not be used for holding it.

5. No shouldering, holding, pushing, tripping, or striking in any way the person of an opponent shall be allowed; the first infringement of this rule by any person shall count as a foul; the second shall disqualify him until the next goal is made or, if there is evident intent to injure the person, for the whole game. No substitute allowed.

6. A foul is striking at the ball with the fist, violation of Rules 3, 4, and such as described in Rule 5.

7. If either side makes three consecutive fouls, it shall count as a goal for the opponents.

8. A goal shall be made when the ball is thrown or batted from the ground

into the basket and stays there, providing those defending the goal do not touch or disturb the goal. If the ball rests on the edges and the opponent moves the basket, it shall count as a goal.

9. When the ball goes out of bounds, it shall be thrown into the field of play by the person first touching it. In case of a dispute, the umpire shall throw it straight onto the field. The thrower-in is allowed five seconds; if he holds it longer, it shall go to the opponent. If any side persists in delaying the game, the umpire shall call a foul on that side.

10. The umpire shall be the judge of the men and shall note the fouls and notify the referee when three consecutive fouls have been made. He shall have the power to disqualify men according to Rule 5.

11. The referee shall be the judge of the ball and shall decide when the ball is in play, in bounds, to which side it belongs, and shall keep time. He shall decide when a goal has been made, and keep account of the goals.

12. The time shall be two fifteen-minute halves, with five minutes' rest between.

13. The side making the most goals in that time shall be declared the winner. In case of a draw, the game may, by agreement of the captains, be continued until another goal is made.[1]

Jim got the department secretary, Miss Lyons, to type up the formal rules to his as-yet unnamed invention, then returned to the gymnasium, where he tacked up the neatly typed pages on a bulletin board. Moments later, members of his 11:30 class began to arrive. Several students noticed the peach baskets nailed to the balcony rails on their way to the locker room and began to snicker. Frank Mahan, the ringleader of the group according to Jim, even went so far as to say, "Huh! Another new game!"[2]

Naismith remained impervious. When the students returned to the gym, dressed and ready for class, he chose two captains and instructed them to divide the remaining students into two groups. The class of future secretaries consisted of 18 men, thus each team would have nine players: three forwards, three centers, and three backs (by today's standards, the backs would be equal to guards). Jim took a few minutes to go over the rules he'd posted on the bulletin board. As the students responded with their usual skepticism, their teacher made a pledge: "I promised them that if this was a failure, I would not try any more experiments."[3] He then instructed the dubious bunch to get out on the court, picked a center from each team, and tossed a soccer ball up between them.

And the very first game of basketball was under way.

Lighting in the gym was poor. Gymnastic equipment sat off to the sides of the playing court, which measured a scant 35 feet wide by 50 feet long.[4] The boundaries were unmarked. The "baskets" hung crooked, lopsided and tilted downward because of their awkward size. Players wore their regular gym class outfits, which consisted of long pants, short-sleeved jerseys, and soft-soled everyday shoes. Jim served as both referee and umpire for his game's trial run.

No rowdy fans rocked the bleachers on that cold December day in Springfield. No cheerleaders in skimpy outfits hopped up and down. There wasn't a vendor or cameraman in sight. Not one participant on the floor that day knew — or cared — what they were supposedly missing.

To Jim's dismay, players quickly disregarded Rule 5 as they pushed, shoved, and slapped each other to get their chance at flipping the ball into the rickety peach basket above their heads. "There was no teamwork," the crafty inventor would later recall, "but each man did his best."[5] So determined were they, in fact, that at times, half the class sat in the penalty area. Amid the ruckus, a calm Mr. Stebbins stood on the sidelines with a ladder, ready to retrieve the ball from the basket should anyone be successful. By most accounts, Stebbins made the journey only once, to retrieve a 25-foot shot (about 15 inches beyond today's three-point line) scored by William Chase. Other sources claim the score was more lopsided: three or four to nothing. In any event, fouls clearly outnumbered the final score of the 30-minute scramble.

No one knows who attempted the most shots, which player was whistled for the most fouls, or if Rule 5 was abused to the point that Naismith disqualified anyone. On that historic day, box scores and stats were irrelevant. All the exhausted participants wanted to know was when they could play again.

For Jim's part, it was largely a feeling of relief. For days he had been dreading the prospect of facing Dr. Gulick and the rest of the faculty only to report that, just as his predecessors, he too had failed to come up with a game to satisfy the infamous group of bored secretarial students. Suffice it to say, his worries were over. "When the first game had ended, I felt that I could now go to Dr. Gulick and tell him that I had accomplished the two seemingly impossible tasks that he had assigned to me; namely, to interest the class in physical exercise and to invent a new game."[6]

Faculty members weren't the only ones impressed. Word of Jim's successful new game spread quickly throughout the student body of the young men's training school. Within days, the gymnastic equipment stowed on the sidelines during Naismith's 11:30 class became invisible behind a shroud of excited onlookers. By the time the students returned from Christmas break, the game's popularity had spread to such an extent that spectators (not all of them from within the YMCA) filled the 200-seat balcony while the class was in progress. Everyone, it seemed, wanted to get a look at this new so-called sport, which one of Jim's students — later identified as Frank Mahan — had appropriately named "basket ball."

In mid–January, the training school's newspaper, *The Triangle*, ran an article written by Naismith titled "Basket Ball."[7] In it, his 13 rules were reprinted for the very first time, along with more detailed instructions stemming from the personal experience he'd gained while refereeing his class. *The Triangle* was

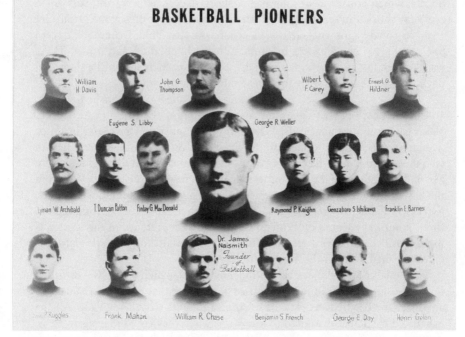

BASKETBALL PIONEERS

William H. Davis

John G. Thompson

Wilbert F. Carey

Ernest G. Hildner

Eugene S. Libby

George R Weller

Lyman W. Archibald

T. Duncan Patton

Finlay G. MacDonald

Raymond P. Kaighn

Genzabaro S. Ishikawa

Franklin E. Barnes

Dr. James Naismith Founder of Basketball

Ruggles

Frank Mahan

William R. Chase

Benjamin S. French

George E. Day

Henri Gelan

Dr. James Naismith founded basketball when he drew up the original 13 playing rules, and the above 18 Springfield College students made history when they participated in the first basketball game ever played, in December 1891 (Basketball Hall of Fame, Springfield, MA).

distributed to other YMCAs across the country, so it wasn't long before students from New York to California were throwing balls into baskets of one type or another.

Naismith was so thrilled with the game's growing popularity that he chose a team of 9 players from his original class of 18 and took them on the road to promote the sport in neighboring eastern states. Most sources credit the group, dubbed the Flying Circus, as the first organized basketball team in history.

Basketball fever continued to spread at the Young Men's Training School in Springfield, where an intramural contest between students and teachers was brewing. Jim and his pal Lonnie Stagg were among the seven instructors who took to the court that eleventh day of March 1892, in what is thought to be the first ever public basketball game. Stagg, later criticized for his overly rough, football-like play, scored the teachers' only point. The students finished with five. Oddly, the event marked the first of only two games in which Naismith appeared as a player. (The other occurred at the University of Kansas in 1898.)

The up-and-coming sport received a huge boost in April when New York christened the opening of a new athletic grounds for its YMCA and presented the game as an alternative to football. The event garnished reviews in all the local papers, including the *New York Times*. Soon after, rival Y's began organizing teams and playing against each other. In big cities and small towns alike, people all over the country were going nuts over Jim's invention. And it wasn't just Americans. The Springfield training center was an international school attended by students from all over the world, students who could hardly wait to tell their families and friends about the exciting new fad called basketball.

Naismith completed his two year program at the International YMCA's training school in spring 1892 and, thanks to a persuasive Dr. Gulick, agreed to remain on staff as a physical education instructor. Naturally, basketball became a major part of the curriculum — and the Springfield school was not alone. In response to huge demand from Y's across the country, Naismith wrote an extended guide of rules and regulations for his fast evolving game. The handbook was printed in pocket editions by Triangle Publishing Company. Revised editions followed in 1893 and 1894, with Dr. Gulick assisting on the latter.

Despite all the hype surrounding his invention, Naismith was not one to think and breathe basketball 24 hours a day. There were more important things in his life, among them Maude Evelyn Sherman, a young lady he had met at the school while helping supervise one of the first-ever women's basketball games. Jim and Maude became Mr. and Mrs. Naismith on June 20, 1894. On July 1 of the following year, the couple's first child, Margaret, was born. About that same time, Naismith decided he could become a more effective teacher with a medical degree in his pocket and bid Dr. Gulick and the training school goodbye.

Naismith had always loved — perhaps *needed*— a challenge. And so he left town with his new family and headed west to Colorado, leaving Dr. Gulick in charge of the national YMCA program that had been set up to govern his game.[8]

But overseeing basketball's many and changing rules and regulations on such a grand scale was an enormous responsibility for one person. Organized games were no longer confined to YMCA gyms. The sport was popular with high school and college students, military forces, church groups— just about every*one* every*where*. An overwhelmed Dr. Gulick prepared a questionnaire regarding possible rule changes and additions and mailed it to other Y's across America. The result was so encouraging that he decided to form a committee made up of various respondents from different parts of the country. Known as the Basketball Co-Operating Committee, the group became the first neutral organization to govern Naismith's game.

It was a noble effort, but basketball's popularity continued to soar at such a rate that neither Dr. Gulick nor his group could keep pace. Control was passed to the Athletic Union of America (AAU), a national sports overseer with a reputation for stability. The union had been established in 1888 to govern all organized amateur teams. Overseeing basketball presented a major challenge, as it was being played by so many different types of groups. After some deliberation,

Basketball's inventor, James Naismith, and his wife, Maude, reminisce about the early days of the game. Maude was one of the first women to play basketball (courtesy YMCA of the USA and Kautz Family Archives).

the union decided it would have to split the sport into three categories: those who registered with the AAU, those who proclaimed to be amateurs but declined to register, and those teams who considered themselves professional. Since the union insisted its members follow very strict guidelines, games between AAU-registered and nonregistered teams were forbidden. Those teams omitted from union play saw no reason to adhere to AAU rules and in many cases made up their own.

So much for standards. For better or worse, Naismith's game seemed destined to follow its own path. And what an amazing path it was. A mere five years after its invention, basketball had taken over as *the* sport on university campuses, especially in the East and Midwestern states, where freezing temperatures chased all but the most avid sports enthusiasts indoors from November to March.

As with any new game, rules were tweaked here and there as the sport progressed. In 1894, Rule 7 gave way to the free throw system. Different numbers of points were experimented with before it was decided that each foul shot would count one point. The distance from the foul line to the goal was originally set at 20 feet, but later reduced to 15 to improve accuracy. One player was usually responsible for shooting all free throws, regardless of whom the foul had been committed against, leading to the term "free throw specialist."

Coaches regularly experimented with the number of players per team allowed on the court. While Jim thought the ideal number was 9, he believed the game could support teams as large as 40. Records indicate he was not alone in that mindset. In an article titled *Paid to Play* featured on the Naismith Memorial Basketball Hall of Fame Web site, author Douglas Stark quotes a reporter's firsthand account of an 1890s game in which 80 players participated in the action. By 1897, however, the competitive level had become such that it was obvious a set number of players had to be established to maintain the sport's credibility. The AAU settled on five, which remains the current standard in all variations of competitive play.

Additionally, the game's equipment was added to and improved on. In early 1892, the clumsy, nonuniform peach baskets were replaced by a cylindrical basket made of heavy woven wire. The new goal measured 18 inches across the top and had several wire cords across the bottom. The improved style eliminated the forward slant caused by nailing peach baskets to rails but still left much to be desired. Later that year, Narragansett Machine Company of Providence, Rhode Island, produced a goal with an iron rim and a cord basket. The bottom of the net remained closed, but it featured a pull chain assembly used to remove the ball, reducing the time needed to do the job manually. More than a decade would pass before the first open net basket was introduced. The AAU did not deem the design official until 1912.

In the 1893-94 season, Overman Wheel Company, a bicycle manufacturer from Massachusetts, produced the first ball specifically created for the game.

Larger than the soccer ball being used by most teams, its sphere had a circumference of 30 to 32 inches. Early designs were made from leather panels stitched together with a rubber bladder inside. The laces could sharply affect a shot, depending on whether or not the ball hit the rim. Free throw shooters of the day were lucky to hit 70 percent of their shots.

The first backboards were introduced in 1895, though their purpose had nothing to do with helping players align shots. Most gyms were much smaller than today's facilities, so balconies were relied on for extra seating. Basketball fans quickly noted the upper level front row seats were conveniently located within reach of the goals. All the exuberant supporters had to do was reach down and *presto*, they could block the shot of an opponent, or give the home team a balcony assist. To put an end to the folly, a heavy wire gauge was installed behind the goal, effectively blocking fans from touching the ball or interfering with movement of nearby players. The backboard became a staple in most games by 1896, and carried a fixed size of four by six feet.

Many changes were yet to come as the twentieth century neared, but none bigger than that which occurred at the Masonic Temple in downtown Trenton, New Jersey, on November 7, 1896, where, for the first time in history, a group of men were *paid* to play Naismith's game. Basketball, the first true American sport, was about to venture into the spotlight of professional athletics.

To Pay or Not to Pay

AAU direction did nothing to hamper the frenzied growth of basketball at YMCAs across the country. Local memberships soared, competition between teams intensified. Although Naismith had done his best to create a game less physical than rugby or football, by its five-year anniversary, the sport was fast adapting to the style of its participants. And that style was not for the squeamish. "The way it worked was this," explained basketball historian Bill Himmelman. "If a guy got past you to score, you would lay into him and send him to the floor."[1] Not exactly the type of game the Young Men's Christian Association wanted to promote.

Volleyball, on the other hand, was an activity the organization could get behind 100 percent, especially given how it, too, was YMCA–grown. The game, originally known as mintonette, had been invented in 1895 by William Morgan, an instructor at the Y in Holyoke, Massachusetts. Ironically, Morgan had devised the sport as an alternative to basketball, which he felt had become too strenuous for the typical businessperson looking for after-hours recreation. "Mintonette" became "volleyball" in 1896, when the International Training School in Springfield hosted an exhibition showing how the ball was volleyed over a net.

While volleyball drew its share of fans, it never threatened to replace Naismith's game as the Y's most popular sport. Among those basketball teams organized through local branches, the most famous was a squad out of Trenton, New Jersey. Appropriately named the Trentons, the group of undersized men (their starters averaged about 160 pounds), tore up the East, manhandling any and all teams who dared to get·in their way.

Fittingly, it was the Trentons who became the first team to collect a paycheck for playing basketball. The group squared off against the Brooklyn Y team at the Masonic Temple in downtown Trenton on November 7, 1896. The contest had been advertised in advance via a one-column, two-inch ad in the Trenton *Daily True American*, another probable first for basketball history. Admission was priced at 15 cents for standing room, 25 cents for a seat on the newly constructed risers.[2]

Early basketball court with caged enclosure (Basketball Hall of Fame, Springfield, MA).

By all accounts, the top floor of the three-story temple, a social hall that had been converted to a basketball court for the night, was packed to the hilt with some 700 boisterous fans. The court itself featured another first: it was surrounded by a 12-foot-high wire mesh fence. Thereafter known as the cage, the apparatus was intended to speed up the game by keeping the ball in play at all times. Without the fence, play was interrupted each time the ball rolled off the court, as the out-of-bounds rule had yet to be established. Once the ball was considered out of play, possession was granted to the first man who was able to get his hands on it, a situation that often resulted in a frantic free-for-all. Players pushing, shoving, and slapping each other did not make great advertising copy for family entertainment, especially when unsuspecting patrons were drawn into the fray. Theory had it the cage would also serve to protect players by preventing overzealous fans from intentionally interfering with game play — a logical assumption, though it proved premature. Sources of the day spoke of rowdy fans who stood at the fence and poked passing players and refs with hat pins and even lit cigars.

But the Trentons were ready for whatever might come their way on that crisp November evening. Clad in uniforms of black padded knickers and sleeveless red jerseys, they won in their usual fashion, flattening their opponents by a score of 16 to 1. The Trenton's starting seven played all 40 minutes while their opponents used only one substitution. Brooklyn's lone point came with three minutes left to play in the game, via a free throw by Simonson. Forward Fred Cooper, the Trentons' captain and leading scorer, finished with three baskets for a game high six points, an honor which netted him an extra dollar in pay. The amount the players collected that night remains in dispute today, but is believed to have been between $10 and $15 each.

The amount wasn't important, of course. The fact they collected *any* pay elevated them from amateurs to professionals—an idea that didn't set well with most YMCAs. Growing discontent between Y's and their basketball teams had been building for years prior to the November 7 contest. The rough, win-at-any-cost style of play that had evolved went against the organization's wholesome image. Naismith had intended his game to be played for fun, a concept many Y officials believed had been lost over the years. They argued players were taking the game too seriously, and their concerns were not without basis. Basketball had all but taken over their facilities, causing tension among those members who wanted to use the gyms for other activities. Once word got out that the Trentons had been paid to play a game, it was impossible to reverse course. As a result of the dispute, the Trentons parted company with their YMCA host and declared themselves professional. The bad feelings brought on by the incident caused some Y's to ban the game from their premises altogether.

Nonetheless, basketball continued to gain momentum worldwide, a fact that did not go unnoticed by the businessmen and sports promoters of the day. Many Y teams chose to follow the Trentons' lead, terminating their memberships in the organization so they were free to play against each other for money. The players rented whatever facilities were available, mostly assembly halls and dance floors, charged admission to their games, and split the proceeds. In 1898, a group of New Jersey newspaper sports editors took notice of the practice and deemed it lucrative enough to form a professional organization.

And so began the first National Basketball League.

The league's name was deceptive, as there was nothing "national" about it. All six teams were located within 70 or so miles of each other. Included in the original group were the Trentons, Millville, and Camden Electrics, all from New Jersey, and from Philadelphia, the Clover Wheelmen, Germantown, and the Hancock Athletic Association. Team owners disagreed in regard to standardized rules, but eventually several were agreed on: No more than eight men per team could play in any game; the courts would be 65 feet long by 35 feet wide and would include at least a 10-foot-high caged enclosure; backboards were to be wire and 4 feet square, with the basket's rim extending 1 foot beyond the board.[3]

Of the original six teams, only the Trentons, Millville, and Camden made it through the NBL's inaugural 1898-99 season. Trenton finished the year with 18 wins, 2 losses and 1 tie (overtimes were not played). Millville wasn't far behind with its 14-6-2 record, but the Trentons prevailed in the championship game.

Several new teams were added in the 1899-1900 season, among them a scrappy group from New York who called themselves the Wanderers. Probably due to the volatility of the teams, it was decided the season would be split into two halves. Trenton rolled over its opponents in the first, compiling an impressive 8-0 record. Although the rookies from New York posted an impressive 13-7-1 showing in the second half, it was good enough for only third place. A best-of-three tie-breaker was held between the Trentons and Millville, the Trentons prevailing two games to one. The Trentons would remain competitive over the next few seasons, but their NBL championship years were over. They were defeated by the Wanderers the following year, and failed to make the playoffs in either of the next two seasons.

No one could argue that the NBL had broadened the game's fan base in the East; unfortunately, that interest hadn't translated into even a fraction of the profits eager owners had anticipated. Gate receipts weren't high enough to meet operating expenses for most teams. Adding to the dilemma, numerous competitive leagues emerged. Though most proved fly-by-night operations, they lasted long enough to raid the NBL of some of its best players. Since NBL rules barred members from playing on other teams, it became difficult to keep squads together for an entire season. The struggling organization closed shop for good midway through the 1903-04 season. Other leagues came and went over the next few years, among them the Philadelphia League, the New England League, and the Western Massachusetts League, none of which established a large enough fan base to stay afloat.

While a lack of revenue was clearly the major stumbling block for early pro leagues, other factors played supporting roles. Leagues were territorial, featuring teams only from their area, and all of those were concentrated in the East and Midwest. With the Civil War still fresh in many people's minds, Southerners weren't all that anxious to embrace a sport of Yankee origin, let alone willing to pay for the privilege. Amateur play had begun to catch on in some Southern states, but Y's weren't nearly as prevalent there as in other areas of the country. Few schools on the high school or college level had *outdoor* playing fields, let alone indoor space devoted exclusively to athletics. Although basketball was a hot commodity at many Western universities, much of the West was still uncharted, considered "wild" by Eastern city dwellers who conjured up images of cowboys, brothels, and gunfights in the streets.

Even if leagues had been organized in other parts of the country, the distance would have made nationwide interleague play impossible. Today, teams cover thousands of miles in a few hours' time via the luxury of private jets; in the early 1900s, it took several hours by bus or car to travel a hundred miles, and there was nothing luxurious about the journey. Playing conditions were substandard and the pay was low, averaging about $40 per week. Some players took to moonlighting in other leagues under false names to supplement their incomes, an action that ultimately contributed to pro ball's instability.

Looking at it from a fan's prospective, league schedules featured a total of six to eight teams facing off against each other several times a week over the course of a season. Paying customers watched the same players make the same plays over and over again. Star players weren't thought of as the celebrities they are today. There were no breathtaking slam dunks or brilliant spin moves in mid-air. Players shot the ball from a stationary spot on the floor, usually with a two-handed push shot. Long balls heaved from beyond the current three-point line connected rarely and were good for only the same two points as any other goal. Often, 10 minutes or more would pass without a basket being scored. Die-hard basketball fans may have been satisfied, but the game proved a dead end at the mainstream box office, even for winning teams.

Fortunately for hoop fans, the early failure of professional basketball was solely a victim of its time and in no way reflected the public's attitude toward the sport in general. Naismith's game continued to flourish at athletic clubs, universities, and YMCAs across the nation and throughout the world. According to *Spaulding's Official Guidebook*, as the first decade of the twentieth century wound down, organized basketball had spread from European countries to shores as far away as Japan, South America, China, and the Philippines.

Back in the United States, discontent over AAU control continued to build, especially on the collegiate level. "The Amateur Athletic Union and the intercollegiate authorities in conference have decided that the best interests of the sport will be conserved by two separate codes," the *New York Times* reported on June 30, 1907. "The reason assigned is that the game which the collegians play is too strenuous to be adapted for the use of men in athletic clubs and YMCAs who are not in constant training, and the college men do not want a less vigorous game."[4] Y officials who had campaigned for an end to the sport's roughness were elated, but the split did little to discourage the game's physical evolution.

In December, the Intercollegiate Athletic Association of the United States (IAAUS) stepped in. The group had been established in March 1906 with a mission of reforming college football, a game that had become so violent a number of fatal injuries had occurred. The IAAUS had since become responsible for establishing and enforcing rules and regulations for all collegiate sports programs nationwide, thus its intervention in the AAU dispute. Following a lengthy discussion, the IAAUS formed the Collegiate Basket Ball Rules Committee and granted it jurisdiction over all college games for a period of three years. In addition to overseeing the rules of the game, the committee was to organize a staff of qualified umpires and officials.

Despite their many differences, the AAU and the Collegiate Basket Ball Rules Committee agreed on one thing: professionals and amateurs did not mix. College teams were forbidden from scheduling games against pro teams, even exhibition matches. Furthermore, no student who had ever played ball on a professional level, regardless of how short-lived his career, was eligible for collegiate

The Buffalo Germans, one of the earliest known organized basketball teams, began play at a YMCA on Buffalo's East Side in 1895. The Germans went undefeated in 5 of their first 18 seasons, including a stretch of 111 straight wins (Basketball Hall of Fame, Springfield, MA).

play. In 1899, the AAU backpedaled a bit by allowing amateur teams from Y's and other athletic clubs to schedule games against pro teams as long as the players were registered with the union as professionals. Many players refused to do so, however, as it meant they would be permanently banned from playing college ball. Thus, intentionally or not, the AAU effectively slowed the emergence of pro basketball.

Conversely, the union's strict guidelines did little to hinder academic play, and in fact, likely contributed to its growing popularity. As the first decade of the twentieth century neared an end, basketball had become a staple for many schools, the number of which was growing at an incredible pace. The same could not be said for non–AAU sanctioned amateurs or professional teams, most of which had taken to barnstorming across the country, playing whatever team they could hook up with on any given night.

The most successful of these early independent franchises was the Buffalo Germans. The original members consisted of six teenage boys from Buffalo's

East Side who met while playing basketball at a local YMCA in 1895. The young men enjoyed playing together and decided to form a team — a sound idea, as it turned out. Local fans were rarely disappointed, seeing their squad lose only 2 of its first 51 home games. Some purists claim the team's success is overblown, given how they played as amateurs for nine seasons before turning professional, thus limiting the level of their competition. While that argument has some merit, the fact is the Buffalo Germans went undefeated in 5 of their first 18 seasons, at one point winning 111 *consecutive* games — a record that is likely to stand forever.

The boys from Buffalo furthered their reputation during the 1904 Olympic Games in St. Louis. The Buffalo Germans were one of several amateur teams from across the United States to attend the competition in what was technically basketball's first appearance as an Olympic sport. The game would not be officially recognized as such until the 1936 games in Berlin, but the tournaments were extremely competitive nonetheless. Each team played five games over a two-day period. The Buffalo Germans took home the Gold Medal by defeating the current national YMCA champs, the Chicago Centrals, by a score of 39–28.[5]

By the time the franchise disbanded in 1925 (then well into its second generation of players), it had racked up an amazing 792-86 win-loss record, earning it a much-deserved spot in the Basketball Hall of Fame.

But the Buffalo team was an exception, not the rule. Most pro players hopped from one team to another, leagues changed names and locales, and through it all only one constant remained: no one banked enough money to make the endeavor worthwhile. Several leagues tried to buck the trend, and might have succeeded had they joined forces. Instead, they undercut each other at every opportunity.

The Central League, named because it featured five teams from Pennsylvania and one from Ohio, debuted with a schedule of 30 games in the 1906-07 season. Following a successful inaugural, the CL played between 60 and 72 games in each of its next five seasons — nearly twice that of most other competitive leagues. Top CL players could earn up to $400 a month, more than *10 times* what the NBL Trentons had made just a few years earlier. Once the word got out — and it's safe to say CL owners were not disappointed when it did — players from other leagues left their teams in droves, hoping to cash in on the advertised bounty. Only the best received top dollar. Others scrambled for the next best deal. The resulting chaos left many teams shorthanded, games canceled, and fans disgusted.

The problem escalated with the debut of the Eastern League in 1909. Determined to beat the CL at its own game, Eastern used dollar signs to lure existing big-name players into their house. Most took the bait, and the cycle began anew. CL attendance fell off steadily until its demise in 1912. The Eastern League managed to stay alive, in one form or another, until 1923, though play was suspended for much of World War I.

In addition to the quandary of players hopping from league to league, there was a growing trend by management to "let players play." As previously noted, the game, both amateur and pro, had long outgrown Naismith's play-for-fun style. As early as 1897, Dr. Gulick had questioned whether YMCAs should continue to promote the sport. "The game must be kept clean. It is a perfect outrage for an institution that stands for Christian work in the community to tolerate not merely discourteous and ungentlemanly treatment of guests, but slugging and that which violates the elementary principles of morals."[6] The following year, Marvin Riley, an early pro official, worked a game between Trenton and Millville in which it was understood, *prior to tip-off*, that no fouls would be called. Fifteen years later, the Eastern League's president, William Scheffer, predicted the increasingly rough play would eventually lead to pro basketball's demise. "If the officials are not backed up, the games become regular indoor foot ball contests, players being injured and spectators becoming disgusted. The latter are the ones to look after, as without public support, no sport will last."[7]

The pro game's roughness may very well have turned off some fans, but the sport was not much tamer on the collegiate level. In 1908, the president of Yale remarked that the game had become even more violent than football. Regardless, the sport's popularity continued to soar at universities across the nation. According to Microsoft's *Encarta*, more than 360 colleges had basketball programs by 1914 — an increase of 400 percent in 10 years. How did the college game succeed so handily where the pros failed? In all likelihood, it was because it adapted a universal set of standards. The college game had flourished under the rules set forth by the IAAUS, which was renamed the National Collegiate Athletic Association (NCAA) in 1910. Since all teams played by the same rules, both players and fans knew what to expect once a game was under way.

Pro leagues, on the other hand, had continually rejected such a strategy. Each league retained its own set of guidelines, amateur rules be damned. Some used a cage and played with a backboard, others didn't. Court size varied. Actions that would be ruled fouls in one league were permitted in others. The average fan related to the game as Naismith had invented it: simple and fun. Memorizing half a dozen rule books didn't fit their definition of entertainment, especially when college games were readily available to most for free.

Dejected league owners of the day may have done well to study the success of professional baseball; the sport enjoyed a loyal following largely because its rules were simple and remained unchanging. Then again, perhaps they did — and decided they didn't like what they saw. Whereas present-day Major League Baseball has changed very little since the early 1900s, a pro basketball game from that era would be nearly unrecognizable today. The interesting thing is, the same could be said when comparing that first game played in the Springfield gym in December 1891 to a hotly contested Eastern League game a mere 25 years later.

Basketball, be it amateur or professional, continued to evolve by adapting to the style of its players. In 1915, the AAU, the NCAA, and the YMCAs formed a joint committee to study the game's many changes and establish a set of standardized guidelines to be followed by *all* amateur competition. Regional conferences were formed, and several division championships were played. Travel costs prohibited a true nationwide tournament, but the press often designated their favorite teams by referring to them as "national champions."

As basketball entered its third decade, it had undergone several major rule changes. By far the most important of these revolved around the dribble. Technically, Naismith's original rules did not prohibit a player from dribbling the ball, although the act would not be recognized as such today. A player was allowed to bounce the ball on the court if he wished, but not as a means of passing to a teammate. Nor could he take a shot immediately after bouncing the ball. He would have to catch it on the bounce while remaining in a stationary position, then pass to a teammate, move to the area he wanted to shoot from, receive the ball via a teammate's pass, and then, finally, attempt his shot.

Suffice it to say the early dribble was not considered an effective offensive exercise. Mainly, players used it as a means to escape a double- or triple-team. If a man was trapped by defenders and his passing lane blocked, he could drop the ball on the court away from the defenders, move a few steps while the ball was out of his hands and try to catch it again at a new angle — hopefully one that included an open teammate. Nonetheless, the move progressed. Savvy players soon realized that by repeatedly dropping the ball and retrieving it, they could maintain control while avoiding their defenders. Yale became one of the first teams to make effective use of the maneuver, which, according to Naismith, became known as the "dribble game."[8] The rule was amended in 1908 to allow the dribbler to shoot without passing first. At the same time, the two-handed dribble (today's double dribble) which had been used extensively by some players was banned from the amateur game, though most pro teams continued to allow it.

In 1908, an extra official was added to help curtail the ever-increasing physical style of play. Referees were given the power to disqualify a player if he committed five personal fouls. Two years later, that number was reduced to four. Most pro teams, however, continued their policy of no disqualifications for personal fouls.

A new out of bounds rule was established in 1913 in the hope it would eliminate the turmoil that occurred when the ball rolled out of play. (Cages were rarely found on amateur courts and were in the process of being phased out by the pros.) Initially, the rule was changed so that the opponent of whoever had caused the ball to go out of bounds would put it back into play. The practice often proved too time-consuming, however, so the following year it was changed to award possession to the nearest opponent.

In 1917, the endzone (end line) was established. The area had a radius of

17 feet, using the free-throw line as its center point. Prior to this, the ball was considered out of bounds if it went beyond the point directly underneath the goal — a rule that proved difficult to enforce when there were numerous players scrambling for a rebound.

One of the most significant changes revolved around player substitutions. Previously, any player who left the game for whatever reason could not return *for the duration* of the game. The rule was amended in 1920 to allow players to reenter the game once. The following season, in a move that reflected the growing popularity of the dribble, running with the ball (it was not yet called traveling) was changed from a personal foul to a violation.

By this point, all teams carried an expert free-throw shooter on their rosters, much as the present-day NFL retains a field goal kicker. Judging by today's foul-shot accuracy, these "experts" would be considered anything but, posting percentages in the mid- to high sixties at best. Regardless, they were good enough to draw the attention of the powers that be, and the free throw rule was amended, forcing the player who had been fouled to take his own free throws. Unfortunately for offense-hungry fans, the move did little to increase final scores.

Equipment, too, continued to improve. Open nets became standard in 1913. Wire backboards had given way to wood or plate glass, and were positioned two feet away from the wall of the court to prevent players from climbing up the padded wall to score goals. In 1916, all backboards were painted white to alleviate the disadvantage some teams encountered when trying to bank in a shot on clear glass boards (there were no background markings on these boards, which confused some players).

Despite pro basketball's remarkably swift evolution, one aspect remained stubbornly unchanged; less a few short-lived exceptions, pro rosters remained 100 percent white. But as with most facets of life, African Americans did not let such prejudices discourage them. As their all-white counterparts would soon find out, all-black basketball teams were quite adept at playing Naismith's game. So adept that two of the four teams enshrined in the Basketball Hall of Fame feature *all*-black rosters: the Renaissance Five of New York (more commonly known as the Rens) and the Harlem Globetrotters.

Neither club had arrived on scene as basketball celebrated its 30th birthday, but their time was drawing near. And with it, a glimpse of the future: tremendous players performing magical skills on the court, a combination that would ultimately set the stage for the success of professional basketball.

COLOR LINES

Glossy black Model Ts, gangsters and tommy guns, bootleggers and speakeasies. It's hard to imagine any decade with a more appropriate sobriquet than the Roaring Twenties. In the aftermath of the First World War, America was experiencing an unprecedented level of prosperity, a situation that allowed for major advances in technology. The first radio broadcast of a sporting event — a boxing match between Johnny Dundee and Johnny Ray at Motor Square in Pittsburgh — hit the airwaves in 1922. Two years later, Russian-born engineer Vladimir Zworykin developed the iconoscope, an image-scanner that provided the basis for television. Three years later, Walter Gifford, the president of AT&T, presented the first TV demonstration, and Charles Lindbergh made his legendary transatlantic flight.

On the social front, however, America lagged behind, clinging to policies that promoted segregation. The short-lived Civil Rights Law of 1875, which made racial discrimination in theaters, hotels, and other public establishments illegal, had been struck down by the Supreme Court in 1883 under the guise that Congress could not legislate matters of segregation. The trend continued in 1896 with the infamous *Plessy v. Ferguson* case, and "separate but equal" became the policy oxymoron of the land.

Despite African Americans' treatment during this era, their culture not only managed to survive, it flourished. The number of urban black communities had increased significantly since the turn of the century and remained on the rise. No longer confined to poor rural areas in the South, black leaders worked together to improve their social and educational opportunities. Many published local newspapers and magazines. College-educated blacks denounced the segregation-friendly policies of Booker T. Washington and demanded they be treated as true equals, a crusade that gained momentum in the 1920s as black intellectuals and notable artists of the day gathered in inner-city hubs to promote and discuss their ideas.[1]

Individually, black artists had made great strides, among them novelist and poet Paul Laurence Dunbar, whose parents were former slaves. Dunbar published four novels, numerous short story collections, and several volumes of poetry between 1893 and 1906. Alabama-born composer and bandmaster W. C. (William Christopher) Handy is largely credited with bringing international attention to the blues, while jazz great Louis Armstrong would soon turn the traditional, collective sound of improvisational jazz into a solo affair, paving the way for such future smash hits as "Blueberry Hill" and "Mack the Knife."

Although sports had its place in African American culture, the talented pioneers of the day were not held in the same regard as their artistic and political counterparts. Opportunities for black athletes were sparse. Baseball was the only professional sport of significance, and that via the segregated Negro Leagues.

Nonetheless, Naismith's game had proven as popular among the nation's blacks as it was with whites. Organized play at black YMCAs, athletic clubs, and universities prospered under the guidance of the Interscholastic Athlete Association of the Middle States (ISAA), created in 1906. The organization was the brainchild of six African American high school and college educators, among them Harvard graduate Edwin B. Henderson. Employed as a physical educator training instructor in the Washington, D.C., area, Henderson organized several local black club and YMCA basketball teams, and would go on to write *The Negro in Sports*, the first book to address the topic of blacks in sports.

The Smart Set Athletic Club of Brooklyn — the first all-black pro club of record — debuted in 1906. The Smart Set was joined later that year by the Marathone Athletic Club and Saint Christopher's. Together, the three teams formed the Olympian Athletic Club League. This first all-black basketball league was successful enough to add three teams the following season: the Jersey City YMCA, the Alpha Physical Culture Club, and Saint Cyrian. Clubs boosted crowd attendance by sponsoring after-game dances, a mix that proved a popular winter activity among urban blacks, often drawing Friday- and Saturday-night crowds of several hundred.

In 1916, the Central Intercollegiate Athletic Association (CIAA) was formed. The organization's main goal was to promote the elevation of athletics in black schools across the country. According to historian Charles Thompson, basketball played a significant role in that movement. "It was the game of basketball that served as the catalyst for the growth and development of many black high school athletic associations, for a number of these organizations were founded in conjunction with efforts to establish state tournaments."[2] Indeed, by this point, it was not uncommon for black and white teams to engage in amateur competition against each other in the East and Midwest. The practice was strictly forbidden in the South, however, where new Jim Crow laws appeared with disturbing regularity.

The most prominent black team of this era was the Loendi Big Five from Pittsburgh. The squad was led by organizer and player Cum Posey, an impressive athlete who became better known for his talents as a center fielder for the Murdock Grays of the Negro Leagues. The Leondi Big Five's aggressive, fast-paced style proved a box office hit, making them one of the most financially successful teams of their day.

Although Jackie Robinson is largely credited with cracking the color barrier in major league sports when he took the field for the Brooklyn Dodgers on April 15, 1947, he was not the first African American to play pro baseball on a white team. In 1878, John "Bud" Fowler played on minor league teams in New Castle, Pennsylvania, and Chelsea, Massachusetts. In 1883, Moses Fleetwood Walker and his brother, Welday, played for the Toledo Blue Stockings. When the Blue Stockings joined the American Association for the 1884 season, the Walker brothers became the first African Americans to play in baseball's major leagues. In his informative book *They Cleared the Lane: The NBA's Black Pioneers*, author Ron Thomas reports that blacks played professional football side by side with whites as early as 1920.[3]

In the world of professional basketball, isolated incidents occurred as early as 1902. One such documented case revolved around the Pawtuckerville Athletic Club, a Massachusetts team from the New England Basketball League. According to William Himmelman of Nostalgia Sports Research, Pawtuckerville suffered numerous injuries in the 1902-03 season, leading them to enlist the services of a local player from the neighborhood by the name of Bucky Lew, a talented young man who just happened to be black. Pawtuckerville's manager signed the 18-year-old Lew after assuring him all he would have to do to collect his $5 paycheck for the night was show up and sit on the bench, that he would never be called on to actually *play*.

Lew's addition gave Pawtuckerville a six-man roster for their game against Marlborough on November 7, 1902. Since many pro teams of the day played the entire game using only their starters (in Pawtuckerville's case, five), the manager's remark was not necessarily prejudicial. But it was premature. As fate would have it, one of Pawtuckerville's starters suffered an injury and had to leave the court. The nature of his injury was irrelevant, as the rules then stated any player who left the court for whatever reason was out for the remainder of the game. Initially, Pawtuckerville continued play without making a substitution, but the hometown crowd was not impressed with their manager's 4-on-5 strategy. Lew entered the game and finished it, earning himself a spot on the team for the rest of the season. In 1958, he recalled the experience with reporter Gerry Finn of the *Springfield Union*.

> All those things you read about ... the abuse, the name-calling ... they're all true. Basketball was a rough game then. I took the bumps, the elbows in the gut, knees here and everything else that went with it. But I gave it right back. It was rough but worth it. Once they knew I could take it, I had it made. Some of those same boys who gave the hardest licks turned out to be among my best friends in the years that followed.[4]

Lew played for rival Haverhill the next two seasons. When the New England League disbanded in the 1905-06 season, he organized teams and barnstormed throughout the East for the next years, finally retiring in 1926 at the age of 42.[5]

Bucky Lew's experience, and those of other players who later shared their stories, tend to suggest it wasn't white *teammates* who objected to playing alongside their black peers. The problem resided with management and its reluctance to challenge the status quo. As noted by Lew's quote, basketball was a rough game, and that roughness was not confined to players on the court. Fans embraced the sport with intensity; they wanted, *expected* their home teams to prevail. Losses, especially lopsided ones, brought out the worst in many. Adding racism to the mix was a daring venture few owners were willing to risk.

It is ironic yet fitting that the most violent of all sports was the first to test the racial waters on a national level. Jack Johnson, considered the best African American boxer in the United States during the early 1900s, had struggled for years to arrange title matches with America's top white fighters to no avail. Promoters claimed blacks fighting whites would tarnish the sport's reputation at a time when it was trying to build credibility. But the boxing world outside U.S. borders harbored no such apprehension. In 1908, Johnson traveled to Sydney, Australia, to fight the current heavyweight champion of the world, Canadian Tommy Burns. Johnson won the fight and the heavyweight title, a situation that did not sit well with many white boxing fans in the States.

As Johnson defended his crown five times over the next two years, racist whites in America clamored for someone, *anyone*, to step forward and take back what was rightfully theirs. Former champ Jim Jeffries, who had retired undefeated in 1905, finally answered the call, albeit reluctantly. Dubbed "the Great White Hope" for obvious reasons, Jeffries squared off against Johnson in Reno, Nevada, on July 4, 1910. Promoters got all the fireworks they'd hoped for and more when Johnson knocked Jeffries out in the 15th round.

Within hours of Johnson's victory, enraged whites were rioting and lynching black men across the nation. Many blacks reciprocated with violent acts, putting the nation on the brink of civil war. The armed forces went on standby alert. Amid attempts to calm a frightened nation, President Taft threatened to prohibit boxing in its entirety. A few days later, Congress passed legislation that banned the screening of the Johnson–Jeffries fight in movie theaters throughout the country.

The incident served as a bleak reminder that racism was alive and well, and not just in the South. Even in the so-called liberal East, where African Americans attended such prestigious universities as Harvard and Yale, most were refused service by white-owned hotels and restaurants nearby. There may not have been "No Coloreds" signs on all the doors, but blacks were well aware of the unspoken rules. They were expected to ride in the rear of the bus, give up their seats to whites. Their children dared not play with white children in neighborhood parks let alone drink from the same water fountain.

Black athletes were among those who suffered the greatest indignities, especially when they traveled beyond the familiar borders of their hometowns. Yet amateurs and professionals alike were willing to endure the humiliation of sleeping in cars or buses and eating cold sandwiches out of brown paper bags if it meant they could play ball. They ignored the racial slurs and threats hurled their way from hostile fans. They tolerated on-court abuse from opposing players, the intentional elbows to the face, the hard shots to the ribs, all in plain view of referees who looked the other way.

Promoters took note. There was no question blacks could play basketball every bit as well as whites. Why let a little thing like skin color stand in the way? As future NBA player John Salley remarked years later, "The color of money is green."[6]

British West Indies immigrant Robert L. Douglas had the business sense and vision necessary to ignore the limitations of his own color. Douglas arrived in the States in the early 1900s and settled in New York, where he formed the Spartan Field Club. The athletic club featured several black sports teams, among them the Spartans who played in the local Metropolitan Basketball Association. Teams in the MBA faced off against each other as well as other prominent teams of the day, including the Loendi Big Five. The Spartans were one of the most successful amateur teams of their era until they were cited for using professional players in late 1921. The MBA ordered Douglas to remove the two players in question, Frank Forbes and Leon Monde. He refused, and the Spartans' MBA days were over.

By this point, Douglas knew there was money to be made in basketball. He had the experience and the players, all he needed was a court to call home and he would be in business, the professional basketball business. In 1922, Douglas learned of a new entertainment center that had recently opened in Harlem: the Renaissance Casino. The facility, located at 138th Street and 7th Avenue, was not a casino by today's terminology. The building featured a ground-floor theater and a second-story ballroom available for private parties and banquets. The Renaissance was owned by Harlem real estate agent William Roche, who just happened to be another West Indian immigrant. Douglas arranged a meeting, and the Harlem Renaissance basketball team was born. For his part in the deal, Roche received a percentage of the gate and a promise from Douglas that his team would not tear up the dance floor. Douglas got his home court base in the center of downtown Harlem.

The Harlem Renaissance, known as the Rens for short, was a success from the opening tip, beating the Chicago Collegians 28–22 on November 30, 1923. Joining the MBA-banned Frank Forbes and Leon Monde that night were teammates Harold Mayers, Jack Anderson, and Hy Monte. The Rens finished their first season with an impressive 38-10 record. Bob Douglas managed all home games. On the road, the squad was coached by Eric Illidge, a no-nonsense type who demanded his players be paid upfront and in cash on arrival at the gate.

During their early years, the Rens played the majority of their games in

The Renaissance, later known as the New York Rens, was one of the most successful barnstorming team, black or white, in the history of professional basketball. *Left to right:* Clarence "Fat" Jenkins, Bill Yancey, John Holt, James "Pappy" Ricks, Eyre Saitch, Charles "Tarzan" Cooper, "Wee Willie" Smith. *Insert:* Owner Robert L. Douglas (Basketball Hall of Fame, Springfield, MA).

the New York area, but by 1930 they were traveling extensively throughout the East, Midwest, and South with a schedule of 130 games or more per season. Much of that time was spent on the road, sometimes for periods of two to three months straight. Travel conditions varied. Major cities in the East and Midwest presented the fewest problems insofar as the players' ability to find a decent meal and accommodations for the night, but as was the case for most barnstorming teams of the era, to post a profit, the Rens had to play *every* night, usually twice on weekends. As such, a good percentage of games were scheduled against amateur and semi-pro teams, most of which hailed from small towns. Many residents in these communities had never seen a black person, let alone shared a meal with one. And they were not about to start with the Rens.

The team made the best of a bad situation, using the bigotry as motivation on the court. Once the game was under way, the Rens were clearly the team to beat, whether they faced amateurs or professionals, blacks or whites. Their style featured short, crisp passing, suffocating defense, and foot speed that left most opponents gasping for air between possessions. The club was led by such early stars as 5'7" playmaker Clarence Jenkins and his backcourt mate, Bill Yancey, both of whom spent their summers playing baseball in the Negro Leagues, and James "Pappy" Ricks, the team's star shot-maker. Future original Celtic great Joe Lapchick described the Rens' pivot man, 6'4" Charles "Tarzan" Cooper, as "the best center I ever saw."[7] So good were the Rens that they often held back, allowing their opponents to remain in the game — a necessary strategy when dealing with opponents they hoped to play again soon. "After all," explained Ren player Puggy Bell, "we had to make money."[8]

Following the game, the usually victorious Rens boarded their team bus to a chorus of racial slurs and boos and returned to the nearest big city hub — often two or three hundred miles away — to grab a shower, a meal, and a few hours sleep, after which they got up and did it all over again. In the South, where they were not welcome at hotels or restaurants anywhere, they stayed at black YMCAs or churches, or slept on the team bus where meals of bologna sandwiches, crackers and cheese were passed around.

The racism encountered by the Harlem Rens was not confined to small town borders or ignorant fans in the seats. Whistles rarely sounded when a Ren player was fouled by an opposing player who happened to be white. The biased officiating led to the team's road motto, "Get Ten," which meant once the game was under way, players gave their all until they had established a 10-point lead, the spread they expected to lose to noncalls by referees during the game.

Despite the Rens' remarkable on court success, professional basketball seemed destined to remain a white man's game. The top-ranked barnstorming team of the Roaring Twenties was not Douglas's New York Rens but a group of Yankees who called themselves the Original Celtics. The team had enjoyed limited success as semi-pros during World War I, when they were known as the New York Celtics. Local promoter James Furey changed the team's name to the Original Celtics when he took over in 1918, and the squad, which would soon draw regular crowds of three and four thousand, was on its way to becoming a basketball dynasty.

Furey's team emphasized defense and passing above scoring — they rarely posted 40-point games— and is generally credited for developing the "give-and-go," where a player who has received the ball passes to a teammate while running toward the goal, gets the ball back en route and scores before the defense has time to react. Overall, the early Celtics prided themselves on bulk and strength. Among their most influential players were 6'5" Joe Lapchick and 6'4", 225-pound George (Horse) Haggerty. Lapchick became famous for his play on the center jump, while Haggerty is often called the game's first enforcer for his on-court fearlessness of opponents and referees.

Some historians also attribute the invention of the pivot play to the Original Celtics, in particular bulky forward/center Dutch Dehnert. The maneuver calls for an offensive player to position himself on or around the free throw line, directly in front of the defensive man who is guarding the path to the goal.

Said offensive player roams about the free-throw line waiting to catch a pass from a teammate cutting to the basket. If the defensive man moves to intercept the pass or block the lane, the offensive player holding the ball — in the Celtics' case, Dehnert — simply "pivots" to the other side of the basket and lays up the goal. Although the Celtics used the play more effectively than any other team of their era, evidence suggests the maneuver existed prior to the Celtics, perhaps dating back to the turn-of-the-century New York Wanderers from the old National Basketball League. According to Original Celtic Hall of Famer Nat Holman, the pivot move "came about through a long process of evolutionary change," and the Celtics "did much to bring the play to its present state of comparative success."[9] Nonetheless, the Celtics perfected the play as near art form, causing crowds to ooh and ahh whenever it was performed.

Like the Rens, the Original Celtics played in excess of a hundred games per season and won most of them. But unlike the Rens, they played in regional leagues on occasion. Led by the amazing passing of forward Nat Holman, the Celtics won the Eastern League title going away in 1921–22. The following year, the team played in the Metropolitan League for half a season, but it, too, provided little competition for the increasingly talented group. So the Celtics returned to the barnstorming circuit, where they traveled upward of 150,000 miles per season. Their colossal success eventually translated into salaries of $10,000.[10]

When comparing the Celtics to the Rens, it must be noted the Celtics had existed, in one form or another, for nearly a decade before the Rens played their first game as pros in November 1923. By then, the Eastern League had folded and the Metropolitan League (not to be confused with the amateur Metropolitan Basketball Association), in the midst of its third season, was struggling mightily. The Celtics remained one of the few mainstays in professional basketball, drawing crowds throughout the East and Midwest on the strength of their established record as a powerhouse. The Rens were a new team struggling to find their identity. Although the Celtics' dominance of pro basketball may have overshadowed Douglas's squad during that struggle, and race factored in that dominance, the rivalry that resulted proved advantageous to both teams.

From the beginning, the Celtics relished playing the Rens, whom they viewed as one of few worthy opponents. Games between the two clubs remained intense and competitive until the end; as such, players on both squads respected each other, on and off the court. In the 1925-26 season, the Rens played six games against the Celtics and won three — no small feat, given the Celtics' recent 134-6-1 record on the barnstorming circuit.

The basketball world quickly took notice. The Harlem Renaissance could play ball. They just couldn't do it in a white league.

Things were about to change. A new player was riding into town, proudly waving the successful banner of his *other* professional sports franchise, the five-year-old National Football League.

AROUND THE BEND

The entertainment business boomed like never before amid the prosperity of the early 1920s, and professional sports was not left behind. Fans were attending Major League Baseball games in record numbers, and football was gaining steam via the new NFL (National Football League).

Given the popularity of Naismith's game on the collegiate level, pro basketball should have been thriving as well. But aside from the few successful barnstorming teams, namely the Celtics and Rens, it was not. Most regional leagues had come and gone by 1923. Players from the dissolved Eastern and New York leagues either formed their own teams or signed with a franchise in the eastern-based Metropolitan League that had begun operations in 1921 (and, true to form, had siphoned the best players from the competing Eastern and New York leagues, leading to their demise). Although semi-pro and amateur leagues remained popular in the Midwest, no team from that region had belonged to a professional league since the dissolution of the Central League in 1912.

What did college ball have that remained lacking in the pros? Standardized rules and a diverse circuit. Schools from Chicago often played those in New York or Philadelphia. Boston teams visited Cleveland and Detroit. Fans were treated to different games, different players, and different styles. At the same time, the game itself remained familiar. Enthusiasts could follow the action on both ends of the court and knew what to expect — but not to the level of boredom. The Original Celtics and the Rens were successful for similar reasons; they traveled extensively and took on all comers. To date, pro basketball owners had either been slow to realize the obvious or simply ignored it in favor of making a quick buck. Regardless, as the Roaring Twenties reached their midway point, the light finally went on. Promoters decided the time was ripe for a *uniform* professional basketball league that stretched beyond the regional boundaries of New York and Philadelphia.

And so began the American Basketball League.

The organization was the brainchild of NFL president Joseph F. Carr, who also dabbled in minor league baseball operations in Columbus, Ohio. Carr

appointed himself president and secretary of the ABL and selected three businessmen — Chicago Bears owner George Halas, George Preston Marshal (who
would later own the Washington Redskins), and Max Rosenblum, the Cleveland department store owner — to serve on the executive committee.

Basketball historians deem it likely Furey's Original Celtics were offered
a slot in the new ABL but, for whatever reason, passed on the invitation. Speculation varies. The most plausible theory is one of finances — the revenue from
30 games versus 130 games. With the Celtics doing so well on the barnstorming circuit, why take a chance on what might turn into yet another here-today-
gone-tomorrow pro league? Another conjecture revolves around the Celtics'
respect for the Rens, specifically that the team took offense to the ABL not making a similar offer to the Rens and thus told Carr to stuff it. Either way, the two
elite teams in pro basketball — the Celtics and the Rens — would not be a part
of the new ABL. The nine franchises chosen for the league's inaugural 1925-26
season were: Buffalo Bisons, Boston Whirlwinds, Brooklyn Arcadians, Rochester
Centrals, Washington Palace Five, Chicago Bruins, Cleveland Rosenblums, Fort
Wayne Caseys, and Detroit Pulaski Post.

While all nine squads hailed from the East and Midwest, the ABL was considered "national" insofar as professional sports of the day were concerned.
Neither pro baseball nor football had yet ventured West of the Mississippi. Long
distance travel, while more common than it had been 20 years earlier, remained
a lengthy, expensive proposition. Furthermore, while San Francisco and Los
Angeles were up-and-coming cities, they did not compare to the metropolitan
hubs of Chicago, New York, and Boston. The South, although feasible from a
geographic standpoint, lingered in a time warp. Jim Crow laws strictly prohibited interracial play in sports; not only were blacks forbidden to play on white
squads, it was illegal for black and white *teams* to compete against other on the
same court. Although sports programs in schools and YMCAs continued to gain
popularity in spite of these laws, organizers deemed it unlikely states south of
the Mason-Dixon Line were ready to support a professional basketball franchise.

Despite geographic limitations, the ABL was determined to succeed where
other pro leagues had failed. Owners adapted the AAU's then-current rules, out-
lawing the double dribble and discarding the cages still in use by the Metropolitan League, whose teams would provide the most direct competition. All
players were signed to exclusive written contracts. There would be no "jumping teams" in the ABL, and its players were required to conduct themselves in
a professional manner at all times, on and off the court. Rule-breakers would
be subject to fines and/or suspensions. Gambling was strictly prohibited; any
team caught doing so would be permanently banned from the ABL. In a move
designed to gain favor with universities, no team could sign a college player
before his school eligibility had expired.

The new league began play with a modest 30-game schedule split into halves. All but the Boston Whirlwinds finished the first season intact, a satisfying start given the dropout rate of earlier pro leagues. The ABL's initial playoff series featured the top first-half season champ, the Brooklyn Arcadians, against the second-half winner, the Cleveland Rosenblums. Twenty thousand fans turned out to watch Cleveland's two home games. The Rosenblums whipped the Brooklyn Arcadians three games straight to become pro basketball's "World Series" champions.

The title was immediately disputed by Original Celtics' manager James Furey, who wasted no time challenging the victorious Rosenblums to a best of five series. The Cleveland owner just as swiftly declined. For its part, the Metropolitan League ignored the ABL's claim of World Series title, but owners were nervous, and for good reason. Although the ABL had been successful in keeping its players from jumping teams, many Metropolitan players had abandoned ship, opting to sign with ABL franchises for more money and the promise of stability.

Met owners, however, would not go quietly. The following season (1926-27), they managed to lure the Celtics into their lair and reemerged as the new National Basketball League. Alas, there was little new or national about it. With the exception of the Original Celtics, who received money guarantees above those of other NBL teams, the league was unable to stop its players from defecting to the more lucrative ABL. Furthermore, the "national" namesake was as much a front as it had been for the original turn-of-the-century National Basketball League: all seven teams haled from the New York–New Jersey area. Furey's Celtics tired of the league after compiling a 14–3 first half record and dropped out. The NBL collapsed shortly thereafter.

For all of its player allure, the ABL was hardly on solid ground as it embarked on year two. The winless Detroit Pulaski Post and the Brooklyn Arcadians dropped out midway through the season. The Detroit franchise was not replaced, but the Original Celtics took over for the 0-5 Arcadians. Several factors played into this unlikely scenario, the most important being Furey's absence from the team. The Celtics' owner/manager, who had worked as head cashier at a large New York department store during the off-season, was convicted of embezzling $187,000 and sent to prison for a three-year stint.

The Celtics remained a powerhouse on the court, dominating the ABL for the next two seasons, but they clearly missed their old manager's business savvy. Without Furey around to stop it, the league split up the Celtics at the start of the 1928-29 season in an effort to make its other franchises more competitive. Games no longer drew 10,000 fans, even in basketball-hungry Cleveland, but the league remained profitable through season's end, a sign that professional basketball was finally on the right track as the thirties loomed on the horizon.

The ABL's 1929-30 season was barely out of the gate when the stock market crashed on October 29, and once again, pro basketball fell victim to the times. The league managed to survive, albeit in a weakened state, through the

1930-31 season before succumbing to the Great Depression.[1] By then pro basketball had reverted to the days of old, with regional leagues popping up
throughout the East and Midwest, all vying for the same pool of talented players and a steadily shrinking fan base.

And so, as had been the case prior to the ABL, barnstorming teams
remained the lone success story in the world of professional basketball. The
regrouped Original Celtics were back on the road, though they would never
regain their glory days of the Roaring Twenties. The Rens, on the other hand,
had played together and stayed together. No team, including the revamped
Celtics, could claim superiority. In the 1932-33 season, the Rens posted an
astounding 120 wins—including a streak of 88 straight over a period of 86
days—against a mere 8 losses. Six of those losses came against the Celtics, as
did eight of the wins. These future Hall of Fame Rens included Bill Yancey,
"Wee" Willie Smith, Eyre Saitch, Charles "Tarzan" Cooper, John Holt, Clarence
"Fat" Jenkins, and James "Pappy" Ricks.[2] Saitch was also a nationally ranked
tennis star. Jenkins and Yancey played baseball in the Negro Leagues.

While the Rens were clearly the best team, black or white, to play the barnstorming circuit during the thirties, they were no longer the only show on the
road. Another all-black squad, the Harlem Globetrotters, were stirring things
up in the Midwest.

The Trotters were owned and managed by Abe Saperstein, a 5'3" Jewish
immigrant who had played high school basketball on Chicago's North Side and
later on the semi-pro Chicago Reds. Though his basketball skills were average
at best, the young British native had a great head for promotion. Saperstein
knew a good thing when he saw it, namely the growth of professional basketball via the traveling Rens and Celtics, and the Cleveland Rosenblums of the
up-and-coming American Basketball League. Determined to cash in on the
trend, he decided to start his own barnstorming team.

Previously published accounts state the would-be promoter built his club
around players from the Savoy Big Five, an all-black basketball team that played
weekend games at Chicago's famous dancehall, the Savoy Ballroom. Depending on which sources are consulted, Saperstein either took over management
of the current team or convinced its best members to sign with him, thereby
forming a new club entirely. However, according to evidence recently uncov-
ered by Jay T. Smith, program producer for the media enterprise Network
Chicago, the Savoy Ballroom did not open for business until November 23,
1927—more than a year after the Savoy Big Five was said to have been playing
there. Given that Smith's evidence came directly from the *Chicago Defender*, a
local newspaper of the day, it would seem irrefutable. What appears likely,
though it cannot be completely substantiated, is that Saperstein hooked up
with a local semi-pro team named the Giles Post American Legion—an early
version of the Savoy Big Five. In an article promoting upcoming basketball
games in the Savoy Ball Room on January 3 and 4, 1928, the *Defender* states:

"The Savoy team was formerly known as the American Legion Big Five."[3] Assuming the article was correct, it is probable Saperstein took over management of the Savoy Big Five when they were still known as the Giles Post American Legion, sometime in 1926.

In any event, the team credited with representing the first generation Harlem Globetrotters played its inaugural game as Saperstein's New York on January 7, 1927, in Hinckley, Illinois, a small town about 20 miles west of Chicago, and took home a winning purse of $75 to split among them.[4] Saperstein served as the team's only substitute, as well as coach, general manager, trainer, and driver.

"Home" was and would remain Chicago for the Trotters, even though their name implied otherwise. Saperstein believed inserting New York into the tag would draw bigger crowds by implying that his team, like the Rens, was a well-traveled, sophisticated group from basketball's talent-rich elite East Coast. Whether the strategy proved successful or the New York adage just grew on him is unknown, but in any event Saperstein's New York soon became simply New York, and then Saperstein's Harlem New York. By the mid–1930s, the team played as Saperstein's Harlem Globetrotters. Although Saperstein borrowed the Harlem name from the Rens, he did not infringe on their Eastern territory, confining his team's appearances to small towns in the Midwest and, as the 1930s began, the South and Pacific Northwest.

By far the biggest misconception concerning the Globetrotters is that they did not play serious basketball and thus should not be compared with the truly great teams. In truth, the club was very competitive, beating most opponents — pro, amateur, or college-level — by impressive margins. Because they won so easily, players began clowning around on the floor during games, making circus passes and dribbling between their legs in an effort to keep the score close and to alleviate their own boredom. One of the team's most famous routines was the "circle," a combination of fancy maneuvers performed at the start of every game. The display included smooth passing behind the back, spinning the ball on their fingertips, bouncing it off their head, knees, and elbows, all the while maintaining complete control.

Keeping the crowd entertained while the home club was taking it on the chin would appear sound strategy for any visiting team; for a black team playing against white opponents in the thirties, it bordered on genius. The tactic didn't always work, however. In his book, *Black Hoops: The History of African Americans in Basketball*, author Fredrick McKissack Jr. tells of an experience in Shelby, Montana, where the team was confronted with a no-win situation: A group of gamblers threatened to shoot them if they won the game. The local sheriff warned of a similar fate if they lost. The Trotters emerged victorious and fled the building in their uniforms, carrying their clothes under their arms. "You did not accept it," Hall-of-Fame Globetrotter Marques Haynes said of the racism the team encountered, "but at the same time you went along with it.

The Harlem Globetrotters are known for their entertaining, comedic routines, but the club played serious, competitive basketball in its early days, beating most opponents, amateur and pro, by substantial margins. The 1940 team won the World Professional Basketball Tournament in Chicago (Basketball Hall of Fame, Springfield, MA).

Because you had that feeling that some day, some day things would become better."[5]

The Globetrotters began incorporating more elaborate moves into their routine as the 1930s wound down, but they remained competitive enough to be invited to the first basketball World Tournament held in Chicago in 1939. The tournament, sponsored by the Chicago *Herald-American*, attracted the top professional teams in the country. In a preview of things to come, the all-black Trotters faced off against the all-black Rens in the second round with the Rens prevailing 27–23. The Rens went on to beat the white Oshkosh All-Stars of the newly refurbished National Basketball League, 34–25, and were crowned champions of the world. The Globetrotters avenged their loss the following year, beating the Rens in the quarterfinals 37–36, and the Chicago Bruins (also from the revived NBL) 31–29 in overtime to win the world title. The champion Trotters, who had amassed an eye-popping 159-8 win-loss record that year in surpassing their 2,000-career game mark, featured such stars as Babe Pressley, Sonny Bowell, and Bernie Price.[6]

The Harlem Globetrotters competed in the tournament until 1946 but never returned to the finals. By that point, the team had worked numerous comedy routines into their act to supplement their fancy ball maneuvers, making them an even bigger draw at the box office. Saperstein's club began traveling abroad after World War II, drawing sell-out crowds from Rio de Janeiro to Berlin. The team remains a popular attraction today. Enshrined in the Naismith Basketball Hall of Fame in September 2002, the Trotters have visited over 100 countries and played in excess of 20,000 games.

Despite the team's success, Saperstein himself acquired a mixed reputation. Some critics felt the Trotters' comedy routines were demeaning to African Americans, that their sole purpose was to portray blacks as simple-minded Uncle Toms who would do anything to get a laugh. Others theorized it was a matter of financial survival, that white fans would not pay to see their home teams embarrassed by blacks in straight, one-on-one basketball games. Many black NBA players, however, believe the Globetrotters' effect on the sport was a positive one.

"I had never seen anybody dribble the ball like that before," Philadelphia All-Star Walt Hazzard said of Trotters guard Marques Haynes, who played for the club in the late 1940s. "He'd be on the floor, on one knee and people couldn't take the ball from him ... I was seven or eight years old, and Marques had an immediate impact on me."[7] Former Los Angeles Lakers showtime guard Magic Johnson harbors similar feelings. "Marques Haynes was my hero when it came to dribbling."[8] Magic's Eastern rival of the day, 12-time NBA All Star point guard Isiah Thomas, thinks the team was simply ahead of its time. "The skills that they displayed and they played with, other people weren't thinking on that level. What they were able to do from the skill standpoint was to inspire others to dribble, to pass. Everyone found some way to incorporate the skills of the Globetrotters into their own personal game."[9]

Some historians go so far as to say Saperstein encouraged professional leagues to remain segregated because he wanted to sign the most talented African American players to Trotter contracts, a theory that, at first glance, has some merit from a fiscal standpoint. Most pro basketball teams of that era were anxious to schedule games or doubleheaders with the Globetrotters because the event usually sold out. Without such promotions, many struggling teams would not have survived. Enlightened by that knowledge, Saperstein may very well have threatened to keep his club from appearing at such events in an effort to thwart league teams from signing black players. Whether he actually would have done so, however, seems unlikely, given the two were interdependent. Pro teams constituted a good percentage of the Trotters' opponents. Without them, the Globetrotters would have played fewer games and made substantially less money. In any event, there is no question basketball fans of all skin colors enjoyed watching the Trotters play and were willing to part with their hard-earned cash for the privilege — a fact that remains true today.

As the thirties neared an end, basketball had become more fast-paced than its creator ever imagined. The 10-second rule implemented in 1932 established a line across the center of the court and required the offense to get the ball across it before the allotted 10 seconds had expired. It became a violation for an offensive player to hold the ball in the six-foot-wide foul lane for more than three seconds without passing to a teammate or dribbling out of the painted area. In 1936, that three-second violation was amended to include *every* player in the lane, making for a blur of constant movement under and around the basket. The following year, the center jump to determine possession after every score was scrapped, paving the way for slick full-court passes and crowd-pleasing break-away baskets. Rather than jump the ball after a score, the team that had given up the basket was awarded the ball and five seconds to inbound it from behind the opponent's end line. Failure to do so resulted in a turnover.

Equipment, too, was changing. The ball was smaller, with a specified circumference of 29.5 to 30 inches. It bounced better and passed more easily. Shoes were made of canvas uppers with cushioned arches and soles specifically designed to provide good traction.

Of all the changes the game had undergone in its 45-year history, abolishing the center jump was by far the most controversial. No one was more opposed than the game's inventor himself. Doctor Naismith, about to retire from his teaching days at the University of Kansas when the rule was implemented, believed it would slow rather than quicken the game's pace. "In the old days it took the referee four seconds to throw the ball up after a score. Now the team scored against can take 15 seconds to bring it beyond the center line."[10] Naismith thought the game would become monotonous if the ball was simply awarded to the opposing team after a score, and many basketball purists agreed. Nonetheless, the change was in the rule books to stay.

So too was professional basketball. Although the game would continue to struggle under the tutorage of its new overseer — the fifth organization to call itself the National Basketball League — *this* NBL would finally get it right.

DOUBLE TROUBLE

The last organization to call itself the National Basketball League was the Midwest Basketball Conference (MBC), a loosely run pro/semi-pro league which began operation in the 1935-36 season. The league was composed of independent teams such as those from YMCAs and athletic clubs, company squads whose players were regular employees of the business (and thereby collected no extra pay for their efforts), and teams owned by businesses or corporations.

Most MBC teams were located in small or mid-market areas stretching from Fort Wayne, Indiana, to Buffalo, New York, and included a schedule that was confusing at best. Each club was responsible for setting up its own games and was to play a minimum of 10 per season within the league. Each team had to play at least four games on the road, and no club could play another more than four times. The result was a hodgepodge of win-loss records and a playoff structure that left fans wondering how the Chicago Duffy Florals could be crowned champions when they had played a mere 5 league games all season, whereas teams like Akron and Toledo had played nearly 20.

Regardless, the league continued play under similar conditions after opting to change its name to the National Basketball League at the start of the 1937-38 season. Owners later confided the decision was approved with the hope it would generate more attention in the media, though the formal explanation given at the time was the league wanted to distinguish itself from the Big Ten college conference, often referred to in print as the Midwest Conference. The name change was lost on most fans and even some players. So disorganized was the first year that Gene Scholz of the last-place Columbus Athletic Supply confessed he wasn't even aware his team was in a pro league. "I didn't know what was going on," Scholz recalled. "I was just picking up a few bucks on the side playing basketball."[1]

Thanks to several strong clubs with sound financial backing, the NBL made it to season two, though its 13 teams had been pared down to 8. Two squads from Akron, Ohio, the Goodyear Regulars and the Firestone Nonskids, were funded by their namesake corporations, while Wisconsin claimed two successful

47

independent clubs in the Oshkosh All Stars and Sheboygan Redskins. The All Stars were owned and operated by local businessman Lon Darling, who also served as manager and coach. The team, which had played on the semi-pro circuit since 1929, joined the NBL in 1937 and realized instant success, winning five consecutive Western Division titles from 1937-38 to 1942-43. The Redskins were formed by a group of city locals hoping to mirror Oshkosh's success with a pro basketball team of their own. While nowhere near as dominant as the All Stars, the Sheboygan franchise was good enough to win one NBL championship and two division titles during its 11 years in the league.

By this point, average player salaries had escalated from a meager $5–10 per game in the league's early Midwest Conference days to $300 per month in the NBL, with some players receiving monthly salaries as high as $1500. Fans were treated to faster games with average scores in the thirties and forties. It was no longer unusual for top players to post scoring averages in the high teens.

Although the new NBL had yet to become the talk of the professional sports world, the league was making enough noise to stay afloat and appeared on track to buck the trend of its failed predecessors. There was every reason to believe it would happen. Globally, basketball fever had reached an all-time high following the sport's first official appearance at the 1936 Olympic Games in Berlin, where 74-year-old Dr. Naismith witnessed the United States defeat Canada 19-8 for the gold medal.

The experience clearly inspired the game's creator. Upon his return to Kansas, where he was employed as a coach at Baker University in Baldwin, Naismith and fellow hoops enthusiast Frank Cramer decided Kansas City should hold its own small college basketball tournament. Working in concert with the school's athletic director, Emil Liston, and several prosperous local businessmen, the National Association for Intercollegiate Athletics (NAIA) became reality in 1937. Eight regional teams participated in the first tournament, with Warrensburg College (Central Missouri) beating Morningside (Iowa) 35–24 in the finals. Naismith also designed the trophy awarded to the winners, a replica of which remains the take-home prize for NAIA champions.

Tournament fever quickly spread throughout the collegiate circuit. The following year, the Metropolitan Basketball Writers Association organized the National Invitational Tournament (NIT) in New York. The event was held at Madison Square Garden where a packed house watched Temple clobber Colorado 60–36 in the finals. Not to be outdone, the National Collegiate Athletic Association (NCAA) launched its own basketball tournament in 1939. Teams from Oklahoma, Villanova, Oregon, and Ohio State made up the conference's initial Final Four. In the championship game, Oregon beat Iowa State 46–33 to win the first NCAA title.

The decade ended on a somber note when Naismith died of a stroke on November 28 at the age of 78, having reaped, in the words of *Time* magazine, mere "pennies" from his invention.[2] Much discussion has ensued as to whether

The USA Basketball team of 1936, the first year basketball was recognized as an official sport of the Games. *Front row, left to right:* Jimmie Needles, head coach; Sam Baiter; Dwayne Swanson; Art Moliner; Francis Johnson; Jack Ragland; Don Piper; Gene Johnson; Dr. Joseph Reiley, assistant coach. *Back row, left to right:* Carl Shy; Carl Knowles; Frank Lubin; Willard Schmidt; Joe Fortenberry; Ralph Bishop; Bill Wheatly; Tex Gibbons (USA Basketball).

basketball's inventor was simply not shrewd enough to capitalize on his invention or made a conscious effort not to do so. According to Naismith's grandson Stuart, "Papa Jimmy" was never interested in money. "He never made any and he never had any," Stuart recalled.[3] "My grandfather was a kind, very nice man and a lot of fun."[4] He was also a man of strong morals, the reason cited for his refusal to endorse a tobacco company following the success of his game at the 1936 Olympics—an endorsement that would have been worth anywhere from $75,000 to $500,000 according to *The Basketball Man* author, Bernice Webb. Most likely, James Naismith reaped exactly what he'd wanted out of his game—the knowledge that people were having *fun* when they played it.

And indeed, they were. As the 1940s got under way, the Basketball World Tournament sponsored by the Chicago *Herald-American* continued to pull in the best of the best professional teams from across the nation, playing to packed houses of 20,000 cheering fans. It seemed inevitable Naismith's game was poised to join its illustrious counterparts—baseball, football, and hockey—as a legitimate professional sport. Yet if one constant existed in the world of pro basketball, it was timing. Bad timing. Just as the NBL had begun to stand on solid ground, the Japanese bombed Pearl Harbor, forcing the United States into the Second World War.

How could Americans justify interest in professional basketball — or any sport, for that matter — when a madman was threatening the very existence of free society? Young men across the country answered the president's call and headed off to war. More than a few came from the ranks of professional sports teams, be it of their own decision or courtesy of the draft. The NBL managed to keep seven teams up and running through the end of the 1941-42 season, but only five made it through the summer intact. Bottom line: there were simply not enough good players left to go around.

World War I had taken its toll in similar manner, slowing the progress of several regional leagues of the day and eliminating most of them. The dwindling NBL had two choices: risk a similar fate by suspending operations during the war or sign whatever talented players they could get their hands on.

Despite the proven talent of black athletes, be it in baseball's Negro Leagues or on world champion basketball teams, professional sports had continued to resist integration. It mattered little that blacks had earned the respect of their white colleagues on and off the playing field or that people of all colors came to watch the Rens and Globetrotters play. Promoters remained convinced the majority of fans would not accept blacks playing alongside whites, let alone pay for the privilege of watching.

With the exception of the National Football League's early years (1920–32), on the rare occasion when integration had occurred it remained an isolated affair — one or two black players amid an entire league of white teams. Technically, the first black to suit up for the NBL was Hank Williams, a 6'4" center who played for the Buffalo Bisons in 1935, when the league debuted as the Midwest Basketball Conference. But the move did not catch on. The Bisons were absent from the Midwest Conference the following season, and when they joined the NBL in 1937, Williams was no longer part of the squad.

As the NBL's first wartime season hobbled to an end in spring 1942, not one team carried a black player on its roster. There was, however, no specific rule in the league charter prohibiting the practice. And so, in an attempt to keep their ball clubs running amid the ever-dwindling circle of available players, the Toledo Jim White Chevrolets and the Chicago Studebakers announced they were adding blacks to their rosters for the upcoming season. "Some of them (owners) didn't relish it," recalled Sid Goldberg, the Toledo team's owner, "but I don't think any of them objected."[5]

The Chicago Studebakers made it through the season by signing several Harlem Globetrotters. The franchise held a distinct advantage over most pro teams because its club was made up of regular company employees; since the auto manufacturer had converted to wartime production, its players were not subject to the military draft. The Toledo franchise was not so fortunate. After losing its star player, Chuck Chuckovitz, to the army, the team amassed a dismal

0-4 record and folded in December. Chicago finished 8-15 and disbanded that summer. The league shrunk to an all-time low of four teams for the 1943-44 season, but its spotty integration managed to survive; former Ren star Willie Smith played center that year for the Cleveland Chase Brass.

As groundbreaking as the move had been for professional sports, the NBL's integration went largely unnoticed. No doubt the war contributed to the lack of publicity, but the reality was the NBL had yet to catch on with mainstream America. Several age-old factors continued to impede its progress—college ball's astounding popularity (now complete with national tournaments), the instability of the pro teams, and a league that had yet to excite fans beyond the borders of the East and Midwest.

The latter remained the biggest road block. Coast-to-coast travel had become more common, spurred on by the emergence of the big three college tournaments, but remained far too costly to consider on a weekly basis. Even without that hindrance, wartime policy would have prohibited it. Adding more teams to the NBL seemed the obvious solution, but it simply was not a viable option at the time, given the shortage of available talent.

Ironically, what seemed like the worst thing that could have happened to the NBL—the escalation of World War II and the military's subsequent raid of its best players—is largely credited with saving the league. While the first 50 years of basketball had undergone many changes, it remained a simple game played with simple equipment: a ball, two baskets, and a court. Thanks to the massive pool of talented athletes available to the military, every branch was able to form its own teams. They did so in broad numbers, across the nation and around the world. Nearly every military base, hospital, fort, and training station had a basketball team. Squads played each other as well as teams from the AAU, YMCAs, colleges, even pro and semi-pro clubs. As a result, organized basketball was in the spotlight like never before. Different styles blurred together, making for a more universal game.

When the war finally ended in August 1945, eager NBL owners looked forward to a robust year ahead. And with good reason. No more travel restrictions to worry about when scheduling games and plenty of players to fill their depleted rosters. The rejuvenated league returned to eight teams for the 1945-46 season, with the franchises evenly split between the Eastern and Western Divisions. The addition of the Rochester Royals, a former semi-pro team from Illinois, gave the NBL its first franchise outside traditional Midwest borders.

The NBL's first postwar season was every bit as successful as owners had hoped. Four new teams were welcomed into the league for the 1946-47 season, and the schedule was increased from 34 to 44 games. Slowly but surely, the organization was becoming prime time. Despite competition from semi-pro circuits and barnstorming teams, the NBL had become the preferred choice for the majority of college stars looking to turn pro.

NBL owners were not alone in their optimism regarding the future of professional basketball amid the fast-improving postwar economy. As had been the case following the end of World War I, Americans were hungry for entertainment. Facilities to house that entertainment were plentiful, especially in major cities; unfortunately, there were not nearly enough circuses, ice shows, concerts, or rodeos to go around during the long winter months. Hockey, boxing, and college basketball filled some of the void, but stadium owners were still faced with far too many empty dates on their calendars. A source of steady revenue would have to be found if they were to remain in operation. Pro basketball seemed like a viable option.

Without exception, the latest NBL was a product of basketball people from top to bottom, sports enthusiasts whose main goal was to put professional basketball on the map via nationwide competition. Making money was an important but secondary objective, as proven by the number of rural entries. The then-current powerhouses of the league — the Sheboygan Redskins, Oshkosh All Stars, and Rochester Royals — were all small-town teams, franchises that had earned the loyalty of their fans in the usual way: by winning games and competing for championships. Alas, prestige did not equal fiscal rewards. A packed house in Sheboygan and Oshkosh meant 3,000–4,000 paying customers with an average ticket price of under $1. Less successful teams were lucky to draw a thousand fans on any given night. NBL teams survived only because their owners *wanted* to remain in the game.

Savvy businessmen had never given up on the idea of pro basketball for profit, however. Arena owners such as Madison Square Garden's Ned Irish and Walter Brown of Boston Garden had been kicking the idea around for several years. The NBL's ability to survive during the lean years and its strong resurgence in the postwar economy convinced them the time had arrived. One option was to approach the existing NBL with the idea of expanding into a larger base via the metropolitan market. The idea was appealing in that the new teams would gain immediate credibility and play against well-established clubs with proven stars. On the downside, as newcomers, owners would have little clout regarding league operations.

In the end, Ned Irish and his cohorts from the Arena Managers Association of America decided their money and business expertise would be better spent on creating a new pro league of their own, and thus was born the Basketball Association of America (BAA). The league opened play in the 1946-47 season with 11 teams onboard. The St. Louis Bombers, Chicago Stags, Detroit Falcons, Cleveland Rebels, and Pittsburgh Ironmen made up the league's Western Division. In the East were the Washington Capitols, Philadelphia Warriors, Boston Celtics, New York Knickerbockers, Providence Steamrollers, and Toronto Huskies.

Most of the new owners already had hockey franchises that played in their arenas, so they were not new to the world of professional sports. Their teams came with ready-made home courts in the form of large-capacity arenas. All that remained was devising a strategy to fill the seats with paying customers.

To assist with that ambitious task, owners chose Russian immigrant and Yale law school graduate Maurice Podoloff, then the top man in the American Hockey League, as their president-commissioner. Podoloff was known throughout the business community for his strong leadership and negotiating skills. His BAA appointment made him the first person in the history of professional sports to simultaneously lead more than one pro sports organization.

The new league promptly distinguished itself by announcing its teams would play four 12-minute quarters for a total of 48 minutes of basketball — a full 8 minutes longer than college and other pro league games. Its schedule was also more ambitious: 60 regular season games to the NBL's 44. In a move that was likely meant to align teams more closely with their hometown fans, clubs were named for their respective cities rather than the business or corporation that supported them.

On the long-standing matter of integration, the BAA chose to adapt an open policy similar to that of the NBL. The racial issue had finally resonated on a mainstream level that year thanks to Jackie Robinson's groundbreaking season with the Montreal Royals, a farm team for the Brooklyn Dodgers. Several blacks were scattered about the NBL as the 1946-47 season got under way: former Globetrotter Willie King, Kentucky State standout Bill Farrow, William King from Long Island University, and ex–Ren star William (Pop) Gates.

Despite its presence in more racially mixed metropolitan hubs, the BAA remained 100 percent white for its inaugural season. Clubs filled their 12-man quotas by snapping up the best players from the regional ABA, which had finally suspended operations for good at the end of the 1945-46 season. A few players from the NBL defected to the new league, but most rosters were a mix of aging stars from independent and semi-pro squads, regional leagues, and graduating collegians. Salaries ranged from $3,500 to $6,500 — decent money for the era, though still not enough to keep most players from seeking regular employment during the summer.[6]

The NBL took a wait-and-see attitude toward its newest rival, a logical strategy given they had managed to coexist with the eastern ABA for years without significant problems. Only the new Chicago Stags would compete directly with an NBL franchise for hometown fans. BAA owners insisted they weren't interested in the National League's small-town market, so where was the threat? If anything, the new league would enhance the NBL's status by bringing more attention to the professional game. With teams in such key hubs as Boston and New York, the pro game was sure to grab its share of media attention.

The potential was promising. Both sides wanted it to work. Owners went so far as to predict they would emulate Major League Baseball by holding a basketball World Series between the two leagues at year's end. An interleague All Star Game was also a possibility. A month into the season, Podoloff and NBL commissioner Ward Lambert agreed to honor each other's contracts, a practice that put an end to the threat of players jumping leagues midseason. Rather than follow the strategy of their predecessors by undercutting each other at every opportunity, the NBL and BAA vowed to work in harmony toward a common goal: establishing their game as a legitimate professional sport.

The *New York Times* coverage of the Knickerbockers' home opener in Madison Square Garden against the Chicago Stags on November 11 was an early sign the NBL was indeed likely to benefit from the BAA. "Aside from the unexpected and — from a local viewpoint — the unhappy outcome, the first major-league professional basketball game to be played at Madison Square Garden since 1929 couldn't have done more to pave the way for the success of the newly formed Basketball Association of America if the script had been prepared in advance," wrote *Times* reporter Louis Effrat. A photo with the caption "A Scramble Under Basket In Garden Game," accompanied the four column article. According to the *Times*, 17,205 fans saw the Knicks lose to the Stags 78–68 in what proved to be the league's first overtime game.[7]

Radio station WHN in New York paid Garden/Knicks owner Ned Irish $250 per game for first season rights to broadcast Knicks games. Although radio was not totally new to basketball — a few games had been broadcast in the past, namely, college doubleheaders at the Garden — the practice itself was in the learning stages.

"I used to spend time thinking about how to broadcast basketball," sportscaster Marty Glickman recalled. "To set the scene in baseball, you give a pitch count, the number of outs, what runners are on which bases, and everyone can visualize the scene of the action. In football, you give down and yardage, set the line of scrimmage and the formation.... Basketball, however, is a fluid game, without the pauses between pitches or plays, so I had to set up a geography of the court, using the vernacular of the game, to set the scene. Then I could describe the dribbling to the top of the circle, cutting from the sideline through the lane, passing to the baseline, right-hand hook off the glass and the listeners could visualize the action just as it happened."[8] The Knicks' initial broadcasts proved a rousing success. In keeping with the BAA's we're-in-it-for-the-profit philosophy, Irish raised his price to $1,750 per game for the 1947-48 season.[9]

Style-wise, there was little difference between BAA and NBL games; both featured a slower pace and less scoring than the average collegiate contest. The jump shot was still in its infancy. Most players continued to score via the two-handed set shot with feet planted squarely on the court, often from a distance of 30 or more feet from the basket, thus it was not surprising that shooting percentages hovered in the twenties and thirties. Action within the six-foot-wide lane under the basket was as rough-and-tumble as ever, and the stalling technique often utilized in the fourth quarter by the leading team kept most final scores in the fifties.

Largely because the new league offered very little that was actually new to pro basketball, most BAA teams were fortunate to average 2,000–3,000 fans per game during season one. Some had trouble pulling in 1,000. Give-aways and gimmicks to entice fans became commonplace: a free oil change for a lucky number scorecard, ladies night reduced admissions, discount clothing certificates. When all was said and done, the BAA finished its opening season with a meager total of $1,089,949 in net receipts.[10] Not quite the bounty hopeful owners had expected, but there were a few bright spots to focus on. All 11 teams had completed the 60-game season. A few had actually posted a profit. And along the way, several new stars had emerged to compete with the top draw in the National Basketball League, Chicago American Gears' big man George Mikan.

Mikan was, of course, *the* player in pro basketball. A three-time All American at DePaul University from 1941–45, Big George signed a five year contract with the Chicago American Gears straight out of college worth $60,000 plus bonus incentives—an astounding amount for the day, especially given he had yet to set foot on a professional court.[11] The 6'10", 245-pound giant did not disappoint. Joining the American Gears at the end of the 1945-46 season, the collegiate National Player of the Year took his new team five games into the World Tournament in Chicago before fouling out in a decisive game against the Oshkosh All-Stars in the semi-finals. Mikan's 100 points over those five games earned him the tournament's Most Valuable Player award.

Like most big men of his era, Big George would be considered slow on his feet by today's NBA standards, but he possessed strong defensive capabilities and a passionate dedication to the game. His relentless shot-blocking skills at DePaul had so altered the college game that in 1944 the NCAA amended its rules to outlaw goaltending. Offensively, Mikan was a tyrant under the basket and devastated opponents with his ability to score a hook shot with either hand. His arrival in the NBL gave the league — and the game of pro basketball — its first player worthy of superstar billing.

While the new BAA had no star of Mikan's caliber, several players helped the league establish itself at the box office. By far the most noteworthy was Philadelphia Warrior Joe Fulks, a groundbreaking player largely credited with establishing one of today's most popular offensive weapons: the jump shot. Fulks spent his collegiate days at small-time Murray State, a teacher's college in western Kentucky, before playing service ball for the Marine Corps. The 6'5" forward led the league in scoring during the BAA's inaugural season with an average of 23.2 points per game. Although a good percentage of Fulks's scoring came from the traditional hook shot, it was his innovative turnaround jumper, which he arched over his head while hanging around in the pivot, that dazzled fans.

The league featured another of the game's premier scorers in Max Zaslofsky, whose predictable but deadly set shots helped the Eastern Division Champion Stags post a league-high team scoring average of 77 points per game. Former NBL star Bob Feerick, who finished the season second to Fulks in scoring average (16.8 ppg) and number of points scored (929) helped the Washington Capitols run off a 17-game winning streak during the regular season.[12] The Caps wound up winning the East by 14 games, only to lose in the first round of the playoffs. Coaching the Capitols that year was young Red Auerbach, who would soon begin construction of the Boston dynasty. Fulks's Warriors took home the BAA's first title, beating the Chicago Stags four games to one.

Others players who boasted more name recognition than impressive stats during the BAA's early years were Press Maravich, the father of future NBA great (Pistol) Pete Maravich, and Chuck Conners, whose mediocre basketball career would give way to fame and fortune as TV's Rifleman.

The BAA's poor financial showing during the first year of operation convinced four teams to close shop. The failure of the Detroit, Cleveland, and Pittsburgh franchises, all of which hailed from the league's Western Division, was probably related to the NBL's stronghold in that area of the country. In the East, only the Toronto Huskies called it quits, squashing the league's hope that hockey-loving Canadians would embrace pro basketball with similar vigor. As the BAA prepared for season two, it added the Baltimore Bullets to the Eastern Division and moved the Washington Capitols to the West, leaving each division with four teams. Owners cut their rosters to 10 players and reduced the league's schedule to 48 games.

Meanwhile the NBL, which remained 12 teams strong through the summer, decided to increase its schedule to 60 games for the upcoming 1947-48 season. Jubilant owners threw their competition a few bones during the off-season. The new league was permitted to share in the NBL's college draft, with each BAA team afforded the right to select one player. A uniform player contact was agreed on, and interleague trading during the season would be permissible.

The NBL's upbeat mood shifted dramatically later that summer when Chicago Gears owner Maurice White announced he was withdrawing his club from the league. White was certain his team's star, George Mikan, was the reason for the NBL's growing success— so certain that he decided to form his own professional basketball league. White's ambitious 16-franchise project, which he dubbed the Professional Basketball League of America, spread over 13 states in the South and Midwest. In addition to his Chicago Gears, the Northern Division had the St. Paul Saints, Grand Rapids Rangers, Louisville Colonels, Omaha Tomahawks, Kansas City Blues, Waterloo Pro-Hawks, and St. Joseph Outlaws. New to the world of professional basketball was an all–Southern Division: Houston Mavericks, Atlanta Crackers, Birmingham Skyhawks, Tulsa Ranchers, Chattanooga Majors, Oklahoma City Drillers, New Orleans Hurricanes, and Springfield (MO) Squires.

The Houston team lasted two games. Oklahoma City dropped out after five. The St. Paul Saints played a league-high nine games before the entire operation went belly up. A humiliated White disappeared from the basketball scene,

Big man George Mikan (6'10", 246 lbs.), the first true superstar of the NBA, is pictured here in his 1947 Chicago Gears uniform. Mikan moved on to the Minneapolis Lakers when the Gears were dismantled, and led the team to five championships in six years (Basketball Hall of Fame, Springfield, MA).

$600,000 poorer for his efforts.[13] Players from 15 of the league's 16 teams were declared free agents, allowing them to sign with the NBL or BAA teams of their choice. The exception was the Chicago Gears, which White had operated as a separate company. The Gears' former association with the NBL afforded the league the right to assume title to the team and all its players. The new

Minneapolis Lakers, formerly the financially impaired Detroit Gems, won the grand prize in George Mikan.

Despite the slow start, the NBL's 1947-48 season was a good one. Mikan led the new Lakers to the Western Division crown, finishing a full 13 games ahead of second-place Tri-Cities. The Lakers took home their first championship, beating the Eastern powerhouse Rochester Royals three games to one. Mikan and company capped off their banner year by winning what proved to be the last World Tournament in Chicago. The Lakers beat the aging New York Rens 75–71. Big George topped all scores with 40 points. Nat "Sweetwater" Clifton was high man for the Rens with 24.

Things were not as rosy for the two-year-old BAA. Attendance was up from the previous year, but barely. While the league was averaging about 3,000 fans per game, the numbers were deceptive as they included complimentary tickets used for promotion. Overall operating expenses had been reduced with the shorter schedule, but fewer games translated into less revenue. Although the BAA held an advantage over its rival insofar as team locations in big cities — the *potential* for a huge fan base was there — the NBL had the best players and thus better teams. The fact that its clubs played in small town markets was actually a plus on the financial end in that travel costs were far less than those of the more ambitious BAA. In a straight line-by-line comparison, the more experienced NBL retained the upper hand and looked poised to continue the trend for years to come.

Appearances, of course, are often deceiving. Despite all its shortcomings, the BAA held the advantage where it mattered most: on the business end. Commissioner Podoloff's immediate job was to keep the BAA in operation, the end goal to make a profit for its owners. He needed only to look at the fate of the disastrous Professional Basketball League of America to realize time was of the essence. Changes would have to be made, cutthroat changes that would ignite yet another war in the world of professional basketball.

ONE FOR THE MONEY

Two months into the BAA's second season, Podoloff knew his league was in trouble. Travel expenses and player salaries were on the upswing, while attendance continued to hover around the 3,000 mark — about the same as most teams in the smaller market NBL. It was obvious BAA owners had overestimated the metropolitan appetite for professional basketball; the only games that drew crowds of 10,000 fans were doubleheaders against popular college teams or Saperstein's Harlem Globetrotters.

The problem was obvious: less a few exceptions, the BAA was a league of leftovers, players who hadn't caught on with an NBL squad. Pro basketball fans wanted familiar teams, winning clubs with players they recognized. The NBL had both. So what if the BAA had impressive arenas that could seat 20,000? It was the small-time NBL teams playing in armories and social halls that had won the hearts of paying fans. And the players appreciated them. "In Sheboygan, we had a capacity of about 3,000 people, and the fans were right off the floor," NBL veteran player/coach Mike Todorovich recalled. "The fans were fanatical. If you won a game, it took you five or six minutes to get back in the locker room."[1]

Once Podoloff identified the problem — BAA fans were *not* fanatical — he knew what had to be done. Sometime in the early part of 1948, the BAA leader made a few phone calls. Among the recipients were the owners or leaders of NBL teams in Minneapolis, Fort Wayne, Indianapolis, and Rochester, not coincidentally four of the NBL's strongest clubs. The Indianapolis Kautskys had been with the league since its inception. The Rochester Royals and Fort Wayne Zollner Pistons were strong playoff contenders, and the Minneapolis Lakers had the game's only true superstar in George Mikan. How would they feel about joining the BAA, Podoloff asked. A primetime league in big-name cities, gorgeous arenas that could seat thousands more paying customers, and all the media attention they could ever want.

By February, it was no secret all four clubs were strongly considering Podoloff's proposal. Sensing the inevitable, Paul Walk, NBL president and head man of the Indianapolis franchise, met with Podoloff in April to discuss a possible merger of the two leagues. No formal announcement was made until the governors' meeting on May 10, 1948, at which time the BAA revealed it was granting franchises to Indianapolis, Fort Wayne, Rochester, and Minneapolis. In a move that made it clear the BAA was about profits first, requests for entry into the league by the small-market Oshkosh All Stars and Toledo Jeeps were denied.

Remaining NBL owners cried foul and threatened swift and severe retaliation. Forget the joint agreement hammered out the previous summer regarding the upcoming college draft. Respect each other's player contracts? No way. If it was a war the BAA wanted, it was a war they would have. Newly appointed NBL president Leo Ferris insisted all players from the defecting teams were the property of the National League and threatened legal action if owners went through with the move.

Tempers cooled slightly over the summer, during which leagues officials met several times in an attempt to work out their differences. By September, however, it was obvious there would be no truce. The BAA's governing board voted to ban all NBL teams from its arenas. Interleague play, even on an exhibition basis, was strictly forbidden.

The crippled NBL entered the 1948-49 season determined to stay alive. The defecting clubs were replaced with new franchises in Waterloo (Iowa), Denver, Detroit, and Hammond (Indiana). When the Detroit Vagabond Kings folded after only nine games, the team was promptly replaced by the New York Renaissance, who would play as the Detroit Rens.

Given the media wave surrounding Jackie Robinson, it followed that an all-black team entering a white pro league would grab its fair share of headlines. And headlines, of course, was exactly what the NBL was after. "They wanted to put an all-black team in the league, hoping they could draw the attendance up," recalled former Ren star Pop Gates.[2] Perhaps the strategy would have been successful in the media-heavy BAA, but the National League was fast becoming an asterisk since the loss of Mikan and its four best teams, thus no one really seemed to notice, let alone care. The lack of fanfare may have been just as well for the Rens, who compiled a mediocre 14-26 league record during their shortened season.

Meanwhile the BAA, drawing on the strength of its new former NBL teams and stars, enjoyed its best season to date. The Minneapolis Lakers and Rochester Royals battled it out for the top spot in the West during the expanded 60-game regular season. The Royals took the division by a game, but Mikan's team prevailed in the playoffs and went on to defeat the Eastern Conference champion Washington Capitols in the finals, four games to two.

The weakened NBL vowed to regroup. It still had Oshkosh and Sheboygan, old favorites that continued to draw sellout crowds in their respective hometowns. The Syracuse Nationals remained popular, as did the Tri-Cities Blackhawks and the NBL champion Anderson Duffey Packers. Additionally, the league had a commitment from the NCAA champions, the University of

Kentucky. The squad, which featured several players from the U.S. Olympic team of 1948, had agreed to turn pro and join the NBL for the upcoming season.

The closer that season got, however, the less confident remaining NBL owners became. A majority wanted to place their teams in the more lucrative BAA, and in the end, they could not be dissuaded. On August 3, 1949, the Basketball Association of American and the National Basketball League formally merged into the National Basketball Association (NBA). Not all NBL teams were accepted into the fold, however. The Oshkosh All Stars were denied yet again, as were the aging Rens. For its part, the BAA dropped two teams: the Providence Steamrollers and Indianapolis Jets. Maurice Podoloff remained at the helm as president. The NBL's head man, Ike Duffey, was appointed chairman of the NBA's Board of Governors.

The new league announced it would begin play with 17 teams split into three divisions. Original BAA teams comprised the majority of the Eastern Division: the New York Knickerbockers, Philadelphia Warriors, Baltimore Bullets, Washington Capitols, and Boston Celtics were joined by only one former NBL team, the Syracuse Nationals. The Central Division featured two BAA franchises in the Chicago Stags and St. Louis Bombers. Joining them were three previous NBL strongholds: the Minneapolis Lakers, Fort Wayne Pistons, and Rochester Royals. The remaining National League teams— the Sheboygan Redskins, Tri-Cities Blackhawks, Anderson Duffey Packers, Waterloo Hawks, and Denver Nuggets— made up the Western Division, which also featured the only new club in the league, the Olympic team from Kentucky, which would play as the Indianapolis Olympians.

Given how most interstate travel still occurred by automobile or train, the ambitious 17-team roster proved a nightmare where scheduling was concerned. When the details were finally hashed out, 10 teams had a 68-game schedule, 4 were assigned a total of 64 games, and the 5 remaining clubs would play only 62. All teams managed to complete their respective schedules, thanks to sheer determination on the part of the players. "It was an overnight train ride to the next city," former Laker Arnie Ferrin explained. "Meal money was seven dollars per day.... Sometimes we'd be gone for three weeks, traveling by train at night."[3] Laker town was one of the least favorite stops for visiting teams, especially during the winter months. "Minneapolis always had taxicab strikes," Bill Tosheff, the NBA's first Rookie of the Year, recalled. "We would have to walk from the train station to the hotel. If you played the night before, your uniform was still wet. You'd get to the hotel, open up your satchel, and your clothes were frozen stiff. They were like big ice sheets. We put them on a radiator to thaw them out."[4]

When spring finally arrived, 12 teams qualified for the playoffs. Of the nine with winning records, only two— the Chicago Stags and New York Knickerbockers— were of BAA heritage. Chicago lost to Minneapolis in the first round, unable to win a game. New York fell to Syracuse, two games to one, in round two. The Mikan-led ex–NBL Champion Lakers took home the first NBA title, beating the former NBL Syracuse Nationals four games to two. Was a pattern emerging? "The BAA was a high school league," scoffed Nat Al Cervi, who played on the Rochester and Syracuse teams. "If they don't steal four clubs from the NBL, they're out of business. That's how they perpetuated their league."[5]

Cervi would have received little argument from most NBL owners, especially those left to ponder whether their admittance into Podoloff's league had been a ploy to dissolve the remainder of the National League prior to the start of the 1949-50 season. Had the initial four defecting teams opted to remain in the NBL that fateful spring of 1948, it was probable the league would have emerged as the sole surviving pro organization, looking to expand via the newly formed team of young Olympians and a wave of up-and-coming college stars. Instead, as the NBA prepared for year two, it became painfully obvious to several of the old school we're-in-this-for-the-love-of-the-game National League clubs that they did not possess the financial means to play ball in the big leagues. The Denver Nuggets, Sheboygan Redskins, Anderson Duffey Packers, and Waterloo Hawks all incurred extensive losses, forcing them to withdraw from the league.

Returning for the NBA's second season would be all six teams from the Eastern Division: Boston, New York, Philadelphia, Syracuse, Baltimore, and Washington. The lone survivors from the Western Division — Indianapolis and Tri-Cities — would be joined by Minneapolis, Rochester, and Fort Wayne. The Central Division was eliminated.

Realignment was only the first step in a busy off-season. As teams prepared for the upcoming college draft, Knicks owner Ned Irish shocked the Board of Governors by announcing his intention to buy the rights to Harlem Globetrotter star Nat "Sweetwater" Clifton. Should the Board attempt to stop him, Irish reportedly threatened to "walk out of this room and withdraw from the NBA."[6] Irish's threat, empty or not, signaled an awakening was at hand. Winning games had finally become more important to owners than the color of a player's skin.

Clifton, nicknamed Sweetwater because of his fondness for soft drinks, had been a Globetrotter for two seasons at this point, having joined the club after finishing a three-year stint in the army. Prior to signing with the Globetrotters, Clifton toyed with a professional baseball career, where he played first base for several minor league clubs. Saperstein eventually convinced the 6'7" forward that basketball was his game — to the tune of a reported $10,000 annual salary.[7] Sweetwater excelled at rebounding and possessed a variety of impressive ball-handling skills perfected during his time with the Trotters. Although he was one of the team's more popular players, rumor had it that he had become expendable because of a personal dispute with Saperstein.

Irish followed through on his pledge to purchase Clifton's contract from the Trotters that summer, but not before Celtics owner Walter Brown stunned associates by choosing Charles (Chuck) Cooper, a black All American forward from Eastern powerhouse Duquesne University, in the second round of the draft on April 25. When a rival owner reminded Brown that Cooper was a black man, Brown responded, "I don't care if he's striped, plaid, or polka-dot! Boston takes Charles Cooper of Duquesne."[8]

Cooper was on tour with the Globetrotters when he was informed of Brown's decision. The news was not a total shock to the 24-year-old, given that Celtic scout Art Spector had told him it might happen; still, to be the first black player chosen in the NBA draft was an achievement he did not take lightly. "He was excited and proud to have been the first one," said Harold Brown, one of Cooper's best friends from high school.[9] According to Brown, Cooper carried a small printed article noting the achievement in his wallet for years.

Once the racial drawbridge had been lowered, other teams fell in line. Earl Lloyd, a tough, defensive-minded forward from West Virginia State, was taken by the Washington Capitols in the ninth round. The Caps also chose Harold Hunter from North Carolina, while Kentucky State's Ed Thompson was selected by the Fort Wayne Pistons.

As NBA owners contemplated what effect their off-season changes would have on the year ahead, the disgruntled group of dropout teams vowed to continue play in a new Midwestern circuit, which they dubbed the National Professional Basketball League. Former NBL leader Doxie Moore was appointed commissioner of the aspiring league, which opened play in the fall of 1950 with nine teams on board. Joining Sheboygan, Anderson, Denver, and Waterloo were new teams in Kansas City, St. Paul, Evansville, Grand Rapids, and Louisville.

By midseason, it was obvious the time for competing professional basketball leagues had come and gone. The St. Paul Lights appealed in vain for NBA admittance before dropping out with a 12-8 record. The Denver Refiners transferred to Evansville, taking over for the 0-6 Agogans. Kansas City, Grand Rapids, and Louisville all closed their doors before season's end. The murky playoff structure crumbled. Both Sheboygan and Waterloo, winners of their respective divisions, claimed title to the championship, but it mattered little as by summer's end, there was no NPBL to be champion of.

Meanwhile, the NBA's 1950-51 season proved a mix of ups and downs, none more noteworthy than its decision to adopt integration. Cooper, who was highly coveted by the Trotters after the Celtics drafted him, eventually rebuffed a more lucrative offer from Saperstein in favor of becoming a Celtic. Saperstein retaliated by refusing to schedule Trotter games in any of the cities that had drafted blacks, but the page had turned and there was no going back. Saperstein's monopoly on the nation's most talented black players had gone the way of the defunct regional leagues.

Earl Lloyd became the first black to actually play in an NBA game, scoring six points in the Capitols' 78–70 loss to Rochester on October 31, 1950.

Because Lloyd left the team after only seven games—courtesy of Uncle Sam's draft—his impact in the league would not be fully realized for several years and would not come as a Capitol; Washington became the only NBA franchise to close shop midseason, after compiling a dismal 10-25 record.

Chuck Cooper had nine points and two rebounds in his debut with Boston on November 1, in a contest that saw the Celts fall to Fort Wayne 84-107.[10] Stats-wise, Cooper would have his best professional year as a rookie, averaging 8.5 rebounds and 9.5 points.[11] He would remain a Celtic for four seasons before moving on to the Milwaukee Hawks.

Sweetwater Clifton was the first black player whose name sold tickets at the box office. By the time he joined the Knicks, his résumé included two years of traveling internationally with the Globetrotters. His early influence on the Knicks was limited by the team's style of play, which, unlike the Trotters, featured a slow, defense-minded type of game. Clifton fit in well enough to remain with New York for seven seasons, however, highlighted by his 1956 All Star appearance, where he scored eight points in 23 minutes off the bench.[12]

It is difficult to measure the impact integration had on the NBA that first year insofar as the fans were concerned. Attendance was up slightly from the year before, with most teams averaging 3,000–4,000 per game—not enough to make a determination one way or the other. "I'm sure there were a lot of white guys who harbored ill will," Earl Lloyd said of his experiences, "but there were enough guys who didn't."[13] If tension existed between black and white teammates, it was kept in check. Celtic coach Red Auerbach recalled, "When Chuck Cooper joined us, some players came to me and said, 'this is a little unusual, but we'd like to room with him.' So I changed roommates every three or four weeks.... They wanted to make sure he was a part of our group."[14]

Off the court, however, racism remained commonplace. Black players continued to be treated as second-class citizens by hotel and restaurant owners from Syracuse to Fort Wayne. "I remember in Fort Wayne, we stayed at a hotel where they let me sleep," Lloyd recalled, "but they wouldn't let me eat. They didn't want anyone to see me. I figured if they let me sleep there, I was at least halfway home.... If adversity doesn't kill you, it makes you a better person."[15]

The same could be said for the NBA itself, at least as far as the players were concerned. For nearly half a century, pro basketball players held summer jobs to make ends meet. Others collected unemployment. But those days were over. The average professional basketball player now made from $4,000 to $7,000 per season for six months' work in the NBA. Eight stars had reached the five-figure mark, with Mikan topping the list at $17,500. Pocket change for today's players, but not bad for the era, considering the median income for an average family in 1951 was $3,709.[16] Unfortunately for owners, game attendance was not keeping pace with swelling payrolls. The average ticket price remained under $2. Only Minneapolis, Syracuse, New York, and Philadelphia were averaging more than 4,000 fans per game as the second season wound down. Small-town

Syracuse, a favorite since its NBL days, continued to lead the pack with 5,185.[17] And even it lost money.

The disappointing figures gave Commissioner Podoloff cause to rethink the league's first All Star Game, which was scheduled for March 2, 1951, at Boston Garden. Most owners agreed it was a dangerous gamble. Showcasing the biggest NBA stars would be great for the game if fans showed up at the gate, but what if they didn't? The resulting publicity would damage the league and humiliate its most visible players. But Celtics owner Walter Brown was willing to take the risk–so willing he offered to foot the bill for all expenses, as well as make up any losses, if the game was a flop.

By the end of the night, Brown was one of the happiest people in the building. Boston Garden was packed with 10,094 eager fans who witnessed 10 of the East's best players beat the West's top 10, 111–94. In a crowd-pleasing finish, hometown boy Ed Macauley of the Celtics was voted the game's Most Valuable Player. Macauley scored a game-best 20 points and was credited with holding a frustrated George Mikan to a lowly four field goals on the night. Philly's jump-shooting Joe Fulks added 19 to the winning cause. The West was led by Indianapolis Olympian Alex Groza, who pumped in 17 points and grabbed 13 rebounds in a losing effort.[18]

The season continued on a downturn for Mikan when his defending champion Lakers made an early exit from the playoffs, ousted by Indianapolis in the semi-finals, two games to one. Meanwhile in the East, Joe Fulks's shocked Warriors fell to Syracuse, a squad that had accumulated a mediocre 32-34 regular season record. In the end, it was the New York Knicks against the Rochester Royals in a heated match-up that produced the NBA's first seven-game Finals. The deciding game went to the Royals, 79–75, in front of an exuberant hometown crowd of 4,200 fans. Slowly, steadily, the pro game was finding its niche; a lengthy, two-column story on Game 7 appeared the following day in the sports section of the *New York Times*.

Although Mikan's Lakers had stumbled as a team, Big George captured the scoring title for the third straight year, averaging a career-best 28.4 points per game. Andy Phillip of the Warriors tied with New York's Dick McGuire for the top assist spot at 6.3. In the rebounding category — a stat new to the list for 1950-51 season — it was Syracuse big man Dolph Schayes beating out Mikan by more than two boards per game at 16.4.[19]

Season two had proven a mixed bag overall, but owners felt optimistic the worst was behind them. The Eastern Conference remained five teams strong with Boston, Philadelphia, Baltimore, New York, and Syracuse all choosing to return for another year. The Washington Capitols, a midseason casualty, was not replaced. In the West, the new Milwaukee Hawks took over for struggling Tri-Cities, joining mainstays Minneapolis, Rochester, Fort Wayne, and Indianapolis. The league would tip off its third season with 10 teams in two divisions, a format nearly identical to that of its second-generation ancestor, the Midwest Basketball Conference. But the similarities ended there.

After 53 years of bitter, interleague battles, pro basketball had come down to one make-or-break organization: the NBA. It was now up to Maurice Podoloff to prove Naismith's game could hold its own in the gritty world of professional sports.

TICK TOCK

The first All Star Game had injected the NBA with a much-needed booster shot as the league looked ahead to season three, but it took a twist of fate for the professional game to overtake its age-old rival, college basketball, in the hearts and minds of mainstream America. Ironically, when the switch finally occurred, it was more a case of the collegiate game self-destructing than anything the NBA did or did not do.

From the very beginning, college ball's major draw had been its love of the game. Players received no monetary compensation for their efforts; they played for the thrill of the competition, a sense of pride in their school, a passionate desire to win.

Or so the game's loyal fans had always believed.

Doubts regarding the purity of the amateur game first surfaced in January 1951, when the Bronx District Attorney's office was informed by Junius Kellogg, a player from New York's Manhattan College, that he was offered $1,000 from teammates John Byrnes and Henry Poppe to throw an upcoming game against DePaul at Madison Square Garden.[1] Poppe eventually confessed to police that he and Byrnes had been paid $5,000 each to alter the outcome of several contests during the 1949-50 season by throwing the games or shaving points from the margin of victory. They, along with three professional gamblers tied to the scam, were arrested on bribery and conspiracy charges.

Initial public reaction was to dismiss the case as an isolated incident, but alas, it proved only the first of many. The following month, players from New York's Long Island University and City College faced similar accusations. In March, the NCAA council met on the subject and recommended its members schedule all future games on college campus facilities, or at the very least, "play only on fields or in buildings of which the collegiate institution has effective control." When asked whether the NCAA had "effective control" of games being played at Madison Square Garden, including the upcoming NCAA tournament, executive secretary-treasurer Kenneth Wilson replied, "No."[2]

Any hope the scandal would be confined to New York vanished in July when eight players from Bradley University of Peoria, Illinois, admitted they had also fixed games for cash. Ohio's University of Toledo soon joined the list. The most shocking revelation, however, came just as the NBA was about to begin play for the 1951-52 season. Three players from the University of Kentucky, two of them former All Americans, confessed to having received $1,500 to throw a 1949 NCAA tournament game. The two All Americans, Alex Groza and Ralph Beard, had since been drafted by the NBA and were teammates on the Indianapolis Olympians when the news broke. Beard and Groza were immediately suspended by the league. Two other Olympian players were questioned and released.

Commissioner Podoloff made the NBA's position clear immediately thereafter: any player so much as *implicated* in point shaving or betting on games, college or professional, would be permanently banned from the league. In retrospect, the policy may have been too strict, as some very talented players were denied entrance into the NBA via unsubstantiated accusations or guilt by association. Unfortunately, for an organization not yet standing on solid ground, financially or otherwise, it was the only way to preserve the integrity of professional hoops.

While there is no question the college scandal helped expand the NBA's fan base, Podoloff realized the pro game would not win the popularity contest solely by default. College basketball was still the preferred style for spectators, the majority of whom had never embraced the rough-and-tumble play that went on beneath the basket during professional games. Fans craved an upbeat tempo: crisp passing, good ball handling, and scoring. Lots of scoring.

Increasing the game's pace remained at the top of the league's wish list. Nowhere had the need to do so been more strikingly apparent than a November 22 contest between the Lakers and the Pistons in Minneapolis the previous season. By the end of the night, a total of eight field goals had been recorded — four by each team. The Pistons won 19–18, setting a new NBA record low for total points scored in a game. Only one field goal was made in the entire fourth quarter. Mikan was responsible for 15 of Minneapolis's points; no teammate had attempted more than two shots. "After the game, the fans wanted their money back," recalled former Laker guard Slater Martin, "and I didn't blame them."[3]

The league responded to the debacle with a new rule allowing referees to call a technical foul (which would result in a free throw) if they felt a team was purposely stalling the game to protect a lead. The policy all but assured the Pistons-Lakers score would retain its lowly spot in the record books, but teams continued to employ the strategy at various levels. Some referees called them on it, others didn't. Regardless, most coaches were willing to concede the technical free throw; even if the attempt was successful, it was worth only one point rather than the normal two that would result from a made field goal.

Owners agreed something had to be done to stop the stalling; it was the *what* that continued to elude them. Several possibilities were discussed during the league's summer meetings, but only one major rule change went into effect for the 1951-52 season: the painted lane under the basket was widened from 6 to 12 feet. The move was intended to help neutralize the size advantage of big men, namely, George Mikan, whose dominance around the goal completely overwhelmed smaller teams. A wider lane meant the Lakers big man could no longer set up in his comfort zone — three feet from the basket — and wait for the inevitable pass to arrive; he had three seconds to shoot, pass, or get out of the paint.

Pundits insisted the rule had worked as expected, citing a 4.6 ppg drop in Mikan's scoring average that year. But they neglected to mention a major side effect: Big George became a better all-around teammate. With more room to work in the lane, he was able to increase his shot selection *and* become a more efficient passer, hitting open teammates as they cut to the basket through a wider, less populated lane. "It's the best thing that's happened to basketball since the elimination of the center jump," a gleeful Mikan said after learning to adjust.[4]

There would be no early exit for the Lakers in 1952 playoffs. After eliminating the first place Rochester Royals 3-1 in the division finals, Mikan's squad overpowered the New York Knicks in the league's second consecutive seven-game championship series.

Big George wasn't the only player upgrading his game. The jump shot, ridiculed by many basketball purists since its inception, was fast becoming the weapon of choice for offensive players. One of the game's most adamant believers was Philadelphia forward Paul Arizin, whose teammate was none other than Jumpin' Joe Fulks, the player responsible for popularizing the technique. Arizin made such effective use of the shot it earned him the season's top scoring (24.4 ppg) and field goal percentage (.448) titles. The flying hook was one of point guard Bob Cousy's favorite weapons. He stopped at the top of the key, took a few dribbles toward the basket, then angled to the side and released a sweeping hook off the backboard. Other guards were creating their own variations of the move. A few set shooters picked up on the one-handed strategy, launching bombs from well beyond today's three-point line.

Slowly but steadily the NBA's product was improving. Owners were optimistic the third year would prove the charm, and they had reason to believe. For once, the pressure was on the collegiate game to dig itself out of the dirt — and the excavation was not going well. Betting scandals remained in the headlines throughout the season. Numerous fines were doled out, coaches were fired, schools stripped of their eligibility. College fans were one disgruntled bunch, ready and willing to be lured into the nearest NBA arena so they could see what they'd been missing. Unfortunately, the league's new offensive show gave way to a familiar scene: the fourth quarter stall and foul. Hoop fans were not impressed.

There was an upside to what proved yet another disappointing year; every team that started the 66-game season finished it intact — a league first. But only the New York Knicks were earning their keep. Smaller markets found themselves deep in red ink. The Celtics, for example, took in a respectable $167,927 in gross receipts, yet lost $64,031 for the year.[5]

Arenas did not overflow with excited fans because the final act was a predictable affair: One team gained an advantage and attempted to hold it until the final buzzer. The strategy, particularly glaring in the final quarter, was sound on the surface, of course; regardless of the sport being played, the objective is to come out on top. But the action must continue in the meantime, and that was where the NBA failed to deliver. Other sports set limits on offense. Football allowed four downs to advance the ball a minimum of 10 yards. Baseball had three strikes and three outs. In basketball, however, once an offensive player advanced the ball across the midcourt line within the allotted 10 seconds, his team could retain possession for an unlimited period of time. Bored fans looked on in disgust as a player held or dribbled the ball in keep-away fashion until an opposing player finally committed a foul to force a possession change. Since no time elapsed from the clock during free throws, the final few minutes of a game could take 20 minutes to play. The league's attempt to discourage the practice by calling for a jump ball at center court after made free throws in the last three minutes had little benefit. Spectators rose to their feet — en route to the nearest exit.

Nonetheless, winning remained the name of the game. By the time the NBA entered its fourth season, the intentional foul had become an art form. Most teams had at least one player who specialized in the tactic, much the same as the early era teams had done with free throw shooters. "We'd just clobber guys," former Hawks player/coach Alex Hannum confessed. "I was as guilty as anyone of that because when I played, I was correctly labeled a hatchet man."[6] The dubious tactic became so prevalent that a new league high of 58 fouls per game was recorded by season's end.

The trend continued into the playoffs. On March 21, 1953, an astounding 107 fouls were whistled during Game 2 of the Eastern Division semi-finals between Syracuse and Boston. Players shot a combined 138 free throws during the quadruple-overtime affair.[7] Backcourt Celtic great Bob Cousy, in the early stages of his Hall of Fame career, logged 30 of his game-high 50 points — an NBA high for a playoff game that year — from the line. The Celtics prevailed in the three-plus-hour marathon, 111–105.

The up-and-coming Celtics eventually lost to Eastern Division winner New York in the second round. In the West, the Division champion Lakers outlasted the Fort Wayne Pistons, marking the first time in NBA history that division winners would meet in the finals. (Both teams had met in the finals the previous season, but neither had won its respective division.) New York wrestled away home court advantage with a surprise win in Game 1, but the Lakers stormed back, taking four in a row to deny Ned Irish's Knicks a championship yet again. When it came to the numbers game, however, Irish was all smiles; his team recorded a season-high profit of $46,042.[8] Unfortunately for the league, no other team came close to matching New York's numbers. Most continued to lose money. Even the three-time World Champion Lakers posted a net loss of more than $11,000 by season's end.

The media was not shy in its criticism. "The NBA is playing ostrich if it continues to hide its head in the sands of victory alone and forgets the men and women who pay the freight," fumed Ben Tenny, a sports writer from Fort Wayne. "There won't be enough fans to warrant an NBA unless they wake up to the dangers around them. And by they I mean players, coaches, officials, club owners, etc."[9]

Despite all the pessimism, the NBA had at least one thing going for it: integrity. While college ball continued to suffer backlash from the betting scandals via suspensions and penalties, the pro game remained amazing clean. And Podoloff made good on his promise to keep things that way. In addition to the two Indianapolis stars, Ralph Beard and Alex Groza, only one other NBA player was ever caught gambling: Jack Molinas of the Fort Wayne Pistons. Molinas was suspected of shaving points during his rookie season (1952-53), investigated, and permanently banned from the NBA. "After seeing what happened to all the college players who were caught in the scandals the NBA guys were scared of gamblers," Alex Hannum admitted. "The owners told us, 'You hang around with gamblers, you're through.' The Molinas case proved their point."[10]

Indeed. And the Indianapolis Olympians served to further emphasize it. The franchise, already struggling to survive in one of the league's smallest markets, was forced to close shop at the end of the NBA's fourth season, unable to overcome the cheater stigma that had penetrated its once promising organization.

The remaining owners limped into season five on the same worn track, opting for small rather than drastic changes. The most noteworthy was an increase in the schedule, to a league-high 72 games. Even the decision to enter the fast-growing medium of television was done at such a snail's pace it wound up doing more harm than good. The original contract, set up by the league's publicity chief, Haskell Cohen, called for 13 NBA games to be broadcast on DuMont, a network struggling to compete with CBS, NBC, and ABC.[11] At $3,000 per game, the deal meant an extra $39,000 in revenue to the struggling league, enough to convince skeptical owners to get on board.

The contract appeared to be just what the doctor ordered, a chance for the league to strut its stuff in the national spotlight. But rather than use that spotlight to showcase its top talent, owners opted to televise the games they thought spectators would be least likely to attend. Their shortsighted reasoning — that fans would be less inclined to come to the games if they could stay home and watch them for free — seemed sound on the surface, but hinted at an overall lack of faith in their own product. As a result of the poorly thought out strategy, viewers were few, and those who did watch saw exactly why NBA attendance was spotty.

The low point of the season came on March 20, 1954, during a playoff contest between the Celtics and the Knicks. Boston needed 3 hours and 5 minutes to squeeze out a 79–78 win, including a foul-plagued 45-minute fourth quarter that sent fans to the exits in droves. And they weren't the only ones who left early. So dubious was the contest that DuMont execs ordered TV crews to pull the plug before the outcome had been decided.

The broadcasting fiasco culminated yet another disappointing end to a promising year. The league's attempt to discourage the intentional foul by disqualifying players who committed more than two personals in a quarter had done little to achieve its goal either. As with most of the league's recent tweaks, it was too little, too late. Coaches were convinced possessions were the key to winning basketball games. As long as the strategy conditioned to work, they had no incentive to change.

Bottom line, rules are effective only if they are enforced. While there is no question coaches were responsible for *developing* the possessions over points strategy that was ruining the professional game, it was the officials who ultimately controlled whether it was successful. Referees had the power to take control of the game — whistle the fouls, set the hackers on the bench, and get the game moving — yet they were less willing to do so.

Low pay was certainly part of the problem. Refs had averaged $25 per game in the American Basketball League during the 1920s — more than some of the players themselves. Thirty years later, the NBA was paying its top referees $40 to $50 per contest.[12] Players, meanwhile, were making an average of about $6,560 per season, or just under $100 per game.[13] Rules had become far more complicated since the old ABL days. Games were more difficult to referee, yet the pay ratio for its officials had failed to keep pace. College ball, on the other hand, knew full well the importance of good officiating, especially in lieu of the betting scandals. Schools in the Big Ten conference paid their refs $75 per game. "That's where we went and stayed," recalled Chuck Chuckovits.[14] Suffice it say, he wasn't alone.

In Podoloff's defense, his league was operating on a shoestring budget. "Rumor had it that Ned Irish of New York lent the league money to make the referees' payroll," former ref Norm Drucker recalled.[15] But the problem wasn't limited to finances. Pro basketball fans remained among the most boisterous in all pro sports. Many officials were intimidated by the crowds, literally fearing for their safety should they make an unpopular call against the home team. Even Sid Borgia, nicknamed the Godfather of officials for his work of 20 years, admitted the job was a dangerous one. "Fans believed they had the right to come to a game and hang the officials on a cross. It took a lot of intestinal fortitude to stand up to all that pressure."[16] Drucker walked off the court prepared for the worst. "We'd take off our belts and wrap them around our fists with the buckles obvious to everyone. This was going to be our protection."[17]

If lousy pay and threats of bodily harm were not bad enough, there was the added pressure from the league to let players play. Much of this stemmed from the owners' background in hockey, where fights remained a normal part of the game. Not only were refs berated by owners for calling too many fouls or ejecting star players on the new foul rule, they were regularly criticized for *not* making calls. All things considered, it was a no-win situation for the men in stripes.

Meanwhile, basketball fans strived for a reason — any reason — to fully embrace the professional game. The league's integrity gave them reason for hope, but there was little else to be optimistic about. Coaches had adapted to the new foul rule, rendering it basically ineffective. Roughness under the basket remained commonplace, and free throws continued to decide close games. Largely because of these failures, the league's first television contract had brought few if any new fans into the fold.

Owners knew they had reached a crossroads as they prepared for season six. Desperate times called for desperate measures. In addition to all the negative publicity the league had received of late, it also faced a changing of the guard: George Mikan decided to retire. Either owners faced the fact their game had to change, and change drastically, or they continued to lose fans and money. Wisely, they opted for the former. By the time the 1954-55 season got underway, two major rule changes were in the books.

The first was yet another attempt to stop the stalling game by limiting fouls, and this time, the league got it right. *Teams* would now be limited in the amount of fouls they could commit per quarter. The number settled on was six, after which a penalty would result in two free throws for the opposing team. If a player was fouled in the act of shooting, he would get three chances to make two shots.

The second, more radical rule imposed a time limit on how long a team could hold onto the ball without taking a shot. The idea had been floating around for years, but the league had been reluctant to embrace it for fear it would alter the game *too* much.

As new of Mikan's retirement broke, Critics were quick to cite his career-low 18.1 ppg scoring average as the reason. More likely, it was a matter of the big man's aging body. Over the course of his career, the center had suffered broken bones in both feet, two broken legs, and numerous fractures of his wrists, fingers, and nose. Yet he never used them as an excuse to ride the bench. After suffering a broken wrist in Game 4 of the 1949 playoffs against the Washington Capitols, he appeared in Game 5 with a cast on his wrist and poured in 22 points. He spent the majority of the 1950-51 season playing with a fractured leg. "The doctors taped a plate on it for the playoffs," he recalled. "I couldn't run, sort of hopped down the court."[18] He hopped well enough to score in the twenties during the Lakers' postseason run.

That's what superstars are supposed to do. Mikan had done it since day one.

During his nine-year professional career, Big George won seven championships and accumulated a 22.6 ppg career scoring average — 30.3 in the
playoffs. In 1950, he was named the greatest player in the first half of the century by the Associated Press. He played in four All Star Games (1951–54), won
the Game's first MVP in 1953, and was named to the All-NBA First Team six
times. His college résumé included similar achievements: NIT title, College
Player of the Year (twice), and three-time All American. His records at DePaul
University and the Laker dynasty he had established in Minneapolis were likely
to live forever, but Mikan's battered body would not. It was time to bid his life
on the hardwood goodbye.

The NBA feared basketball fans would adopt a similar outlook in the
Mikan-less era unless they acted quickly. The magic number settled on was 24
seconds — the team in possession of the ball would have exactly that long to run
their offense with the game's new rule. If no shot was attempted during the allotted time, the ball would be awarded to the other team.

Some owners remained skeptical a time limit could be enforced during
actual play, but they agreed to try it out during preseason exhibition games.
Afterward, the vote was unanimous: the 24-second clock was a go. The results
were immediate and astounding. Scoring for the 1954-55 season increased by
an average of 13.6 points per game over the previous year. The Cousy-led Celtics
wound up averaging better than 100 points per contest, an NBA first.

There is no doubt within the basketball world that the 24-second clock
rescued the professional game. Podoloff later called it "the most important
event in the NBA."[19] Credit for the save went to Danny Biasone, owner of the
Syracuse Nationals. "It's something that should have been done a long, long time
ago," said Nats Hall of Famer Dolph Schayes. "It paved the way for the modern era."[20] How and why did the game's hero arrive at 24? "I looked at the box
scores from the games I enjoyed," Biasone explained, "games where they didn't
screw around and stall. I noticed each team took about 60 shots. That meant
120 shots per game. So I took 48 minutes — 2,880 seconds — and divided that
by 120 shots. The result was 24 seconds per shot."[21]

Biasone felt the rule would have worked just as well if the limit had been
30 or 40 seconds, but Schayes is convinced 24 was the perfect number. "We
realized we could pass the ball half a dozen times at least, or more," he recalled
during an interview on Biasone's induction into the Basketball Hall of Fame in
October 2000. "The amazing thing is, that was 45 years ago, and yet it's still
the magic number."[22]

Spurred on by the new rules, Biasone and his up-tempo Nats won their
first NBA title, beating the Fort Wayne Pistons in an exciting seven-game series.
Unfortunately for the league, the small town match-up drew little interest
nationwide. Mikan was gone and his Lakers had made an early playoff exit, losing four straight to the Pistons in the Division Finals. Nonetheless, the Nats-
Pistons series served as validation for league's new rule. Schayes's Nats fell

Danny Biasone, owner of the Syracuse Nationals, is credited with convincing owners to implement the 24-second clock into the professional game. Most experts agree
the clock, put into play for the 1954-55 season, saved the NBA from collapse. The
time limit made an immediate impact, increasing league scoring by an average of
13.6 points per game in its first year (Basketball Hall of Fame, Springfield, MA).

behind by 17 points in the second quarter of Game 7 but wound up winning
in the final seconds—a scenario that would have proved nearly impossible in
previous years.

The game's new tempo came too late for the Baltimore Bullets, who folded
early in the season after compiling a dismal 3-11 record. Their demise left the
NBA with a scant eight teams going into the 1955-56 season, but finally there
were concrete signs the league was turning the corner. Most organizations still
posted a net loss for 1954-55, but the figures had improved from the previous
year, in some cases dramatically. Fort Wayne cut its losses by more than 60 percent, the World Champion Syracuse Nats by almost 80 percent. New York,
denied a title once again, boosted its league-leading profit margin by an additional 18 percent.[23]

Ironically, the up-and-coming Celtics proved the major exception. Boston
had posted a net loss of $5,127 the previous season, a mild amount by compar-
ative standards. For the 1954-55 season, however, the team lost an astounding
$53,385.[24] Much of the increase was due to player salaries, not surprising

considering their payroll included the likes of Bob Cousy, Bill Sharman, and Ed Macauley, all of whom ranked among the top 10 in scoring average, assists, and free throw percentage. Sharman and Macauley also finished among the top 10 in field goal percentage. But youth over experience rarely wins out, thus the team managed only a mediocre 36-36 record for season six, good for third place in the Eastern Division. Attendance remained about the same as the previous year, hovering around 7,000 fans per game.

Given all that, Celtics owner Walter Brown wasn't smiling on his way to the bank just yet, but deep down he knew what the rest of the league was about to discover: Boston's time was nearly at hand. And what a glorious time it would be.

DYNASTY BY COMMITTEE

Since the dawn of professional sports, every game has had its mega-stars—gifted athletes able to draw huge crowds on and off the playing field. Babe Ruth, Joe Montana, Wayne Gretzky, Mohammad Ali, Chris Evert, Michael Jordan, Tiger Woods ... all became household names because of their individual talent. But while Ali, Everett, and Woods claim sole responsibility for their successes and failures, the personal accomplishments of stars such as Ruth, Montana, Gretzky, and Jordan were at least somewhat dependent on the performance of their teammates. No one player on a team can ensure a championship. A true superstar, therefore, must possess not only extraordinary talent, but the ability to make those around him better.

The early barnstorming giants of professional basketball — the Rens, Original Celtics, and Trotters — all featured talented players who relied on each other to get the job done. Clearly there were bona fide dynasties of the era, as proven by their Hall of Fame status, yet it must be noted that they did not belong to an organized league — a technicality that allowed them to control the quality and number of their respective opponents. Such was not the case in the NBA, or the NBL or BAA which preceded it. Although quality teams such as the Oshkosh All Stars, Rochester Royals, and Fort Wayne Pistons had their share of success, it was not until Mikan joined the Chicago Gears midway through the 1946-47 season that any one team completely overshadowed its rivals. So bright was Chicago's future with Big George that Gears owner Maurice White pulled out of the NBL to start his own pro league. As previously noted, Mikan wasn't enough to save the poorly thought-out Professional Basketball League, but his subsequent arrival in Minneapolis via the NBL dispersal laid the groundwork for the first dynasty in *organized* professional basketball history.

Mikan's Lakers won five championships in six years, dating back to their BAA title in 1949. Their lone failure came in 1951, when Mikan was hampered by a foot injury for much of the season and into the playoffs. The team's 1954 championship was their last with Big George, who retired shortly after the title celebration.

As with all championship teams, there was more to the Lakers than Mikan.

Playing alongside Big George in Minneapolis were future Hall of Famers Jim Pollard, Slater Martin, and Vern Mikkelsen. Pollard was considered one of the most
gifted athletes to ever play the game. Dubbed the "Kangaroo Kid" for his impressive jumping abilities, the 6'5" forward was among the first players to dunk the
basketball during practice and pregame warm-ups.[1] Martin, a feisty 5'10" point
guard who would rather pass than shoot was exceptional at running the court
and getting the ball to Mikan and Pollard for easy scores. Rounding out the Lakers' talented front line was muscular 6'7", 230-pound Vern Mikkelsen, a durable
All Star power forward who led the league in foul disqualifications.

Despite the formidable leftovers, however, Minneapolis was unable to get
it done in Mikan's absence. In the team's first season without him (1954-55),
they finished second in the West at 40-32, three full games behind the division-
winning Fort Wayne Pistons. The introduction of the 24-second clock presented an additional challenge to the Lakers, as even without Mikan the team
remained a power-orientated squad, dependent on rebounding and inside scoring to win games. The slow-footed group managed to survive the first round
of the playoffs, but fell 0-4 to the quicker Pistons in the Division Finals. Adding
to the team's postseason disappointment, Pollard retired.

The depleted Lakers entered 1955-56 looking and playing old. Mikan's
replacement in the middle, Clyde Lovellette, was the youngest member on the
team at age 26. By midseason, the squad was so desperate for wins that they
lured Big George out of retirement. But the layoff had clearly taken its toll;
Mikan averaged only 10.5 points and 8.3 rebounds in 37 games. The team
finished under .500 for the first time ever (33-39) and lost to St. Louis in the
opening round of the playoffs, two games to one.

By the end of the 1957-58 season, Minneapolis had slid to the bottom of
the league with a dismal 19-53 record. Even the infamous Mikan, enticed to
return yet again, this time as coach, was so discouraged with the squad he left
midseason after compiling an embarrassing 9-30 record. Fortunately, there was
a bright spot to finishing with the league's fewest wins: the Lakers were afforded
the number one draft pick that spring. The staff chose wisely in Elgin Baylor,
a high-scoring 6'5" forward from Seattle University who rebounded like a
seven-footer and passed with the skills of a point guard. Baylor would prove
instrumental in the team's rebuilding efforts when it moved to Los Angeles two
years later, but the tumultuous sixties would come and go before the Lakers
were crowned NBA champions again.

From a technical standpoint, there is no question the Lakers were the first
dynasty in the NBA —five titles in six years is no fluke. The team's swift decline
following Mikan's retirement, however, proved how overly dependent the team
had been on its superstar. Clearly, they could not compete on the same level
without him. As such, it can be argued the Minneapolis's dynasty was in fact
George Mikan's Lakers— hardly the concept Dr. Naismith had in mind when he
invented the game.

Naismith saw basketball as a team affair, whether that team was made up of 5 or 25 players. The new coach of the Boston Celtics, Arnold "Red" Auerbach, shared a similar philosophy. "Individual honors are nice," he would say years into his tenure at Boston, "but no Celtic has ever gone out of his way to achieve them."[2] Players confirmed Red's system was built around one collective attitude: winning. "With the Celtics, the box scores sat on the table where they were left by the stat people," recalled Carl Braun, longtime NY Knicks All Star guard who finished his career in Boston. "The Celtics only cared about the final score."[3]

Auerbach learned the meaning of teamwork early in life. His father, Hyman, who had emigrated from Russia, ran a small business in Brooklyn with his American-born wife, Marie. The hard-working couple was skeptical when their son informed them he was going to make a living at basketball, but Red proved good enough to make the second all-scholastic team his senior year in high school and went on to play college hoops at Seth Low Junior College. His sophomore year he transferred to George Washington University, where he became a three-time letter winner. The young man was a workhorse on the academic end as well, earning a bachelor's degree *and* a master's.

But the only business that truly interested Red was basketball. His love of the game led to high school coaching positions at St. Albans Prep in 1940 and Roosevelt High from 1941–43. He played a year of pro ball with the ABL Harrisburg Senators before entering the navy, where he served as an assistant coach at the Norfolk base. When his military commitment ended, Red landed a coaching job with the BAA Washington Capitols and led the team to two division titles in three years. After the Caps folded, he spent one season at the helm of the Tri-City Blackhawks before moving to the Celtics.

As Red prepared to take over the reins in Boston, team owner Walter Brown was under heavy pressure from hometown fans to draft Bob Cousy, a flashy playmaking guard from nearby Holy Cross, with the team's number one pick. Later known as the "Houdini of the Hardwood," Cousy was clearly ahead of his time. In a game still dominated by the chest pass and two-handed set shot, Bob played like a 1980s Magic Johnson: behind-the-back dribbles and sweeping one-handed hook shots that pulled fans out of their seats. The three-time All American led Holy Cross to 26 straight victories his senior year, capping it off with a second-place finish in the NIT. Every NBA coach assumed the backcourt star would go to Boston with the team's 1950 number one pick — a sensible conclusion given the Celtic's dismal 22-46 record that year.

But in a sign of things to come, Auerbach's first decision as the Celtics' coach was to defy the obvious. Forget the media hype; Red was convinced what his squad *really* needed was a good big man who could rebound and block shots. The fact that Cousy was a hometown boy did nothing to alter his opinion. "I'm supposed to win," he grumbled, "not go after local yokels."[4] Red settled on 6'11" center Charlie Share from Bowling Green.

Bob Cousy, dubbed the "Houdini of the Hardwood," was an early Magic Johnson, dazzling fans with his court vision and fancy ballhandling abilities. Cousy played 13 seasons in Boston, teaming with Russell for six of those to produce six titles. He led the NBA in assists for eight straight years (1953–60) (Steve Lipofsky Basketballphoto.com).

Cousy was drafted by Tri-Cities, but he never signed a contract with the team, opting instead to remain in Worcester, where he and a partner opened a gas station and a chain of driving schools. "I had never seen a pro game when I was in college," Cousy later admitted. "The league (NBA) had little prestige and received little publicity. I figured my basketball days were over and I was going into business."[5] His rights were eventually traded to the Chicago Stags, one of six teams that folded later that summer.

As the start of the next season approached, the NBA's three worst clubs — Boston, Philadelphia, and New York — were in the running for the most coveted player from the defunct Stags, league scoring champ Max Zaslofsky. In addition to the high-scoring guard, two other backcourt players were up for grabs in the three-way lottery: proven All Star Andy Phillip and the as-of-yet unsigned rookie Bob Cousy. Luck was seemingly with New York's Ned Irish, who pulled Zaslofsky's name out of the hat. Philadelphia drew Phillip, leaving Walter Brown with the rights to Cousy.

Bob had said all along he would consider the NBA if he were drafted by the Celtics because playing in Boston would allow him to remain close to home. When Auerbach was able to acquire big man Ed Macauley from St. Louis, Brown decided to take a chance on the flashy playmaker. Cousy agreed to a one-year $9,000 contract with the team, $1,000 below his asking price. Auerbach wasn't thrilled with his new floor general, but Boston fans were quick to voice their approval where it mattered — at the box office. Cousy led the team to its first ever winning record at 39–30 while averaging nearly 16 points and 5 assists per game.

Ed Macauley, another decorated college All American whose awards included AP Player of the Year and NIT Most Valuable Player, complimented Cousy's fast-paced style. Ed began his pro career with the St. Louis Bombers in 1949-50, where he devastated opponents with his quickness in and around the lane. Most of his points came on layups and hook shots in the paint, thus his nickname "Easy Ed." When the Bombers folded, the Celtics acquired the 6'8", 195-pound center via the dispersal draft. Macauley fit in perfectly with Auerbach's up-tempo style, averaging 20.4 points and 9.1 rebounds per game during his first year with the team.

Also on the squad during Cousy's initial season with the Celtics was Charles (Chuck) Cooper, one of three blacks playing in the newly integrated league. Cooper averaged 9.3 points and 8.5 rebounds, helping his team to an impressive second place finish in the East, 2.5 games behind the Philadelphia Warriors.[6] Boston finished first in the league in team assists and points scored, but its season ended on an ugly note when it was swept by New York in the first round of the playoffs. None of the three games was close.

Auerbach responded to the thrashing by acquiring 6'1" shooting guard Bill Sharman from the Pistons during the off-season. Sharman spent his college years in Los Angeles at USC, where he excelled at both basketball and baseball.

The latter was closest to his heart. Despite being named the Pacific Coast Conference Most Valuable Player his junior and senior years, the All American opted to sign a minor league deal with the Brooklyn Dodgers following his graduation in 1950. When the Washington Capitols drafted him in the second round that same year, Bill decided to keep his USC trend alive by playing both sports.[7] His rookie numbers with the Capitols were not all that impressive — he averaged a little over 12 ppg for the season. Still, Auerbach liked what he saw. In what turned out to be one of the most lopsided deals ever, the shrewd Boston coach snared Sharman and inside muscle man Bob Brannum from the Pistons in exchange for the rights to Charlie Share. Although Share had signed with the Celtics, he wound up sitting out his rookie season due to a contract dispute. "Fort Wayne wanted Share and I knew that," Auerbach recalled, defending his decision to take the big man over Cousy. "If I didn't draft Share, we never would have gotten Sharman."[8]

Bill saw limited action during his first season with the Celtics, but his pairing with Cousy stands as one of the game's most impressive backcourts ever assembled. By year two, the sharp-shooting guard led the league in free throw accuracy at 85 percent and ranked sixth in scoring at 16.2 ppg. In 1953, he made the first of eight consecutive appearances in the All Star Game, winning the game's MVP in 1955.

The Celtics remained a formidable regular season opponent during Auerbach's first six years, winning more games than they lost with their dynamic backcourt and high-scoring center leading the way. Auerbach's squad consistently placed second or third in the Eastern Division and went on to make the playoffs. Once the postseason got under way, however, they continued to fall short in the first or second round. From 1951–56, the Celtics accumulated an unimposing 10-17 postseason record.

Needless to say, a lack of points wasn't the problem; the team had three of the league's top 10 scorers in Sharman, Cousy, and Macauley. What they lacked was a strong defensive presence in the middle, a player who could block a shot when it really mattered, or grab an all-important rebound to seal a close game. This void became even more apparent after the advent of the 24-second clock in 1954-55. Although the Celtics led the league in scoring *and* assists that year, their record plummeted to .500 at 36-36, the fist time the team had not posted a winning record under Coach Auerbach. The freefall continued in the postseason, with the Celtics losing to rival Syracuse in the first round, 0-3. The team acquired hard-working forward Jim Loscutoff in the draft that spring, a move that helped them climb back over the .500 mark the following season at 39-33, but the playoff result was the same: yet another discouraging defeat at the hand of the Nats.

Auerbach had seen enough. In a move that shocked the local media and Celtic faithful, he sent Ed Macauley and the rights to Cliff Hagan, the popular Kentucky star about to be discharged from the army, to the Hawks for their 1956 first-round draft pick, 6'9" defensive standout Bill Russell.

And thus began the most remarkable dynasty in the history of professional sports.

William Felton Russell was born in Monroe, Louisiana, on February 12, 1934. His family later moved to California and settled in the Oakland area, where his father found work at one of many local military bases. Bill attended high school at McClymond but didn't play much basketball until his senior year, when he started at center. By most accounts, he was nothing special aside from his size, which proved good enough to land him a scholarship at the University of San Francisco.

Bill made the most of his opportunity with the Dons, where he played alongside future Celtic teammate K. C. Jones. During the duo's years together in San Francisco, the team won an amazing 56 straight games and captured back-to-back NCAA titles in 1955 and 1956. Russell posted an impressive 20.7 ppg scoring average during his collegiate career, but what drew Auerbach's interest was the big man's rebounding. Russell *averaged* more than 20 boards per game. Just the type of player who could take over the game on the defensive end.

Auerbach knew Russell would go too high for the Celtics to draft him, given how the team had forfeited its first-round choice to claim Holy Cross star Tom Heinsohn as a territorial pick. The Territorial Rule afforded teams the opportunity to sign a local college star before he became available via the league-wide draft, a rule that had proven exceedingly popular with hometown fans. But Heinsohn was not chosen simply to appease the locals. He was a proven talent at Holy Cross, averaging a record 27.4 ppg during his senior year. The All American excelled on the academic front as well, appearing on the dean's list for his final four semesters. Auerbach was happy to add Heinsohn to the team, but he still wanted Russell badly enough to trade away Easy Ed and the draft rights to Hagan to get him.

Auerbach's willingness to give up such a proven talent as Macauley in exchange for a player who had never set foot on a pro court was in itself astounding. Even more amazing, given the era, was how little was made of the fact that Russell was black. Although the NBA had been integrated for six years by this point, the league still had no real black stars to speak of. Whether that was due to a lackluster interest in pro basketball among black athletes or simply a matter of prejudice among white owners remains up for discussion. Either way, there is no question that Russell's arrival opened the door to true integration in the NBA.

Bill's teammate on the Dons, K. C. Jones, also African American, was drafted by the Celtics in the second round. It would be two years before he and Bill played together in Boston, however, as Jones had made a two-year commitment to the military.

Russell became a Celtic in the summer of 1956, but the early part of his rookie season was spent in Melbourne, Australia, where he helped the U.S.

Olympic team capture the gold medal. Boston got off to a hot 13-3 start without him, energized by Heinsohn's addition and the continued jelling of Cousy and Sharman in the backcourt. Russell finally made his debut on December 22 and went on to average 14.7 points and a league-best 19.6 rebounds over the remaining 48 games. Most of his scoring came in the paint. "Russell was the first player to dunk regularly," a nonchalant Slater Martin recalled. "There was no finger pointing or talking like you see today. We didn't consider the dunk a skilled shot. If you could jump high, then you could throw the ball through the rim. So what?"[9]

The Celtics cruised to the league's top record at 44-28 and for once appeared on track to win it all. The rival Nats provided little competition in the Division Finals against the Celtics' powerful starting squad of Russell, Heinsohn, Sharman, Cousy, and Loscutoff, losing three games to none, but the revitalized St. Louis Hawks (formerly of Milwaukee), led by former Celtic Ed Macauley and emerging great Bob Pettit, gave Boston all it could handle in the championship series.

The Finals began March 30 in Boston Garden with a shocking two-point, double-overtime victory for the visiting Hawks. The Celtics took the next game by 20 points, but lost another 2-point thriller in St. Louis on April 6. Boston tied the series at 2-2 the following day and returned home, where they won 124–109 on April 9. The series returned to St. Louis for Game 6, which turned into another two-point heartbreaker for the Celtics when a missed shot by Pettit was tapped in by Cliff Hagan for the winning margin. The deciding Game 7 on April 13 provided all the drama fans and players could hope for, with the Celtics eventually prevailing 125–123 in double overtime. Although the contest proved a nightmare for Boston's All Star backcourt — Cousy and Sharman shot a miserable 12.5 percent for the night on 5-for-40 shooting — the Celtics' prize rookies had come to play. Russell and Heinsohn combined for 56 points and 55 rebounds en route to the Celtics' first NBA championship. It was indeed Boston's year. In addition to taking home the title, the Celtics claimed the 1957 Rookie of the Year in Heinsohn and the league's Most Valuable Player, top assist man Bob Cousy.

Boston looked poised to repeat as champions the following year as they cruised to a league-best 49-23 record, eight full games ahead of the nearest competition. Cousy remained the number one assist man (7.1 per game) and an improved Bill Russell won top rebounding honors (22.7 per game) and the league's regular season MVP award. But the team's rosy season wilted when Russell hurt his ankle in Game 3 of the Finals, and Boston wound up losing the series to archrival St. Louis, four games to two. The Hawks' 110–109 victory in Game 6 featured a 50-point outburst by Bob Pettit, tying the NBA playoff record set by Cousy in 1953.[10]

To what degree Russell's injury had affected the outcome of the series became a talking point for years to come. "You can't dismiss the fact that the one year Russell was hurting, Boston didn't win,"[11] Ed Macauley admitted. The debate is testament to how radically the NBA had changed in regard to race: Russell was being discussed solely on his talent and contribution to the team. Anyone who doubted whether a fully integrated league was here to stay need have looked no further than the 1958 Hawks, as they would be the last all-white team to capture an NBA championship.

Auerbach's failure to retain the title made his team all the more determined to recapture it the following year. Their cause was aided by the addition of Russell's old teammate from the Dons, K. C. Jones. Boston also featured an emerging star in second-year player Sam Jones, who spotted Sharman in the backcourt. The mixture of old and new jelled to win a record 52 games in the regular season. Cousy held court as the league's leading assist man at 6.8, and Russell upped his rebounding average to an amazing 23 boards per game — nearly 7 more than second place Bob Pettit.

Auerbach's squad faced a surprisingly stubborn Nats in the Eastern Division Finals. The series went the distance, but the Celtics won big in Game 7 and went on to sweep the newly revitalized Elgin Baylor–led Lakers in the Finals to reclaim the Championship. The series marked the first sweep in NBA Finals history.

Eight years would pass before Boston relinquished the trophy again.

But that is not to say the Celtics were without competition as the 1950s wound down. A new era was about to dawn in nearby Philadelphia as the Warriors welcomed their 1959 first round draft pick, 7'1", 285-pound Wilt Chamberlain.

STARLIGHT, STAR BRIGHT

When the talking points of a professional athlete's career are discussed, his or her hometown is rarely little more than a footnote. In the case of Wilt Chamberlain, however, the fact he was born and raised in Philadelphia proved instrumental in the salvation of Eddie Gottlieb's struggling Warriors.

Gottlieb's love for basketball had kept him in the game for years, but he was a businessman who ultimately dealt in reality. The costs of running an NBA franchise continued to escalate with rising salaries and extended travel. Eddie knew if he expected to keep pace, he would have to find a way to excite local fans so they would support his team at the box office. The ultimate solution nearly dropped into his lap via a local high school student by the name of Wilt Chamberlain. It was obvious to anyone with a basketball eye that the sprawling young man, also a top-notch track star at Overbrook, would grow into one of the best players to hit the court since the invention of Naismith's game. The question for Eddie was how to ensure Wilt would become a Warrior.

Gottlieb knew the high school senior was being wooed by universities across the country (sources later estimated the number at 200) and would definitely go on to play college ball at one of them. It was unheard of at the time for a high school player to jump directly to the NBA, regardless of how promising his talent. Furthermore, 1955 NBA rules stated that once a player committed to a university, he could not join the NBA for the remainder of his college eligibility, regardless of whether he remained in school.

Four years was an incredibly long time to wait. Much could happen in that interim; Wilt might suffer a serious injury or decide to pursue a career outside of sports. But Eddie Gottlieb would not be dissuaded. The Philadelphia Warriors chose the prep star in the first round of the 1955 draft, claiming his rights under the Territorial Rule. Several teams later objected, but the league sided with the Warriors, who argued that since Kansas had no NBA team, Chamberlain's territorial rights belonged to the city where he had played high school ball. Wilt's selection marked the first time in NBA history that a player — black or white — was drafted while he was still in high school.

The Christian Street YMCA team from Philadelphia, National YMCA Basketball Champions, 1952–53. Note 16-year-old Wilt Chamberlain in the center, back row (courtesy YMCA of the USA and Kautz family archives).

It is difficult to dispute Gottlieb's foresight. During Chamberlain's years at Overbrook, he accumulated an astounding 2,206 points while leading his team to two city titles and an overall record of 56-3.[1] When he was not busy mesmerizing fans on the basketball court, he was displaying his athleticism in track, where he took top honors in the high-jump and shot put. As former classmate Jimmy Sadler would later recount, "He would be great not because he was tall, but because he could do so many things."[2]

Fittingly, Chamberlain decided to play his college ball at Naismith's old stomping grounds, the University of Kansas, where he was coached by the "Father of Basketball Coaching" legendary Hall of Famer Forest "Phog" Allen. Local fans watched in awe as the lean seven-footer scored 50 points in his freshman debut in a game against the school's varsity squad. (At the time, NCAA rules prohibited freshman from playing on varsity teams.) The following year, Wilt led the Jawhawks to the 1957 NCAA finals, where they lost to North Carolina in a triple-overtime thriller, 54–53. Despite the defeat, Chamberlain was voted the tournament's MVP. In 48 varsity games, the First Team All American grabbed a total of 877 rebounds and averaged 29.9 points per game.

Wilt's enormous impact on the game was directly responsible for several rule changes in NCAA play. One of the big man's trademark moves, leaping from the foul line to slam in his own missed free throws, became illegal; free throw shooters were hence required to remain stationary behind the line until the shot was complete. In a related move, the offensive goaltending rule was amended to forbid any player from touching the ball while it was still in the cylinder. Inbounding the ball to a teammate by lobbing it over the backboard was no longer permitted, effectively stopping still another of Wilt's favorite moves. Finally, only the opposing team was allowed to line up players closest to the basket during foul shots.

Some claim the rule changes were responsible for Chamberlain's decision to forgo his senior year. Wilt said it was because he had accomplished all he could at Kansas and was anxious to move on to the professional game. In any event, because NBA rules prohibited him from joining the Warriors until his class had graduated, he spent the 1958-59 season with Saperstein's Harlem Globetrotters. According to numerous sources, his salary hovered in the $50,000 range, an astronomical amount for the day. Chamberlain added another first to his résumé when the Trotters traveled to the Soviet Union in 1959. The sold-out tour included a face-to-face greeting from Nikita Khrushchev at Moscow's Lenin Central Stadium.

Wilt's NBA career began the following season in the spotlight at Madison Square Garden, where he debuted with an extraordinary 43-point, 28-rebound effort against the Knicks. He went on to average 37.6 points and 27 rebounds for the season while racking up numerous individual awards, beginning with the All Star Game, where he was voted MVP. The 1960 Rookie of the Year was also named league MVP, becoming the first player to receive both prestigious awards in one year. As of this writing, only Wes Unseld of the 1969 Washington Bullets has duplicated that feat.

Chamberlain led the previously last-place Warriors to a second-place finish in the East his rookie year. The revitalized team went on to meet Auerbach's champion Celtics in the 1960 Division Finals. The series featured the first match-up between Chamberlain and Russell, a rivalry that would grow into one of the most hotly contested events in all of professional sports. Wilt averaged a series-high 30.5 ppg, bolstered by a 50-point effort in Game 5, but Boston claimed the series in six and went on to edge the Bob Pettit–led St. Louis Hawks in the Finals, four games to three.

Meanwhile, over in chilly Minneapolis, the Lakers were in the midst of their own revival, led by the high-flying skills of their emerging star, Elgin Baylor. A standout forward in college, the 6'5" Baylor had led Seattle University to the NCAA Finals in 1958. In a situation that mirrored Chamberlain's, Baylor

Elgin Baylor, chosen by the Minneapolis Lakers with the number one pick in the 1958 college draft, was one of the earliest stars to play above the rim, and thus is often referred to as an early Michael Jordan. He averaged 27.4 points, 13.5 rebounds, and 4.3 assists over his 14-year career (Basketball Hall of Fame, Springfield, MA).

won Tournament MVP honors even though his team lost the championship game. The downtrodden Lakers (19-53) chose him with the overall number one pick in the 1958 draft and shelled out a then-hefty $20,000 salary to sign him. All within the organization soon agreed it was money well spent.

The Washington, D.C., native was the first NBA player to make a name for himself above the rim. In the words of the late Chick Hearn, who spent 42 seasons broadcasting Lakers games: "He would hang in the air for so long that you'd worry that he'd get hurt when he came down."[3] Later nicknamed "the man with a thousand moves," Baylor possessed tremendous offensive skills, freezing opponents with a quick first step en route to a driving layup, or pulling up for a springboard jumper from 20 feet. "A lot of the moves people say were invented by Michael Jordan or Julius Erving, I saw Elgin do first," Hearn added. "People ask me, how good was Elgin ... well, he may have been the greatest player ever."[4] Former Celtics great Bill Sharman, who went on to coach the Lakers during Baylor's final years, called him "the greatest cornerman who ever played pro basketball."[5]

Adding to Baylor's game was his physical strength, well above average for his 225-pound frame. Hot Rod Hundley, who played with Baylor for several years, compared him to a modern-day Karl Malone. "He'd pound the boards for a rebound, throw an outlet pass to a guard, fill the lane on the fast break, catch the return pass and go to the basket like a steam engine, daring anyone to get in his way."[6] Longtime teammate Jerry West said Baylor was the strongest forward he had ever seen. "At 6-5 he wasn't a giant," West wrote in his 1969 autobiography, *Mr. Clutch* (p. 78), but he was bull-strong and quick and very daring."

Baylor led the Lakers to a 33-39 record during his rookie year, 14 wins better than the previous season. But the revitalized squad didn't stop there. Upset victories over Detroit and St. Louis in the playoffs earned the former champions a Finals match-up with Boston. Elgin's heroics were not enough to lead his tired squad past the experienced Celtics, however, and they lost the series in four straight. Nonetheless, the 1959 NBA Rookie of the Year had gained important postseason experience to go with his impressive debut. Voted All Star Co-MVP (with Bob Pettit) in his first year, Elgin finished the season fourth in scoring (24.9), eighth in assists (4.1) and fifth in rebounds (15). No one suggested it was beginner's luck.

The following year, Baylor upped his regular season scoring to third best in the league (29.6) and poured in 33.4 ppg in the Lakers' two playoff series. Minneapolis was unable to duplicate the previous season's success in the Division Finals, however, and fell to the Hawks in seven games. Nonetheless, Baylor had left his mark on the year by setting a new NBA record for points scored in a game. Elgin's 64-point performance against the Celtics on November 8 had surpassed the league's 10-year-old record of 63, held by Philadelphia's Joe Fulks. The game also made Baylor the new Lakers' scoring champ, eclipsing George Mikan's 61, set in 1952.

Despite the excitement of Baylor and the team's overall improved play, the Lakers failed to re-create the magic of the Mikan era insofar as the fans of Minneapolis were concerned. Attendance hovered around the 4,000 mark, well below the league average of 5,008.[7] Although Eastern and Midwestern cities still housed most professional sports franchises, some owners had begun to venture West. The most recent success story belonged to the Dodgers, who had abandoned downtown Brooklyn for sunny Los Angeles in 1958. The fact the Dodgers were reaping hefty profits since their move was not lost on Lakers owner Bob Short. If Major League Baseball could win the hearts of Los Angeles' sports fans, why not the NBA?

Short's decision to move his team across the country at the beginning of the 1960-61 season was met with skepticism by the league, which initially declined the proposal. Understandably, owners were concerned about the added travel expenses necessary to support what would be the only West Coast team in the league. But Short was so convinced his club would find new life in L.A. he agreed to foot the bill for whatever extra expenses were incurred by the rest of the league. A second vote was taken, and the move was approved. Knicks owner Ned Irish was the lone dissenter. Word had it Irish was hoping Short's financial troubles would escalate to the point the Lakers would be forced to sell Baylor's rights, in which case he would be waiting on the sidelines, cash in hand.

A public announcement that the Lakers were moving to Los Angeles came several months after the team had drafted yet another promising young player with its first-round draft pick, 1960 Gold Olympian star Jerry West.

The son of a coal-mine electrician, Jerry grew up Cheylan, West Virginia, a town of 500 folks some 14 miles south of Charleston. His rural heritage led to the nickname "Zeke from Cabin Creek," so named because the West family received their mail from the nearby town of Cabin Creek. It was a name West would never be comfortable with, as he believed it carried with it the stigma that he was a country bumpkin.

Jerry played his high school ball at East Bank, where he became the first prep player in the state to reach a career total of 900 points. His senior year, he led his team to the state championship while averaging 33.6 points per game. The smallish, slender guard would later confide that winning the 1956 state title was the happiest moment of his life.

West attended West Virginia University, also the playground of future Lakers teammate Hot Rod Hundley. When Jerry arrived as a freshman, Rod was in his senior year and expected to be among the NBA's hottest draft picks. Hundley held most of the school's scoring records, and, according to West, had done so "in such a showy way that he was bound to be missed."[8] As it turned out, Jerry filled the void nicely. During his time with the Mountaineers, he was named an All American twice while averaging 24.8 points per game. West led his team to the NCAA Finals his junior year, racking up a total of 160 points

Jerry West signified the ultimate NBA workaholic. The 6'2" shooting guard's tireless, winning attitude helped keep the Lakers in the title hunt for most of his 14-year career, over which he averaged 27 points, 6.7 assists, and 5.8 rebounds. West is currently the GM of the Memphis Grizzlies (Dick Raphael).

in five postseason games. The season ended on a sour note when the Mountaineers lost the championship game to the University of California 70–71, but like Chamberlain and Baylor before him, West was named Tournament MVP. He did not view it as much of a consolation. "It was hard not to cry," he recalled years later. "I mean, what good are the fancy records and the high honors if you lose the championship by one point?"[9]

Jerry won many other awards that year, including conference Basketball Player of the Year and Athlete of the Year, but his proudest achievement was being named to the team that would represent the United States in the upcoming Pan American Games in Chicago. The U.S. team breezed past the likes of Cuba, Mexico, and Canada en route to the gold medal. The following year, West realized a longtime dream when he was selected for the 1960 Olympic Team. Jerry described accepting his gold medal in Rome as a thrill he would never forget.

Prior to the Olympic Games, Jerry had been drafted by Short's Lakers and thought he was headed to Minneapolis. "I knew nothing about the city," he would later admit, "except that it got real cold there. But it wasn't New York ... I had to talk myself into enthusiasm." West's mood improved substantially when he learned the team was moving to Los Angeles. "It was a big town and an exciting town."[10] Adding to the good news, West learned his college coach, Fred Schaus, had been hired by Short to take over the team.

Although West was the second player selected overall, he was offered a contract for $5,000 less than Elgin Baylor had received two years earlier. It was common knowledge throughout the league that Short was strapped for cash, and Jerry wasn't discouraged by the offer. Money was a secondary issue to him. What mattered was the prospect of winning championships, regaining that euphoria he had experienced with his East Bank squad in 1956. Convinced the Lakers could become a title contender with the threesome of himself, Baylor, and Hot Rod, Jerry signed the contract and headed to L.A.

The rookie's enthusiasm was tethered when Coach Schaus announced Jerry would start the season by coming off the bench. West admitted he was surprised and frustrated, especially given how the Lakers guards were considered among the teams' weakest positions. Perhaps Schaus was attempting to protect Jerry from the rigors of NBA initiation, or maybe he was hoping to avoid the disappointment that had surrounded Hot Rod, who had not yet lived up to expectations in the pros. In any event, West finished the year averaging 17 ppg — not bad for a first-year player, but far below that of the NBA Rookie of the Year, Jerry's friend and Olympic teammate cocaptain Oscar Robertson.

When discussing the most complete player the NBA has ever seen, most fans think of Michael Jordan, Larry Bird, and Magic Johnson — all exceptional players of the modern era. But ask the majority of legendary players, coaches, and basketball historians the same question, and nearly all will answer "The Big O" from Cincinnati, the only player to ever *average* a triple-double (double

Oscar Robertson, nicknamed the Big O, remains the only NBA player to *average* a triple-double for an entire season (1961-62; 30.8 points, 12.5 rebounds, 11.4 assists). The feat is all the more amazing, given how he achieved it during his second year in the league. Robertson played 10 years with Cincinnati before being traded to the Bucks, where he teamed with a young Lew Alcindor (Kareem Abdul-Jabbar) to bring a championship to Milwaukee in 1971 (Dick Raphael).

figures in scoring, rebounding and assists) for an entire season. Oscar Robertson accomplished the amazing feat in 1961-62, his second year in the league, posting averages of 30.8 points, 12.5 rebounds, and 11.4 assists. "He is so great he scares me," Red Auerbach once confided.[11] Legendary Celtic John Havlicek, who played against Oscar most of his career, added, "There was nothing Oscar Robertson couldn't do."[12]

Born Oscar Palmer Robertson, the Tennessee native grew up in the poor, segregated projects of Indianapolis, where he learned and perfected the skills that would carry him to fame and fortune in the NBA. Taking a page from history, Oscar's journey began in the same manner of those in Naismith's era, by mounting a peach basket in the family's backyard. His first "basketball" was actually a tennis ball wrapped in rags and tied together with rubber bands.

Robertson's talent to improvise would carry through to the game itself. By the time he walked through the doors of Crispus Attucks High School as a freshman in 1952, he possessed amazing skills in nearly every aspect of the sport — a fact not lost on the school's coach, Ray Crowe. Realizing he was going to be part of something special, Crowe encouraged the budding star to improve the fundamentals of his game: dribbling, passing, rebounding, and above all, *thinking* about the game from a team concept. The partnership was an immediate success. The all-black Crispus Attucks, previously shunned by white opponents, became the hottest draw in the state. Oscar led his team to an remarkable 62-1 record en route to consecutive state titles in 1955 and 1956.

Sports fans of Indianapolis were elated at their first-ever state titles, yet racism continued to conquer and divide. Citing fears that blacks would "tear up the town" amid any celebratory activities, city officials informed Crowe his team would have to hold its victory party outside of town. The double-standard treatment continued through Robertson's college years at the University of Cincinnati, where he averaged an extraordinary 33.8 ppg on the varsity Bearcats. Hometown fans roared their approval as the three-time College Player of the Year led the Bearcats to a 79-9 record while establishing 14 NCAA records, including 3 consecutive scoring titles. Off the court, however, his accomplishments often faded beneath the color of his skin. "There was a movie theater a half block from the campus that would not sell a ticket to a black," Bearcats mascot Ron Grinker recalled, "even if the black was the great Oscar Robertson. This was the late 1950s and there were restaurants in town that would not serve the great Oscar Robertson."[13]

Although the Civil Rights Act had yet to be enacted, the success of Russell, Chamberlain, and Baylor had made race irrelevant within the confines of the NBA. Players were drafted solely on the level of their talent. As such, the Cincinnati Royals used the Territorial Rule to snare Robertson with the number one pick and promptly signed him to a generous $33,000 salary.

Oscar responded by averaging 30.5 ppg his rookie year, third highest in the NBA. He dazzled fans at the All Star Game with an MVP performance of

23 points and 14 assists, bettering rival Bob Cousy's assist record by one in the process. The 1961 Rookie of the Year also ended Cousy's string of league-leading assists at eight seasons with a 9.7 per game average. Unfortunately for the Royals, Oscar's brilliant play was not enough to pull them out of the Western Division cellar, though the team did improve from its dismal 19-56 showing the year before to a more respectable 33-46 record. As with Jerry West in L.A., Oscar's impact on the league had just begun.

Atop the Western Division that year, the 51-28 St. Louis Hawks featured a prize rookie of their own in playmaking guard Lenny Wilkens. A former defensive standout at Providence, Wilkens had been drafted by St. Louis in the first round, but had not expected to make the team, let alone earn a starting job in the backcourt. His skepticism was understandable. Prior to his arrival, the club was heavy on talent with Bob Pettit, Clyde Lovellette, and Cliff Hagan, all of whom ranked among the league's top 12 in scoring *and* rebounding. The Hawks would have a hole to fill at point guard, however, as future Hall of Famer Slater Martin had announced his retirement.

Hawks veterans were less than thrilled with the idea of a rookie replacing the stellar Martin, but Lenny impressed with his ability to see the court, find open teammates, and pass the ball at precisely the right time and place. "Ball-handling is not natural like jumping," Wilkens said when explaining his approach to the game. "It's a learned skill, and it was the reason I had success."[14]

Wilkens learned quickly enough to earn his way into the starting lineup midway through his rookie season. Although he averaged a modest 11.7 ppg that year, his defensive intensity and ballhandling capabilities made it obvious he would grow into a steady floor leader. Under his guidance, the team won five more games than it had with Martin the previous year and went on to defeat the Lakers in the Western Division Finals, four games to three.

The Hawks moved on to face Boston in the Finals that year, a series that began a mere *one day* after the team's exhausting 105–103 victory over the Lakers in Game 7 of the Division championship. The Celtics put 129 points on the board in Game 1, compared to the Hawks' 95, a score that would prove indicative of the lopsided series. Mercifully, it was over in five. The Celtics retained their crown for the third straight year, winning their fourth title in five years. Russell won league MVP.

Although integral to his team's success, Bill Russell was not the only reason the Celtics continued to collect championship banners. The club was stocked with above-average talent at nearly every position. Sharman and Cousy remained the most formable backcourt in the league, backed up by the able up-and-coming Joneses, Sam and K. C. On the frontline, starting forwards Tom Heinsohn and Frank Ramsey averaged more than 36 points between them. Every game was a collective effort. No starter ever put enough points on the board to claim the scoring title at the end of the season, but all five averaged at least 15 ppg. Under the guidance of Auerbach, Boston's game was old-fashioned basketball, Naismith style.

Over in Philadelphia, the name of the game was Wilt the Stilt. Chamberlain led the league in rebounding and averaged more points than three of Boston's starters combined. The Big O was tearing up the record books in Cincinnati, consistently placing among the league's best in scoring, rebounding, and assists. The revitalized West Coast Lakers featured the league's best scoring duo in Jerry West and Elgin Baylor, while St. Louis had one of the NBA's top floor generals in Lenny Wilkens. Yet when the curtain closed on the regular season and the playoffs began, not one of those stars could lead his team past Auerbach's Celtics in a seven-game series.

Fortunately for most owners, capturing a world title is not the only way to be crowned a winner at the box office. When all is said and done, there is room for only one champion, one team that has managed to claw its way through the adversity of the regular season and still have enough game left to come out on top. The remainder of the league must be content to compete. On that end, the arrival of stars like Baylor and Chamberlain signaled a new era in the world of professional basketball. Be it for better or worse, the age of the superstar was here to stay.

TREMORS

By the early 1960s, the NBA appeared to have proven the staying power its predecessors lacked. Although a few teams continued to struggle financially, attendance was steadily growing. Several clubs had changed locations, but the league had not lost a franchise since the Baltimore Bullets called it quits midway through the 1954-55 season.

Owners' confidence in the NBA's resilience was reflected in the numbers. Unlike previous leagues, which had decreased the number of games played to stay afloat, the NBA's regular season schedule had inched upward since its initial 60-game mark in 1949-50. Half a decade later, teams were playing 72 games. By 1961-62, the total had risen to 80. Spotty attendance had leveled out. Clubs were averaging more than 5,000 fans per game and the numbers were on the rise at most arenas, enough so that the league opted to add a franchise — the Chicago Packers — to compensate for the Lakers' move to L.A. the previous year.

On the marketing end, hoops fans who had bemoaned the loss of Mikan as the end of the professional game were being reintroduced to star power via the likes of Elgin Baylor's spectacular high-wire acrobatics, Oscar Robertson's triple-double highlights, Lenny Wilkens's steady playmaking skills, the never-quit attitude of sharp-shooter Jerry West, and the absolute dominance on both ends of the court by Wilt the Stilt.

It was obvious to owners that individual stars had become and were likely to remain one of the driving forces behind the success of professional basketball. As expected, Chamberlain was impacting the league in a way no player, even the dominant Mikan, ever had before. The 1961-62 campaign, Wilt's third, would prove his career-best insofar as individual stats were concerned. His most astounding feat occurred on March 2, 1962, before 4,124 fans in Hershey, Pennsylvania. Ironically, it was a meager crowd present at the Warriors' 169–147 victory over the New York Knicks that witnessed one of the most spectacular events in the history of professional sports. Chamberlain made 36 of 73 field goals during the regulation game and shot an uncharacteristic 28-for-32 from the free throw line (Wilt's career free throw percentage was a dismal 55 percent) to post a once-in-a-lifetime box score total of 100 points. He went on to *average* 50.4 ppg for the season, more than 12 points ahead of second-place finisher Elgin Baylor (38.3). Chamberlain also captured top rebounding honors, beating out Russell 25.7 to 23.6. Finishing third in both scoring and rebounding was another rising star, Rookie of the Year Walt Bellamy, from the new Chicago Packers.

Given how the popularity of Naismith's game continued to grow within the collegiate ranks as well, it seemed plausible that every NBA team would be able to highlight at least one star attraction at its home gate, ensuring the financial stability of the league. Surely it followed that there was room for more — much more — than the NBA's current load of nine teams.

Such was the mindset of Abe Saperstein, whose Globetrotters continued to play to enthusiastic sellout crowds across America and abroad. Word had it Saperstein was upset with the NBA and its supposedly unfilled promise to award him a franchise, presumably in Los Angeles. When Short's Lakers arrived on the West Coast for the 1960-61 season instead, Saperstein responded by putting together his own professional league.

The American Basketball League began play in October 1961 with eight charter franchises spanning the nation from New York to Los Angeles to Hawaii. Several teams relocated during the 40-some game season (the number varied between franchises) in an attempt to stay afloat. The Los Angeles Jets, coached by none other than retired Celtic great Bill Sharman, folded after accumulating one of the league's best records at 24-15. As great a player as Bill had been, it was obvious basketball fans in L.A. preferred to spend their money watching Lakers legends Baylor and West. Sharman moved on to the Cleveland Pipers when head man John McLendon — the first black to coach in professional basketball — resigned. McLendon cited interference from the team's owner, George Steinbrenner, as the reason for his departure.

As a league, the ABL had credibility problems from the get-go, fueled by Saperstein's decision to appoint himself commissioner, a situation that set up an instant conflict of interest, given how his own Chicago Majors played in the league. Although several former NBA stars were convinced to join Sharman on the coaching front, Saperstein failed in his bid to lure active big-name players from the NBA hardwood. Predictably, most college stars also elected to sign with teams from the established league. The ABL was left with players from the semi-pro Eastern League, various AAU teams, and those would-be college stars tarnished by betting scandals and subsequently banned by the NBA. Of the latter, the most notable was New York playground legend Connie Hawkins, who would eventually be named to the NBA's list of 50 Greatest Players.

Of all the young players whose careers were affected by the notorious betting scandals, it is generally agreed by sports historians that Connie Hawkins suffered the most from the league's no tolerance rule. The Brooklyn native learned the game on the streets, where he dazzled fans from his Bedford-

Stuyvesant neighborhood with high-flying dunks by age 11. Things looked to be well on track when Hawkins was named a *Parade* magazine High School All American in 1960, but the following year as a freshman at Iowa, his name came up in the betting scandals that were currently rocking New York. An investigation turned up no evidence linking Hawkins with the point-shaving scandal. Even those players eventually indicted in the scam insisted he was not involved. Nonetheless, Iowa found Hawkins guilty by association, or the possibility of association, and bid him adieu before he ever set foot on the court. He did a brief stint with the Globetrotters before joining the ABL Pittsburgh Rens at age 19.

Hawkins was named the ABL's Most Valuable Player. In the playoffs, Sharman's Cleveland squad found itself down two games to none before beating the Kansas City Steers three straight games to win the best-of-five playoff series championship. The latter event managed to generate a six-paragraph write-up in the *New York Times*.

The fledging league generated a bit more publicity during the off-season, when the Cleveland Pipers signed collegiate sensation Jerry Lucas to an eye-popping $50,000 two-year deal. Lucas was just the type of player the new league so desperately needed: a leader who knew how to win. The three-time All American and former Olympian had an NCAA title and two tournament MVP awards under his belt. He was expected to make an immediate impact on the pro game, touting career averages of 24.3 points and 17.4 rebounds per game.

Lucas's signing did not go unnoticed by the NBA. Discussions regarding a possible merger between the two leagues took place over the summer but ultimately went nowhere. The NBA was, however, very interested in adding Steinbrenner's Pipers and his newly acquired, sure-to-be superstar to the fold via an expansion franchise. Steinbrenner was more than happy to write a check for the $400,000 NBA franchise fee, but a furious Saperstein blocked the move with a lawsuit, and the Pipers became a team without a league. The loss of its championship franchise left the ABL with six teams heading into the 1962-63 season.

The big preseason news in the NBA belonged to Chamberlain and his Warriors, who left the streets of Philadelphia for the hills of San Francisco. With California now home to three of the NBA's top gate attractions in Baylor, West, and Chamberlain, pro basketball fans saw little reason to follow mediocre ABL teams in Oakland and Long Beach. Saperstein could only hope his league fared better in the East, where perhaps disgruntled Warrior fans would embrace his Philadelphia Tapers and Pittsburgh Rens.

In nearby Boston, the Celtics remained the only pro basketball game in town. Eager fans welcomed rookie John Havlicek into the fold as the team prepared for its final run with 34-year-old Bob Cousy, who had announced he would retire at the end of the 1962-63 season. Meanwhile in Cincinnati, fans were slapped with a double whammy. Saperstein's lawsuit kept the Royals from adding Jerry Lucas to its roster, and the team was switched from the Western Division to the East. The realignment, which ensured the title-heavy Celtics would not run away with the East unchallenged, would serve to frustrate the Big O for years to come. On an obscure note, the Chicago Packers, the only NBA team to face direct competition with an ABL club (Saperstein's Chicago Majors), changed its name to the Zephyrs.

With Lucas's situation in limbo, Connie Hawkins remained the American Basketball League's only big-name draw at the box office. Saperstein scheduled numerous doubleheaders with his Globetrotters as the season progressed, but the lift in attendance was not enough to save his floundering venture. The ABL ceased operations abruptly on December 31, 1963. "Not a single team was operating in the black,"[1] a disheartened Saperstein confessed in a media statement announcing the league's disbandment. All ABL players became free agents, some of whom went on to sign with NBA clubs. Hawkins rejoined the Globetrotters.

Just as the ABL had done nothing to diminish the NBA's supremacy, the Warriors' relocation to San Francisco was unable to provide Chamberlain's squad — runner up to the Celtics the past three years — with an elusive division title. Wilt's 44.8 ppg was more than enough to retain his individual scoring title, but his team finished fourth in the West, 22 games behind the Lakers. There would be no playoffs for the Stilt in the spring of 1963, let alone a much-anticipated Finals match-up against Russell.

The Royals gave the Celtics all they could handle in the Eastern Finals, but the Big O could not quite push his club over the top in Game 7. Meanwhile, the Lakers needed seven games to dispose of a much-improved St. Louis team. No club had improved enough, however, to topple the reigning champions. The exasperated Lakers lost Game 6 at home, sending Auerbach back to Boston with his fifth straight NBA title in hand. Fans, not to mention opposing coaches and players, began to wonder if the guys in green would ever lose a Finals series again.

While there is no question the Russell-era Celtics was loaded with talent, the same could be said of other, less successful teams. Syracuse had five players who finished among the league's 20 most accurate shooters (field goal percentage). The St. Louis Hawks featured four proven stars in Bob Pettit, Lenny Wilkens, Zelmo Beaty, and Cliff Hagan. The Warriors had Chamberlain, a man capable of scoring 100 points on his own.

The difference was not a matter of talent as much as production. On that end, the Celtics coach was in a league of his own. Former Celtic Tom Heinsohn called him the "ultimate sports management" person — an apt description, given how one of Auerbach's greatest strengths was his ability to groom young players, bring them along slowly while teaching the game from a team-orientated standpoint. "He had a way of listening to players and being honest with them," Heinsohn said. "If we had an idea, we knew he really wanted to hear it."[2]

Arnold "Red" Auerbach coached the Boston Celtics to 10 Eastern Division titles and 9 championships in 16 years. He moved to the front office in 1966 and served as the team's president until his death on October 28, 2006 (Steve Lipofsky Basketballphoto.com).

There was also a great sense of security on the Celtics squad. Once a player made the team, he was considered a member of the family, on and off the court. When a star neared the twilight of his career, he was eased out of the starting lineup gradually, exchanging roles with a backup whose abilities he had come to admire and respect. "Red would give a veteran player an extra year when most other teams would have told him to retire or traded him off," Heinsohn explained. "But you also trained your replacement — which was unique in basketball."[3] Unique and effective. Many speculated the Celtics would falter when their legendary guard tandem of Sharman and Cousy retired, but the team continued to win titles with Sam Jones and K. C. Jones in the backcourt. John Havlicek, who joined the team during Cousy's final year, revolutionized the sixth-man role by becoming the first 20-plus point scorer not among his team's starting five. Like all of the Celtics, he believed in his coach. "No matter what Red said," Havlicek related, "I'd say, 'You've got it.'"[4]

And Red *did* have it, title after title, year after year. The rest of the league could only draw solace from the law of averages: the Celtics would have to lose a Finals series eventually. But their title reign would not end under Commissioner Podoloff's rule. For the first time in its 14-year history, the NBA began the 1963-64 season with a new man at the helm. His name was Walter Kennedy.

Kennedy was no stranger to pro basketball, of course. He had served as the BAA's public relations director during its difficult merger with the NBL and later as publicity director for the Harlem Globetrotters. In 1959, he returned to his hometown of Stamford, Connecticut, where he completed a successful run for mayor. His appointment to succeed Podoloff as commissioner in 1963 would make the NBA a major force in the world of professional sports.

The league underwent several changes during Kennedy's first year. The Syracuse Nationals, a mainstay in the small market community since its inception as a NL team in 1946, moved to basketball-hungry Philadelphia where they would play as the 76ers. The Chicago Zephyrs left the Windy City for Baltimore to become the new Bullets. In Ohio, John Lucas's exile ended in great fashion for Royals fans when the 6'8" forward, who had been claimed as a territorial pick prior to signing with the Pipers, joined the Big O in Cincinnati.

Meanwhile out West, the San Francisco Warriors' disappointing 31-49 record in their Western debut had prompted a coaching change. Alex Hannum, who had interrupted the Celtics' run by guiding the St. Louis Hawks to the title in 1957, arrived as head coach with a new philosophy for the struggling Warriors: defense. Under Hannum's direction, the team led the league in fewest points allowed (102.6) en route to a 48-32 record and its first division title. Rookie big man Nate Thurmond was part of the reason, joining Wilt on the front line to grab an additional 10.4 rebounds per game. Hannum delighted in beating his old team in Game 7 of the Western Division Finals, but it was business as usual in Bean Town. The Celtics disposed of Wilt's new look squad in five games to secure their sixth straight NBA crown. It would prove beloved owner Walter Brown's last victory celebration; he passed away on September 7, 1964.

Shockwaves resounded through the league midway through the next season when it was announced that Chamberlain, considered in the peak of his career at age 28, was headed back to Philadelphia. The Warriors received some

cash, reportedly in the $300,000 range, two mediocre players—Connie Dirk-
ing and Paul Neumann—and the rights to a third, Lee Shafer (who was in the
midst of a contract dispute with the 76ers), in return for the most dominant
player in history. The move assured the Warriors it would miss the playoffs
once again.

The 76ers, meanwhile, gained instant respectability, especially from the
Celtics, who needed every minute of the seven-game Eastern Finals to get past
Wilt and his new club. Boston led by seven with only two minutes to play, but
a determined Chamberlain scored six straight points to bring his team within
one. Then the unthinkable happened: a miscue by Russell on the inbounds
gave the ball back to Philadelphia with five seconds to play. But as the 76ers
inbounded the ball under their basket, Havlicek managed to get a hand on the
pass and slap it to teammate Sam Jones, who raced down court, sealing the victory.

The Lakers were back in the Finals for another go at their Eastern nemesis, but without an injured Elgin Baylor, who had been plagued by knee problems the past two seasons. The Celtics finished off Jerry West's shorthanded
squad in five games, and Auerbach won his first Coach of the Year award.

Jubilation filled opposing arenas the following year when Red announced
the season would be his last on the bench. Even worse for Celtics fans, their
coach was not the only one in the organization who was showing signs of age.
Loscutoff, Ramsey, and Heinsohn had already retired; Bill Russell and the backcourt Joneses were now in their thirties. Younger players like Don Nelson and
Larry Siegfried were on their way up but would need to time grow into regular contributors.

Meanwhile across state lines, a title-hungry Wilt and his 76ers were making noise. Lots of noise. New addition Billy Cunningham, a promising rookie
out of North Carolina, provided additional scoring upfront to the tune of more
than 14 ppg. Chet Walker was fast coming into his own as a star, and veteran
guard Hal Greer had reached the prime of his steady career. As with Celtics
squads of previous years, the 76ers had finally acquired the perfect blend of
youth, experience, and star power necessary to win a championship.

Philadelphia gained momentum during the regular season, beating rival
Boston in 6 of 10 attempts on the way to a 55-win season and the Eastern Division title. The achievement marked the first time in 10 years that a team other
than the Celtics had won the division. On an individual level, Chamberlain
passed Bob Pettit to become the league's all-time scoring champ.

Philadelphia appeared ready to take its rightful place as the new Eastern
power going into the playoffs. All that remained was getting past an aging
Boston squad in the Division Finals. At the time, division winners received a
bye in the first round, thus Philadelphia had time to rest and prepare for its
impending match-up. The Celtics, meanwhile, needed all five games to get past
Oscar's Royals in the Semi-Finals. But as often proves the case in professional

sports, too much rest can be worse than no rest at all. The two week layoff left the 76ers out of sync when the series began, and the Celtics, spurred on by a quest to give their beloved coach the ultimate sendoff in the form of an eighth straight title, jumped on them early. A shocked Philly club fell in five games. Coach Dolph Schayes lost his job, and Auerbach's Celtics moved on to meet the Lakers in the Finals.

When Boston lost Game 1 to the Lakers at home in overtime, it appeared as if the club was sputtering on its last drop of gas. But Auerbach had one more rabbit to pull out of his hat. Amid the buzz of his team's pending demise, he made a shocking announcement: Bill Russell would succeed him as coach. The news so inspired his players they won the next three games. L.A. squeaked out another victory in Boston, then took care of business on its home court in Game 6 to tie the series at 3–3. The tiring Celtics regrouped for Game 7 in Boston, where they jumped to an early first-half lead amid the tepid shooting of West and Baylor. The Lakers fought back to a two-point deficit with four seconds remaining in the game, but the guys in green managed to dribble out the clock, denying the Lakers yet again.

Celtics fans spent an anxious off-season wondering how Auerbach's decision to move from coach and general manager to GM only would affect the team. His first step, announcing Russell would take over the coaching duties, had already raised plenty of eyebrows in the media. "Bill Russell became the first Negro to direct a major professional sports team today," wrote Gordon White Jr. of the *New York Times* on March 13, 1966. As previously noted, John McLendon of the ABL Cleveland Pipers had actually been the first, though it would be difficult to argue the defunct league had been considered "major" by any stretch of pro sports standards. In any event, expectations for Russell were high. Bill would remain an active player on the team, making him player/coach, a situation that would gain popularity in the years ahead. The dual title would net him an additional $25,000 per year, in addition to his league-high player salary of $100,001. (Russell's $100,001 salary made him the highest paid player in the league, beating out Chamberlain by $1— an honor Celtics management felt he deserved.)

The money itself was enough to promote discussion. Was anyone who played a *game* for a living really worth that much? And of course the color of Russell's skin added fire to the commentary. Integration had become the norm for professional sports insofar as the playing field, but management remained a white man's game. Skeptics questioned whether white players would actually follow the direction of a black coach. Russell addressed the racial issue in his book, *Go Up for Glory*:

> I have never worked to be well-liked or well-loved, but only to be respected. I have fought a problem the only way I know how. Maybe it was right or wrong in the approach, but a man can only ultimately be counted if he thinks he is doing right. Then, at least, he is a man. I have my own ideas for the future. I have my own

The match-up between Wilt Chamberlain (top right) and Bill Russell (top left) remains the best one-on-one rivalry in the history of professional sports. Russell played his entire career with the Celtics, averaging 15.1 points, 22.5 rebounds, and 4.3 assists in 13 seasons. Chamberlain played 14 seasons, splitting his time between Philadelphia, San Francisco, and Los Angeles (Lakers) while accumulating career averages of 30.1 points, 22.9 rebounds, and 4.4 assists. Russell won 11 titles with Boston. Wilt notched one championship in Philadelphia (1967) and one with the Lakers (1972) (Dick Raphael).

dreams. I believe that I can contribute something far more important than mere basketball. I said before three emotions have always been very real to me: fear, prejudice and bitterness. It is the reactions to these emotions that make a man.[5]

For his part, Auerbach said race had never factored into his decision, that he had simply hired the best man for the job.

Although the hoopla continued throughout the summer, Boston wasn't the only team making news in the off-season. Chicago was awarded a new franchise — the Bulls — to replace the Packers-Zephyrs, which had relocated to Baltimore, making the NBA a 10-team league. The Bullets were switched to the East so the divisions were evenly split at five teams each, and the first-round bye previously afforded division winners was scrapped, adding another best-of-five playoff series to the mix.

As for Russell, he answered the bell and his critics by leading Boston to a 60-21 record, six more wins than the team had posted the previous year. The number tied a mark for the club's second most wins ever. On the court, the 33-year-old Russell averaged 13.3 points, 5.8 assists, and 21 rebounds per game. The team had added some depth in the off-season with veterans Wayne Embry and Bailey Howell, but it wasn't enough to get past the surging 76ers, which won a league record 68 games and the Eastern title.

Philadelphia's new head man was none other than Alex Hannum, Wilt's old coach from the San Francisco Warriors. Hannum was still preaching defense, and this time, Wilt was listening. For the first time in his illustrious career, Chamberlain did not lead the league in scoring; his 24.1 ppg average was a modest fifth, more than 10 points behind the NBA champ, San Francisco's second-year man Rick Barry. Chamberlain still led the league in rebounding at 24.2 per game, and came in third in assists, dishing out 7.8 per contest, an amazing accomplishment for a seven-footer.

Wilt was no longer his club's main focus on the offensive end. Second-year man Billy Cunningham chipped in a solid 18.5 points off the bench. The starting backcourt of Greer and Jones averaged over 35, Chet Walker almost 20, and power forward Lucious Jackson another 12. The team-oriented group swept its way through the playoffs, beating Cincinnati 3-1 in the best-of-five first round, and disposing of the rival Celtics in the Eastern Finals, 4-1. The deciding Game 5 put an exclamation mark on the series, with the 76ers scoring 140 points to the Celtics' 116.

And so Boston's winning streak had finally come to an end, its bid for a ninth consecutive championship smothered, ironically, by Chamberlain playing the very type of team ball that had earned the Celtics its many titles.

Media and fans across the country were elated to pronounce the Boston dynasty a thing of the past, but the Celtics remained a confident bunch. "I kept reminding reporters we were dead only until October,"[6] a defiant Havlicek recalled.

Ironically, Philadelphia went on to face Wilt's old team, the San Francisco Warriors, in the Finals. The Sixers took Games 1 and 2 at the Convention Center, but Rick Barry's 55 points in front of a rocking crowd at the Cow Palace led the Warriors to a 130–126 win in Game 3. Wilt scored only 10 points in Game 4, but his tough defense on rebounder Nate Thurmond sent the Sixers home with a promising 3-1 lead.

Wilt felt the monkey hanging on his back in Game 5, as his squad failed to get the job done in front of a disappointed home crowd. The series headed back to the Cow Palace for Game 6, where Rick Barry did everything he could to stretch the series to a decisive Game 7. Alas, his 44 points were not enough. Philly edged out a 125–122 win, giving Wilt his long-awaited championship.

As 76ers fans celebrated their victory, another challenger was preparing to enter the ring. A serious challenger whose game would turn the world of professional basketball upside down. Walter Kennedy's NBA was about to meet Showtime, American Basketball Association style.

THE REAL DEAL

The American Basketball Association was born with a twist of irony: it was supposed to be a football team. Sports lover Dennis Murphy, then mayor of Orange County's Buena Park, had been working diligently on a proposal that would bring professional football to nearby Anaheim via the up-and-coming American Football League (AFL). In just six short years, the AFL had established itself as a legitimate player. National TV had begun televising the games on a regular basis in 1965, via a five-year deal with NBC worth $36.5 million.[1] Los Angeles already had a pro team in the NFL Rams, but Murphy was confident the L.A.–Orange County area could easily support two professional clubs. He had taken his idea far enough to assemble a willing group of investors, but bad timing squelched the proposition when the AFL agreed to merge its teams with the NFL. The move left little hope Anaheim would be granted a team.

Murphy was disappointed but not dissuaded. After mulling over the situation, he decided to offer his fellow sports-loving investors an alternative: how about a basketball team? Of course the Lakers posed a similar problem to that of the Rams—the NBA was not likely to grant Murphy's group a franchise that would infringe on the Lakers' territory. But Murphy saw a way out of that dilemma: start his own *league*.

Murphy had been a big hoops fan for years. Among his pals was none other than Bill Sharman, fresh from a coaching stint with Cal State. Murphy knew Sharman's name would bring instant experience and credibility to the project. Talks between the two men progressed far enough that they came up with a name — the American Basketball Association — but timing interfered yet again when Bill was offered the Warriors' coaching job for the upcoming 1966-67 season. Although Sharman accepted the job in San Francisco, he encouraged Murphy to pursue the project without him and offered an interesting suggestion on his way out the door: why not give George Mikan a call? Promotion was, of course, all in a name.

Murphy took his friend's advice, only to find someone else had already contacted Big George about starting a new pro basketball league. At Murphy's request, Mikan passed on the phone number of the project's headman, Connie

Seredin, a New York advertising wheeler-dealer whose mouth turned out to be a whole lot bigger than his pocketbook. Murphy soon nixed the idea of working with Seredin and instead paired with fellow Californian John McShane, a local DJ and fellow sports fanatic. The two hired a secretary and set up an office in Orange County. Shortly thereafter, attorney Gary Davidson came on board, mainly as a spokesperson for a group interested in putting a franchise in Dallas.

As the project gained momentum, Murphy continued to touch base with Mikan, who had settled in Minneapolis, where he owned a travel agency. Murphy stressed he wanted George involved upfront, hopefully as league commissioner, but Mikan was adamant the ABA would have to have sound financial backing before he would make any commitments.

By the time the details had been worked out, Murphy's group had settled on a number: anyone with $5,000 cash in his pocket could apply for an ABA team. The amount was in stark contrast to the $1.5 million the NBA was charging, thus it was not surprising that many would-be owners spoke of buying multiple teams. Once discussions progressed, Murphy weeded out the amateurs by explaining the $5,000 was only a down payment; a commitment of $50,000 would be required to actually put a team on the floor. Enough investors remained in the pool to make the league a reality, and Mikan agreed to become commissioner at a guaranteed salary of $50,000 a year for three years. It was big money for the start-up league, but owners realized they needed someone of stature to get their project off the ground.

The strategy proved effective, at least from a media standpoint. "Mikan is Hired as Commissioner by Newly Organized Pro Basketball League," read the headline in the sports page of the *New York Times* on February 3, 1967. The lengthy article included a quote from Mikan, promising the new league would not attempt to raid the NBA of its players, though he quickly added: "We hope, of course, that some big stars and others will be in a position to come to us; if they are free, we want to talk to them."[2] The league was not so gracious where territory was concerned, however. Eleven clubs would begin play in the 1967-68 season; franchises in Anaheim, Oakland, and New Jersey would provide direct competition with established NBA teams. Other cities on the slate were Louisville, Denver, Houston, Dallas, New Orleans, Minneapolis, Indianapolis, and Pittsburgh. The latter retained the services of Connie Hawkins.

Like its NBA rival, the ABA would be split into two divisions, East and West. Mikan said the league hoped to start off with a 70-some game schedule and the rules would be a combination of college and NBA play, though specifics had yet to be worked out. Deals had been arranged with respective cities ensuring that all teams would play in major arenas with a seating capacity of 8,000 to 15,000 fans.

The NBA responded to the news with an announcement of its own: expansion franchises in San Diego and Seattle would begin play at the start of the upcoming season. Both the San Diego Rockets and Seattle Supersonics were situated in the West. To compensate, the Pistons would move to the Eastern Conference as the season commenced. The enlarged 12-team league would play its most ambitious regular season schedule ever: 82 games.

The NBA's official reaction to the start-up league was peppered with upbeat sentiments of welcome and good luck. Privately, owners expected to ignore the challenger, much the way they had Saperstein's failed ABL, and simply await its inevitable demise. Even the declaration the ABA would hold its college draft four to six weeks ahead of the NBA's annual affair presented little cause for concern. The top college seniors drafted by ABA clubs were not obligated to play for those teams, and most did not. In fact, ABA owners had expected as much. Most admitted they couldn't have cared less about the college draft because they fully expected to rob the NBA of its best established players. "We hadn't played a game, but we were deluding ourselves into thinking that all these NBA guys would jump leagues," recalled Dick Tinkham, legal counsel for the Indianapolis team. "Of course, it didn't take long for reality to set in."[3]

And a stark reality it was. The only major player to abandon the NBA that first year was the Warriors' Rick Barry, who signed a lucrative three-year deal with the Oakland Oaks worth $500,000. As an added incentive, Barry's father-in-law and former college coach, Bruce Hale, was hired to coach the team. San Francisco Warriors owner Frank Mieuli said the move "could shatter the whole concept of professional sports in the United States,"[4] and promptly filed a lawsuit to stop it.

Meanwhile, ABA owners gathered over the summer to draw up their rules. The most noteworthy concerned the ball itself: rather than the usual brown leather, the ABA decided its ball would be dyed a combination of red, white, and blue. The idea came from George Mikan himself, who thought the colors would tie in nicely with the name of the league. Some owners found the idea ridiculous, but Murphy liked it. ABA exec Mike Storen agreed. "This was a great marketing tool. In Indiana, one of our first and most successful promotions was with Standard Oil and we gave away a half-million of those basketballs. Kids just loved them."[5]

The color scheme carried over to the uniforms worn by league officials: white pants, blue shoes, and a red shirt. Adding a personal touch to the colorful flare, the officials' names would be printed on the back of their shirts.

The ABA adapted most NBA rules with one major distinction: the three-point shot. Saperstein's ABL had actually been the first to implement the idea, though coaches rarely allowed its use in actual game play. But ABA owners agreed the rule would make a great addition to their game, something that would make them stand out from the NBA while fitting nicely into their plans for creating an up-tempo league. Although most broadcasters would refer to the shot as a 25-footer, the actual distance measured 23 feet, nine inches from the top of the key to the center of the rim, 22 feet to the corners.

Lee Meade, hired as the league's statistician, opted to provide fans with a detailed review of the game and its players. In contrast to the rival NBA, steals, turnovers, blocked shots, and team rebounds would all be tracked and listed in a club's respective box score. Additionally, personal rebounds would be separated into offensive and defensive, another distinction lacking on NBA scorecards. While not all of the stats were accurate that first year (teams did not always keep track of the numbers as requested), it gave basketball fans something new to talk about over their morning coffee.

The new league's first season opened with an ambitious 78-game schedule. Rosters contained a few lesser-known NBA players, such as Bob Love and Jim Barnes, and a scattering of others who had previously retired, but the majority of players came from the regional Eastern League and numerous AAU teams from across the country. Rick Barry's paycheck was hardly representative of the league: most players' salaries ranged from $8,000 to $15,000, with meal money averaging $7 per day.[6] Teams began play on October 13, 1967, whether by design or not, a Friday. In the Bay area, 4,828 fans showed up at the Oakland Coliseum to watch the Oaks beat the visiting Anaheim Amigos, 132–129. Meanwhile in basketball-crazy Indianapolis, a standing-room-only crowd of 10,835 cheered their Pacers to a 117–95 win over the Kentucky Colonels.[7]

Ironically, Rick Barry was not in uniform for the Oaks on opening night, nor would he be for the rest of the year, thanks to the reserve clause in his NBA contract with the Warriors. The clause, also known as an option, was commonplace in NBA contracts of the day. The rule stipulated that a player was obligated to his current NBA team for one full year *after* his contract expired. ABA lawyers were certain the clause would not hold up in court, but they were wrong. A San Francisco court ruled swiftly in favor of the Warriors, forcing Barry to either return to his old team or sit out the season. He opted for the latter and spent the year as a radio broadcaster for the Oaks.

Barry's absence made the league's other superstar, the Pipers' Connie Hawkins, a shoe-in for league MVP. Hawkins topped the ABA in scoring at 26.7 ppg while leading his team to a league-best record of 54-24. The Pipers easily beat Minnesota 4-1 in the Eastern Division Finals and went on to defeat New Orleans in the first ABA Championship Series, four games to three.

In NBA land, favored Philadelphia won the East by eight games and Wilt was named the league's regular season MVP. But the big news was in fact the same old same old once the playoffs got under way. The Celtics squeezed out a tight Game 7 victory against the injury-ridden 76ers in the Eastern Division Finals before moving on to meet the Lakers in the title round. The teams split the first four games, with West suffering a sprained ankle late in Game 4. Although he bounced back two nights later with a 35-point performance, the Lakers fell in overtime and went on to lose the series in six.

Philadelphia's playoff collapse led to a blockbuster trade prior to the start of the 1968-69 campaign. Chamberlain was sent to the Lakers for Archie Clark

(6'2" guard, fourth-round pick, Lakers 1966), Jerry Chambers (6'5" forward, first-round pick, Lakers 1966), and Darrall Imhoff (6'10" center, first-round pick, NY Knicks 1960). All would go on to have solid, albeit not stellar careers. In other NBA news, the league announced teams in Phoenix (Suns) and Milwaukee (Bucks) would be onboard for the upcoming season.

For the ABA, the most amazing postseason feat was that all 11 teams managed to survive. Although Indiana, long a primetime player in the world of college hoops, had averaged nearly 6,000 fans per game, most teams were lucky to hit the league average of 2,800. Likewise, many of the original owners, including Murphy himself, lacked the capital to run their teams and had to sell out for a fraction of their investments. Four teams were relocated via the shuffle in personnel. The Anaheim Amigos became the L.A. Stars, the Minnesota Muskies moved to Miami where they would play as the Floridians, the Pipers abandoned Pittsburgh for Minneapolis, and the New Jersey Americans moved to Commack Arena, where they became the New York Nets.

Despite the league's financial troubles, the ABA could have benefited from its champion Pittsburgh Pipers during the off-season. The team had attracted quite a bit of publicity during the Finals, especially given that Connie Hawkins made the city his home on and off the basketball court. But as Singer Pat Boone, an early investor of the Oakland Oaks, would later say: "Professional sports can make you act irrationally, because you become so wrapped up in it."[8] Speculation as to what Pipers owner Gabe Rubin was wrapped up in was the talk of the league when he announced he was moving the Pipers to Minneapolis that summer, a city that had refused to support its Muskies despite the team's impressive 50-28 record. League executive Mike Storen contended it was Mikan who insisted the league keep a team in Minneapolis, which also housed the ABA's home office. Whatever the reason, the move did not prove popular with Pipers coach Vince Cazzetta, ABA Coach of the Year. When Cazzetta demanded more money to compensate for moving his family across the country, Rubin told him to take a hike.

The incident proved a sign of things to come for season two. Cazzetta's replacement, former college coach Jim Harding, was fired midseason during the All Star banquet after the two men got into a fistfight. Rick Barry, finally free of his contractual obligation to the Warriors, hurt his knee after playing only 34 games and was out for the rest of the year. Connie Hawkins, already upset by the Pipers' relocation, became further disenchanted by his new coach, who became openly critical of Connie's game as the season progressed. Several owners spoke publicly about wanting out of the league. Others, desperate to acquire talented players who would bring fans into their buildings, alienated themselves from the NCAA by approaching collegiate seniors, money and contracts in hand, prior to graduation.

Such was the everyday plight of the new kid on the block — teetering on the edge, just as Saperstein's ABL and those before it. Owners realized they needed a miracle to stave off inevitable demise. All were nothing short of amazed when they found one: multimillionaire Jim Gardner from North Carolina.

When Gardner contacted the ABA early into its second season about acquiring an expansion franchise for his state, he had no idea the league was about to go under, that the organization's two richest owners, T. C. Morrow of the Houston Mavericks and the Pacers' Bill Ringsby, had given Mikan notice they were ready to call it quits. Without them, the league had no hope of staying alive. But thanks to some creative thinking, league execs managed to stall Ringsby long enough to sell the existing Houston team to Gardner on the stipulation he could move it to North Carolina the following (third) season. The $350,000 cash inflow was a Godsend, but Gardner himself proved even more of an asset, injecting the league with a much-needed dose of optimism and imagination. Ringsby agreed to stay onboard, and the ABA made it through its second year intact.

Mel Daniels, the league's highest draft pick from season one, was second-year league MVP, posting season averages of 24 points and 16.5 rebounds per game. The ABA Finals pitted Daniels's Indiana Pacers against the Rick Barry–less Oakland Oaks, which had soared to a league-high 60-18 regular season record without its star player. The Pacers lost the series in five games, two of them overtime contests.

Meanwhile in Boston, the reigning NBA champs had one of their most forgettable regular seasons to date, posting a 48-34 record, good for fourth place in the East. John Havlicek was coming into his own as a leader, but Russell was a tired-looking 34 years old. K. C. Jones was gone, and his longtime backcourt mate, Sam, well past his peak at 35. Nonetheless, the team managed to pull together for the playoffs. Player/coach Russell led his squad past a disappointing Philadelphia team in the division semi-finals, four games to one. Boston needed six games in the Eastern Finals, however, to squash a fast-improving New York Knicks club, which featured three pretty decent rookies: Walt Frazier, Bill Bradley, and Phil Jackson.

In Los Angeles, it took the Wilt-fortified 55-27 Lakers six games to get by the ho-hum .500 Warriors before disposing of Atlanta in the Western Finals 4-1. After years of being undermanned in the middle against their tough Eastern nemesis, the Lakers finally had a capable big man to offset Russell's rebounding. Wilt no longer led the league in scoring — he was nineteenth at 20.1 — but he was still the top rebounder at 21.1 per game. Bill Russell, fighting both injuries and age, posted respectable numbers of 9.9 ppg and 19.3 rebounds, assuring fans they would see yet another classic match up between the former MVPs.

The Lakers were heavy favorites, especially with homecourt advantage, but no one was more determined than Jerry West that his team would prevail. Chamberlain did his job by keeping Russell busy on defense, and West did his, scoring a total of 94 points in the first two games. Elgin Baylor chipped in 56. For Boston, the duo of John Havlicek and Sam Jones countered with 83 and 42, respectively. Russell outscored Chamberlain 25-19 in their modest scoring duel, but the Lakers took a 2-0 lead in the series as it moved to Boston.

A relentless double-team on West and a boisterous hometown crowd helped the tired Celtics pull out Game 3 in the Garden. Two nights later, the Lakers had a one-point lead and possession with 15 seconds to play in the game. A victory would mean a commanding 3-1 series lead heading back to Los Angeles; instead, a turnover on the inbounds allowed the reigning champs to squeak out a one-point win. The home team prevailed in Games 5 and 6, setting up a classic Game 7 match-up at the Forum. West, hindered by a hamstring pull suffered in Game 5, turned in another monster performance with 42 points, 12 assists, and 13 rebounds. But the Lakers missed 19 free throws in the foul-plagued game, including a dismal 4-for-13 night by Chamberlain, and Boston escaped with a 108–106 win.

It was the sixth time in eight years the Lakers had faced the Celtics in the Finals, and the sixth time they had lost, including four Game 7s. Although West's phenomenal play throughout the series earned him the Finals MVP — the first and only time the award has been given to a player on the losing team — he found it little consolation. "I didn't cry," he said, describing the anguish of the moment, "but I wanted to."[9]

Unfortunately for the struggling ABA, the biggest news of the year was more what might have been than what ultimately came to be. The 1969 college draft featured one of basketball's largest prizes in the history of the game: famed UCLA center 7-foot Lew Alcindor, who later changed his name to Kareem Abdul-Jabbar. Lew had been chosen number one by the last-place (17-61) New York Nets during the ABA's February draft. Due to the Nets' prime location, the big man actually considering signing with the club in favor of the NBA team that owned his rights, the second-year Milwaukee Bucks.

According to ABA exec Mike Storen, Nets owner Arthur Brown and George Mikan were set to present Alcindor with their best offer, a $1 million contract, up front. But once talks got under way, Mikan and Brown decided to make a lesser offer, anticipating they would have a chance to increase the amount after Alcindor talked with the Bucks. The plan fizzled when Alcindor accepted the Bucks' initial offer, which was higher than that of the Nets. The bungled negotiations cost the ABA its chance to sign a superstar — a move that would have gained the league instant credibility. Shortly thereafter, Mikan either resigned or was fired, depending on the source consulted.

More changes would arrive before the third season got under way. The Pipers, who proved even less of a hit in Minneapolis than the Muskies had been, announced they were returning to Pittsburgh. An exasperated Connie Hawkins was able to remain behind this time, having finally won the right to enter the NBA.

It was Hawkins's $6 million antitrust suit against the NBA that had gotten Commissioner Kennedy's attention. The suit claimed the league's ban was illegal since Connie had never been charged or convicted in any betting scandal. His case was bolstered by a *Life* magazine article that quickly became the talk of the basketball world. Kennedy agreed to settle out of court for $250,000 in cash and annuities of $1.295 million that would commence when Hawkins turned 45.[10] The ban was lifted immediately after the settlement, and the 27-year-old Hawk, who had accumulated averages of 28.2 ppg and 12.6 rebounds during his two years in the ABA,[11] was on his way to Phoenix. The Suns, recent losers of a coin toss with the Milwaukee Bucks to determine which team got the rights to draft Lew Alcindor, acquired Hawkins via a coin flip with the Seattle Supersonics.

Hawkins's defection was a devastating blow to the ABA. The league retaliated by convincing one of the NBA's bigger names, center Zelmo Beaty, to switch affiliations, but the swap was hardly equal value, especially given that, like Barry, Beaty had an option clause in his contract with Atlanta that would keep him from playing on any ABA team until the following season. Nonetheless, league execs felt they were making progress. Although few NBA players proved willing to switch alliances, the ABA was quite successful in raiding its rival of qualified officials. Four of the NBA's best referees — Joe Gushue, Norm Drucker, John Vanak, and Earl Strom — agreed to jump ship for the 1969-70 campaign. The issue was a simple one: money. The day when players and refs received equal pay had long disappeared. The NBA's minimum salary had risen to over $12,000 a season. Most veterans made much more than that, in the $20,000 to $50,000 range, while superstars were pulling in six-figure salaries. When the Milwaukee Bucks signed Lew Alcindor in the summer of 1969, the contract was reportedly worth $1.4 million over five years—for a rookie. At the same time, most NBA officials were making around $15,000 a year after expenses. The ABA offered the willing defectors a three-year deal that included a $10,000 raise in annual salary, $500 per game for the playoffs, and a $25,000 upfront signing bonus.[12] The group gave the NBA a chance to match the ABA's offer, but Commissioner Kennedy promptly declined.

As for former Commissioner Mikan, his departure was thought to be a good thing by most owners, who felt his basketball talents had not translated well to the front office. Jack Dolph, former headman of CBS sports, was the chosen successor. It was hoped Dolph's connection to the network would eventually land the league a national television deal. The NBA received about $1 million per season from its contract with ABC. In addition to broadcasting a Sunday game of the week, which usually included either Boston or L.A., the network televised the All Star Game and the Finals nationwide.[13]

Prior to the start of the third season, the ABA increased its schedule to 84 games. Three new cities were on the map via relocations. The financially strapped Oakland Oaks changed its name to the Capitols and moved to Washington, D.C., but its star player did not join his teammates on the bus headed East. Rick Barry claimed he had an agreement with the club's original owners that freed him of his contractual obligations if the Oaks left the Bay Area — a situation that would leave him free to return to the NBA should he so desire. He *did* so desire, but his plan to attend the Warriors' training camp was put on hold when the case went to court. The ruling was pretty straightforward. Since there was nothing in Barry's contract with the Oaks to back up his claim, he remained the property of the ABA team. Barry eventually joined the club in Washington, where he played out the season.

Oakland wasn't the only team to pack its tent. The unappreciated Minneapolis Pipers returned to Pittsburgh, minus hometown star Connie Hawkins. As previously agreed, new owner and interim Commissioner Jim Gardner moved the Houston franchise to his home state of North Carolina; the former Mavericks would play as the Carolina Cougars.

The ABA had one more surprise to unveil prior to its third season tip-off. On August 23, the Denver Rockets announced they had signed college sensation Spencer Haywood, a second-year player from the University of Detroit, to a $250,000 contract.[14] Haywood, a former Olympian and All American, was considered one of the best players in the country. During his sophomore year at Detroit, the 19-year-old had led the nation in rebounding at 21.5 a game while averaging an impressive 32.1 points.[15]

The NBA was livid, and no wonder. Their rival had managed to secure one of the most promising young talents in the nation without so much as a competitive bid. NBA doctrine still prohibited college players from joining the league until their class had graduated, a rule that remained on the books mainly to appease the NCAA. Although the ABA had instilled a similar rule upon inception, also to pacify the NCAA, owners decided to make an exception for what they deemed "hardship" cases. Under the rule, a player could be considered a hardship if he was the sole breadwinner for a family with limited means of income. Haywood certainly fit the criteria. He and his nine siblings had spent their childhood in poverty-stricken Silver City, Mississippi. His father was deceased and his mother worked as a domestic.

The NCAA insisted the four-year rule was in place to protect the interests of their students, all of whom were attending college to further their educations. Businessman/agent Steve Arnold saw it a different way. "The NBA agreed not to touch the college players until their eligibility was up. That way, the colleges could make money off them."[16]

Regardless of the reasoning, harsh protests from the NBA and NCAA did nothing to keep Haywood from suiting up in Denver on opening night. The 6'9" 225-pound center-forward quickly silenced his critics, most of whom were associated with college sports, who said he was not ready to compete on a professional level. Spencer would go on to post league-high averages of 30 points and 19.5 rebounds per game — the latter a new ABA high — en route to Rookie of the Year and MVP.

Haywood's Rockets finished the season atop the West with a 51-33 record. In the playoffs, his club slipped past Washington 4-3 in the Western Semi-Finals but lost in five games to the L.A. Stars in the Division Finals.[17] Indiana, which finished the season with a league-best 59-25 record, beat the Stars 4-3 in the ABA's Championship series. Bill Sharman, in his second year with the L.A. Stars, won Coach of the Year.

In the NBA, the Celtics played without the cornerstone of its franchise for the first time in 13 years; Bill Russell had announced his retirement as player and coach following the team's 1969 championship. Longtime teammate Sam Jones also decided to call it a career. Former Celtic Tom Heinsohn took over as coach, but with John Havlicek the only player to score more than 20 ppg and no one averaging double-digit rebounds, the team finished sixth in the East at 34-48 — well out of the playoffs and 26 games behind the once lowly New York Knicks. It was the first time in 20 years the club had missed the playoffs, but no one outside of Boston was shedding any tears, least of all New Yorkers.

Knicks fans had supported their team since its inception without a division title, let alone a championship, to show for it, but 1970 would finally prove their year. Like the Celtics in their heyday, the Knicks found success in team ball. In the middle was 6'10", 240-pound Willis Reed. The talented left-hander had been overshadowed by Russell and Chamberlain during his first few years in the league but had become a star in his own right nonetheless. Reed had been a regular at the All Star Game since his Rookie of the Year season in 1965. In 1970, his All Star performance (21 points, 11 rebounds) led the East to 142–135 victory while earning him MVP.[18]

The Knicks also featured one of the NBA's best young guards, Walt Frazier. The third-year man trailed only Lenny Wilkens in assists, dishing out 8.2 per game while scoring 20.9 points. Two-guard Dick Barnett gave the team a reliable 15 ppg jump shooter. At power forward was defensive-minded veteran Dave DeBusschere, who had arrived the previous season in a trade for Walt Bellamy. DeBusschere supplied plenty of muscle inside while collecting 14 points and 10 boards a game. Playing alongside DeBusschere and Reed on the front line was Oxford graduate Bill Bradley. Bill's contribution of 14.5 points and 4 assists was a world away from his 30 ppg superstar years at Princeton, but the scholarly Bradley often preferred to defer to the club's other stars; his attitude provided steady leadership on and off the court. The selfless squad, led by third-year coach Red Holtzman, won 60 games en route to the Eastern title, including a then NBA record 18-game winning streak.

New York's dream season almost screeched to a halt in the first round of the playoffs when it encountered a surprisingly determined Baltimore club led by "Earl the Pearl" Monroe, a tremendous 6'3" playmaking guard who could best be described as an early Magic Johnson.[19] But the Knicks managed to prevail 127–114 in Game 7 at home and went on to face the 56-win Milwaukee Bucks in the Division Finals. Rookie Lew Alcindor had delivered even more than expected for Milwaukee, collecting 28.8 points and 14.5 rebounds per game while shooting better than 50 percent. The Bucks had disposed of Philadelphia in five games in their first-round series, but the young team's lack of experience proved costly against the veteran Knicks. Milwaukee fell in five games, and New York went on to face the Lakers in the Finals.

Jerry and company hadn't had the best of seasons, finishing second in their division at 46-36. The 33-year-old Chamberlain injured his knee early into the 1969-70 campaign and was out for most of the regular season. Elgin Baylor's worsening knees kept him out for 28 games as well. But West kept the team competitive, averaging a league-high 31.2 ppg, and Baylor and Chamberlain returned for the playoffs. The revitalized team was sluggish against the sub .500 Phoenix Suns in round one but moved on to sweep Atlanta in the Division Finals, setting up the first Los Angeles–New York Finals in NBA history.

It was a show that lived up to the hype. With the series tied 1-1 and the Knicks up by a basket, Jerry West launched a 60-foot bomb at the buzzer to send the contest into overtime. (The NBA had not yet adopted the three-point shot.) The Lakers wound up losing the game, but rebounded with an overtime victory in Game 4. The Knicks took Game 5 in New York, despite losing Willis Reed to a torn thigh muscle in the first half. The injury kept Reed out of Game 6 in L.A., and Wilt capitalized, scoring 45 points and hauling down 27 rebounds. Game 7 was one of heroics, most of it coming from the bench. A hobbling Reed took the floor to thunderous applause as the game began. His injury prevented him from playing more than a few minutes, but his effort rallied his teammates to a 113–99 win at the Garden. The disheartened Lakers returned home empty-handed once again.

All things considered, it had been a great year for pro basketball fans, and the ABA hadn't done too badly, either. Commissioner Dolph's bid for a national TV deal with a game of the week never materialized, but he had managed to get the ABA's All Star Game broadcast on CBS in January, showcasing such talents as Spencer Haywood, Rick Barry, Mel Daniels, Doug Moe, Steve Jones, and Larry Brown. Haywood had turned in a particularly stellar performance with 7 blocked shots, 19 rebounds, and 23 points, earning him MVP. The West won the game, 128–98.

NBA execs viewing the game had most surely recognized their former officials, Earl Strom and John Vanak. They also may have noticed that the Fairgrounds Coliseum in Indianapolis was crammed to the rafters; nearly 12,000 fans had attended — 2,821 *over* capacity.[20] Outside the arena before the game, scalpers had reportedly been selling $4 face value tickets for $10 a pop.

Attendance at the All Star Game was not a fluke. The Pacers pulled in a record 8,500 fans per game during the regular season. Haywood and the Denver Rockets proved a steady draw as well, filling their 7,000-seat facility 24 times. Even the Nets more than tripled their lowly 1,100 mark from the year before. When the final numbers were in, average attendance at ABA games came out to 3,948, up nearly 25 percent from the previous year.[21]

By comparison, NBA attendance for the season had averaged 7,563, an increase of about 16 percent from the 1968-69 season. The biggest jump came in Chicago, where the four-year-old Bulls pulled in 10,050 fans per game, up from 3,790 the year before. The second-year Milwaukee Bucks got a similar boost, thanks mainly to NBA Rookie of the Year Lew Alcindor. The Lakers and the Knicks, already among the league's top draws, continued to show moderate increases, but attendance in Detroit, Philadelphia, and Baltimore declined. Oscar Robertson's Cincinnati Royals, now minus Jerry Lucas (traded to the Warriors) continued to lag behind league expectations, having averaged fewer than 5,000 fans per game for the past four seasons.

Given the ABA's increase in attendance, especially in Indiana and Denver, NBA owners had cause for concern. The longer the new league survived, the better chance it had of attracting the game's high-end players, collegiate and professional. Remembering the lessons learned in the old NBL–BAA days, owners realized a merger was in their best interests. While there was more than enough basketball talent to support two leagues, the ABA being a separate entity had the potential to bankrupt both organizations by driving player salaries through the roof. Competition for officials had already cost them on a smaller scale. League expansion was another problem. The ABA owned teams in several smaller-end markets that had been ignored by the NBA: Indiana, Dallas, and Denver were all drawing well.

Publicly, ABA execs, including Commissioner Dolph, downplayed the idea of a merger, insisting the league did not need the NBA to survive. Privately, however, the idea had been front and center since the organization's inception. The AFL–NFL merger that had squelched Dennis Murphy's dream of putting a football franchise in Anaheim had led him to believe the same thing was possible with the NBA if a competitive league could be firmly established. Three years later Murphy was gone, but the ABA remained alive and kicking. Most owners fully expected their teams to be accepted into the NBA in due time, especially those whose locations did not compete with existing NBA clubs. New Oaks owner Earl Foreman ran into considerable resistance from the rest of the league when he moved his team to Washington, D.C., at the start of the third season. "The NBA's Baltimore Bullets were in the same territory and we were in the middle of the never-ending merger talks," the Pacers' Dick Tinkham explained. "Abe Pollin owned the Bullets and he said he'd never go for a merger if the ABA put a team in Washington."[22] Foreman was denied an expansion team for that very reason, but he was able to purchase the floundering Oakland franchise and move it without league approval.

Talks of a possible merger continued through the third off-season and likely would have come about if not for an unexpected development. The NBA Players Association, headed by Oscar Robertson, decided that a merger would not benefit players of either league. "We're going to fight a merger in every way we know how," Robertson told the *New York Times* in June 1970. "We think it's a violation of the antitrust laws and it clearly eliminates competition."[23] The Players Association filed a lawsuit shortly thereafter. Known as the Oscar Robertson suit, the court case challenged the potential merger, the legality of the NBA's reserve clause *and* the college draft, all of which, the players contended, violated their right to secure the best possible financial deals for themselves and their families.

Players knew a good thing when they saw one. Although the idea of playing for the love of the game might not have disappeared, the enjoyment had certainly become enhanced via the potential for enormous monetary gain. In 1966-67, the average NBA salary was $13,000. When the ABA debuted the following season, that number jumped to $20,000, an increase of over 54 percent. As the NBA prepared to kick off the 1970-71 season, the median had reached $40,000.[24] There was every reason to expect the trend to continue. As long as both leagues remained independent of each other, bidding wars were inevitable. It seems inconceivable that Lew Alcindor, a great college player but nonetheless untested in the pros, would have been offered a contract in excess of $1 million — an unheard of amount in 1969 — if the threat of losing him to the rival ABA had not existed.

Bottom line, both leagues wanted the top players in their fold, and were willing to spend whatever it took to get them, a scenario that spelled disaster up the road. For the NBA, that was disaster with a capital D, as in Dolgoff Plan, the ABA's answer to escalating payrolls.

SURVIVAL OF THE FITTEST

In business, money is generally the driving force behind competition. The world of pro sports is no exception. Today, most professional athletes sign contracts with the team that offers the largest salaries and benefits. The situation is particularly true in Major League Baseball, where no salary cap exists; owners are free to spend as much as they wish to assemble the dream team of their choice. The NFL and NBA operate with salary caps, though the rule's intended objective to achieve league parity remains in question.

No NBA salary cap existed when the Oscar Robertson suit was filed in the summer of 1970; teams spent whatever their owners allowed in an effort to secure the game's best players. The one caveat was the reserve or option clause, which bound a player to his current team for a full season *after* his contract had expired. The rule was meant to provide owners the best chance of keeping their own players by limiting outside competition for their services, and it proved quite effective. Few players were willing to forfeit an entire season, even if they were paid (as had been the case for Rick Barry), as their playing value tended to decrease during such a layoff.

The emergence of the ABA threatened the entire status quo. During its first three years, the new league had dared to challenge both the reserve clause and the NCAA's rule governing college players and their rights to play pro ball prior to their pending graduation date. The reserve clause had held up in court, but the NCAA decree died with Spencer Haywood's case. Legally, the court ruled a college had no right to keep a player from signing a professional contract whenever he wished. That rule, in effect since the dawn of the NBA, had never been a legal rule per se, rather a gentleman's agreement between the NCAA and the NBA. Under the handshake deal, universities groomed players for several years, in effect, serving as modern-day farm teams. By the time a senior graduated, it was expected he would possess the skills to play professional ball from the get-go. Meanwhile, he had done his part to draw paying fans into college arenas.

Initially, ABA owners had feared the NCAA's wrath should they dare to break with tradition. But as time wore on, they came to realize they had little to lose. The league had had very limited success signing top college players via conventional methods. If the ABA was to survive, execs knew they would have to break new ground, which included taking some risks. Unfortunately, signing players in Spencer Haywood's category did not come cheap. That is where the ABA's method of accounting, known as the Dolgoff Plan, came into play.

In essence, the Dolgoff Plan, named after its inventor, ABA exec Ralph Dolgoff, was an annuity. A team would offer a player a certain amount and call it a five-year contract, but much of the actual salary was deferred.[1] So while it sounded as if ABA players were being bombarded with riches—contracts worth $1.5 million — the total they actually collected over those four to five years was closer to $250,000, about the same as the NBA's average salary of $40,000 to $50,000 per year. The remainder of the money would be doled out in yearly installments via payments set to begin 20 years up the road. Some players found the method acceptable, viewing it as a solid pension plan. Others were confused and felt cheated. What mattered to the ABA, of course, was the bottom line, the total amount of the contract, for it was that number that wound up in the media.

The ABA was further able to increase its buying power by pooling resources. In the NBA, once a player was drafted by a certain team, he was obligated to sign with that team if he expected to play in the league. In the ABA, the system was much more flexible. Owners got together and decided which players they would like to see in their league and how much each was worth. Once a player on the list was drafted, he was approached by league officials with a contract. The team a player actually wound up playing for often could be of his choosing, which worked as an added incentive. The ABA was still in business for season four because it had opted for teamwork over competition.

NBA owners, meanwhile, had stepped up their bidding wars against teams from their own league as well as those in the ABA. Any hope of relief from rising salaries sat in purgatory thanks to the Oscar Robertson suit. No merger, no mercy. In the NBA, it was every owner for himself as the 1970-71 season got under way.

As a whole, the NBA embraced the challenge of its rival with vigor, adding three more expansion teams: the Buffalo Braves, Cleveland Cavaliers, and Portland Trail Blazers. All told, the league had added seven clubs since the ABA's arrival in 1967-68, most in cities that had previously been written off as too small to support professional teams. The new additions brought the total number of NBA franchises to 17, enough to warrant division realignments. For the first time in its history, the NBA would play in four divisions. The Eastern and Western Divisions became conferences split into two divisions each. The Knicks, Celtics, 76ers, and new Buffalo Braves made up the Atlantic. The expansion Cavaliers would play in the Central Division, along with the Bullets, Royals, and former Western Division Atlanta Hawks. In the Midwest Division, it was Milwaukee, Chicago, Detroit, and Phoenix. The Pacific was the only division to

feature five teams: Seattle, San Diego, San Francisco, Los Angeles, and Portland. The league opted to stay with its 82-game season schedule.

The ABA remained an 11-team, 84-game league and had its usual share of
relocations. Memphis hosted the Pros, formerly the New Orleans Buccaneers. The
Bill Sharman–coached Stars, unable to compete head to head with the Lakers, set
up shop in Salt Lake City. In the East, Rick Barry's Oaks-turned-Capitols had
agreed to vacate the Baltimore Bullets territory via an agreement that gave owner
Earl Foreman the right to set up a franchise in any city currently without a pro
basketball team. The deal was brokered on the assumption an NBA–ABA merger
was near. When it failed to happen, Foreman had no choice to but to follow
through on relocation, as he had already laid the groundwork for a move. He opted
for Virginia, home to three new arenas, and renamed his team the Squires.

It was a busy summer for the Denver Rockets as well. League MVP Spencer
Haywood, one of the Dolgoff Plan's most dissatisfied customers, was demanding a new contract. The Rockets had already renegotiated his deal several times
during the previous season, but on each occasion a good block of the cash
remained deferred. Haywood eventually hired an agent to argue his case. Meanwhile, he listened to offers from Seattle Supersonics owner Sam Schulman, who
had chosen Haywood in the NBA draft the previous spring.

The situation was murky to say the least. Both Schulman and Haywood
knew the NBA continued to enforce the four-year rule prohibiting college players from entering the league until their class had graduated. For Haywood, that
meant two more seasons. But Schulman, determined to make his young team
a winner, had decided to go the ABA route of challenging the rule if Haywood
would ink his name to a contract. Spencer eventually signed a deal with the
Sonics worth $1.5 million over six years, none of it deferred. When the NBA
threatened to void the contract and implement sanctions against Schulman's
team, Haywood responded by filing an antitrust suit against the NBA, challenging the four-year rule. The pending litigation kept him off the basketball
court when play commenced in November 1970.

Haywood wasn't the ABA's only disgruntled employee. Rick Barry wanted
nothing to do with his second relocation in as many years, especially given that
location was Virginia. He offered to buy back his contract, but Foreman refused.
Barry retaliated by agreeing to an interview in *Sports Illustrated* in which he
was quoted as saying, "I don't want my kids growing up and saying, 'Hi, y'all,
Dad.'"[2] The resulting publicity enraged locals, forcing Foreman to trade his
disgruntled star to the New York Nets.

Denver made up for the loss of Haywood by signing another hardship case,
6'5" guard Ralph Simpson out of Michigan State. Other promising rookies making their professional debut included the Squires' Charlie Scott, a high-scoring guard out of North Carolina, and Dan Issel, a 6'9" center from Kentucky
who would play for the Colonels. Former NBA star Zelmo Beaty finally suited
up for the Stars, having served his required year in limbo for jumping leagues.

The NBA's prize rookie cast included the Celtics' Dave Cowens, Pete Maravich of the Atlanta Hawks, Nate Archibald from Cincinnati, Detroit Pistons big man Bob Lanier, Rudy Tomjanovich and Calvin Murphy from the San Diego Rockets.

By far the biggest preseason news in the NBA centered on a blockbuster trade that sent the Big O from Cincinnati to Lew Alcindor's Milwaukee Bucks. The Royals had already traded away its other homegrown star, Jerry Lucas, to the Warriors at the start of the previous season, shortly after 41-year-old Bob Cousy was hired as coach. Robertson went to the Bucks in exchange for forward Charlie Paulk, the Bucks' first round pick in 1968, and 6'1" Flynn Robinson, a guard who had played for the Royals from 1966–68. Neither player would be on Cincinnati's roster the following year. Critics of the trade, which included just about everyone, speculated Cousy was jealous of Robertson, who had eclipsed so many of Bob's NBA records. Whatever the reason, Royals fans were not pleased with the deal that sent their beloved superstar packing. Milwaukee, of course, was elated. Oscar joined Alcindor's supporting cast of Bob Dandridge, Jon McGlocklin, and Lucius Allen. Together, the group averaged 92.4 points, 21.3 assists, and 34.9 rebounds during the regular season while occupying numerous slots on the Sunday game of the week.[3]

The ABA still didn't have a game of the week, but its deal had improved slightly from the previous year. In addition to the All Star Game, CBS agreed to broadcast up to six regular season games. The deal was of little help financially — each club received a paltry $10,000 — but the exposure was certainly an asset to a league intent on proving its stars were every bit as good as those playing in the NBA. A good share of fans appeared ready to believe. The All Star Game held in Greensboro, N.C., on January 23, 1971, drew 14,407, almost 2,500 more than the previous year's record-setting crowd in Indiana.[4] MVP Mel Daniels led to the East to a 126–122 win with 13 rebounds and 29 points.

The league's former MVP, Spencer Haywood, got a late Christmas present when a judge issued a temporary injunction against the NBA. Haywood was cleared to play in the final 33 games of the season, but his average of 20.6 points and 12 rebounds was not enough to propel his new club into the playoffs. The Sonics, headed by player-coach Lenny Wilkens,[5] finished the year 38-44, 10 games behind the division-winning Lakers. Although Seattle failed to make the playoffs, its season ended on an up note when Haywood's antitrust suit was settled out of court. Under the agreement, the Supersonics retained the rights to Haywood, but the team was fined $200,000 by the league for the privilege.[6]

Not surprisingly, the playoff story in the NBA was the Oscar Robertson–reinforced Milwaukee Bucks. The third-year club, which had won a league-high 66 games against only 16 losses in the regular season, continued its winning ways in the semi-final round of the playoffs, disposing of the Warriors four games to one before meeting the Lakers in the Conference Finals. Wilt's aging team was no match for the young Milwaukee squad, especially with West and

Baylor out with injuries. The Bucks breezed past the sluggish Lakers in five and went on to face the Baltimore Bullets, which had squeezed past the defending champion New York Knicks in a tight seven game Conference Finals. (Cousy's Robertson–less Royals finished the year 33-49, the fourth worst record in the league.)

The Bullets had quite a dominant big man of their own in former University of Louisville star Wes Unseld, the first player since Chamberlain to win Rookie of the Year *and* MVP in the same season (1969). The 6'7" Unseld outweighed Alcindor by 13 pounds, but he was playing on a lame ankle. Likewise, Oscar's counterpart, Earl the Pearl, was hampered by bad knees, as was forward Gus Johnson. A healthy Bullets squad might have made for more of a contest, but as it was, the club became the first since the 1959 Minneapolis Lakers to get swept in the finals. Alcindor was named regular season and Finals MVP. Boston's new center, 6'9" Dave Cowens won co–Rookie of the Year, sharing the award with Geoff Petrie of the expansion Portland Trail Blazers.

In the ABA, the Pacers topped the league again with 58 regular season wins. Sharman's Utah Stars finished a breath behind with 57. These teams swept their first-round opponents before meeting in the Western Finals. Utah took that series in seven. In the East, the newly relocated Virginia Squires topped the charts at 55-29. Ironically, they faced Rick Barry's new team, the Nets, in the Eastern Division semi-finals. The Squires disposed of New York in six but lost to Kentucky in the Division Finals. Utah won the championship in seven games. Kentucky's Dan Issel won the scoring title and shared Rookie of the Year honors with the Squires' Charlie Scott.

Although Robertson's lawsuit pressed forward as the season came to an end, execs from both leagues expected the courts would eventually rule in favor of a merger, making for one big happy basketball family. Toward that end, the first interleague All Star Game was arranged for May 28, 1971, at the Houston Astrodome.

The business angle aside, players had their own ideas about their respective leagues. Sports writer Bob Ryan, who covered the NBA for the *Boston Globe*, put it bluntly: "The common perception in the NBA was that the ABA was a second-rate, offensive-minded collection of people who didn't have the good sense to come into the NBA if they were good enough."[7] But ABA veteran guard Gene Littles saw nothing second-rate about his league. "The difference was that they had television and we didn't. We never felt inferior, because guys from the NBA would jump to the ABA and they didn't tear up the league."[8] *Sports Illustrated* landed somewhere in the middle. In their annual ranking of the top 20 pro basketball teams, 6 were ABA squads. Given the NBA had 17 teams to the ABA's 11, it was a pretty even draw.

The Astrodome contest was a showcase of similarities and differences. The first half was officiated using the more familiar NBA rules, but ABA guidelines (three-point shot, 30-second clock) took over in the second half, which was played with the league's trademark red, white, and blue ball. Among the stars representing the NBA that day were John Havlicek, Walt Frazier, Earl Monroe, and Oscar Robertson. Coaching the ABA squad was Denver's Larry Brown, whose players included Mel Daniels, Steve Jones, Charlie Scott, Zelmo Beaty, and Rick Barry. A crowd of 16,364 saw the Bill Russell–coached NBA team pull out a tight, come-from-behind 125–120 win. Walt Frazier won MVP.

No progress was made in respect to the hoped-for merger over the summer, but the success of the All Star Game paved the way for a series of preseason, interleague exhibition games. Prior to the start of the 1971-72 season, 22 games were played between NBA and ABA teams. All were held in either neutral or ABA territory, with the exception of a September 28 contest between the Sonics and the Pacers in Seattle. Out of a combined total of 28 clubs, only the Lakers and Cleveland Cavaliers refused to join the mix. ABA teams managed to win just 6 times, but most games remained competitive throughout; 13 of the ABA's losses were by 10 or fewer points.

More important than wins or losses was the notable distinction between the two leagues insofar as playing style was concerned. For all its changes over the years, the NBA remained a power league led by frontline bruisers and high-scoring big men. Lew Alcindor picked up where Chamberlain had left off as the most dominant player in the game. Big men continued to occupy the top spots in the draft (Wes Unseld, Alcindor, Bob Lanier), and for good reason: League MVP had not been awarded to a player outside the center position since Oscar Robertson in 1964. A supporting cast of scorers and assist men was imperative, but coaches knew they could not win an NBA title without muscle and size in the middle. As great as Jerry West and Elgin Baylor had been together in their heyday, they had not led the Lakers to a championship. When Russell retired from the Celtics, the team faded into the sunset. It was a league that prided itself on defense and rebounding.

The ABA was more about scoring and technique, and no player in league history better epitomized that style than the Virginia Squires' 1971 first-round pick, 6'7" forward Julius Erving from the University of Massachusetts.

Erving played high school ball in his hometown of Roosevelt, New York, where he established himself as a hard-working player with a great attitude and a solid, all-around game. "He lived and breathed basketball," said Art Flechner, Roosevelt's former district athletic director. "Everybody in the entire community talks about him constantly."[9] Although Julius won the Most Outstanding Player award once and made All Conference his final two years at Roosevelt High, it was not until he moved on to the University of Massachusetts that his name became a household word in the neighborhood. Fans were so enthralled with his athletic style of play — spontaneous, graceful midair twists and spins — that they hung around the Curry Hicks Cage hours before games were scheduled to begin. Capacity crowds watched Erving collect an average of 26.3 points and 20.2 rebounds during his two varsity seasons with the

Minutemen.[10] He started all 52 games, and only once failed to register a double-double. He remains one of only six players in NCAA history to average more than 20 points and 20 rebounds.

Despite his huge local following, Erving was not a hot topic among pro scouts, mainly because he played in the Yankee Conference, which was known for its weak schedule. Those who did manage to see the young man play, however, had nothing but good things to say. Luckily for Squires owner Earl Foreman, that word of mouth spread slowly enough that he was able to purchase the draft rights to Julius for $10,000.

After a lengthy night of contract negotiations, Erving opted to forgo his senior year at Massachusetts to sign with the Virginia Squires. "I felt I had accomplished all I could in college ball and I was ready to turn pro," he told author Terry Pluto in *Loose Balls* (p. 224). The Squires GM, Johnny Kerr, said Julius told him he was concerned about his mother's health and felt it was his duty to help financially. The contract to help him do so looked great on paper: a four-year deal worth $500,000. In Dolgoff numbers, that meant Erving would receive a $75,000 yearly salary with the remainder ($50,000) deferred. Although the yearly amount still fell within the NBA's average salary range, it would soon become obvious to anyone who knew anything about basketball that there was nothing average about "the Doctor," a nickname he picked up while in high school. "A friend of mine kept telling me he was going to be a professor," Erving told the *New York Times*, "so I told him I was going to be a doctor, and we started calling each other that, professor and doctor."[11]

The Doctor so impressed his coach, Al Bianchi, during the Squires training camp that Bianchi sent him home early for fear he might be injured before the season got under way. Years later, Magic Johnson would put the Doctor's early influence on the game into perspective. "There were other big players, talented players, and great players before him. But it was Dr. J who put the 'Wow!' into the game."[12]

Erving began his professional career in 1971-72, playing in tandem with Virginia's high-scoring guard Charlie Scott, the previous season's co–Rookie of the Year. Scott won the league's regular season scoring title with an average of 33.4 ppg. Erving came in sixth with 27.3, and finished third in rebounding at 15.7, only 2.1 behind the league leader, fellow rookie Artis Gilmore of the Kentucky Colonels.[13] Erving's Squires finished second in the East with a 45-39 record and went on to sweep the Floridians 4-0 in the semi-finals. The club took a 3-2 lead against Rick Barry's Nets in the Eastern Finals but lost the next two games. New York met the Championship Pacers in the Finals and lost the series in six.

In addition to Erving, the ABA's fifth season featured several other impressive first-year players: the above-mentioned Artis Gilmore, George McGinnis of the Pacers, and Memphis's Johnny Newman. Of the four prize rookies, only Gilmore, who beat out Erving for Rookie of the Year, was *not* a hardship case.

In the NBA, the Rookie of the Year was Sidney Wicks, a 6'8" power forward with the Portland Trail Blazers. Wicks, the number two overall pick in the draft, averaged a respectable 24.5 points and 11.5 rebounds per game. The league's other high-drafted big man, Elmore Smith of the Buffalo Braves, failed to finish among the league's top 20 scorers. Lew Alcindor, who had converted to Islam during the off-season and changed his name to Kareem Abdul-Jabbar,[14] remained at number one with 34.8 ppg — up 3 points from the previous season. Chamberlain continued to lead the league in rebounding, grabbing 19.2. boards for the Lakers. Abdul-Jabbar was third with 16.6.

While the ABA focused on youth and athleticism, the Lakers went the NBA's conventional route — size and experience — to capture its first title in Los Angeles. The team lost one of its cornerstones when Elgin Baylor retired nine games into the season, but his replacement,

From his high-flying Afro to his magnificent, creative dunks, Julius Erving, aka "Dr. J," epitomized the free spirit of the American Basketball Association. His five-year tenure in the league is generally credited with forcing the ABA–NBA merger in 1976. Erving became the face of the 76ers in the '80s, leading Philadelphia to the Finals three times in four years, culminating with a 4–0 sweep of the Lakers in 1983 (Dick Raphael).

Gail Goodrich, quickly filled in the gap. The backcourt duo of West and Goodrich averaged over 50 points between them, with West adding a league-best 9.7 assists. Chamberlain, still an amazing force at age 35, topped the NBA in rebounding (19.2) *and* shooting percentage (.649). Forwards Jim McMillian and Happy Hairston rounded out the starting five, a group that jelled quickly under the team-oriented approach of new head coach, Bill Sharman. After beginning the season 6-3, the Lakers won 33 games in a row before losing to the Milwaukee Bucks on January 9, 1972. Ironically, it was the Bucks who owned the prior record of 20 straight wins, set during the 1970-71 campaign. (The Lakers' run has yet to be shattered in any American professional sport.)

Sharman's Lakers finished the regular season at 69-13, then the best single-season record in NBA history. The club's dominance carried over to the playoffs, where they beat the Chicago Bulls in four straight and the defending champion Bucks in six. In the East, the Knicks had struggled though most of the season without center Willis Reed, who had developed tendonitis in his left knee. The club compensated for the scoring loss by acquiring Earl the Pearl Monroe from the Bullets. Monroe did not fit well with his new team initially, but the club figured things out by the playoffs, rolling past Baltimore and Boston en route to another title match with the Lakers. But the loss of Reed hit hard against Chamberlain. The undersized Knicks fell in five games, and 33-year-old Jerry West, who had tied his lowest playoff average ever at 22.9 ppg, finally had his championship. Bill Sharman was named Coach of the Year. The Lakers' title made Sharman the only coach in professional sports to win a championship in three separate leagues: the 1962 ABL Cleveland Pipers, the 1971 ABA Utah Stars, and the 1972 NBA Lakers.

As for the world of pro basketball overall, the season ended much the same as it had the year before: in a state of flux. Owners in both leagues still wanted a merger, but until the Oscar Robertson suit was settled, the ground rules remained every team for itself. Suffice it to say, the ABA had already lasted far longer than the NBA had imagined possible. Along the way, the veteran league had lost its chance to tap into some of the country's more lucrative basketball markets such as Louisville, Denver, and Indianapolis. The case could be argued that the ABA was directly responsible for NBA teams in cities such as Seattle, Phoenix, and Milwaukee — small-market areas the league had previously ignored despite strong fan interest.

On a similar front, although the NBA continued to insist the NCAA's four-year rule was in college players' best interests, it could ill afford to stand by helplessly while the ABA bolstered its league with the exciting talents of players like Haywood, McGinnis, and Erving. Prior to Spencer Haywood's settlement with the NBA, the district court judge who granted the injunction allowing Haywood to play for the Sonics while his case was pending had rejected the legality of the four-year rule, stating it violated antitrust laws. Since it was obvious the NBA could not stop players from signing with ABA teams, it had little choice but to implement a hardship policy of its own. Owners had reluctantly agreed to do so during a June 25 meeting the previous summer. As a result, the 1972 draft marked the first time in league history underclassmen would be allowed to play in the NBA.

The NCAA was not happy with the development but certainly must have seen it coming. For years, agents had swarmed the NIT and NCAA tournaments with pro contracts in hand, but it was only after the ABA dared to test the waters that players began signing in earnest. The only question was, what had taken so long? Colleges made millions off their respective players without having to adequately compensate them and defended the practice by insisting it was for the players' own good. In an article titled "Gentleman's Agreement," that ran in the *New York Times* on January 10, 1971, writer Leonard Koppett provided a clear, concise picture of the way the collegiate system operated.

> The desire of college coaches and other officials to protect their charges from "seductive" pro offers would be more impressive if their own activities were less competitive. Colleges seek out, pursue, offer inducement to and sign to "letters of intent" high school athletes, and they do it with more intensive scouting systems than the pros use to evaluate collegians. A significant percentage of big time college athletes do not make normal progress toward a degree, if they get one at all. By openly providing athletic scholarships and other benefits, and by collecting large sums in gate receipts, colleges create an employer-employee relationship in practice no matter how much they deny it in theory.[15]

A number of respected coaches agreed. "The NCAA doesn't want to admit it's running a pro operation," said Doug Moe, who coached three years at Webber State before moving to the NBA. Hall of Fame coach Al McGuire from Marquette presented a more personal view when discussing one of his own players, Jim Chones, who opted to sign with the ABA. "I have looked in his refrigerator and in mine, and mine has meats, pastries, and other goodies. His was empty, so why blame any kid who is tempted by $250,000 to sign. They can always finish college in summer school and be that much richer, too."[16]

Whether a player's mental health and well-being would be enriched by those monetary benefits remained to be seen, but one thing was certain: for richer or poorer, the youth movement in professional basketball had begun.

A MATTER OF STYLE

As the ABA approached season six, its impact on the NBA was undeniable. Whether the idea of retaining two separate leagues was good or bad for pro basketball in general, however, depended on prospective. Players saw the ensuing competition for their services as a boon where it mattered most, in their bank accounts. Owners viewed the sharply rising salaries as eminent danger that threatened the entire future of the sport. But the most important element of the equation — the paying customers— was not concerned with behind-the-scenes economics. Fans cared only about the quality of the game and its players. A rise in attendance for the completed 1971-72 season suggested both leagues were delivering on that end. The average NBA game had attracted 8,061 fans, up 413 from the previous year, an increase of 5.4 percent. In the ABA, the front number looked nearly identical: attendance was up 407 fans per game. When translated into a percentage increase, however, the ABA held a clear advantage, posting a rise of 8.3 percent over the 1970-71 average of 4,924.[1]

The rival league's increasing popularity fueled a second ABA-NBA All Star Game, held at the Nassau Coliseum in Uniondale, NY on May 25, 1972. Former Lakers star Elgin Baylor resurfaced to coach the NBA squad. The ABA was led by the Virginia Squires' Al Bianchi. Baylor's team squeaked out a 106–104 victory in front of 14,086 fans. Detroit's Bob Lanier was MVP.[2] The game proved to be the last time fans saw Rick Barry in an ABA uniform; he would return to Oakland to play for the Warriors at the start of the 1972-73 season.

With owners on both sides still hopeful for a merger, pro basketball had a relatively quiet off-season. The biggest news in the NBA was the relocation of Oscar Robertson's former team, the Cincinnati Royals, to Kansas City for the 1972-73 season. Given how the city already had the Major League Baseball Kansas City Royals, the club changed its name to the Kings. Once again, the ABA's influence came into play as the franchise announced it would split its home games between Kansas City, MO, and Omaha, NE, a practice several ABA teams had instilled early on to increase fan interest and attendance in smaller market areas.

In the ABA, the off-season action was more controversial. Julius Erving wanted to play in the NBA, where he would get more money while showcasing his unique talents to a broader audience that included national TV. Like Spencer Haywood, he was drafted by an NBA team — the Milwaukee Bucks — while still under contract with an ABA club. Unlike Haywood, however, Erving did not have to apply for hardship status because he was drafted the same year (1972) he would have graduated. But rules were being tested by players in both leagues, and the Doctor was no exception. Erving filed for arbitration, claiming his Squires contract was invalid because one of the agents who had negotiated it, Steve Arnold, was also employed by the ABA. Not only did Erving defy the Virginia Squires, he snubbed the Bucks, who clearly owned his NBA draft rights, in favor of signing a contract with the Atlanta Hawks. Perhaps Erving did not find the idea of joining a ready-made All Star cast headed by Abdul-Jabbar and the Big O enough of a challenge. Or maybe it was simply a matter of the Hawks putting more money on the table. In any event, reasons proved irrelevant to the ABA; the league promptly filed a lawsuit challenging his right to play for any NBA team while still under contract to the Squires.

As a whole, the pro game's escapades took a distant second to the *real* hoops news of the summer: the 1972 Olympic Games in Munich. As previously noted, Naismith's game had first appeared as an official sport at the 1936 Summer Games in Berlin, when the gold medal game pitted the United States against Canada. The contest was played on a dirt court in the pounding rain, which probably contributed to the low-scoring affair, won by the United States, 19–8.

No games were held in 1940 or 1944 because of World War II, but the United States again prevailed in 1948, when it routed France 65–21 at the Summer Games in London. Four years later, the Soviet Union made its first appearance at the games in 40 years. Its basketball team lost the gold medal game to the United States 36–35. A rematch in Helsinki four years later gave the United States a commanding 89–55 win. The 1960 Summer Games held in Rome became the first to be televised worldwide. Few were surprised when the United States dominated the basketball court in a round robin tournament, beating the Soviet Union 81–57, Italy 112–81, and Brazil 90–63 en route to another gold. Victories against the Russians in 1964 (73–59) and Yugoslavia in 1968 (65–50) made for seven consecutive U.S. gold medals over a span of 32 years.

There was little reason to believe things would change going into the 1972 Games in Munich. The United States was on a roll, led by swimmer Mark Spitz, who won a world-record seven individual gold medals. But things took an ugly turn when terrorists attacked the Olympic Village on September 5, killing two Israeli athletes and kidnapping nine others. Bad went to worse when German authorities botched a rescue attempt. Several terrorists were killed, but so were the remaining hostages. The games were postponed for a day of mourning. Spitz, a Jew, opted to leave Munich early in fear for his life. In basketball, it was yet another Cold War match-up between the Americans and the Russians in the gold medal game. Tensions, already at an all-time high, spilled over to the game, the outcome of which remains disputed to this day.

Both teams came into the deciding contest with an 8-0 record. The game was tight throughout the first half, which ended with the United States trailing 21–26. The Russians maintained a small lead through the first seven minutes of the second half before things got ugly. A heated scramble for a loose ball between the U.S. top scorer, Dwight Jones, and Dvorni Edeshko, a reserve player for the Soviet Union, resulted in both players being ejected. Shortly thereafter, U.S. player Jim Brewer suffered a concussion after being knocked to the ground on a jump ball.

But the shorthanded Americans refused to fold. The team rallied to get within a point at 49–48 with 40 seconds to play in the game. The Russians managed to work the clock down to 10 seconds before hoisting a shot; it was blocked by Tom McMillen. A Russian player regained control of the ball and attempted to pass off to a teammate at center court, but Doug Collins read the play, intercepted the pass, and drove toward the hoop at full gallop. He was sharply undercut at the basket, resulting in a two-shot foul. A shaken Collins sank his first free throw to tie the game. As he launched the second shot, the horn sounded, signaling the end of the game. Since no time is to elapse during free throws, the clock was reset to three seconds after the second shot went down.

The Soviets inbounded the ball with the United States leading 50–49, but were unable to score as the buzzer went off. The American celebration began, but was cut short when one of the officials stepped in, insisting he had blown his whistle for a timeout with a second remaining on the clock. The Russians then argued they had called for a timeout *prior* to Collins's free throws. The time was eventually reset to three seconds, but the referees put the ball in play before the timekeeper started the clock, negating the play run by the Soviets — a desperation length-of-the-court pass that did not connect. In the midst of the ensuing argument, FIBA Secretary General R. William Jones ordered the clock reset to three seconds yet again. The Russians passed long again. Two U.S. players jumped alongside the intended receiver, Aleksander Belov, but it was Belov who secured possession while knocking his defenders to the floor. No foul was called. Belov scored on a layup, and the buzzer sounded. Final score: USSR 51, USA 50.

The United States launched an official protest, but was denied by the five-member jury consisting of representatives from Cuba, Poland, Spain, Italy, and Puerto Rico. The Soviet Union was awarded the gold medal, ending a 66-game winning streak by U.S. basketball teams in Olympic competition. U.S. team members voted unanimously to refuse their second-place silver medals, which to this day remain locked in a vault in Lusanne, Switzerland. "It was sort of like being on top of the Sears tower in Chicago celebrating and then being thrown off and falling 100 floors to the ground," Doug Collins reminisced. "That's the kind of emptiness and sick feeling I felt."[3]

The 1972 men's Olympic team became the first U.S. squad to lose the gold medal in basketball since the game's arrival as an official sport in 1936. The defeat paved the way for the inclusion of NBA players at the Olympics, beginning in 1992. *Back row, left to right:* A. C. Gwynne, trainer; John Bach, assistant coach; Don Haskins, assistant coach; Herbert Mols, assistant manager; Mike Bantom; Dwight Jones; Tommy Burleson; Tom McMillen; Bobby Jones; Jim Brewer; James Forbes; W. K. Summers, manager; J. McLendon; Henry Iba, head coach. *Front row, left to right:* Kenny Davis; Kevin Joyce; Tom Henderson; Doug Collins; Ed Ratloff (USA Basketball).

Collins did not allow the experience to adversely affect his senior year at Illinois, where he carried on as the team's leading scorer. The 6'6" Redbird guard would graduate with a 29.1 ppg varsity average while having scored a total of 2,240 points—both Redbird all-time records.[4]

Back in the pros, NBA and ABA teams squared off for another round of preseason interleague games. Once again, nearly all were held in neutral or ABA cities. NBA teams prevailed in 25 of the 34 contests, but 14 wins came by 10 points or less, and half of those by 5 or less. Regardless of what the players said on the surface, the games mattered. "Those NBA-ABA games were intense," recalled *Boston Globe* writer Bob Ryan, who remembered a specific game when Celtics coach Tom Heinsohn was assessed seven technical fouls by referee Jack Madden before being ejected.[5] Larry Brown added, "Tommy Heinsohn would say that we were playing to win and they weren't, but I'd check the box score and see that Tommy played his regulars 35 to 40 minutes, so what does that tell you?"[6]

Despite being in the midst of arbitration, Julius Erving played two exhibition games for the NBA Hawks. When the regular season got under way, he continued to hang out in the Hawks arena, ready to don a uniform on a moment's notice. The Doctor's house call in Atlanta proved brief, however. Four games into the season, a court order sent Erving back to Virginia to dribble a red, white, and blue ball for the remainder of the year. The Atlanta Hawks were ordered to pay the Bucks $250,000 for having signed Erving when Milwaukee owned his rights. The Bucks also received a couple of second-round draft picks from the Hawks while retaining the NBA rights to the Doctor. Additionally, the Hawks were fined $50,000 by the league for the two exhibition games in which Erving participated.

Virginia wasn't the only ABA city making headlines as year six began. The 76ers' Billy Cunningham, an All Star considered by many to be the best small forward in the NBA, became a Carolina Cougar.[7] Carolina also welcomed the ABA's all-time leading assist man, Larry Brown, as its new head coach. Brown, who was battling a severely injured hip, ended his playing days in Denver to take the head job, and hired his longtime pal and teammate Doug Moe as an assistant. Both men had spent their entire careers in the ABA.

The league's two weakest teams, the Miami Floridians and the Pittsburgh Condors, had folded over the summer. To compensate, the league added an expansion franchise in San Diego. It was hoped the new Conquistadors, coached by former Celtic K. C. Jones, would fill the void left by the departure of the NBA Rockets, which had relocated to Houston at the start of the 1971-72 season. The league's new geographical structure made for an odd division split of four teams in the East and six in the West, but the league retained its 84-game schedule. Prior to the start of the season, league Commissioner Jack Dolph, who had never delivered on his promise to secure a major television contract, was replaced by Bob Carlson, a legal consultant for the New York Nets.

The NBA season revolved around the reemergence of the Celtics, which was not just John Havlicek anymore. The team had a solid center in 6'9" Dave Cowens, the NBA's 1971 co–Rookie of the Year then in his third season. Jo Jo White was coming into his own as a star in the backcourt, and Celtics veterans Don Nelson and Don Chaney continued to make solid contributions. The up-and-coming group had won the Atlantic Division the previous year, but fell apart in the Conference Finals, losing to the Knicks in five games. The addition of veteran forward Paul Silas would prove instrumental in the team's quest to return a title to Boston.

Meanwhile, the relocated Royals were making headlines in their new digs with budding star, 6'1" Nate "Tiny" Archibald. The 160-pound Tiny, so named after his father, "Big Tiny," would have a breakout year in the team's debut in Kansas City–Omaha, becoming the first player in NBA history to finish the season at the top of the league in scoring (34) *and* assists (11.4).

One of the most noteworthy events of the NBA season took place off the

John Havlicek's speed and constant movement frustrated opponents on both ends of the court. He revolutionized the sixth man role during his early years with the Celtics and went on to become the team's all-time leading scorer with 26,395 points. "Hondo" spent his entire 16-year career in Boston, and retired with eight championships to show for his effort (Steve Lipofsky Basketballphoto.com).

basketball court on March 5, 1973, when Commissioner Kennedy announced the league had reached a comprehensive three-year deal with the National Basketball Players Association (NBPA). The new collective bargaining agreement set minimum player salaries at $20,000 (the highest of any pro sport) and established a player pension fund that would give players $720 for each active year they played in the league. The payments would begin at age 50, and were payable for life. Additionally, teams were required to keep a minimum of 11 players on their active roster at all times. Playoff pools and arbitration procedures were also addressed.[8]

The improved Boston Celtics remained the story in the NBA as the season wound down, winning a league-best 68 games; Dave Cowens won league MVP. The Lakers and Bucks tied for second most wins with 60. Meanwhile in Philadelphia, the loss of Billy Cunningham sent the 76ers into a freefall. The team had its worst year ever, posting a dismal 9-73 record.

The defending champion Lakers started slowly in the playoffs, needing seven games to get by the Chicago Bulls, which featured one of the league's highest scoring forward tandems in Chet Walker (19.9) and Bob Love (23.1). Up north in Oakland, the Rick Barry–bolstered Warriors surprised critics by disposing of the Midwest champion Bucks, four games to two. The 28-year-old Barry fit in well with a solid veteran squad that included Nate Thurmond, Cazzie Russell, Jeff Mullins, and Jim Barnett. But the Lakers, fresh from a wake-up call in Chicago, proved all business in the Conference Finals, beating the Warriors in five. In the East, the Erving-less Hawks took the surging Celtics to six before the men in green moved on to meet New York in the Eastern Finals. The Celtics were clearly improved with the addition of 6'7" Paul Silas, a durable, Russell-type player with an A+ attitude, but it was not enough to beat the determined Knicks with a semi-healthy Willis Reed on the floor. New York prevailed in Game 7 at Boston Garden, setting up a coast-to-coast rematch for the Finals. This time, it was the Knicks who prevailed 4-1 in the duo of aging veteran squads. Chamberlain, noticeably less effective at age 36, credited New York's tenacious defense for the victory. Willis Reed completed his comeback year by winning Finals MVP.

In the ABA, Julius Erving led the league in scoring at 31.9 ppg, but his Squires finished the year at .500, 15 games behind Billy Cunningham's Carolina Cougars. As such, Cunningham nudged out the Doctor for league MVP. In the playoffs, Carolina routed the Rick Barry–less Nets in five games but lost to the Kentucky Colonels in the Eastern Finals, 3-4. The Indiana Pacers disposed of the Utah Stars in six games to advance to the Finals, where they beat Kentucky in a highly competitive seven-game series that saw four contests decided by four points or less. The Pacers' rising star George McGinnis was the series MVP.

Despite the March agreement reached between the players association and the NBA, the Oscar Robertson suit continued to drag on through yet another summer. Owners in both leagues had become skeptical as to whether a merger would ever happen. ABA owners in particular were becoming discouraged, some downright desperate. Fan interest remained on the rise, but increased ticket sales alone could not support the escalating player salaries, even with the help of the Dolgoff Plan economics. Owners who needed an immediate influx of cash to keep their teams up and running had little choice but to sell their most popular assets—star players—if they were to remain in the hunt for an eventual NBA franchise.

The Virginia Squires was among the hardest hit. The club played in a very small market, even for an ABA franchise, yet it had what many felt to be the league's top player in the Doctor. Erving had complied promptly with the court order, returning to the Squires and behaving like a professional for the entire 1972-73 season. But as had been the case with Rick Barry, Julius made it no secret he wanted out of Virginia. As soon as owner Earl Foreman put out the word Erving was for sale, the New York Nets came calling. In Forman's words, Nets owner Roy Boe "couldn't write a check fast enough."[9]

Squires coach Al Bianchi tried to look on the bright side. "The last thing we wanted was to lose him to the NBA. So I was glad he stayed in the league, even if it wasn't with me."[10] The Doctor got a $2 million, five-year deal with the Nets and the chance to showcase his unique talent in the largest market area of the country. In exchange, Earl Foreman received $1 million in cash, enough to keep his team afloat for at least the coming season.[11] "Virginia selling Julius after his second year was like it would be if Chicago Bulls sold Michael Jordan," noted Johnny Kerr, the Squires' GM and future radio voice of the Chicago Bulls. "Today it is unimaginable. In the ABA, it was business."[12]

By far the biggest news of the off-season in either league was Wilt Chamberlain's retirement. Whether he was the best player ever remains open for discussion, but if judged by statistics alone, it is hard to find another who contributed so much in so many different aspects of the game. Over a span of 14 seasons, Chamberlain accumulated a record 31,419 points and 23,924 rebounds. The point total has since been surpassed by several players, but the rebounding mark is likely to stand forever. All told, Chamberlain left the game owning or sharing an astounding 43 records. Among them: single game record for points (100), most 50+ point games (118), highest field goal percentage in a season (.727), most *consecutive* games with 20+ points (126), 30+ points (65), and 40+ points (14), highest single-season rebounding average (27.2) and highest rookie scoring average (37.6 ppg). In addition to his two championships, the 13-time All Star was Rookie of the Year, league MVP four times, Finals MVP, All Star MVP, and made the All-NBA first team seven times.[13]

Chamberlain's absence from the game itself proved short-lived when he announced he had accepted the head coaching job with the San Diego Conquistadors for the 1973-74 season, replacing K. C. Jones. The idea that San Diego would do something so dramatic was not surprising, given the team was having trouble drawing fans. (The club finished the previous season in fourth place at 30-54.) The original idea was for Wilt to become player-coach, a scenario that actually played out on four occasions during the exhibition season in which the big man averaged 18 ppg. But his on-court participation was promptly challenged by the Lakers, claiming ownership of Chamberlain's rights via the option clause. The court agreed, ending the big man's playing days in the ABA. He would, however, be allowed to stay with the Conquistadors as coach.

For the ABA as a whole, the story was not Wilt playing in the exhibition games, rather the outcome of those exhibition games. For the first time in three years of interleague competition, the ABA was victorious in the majority of contests, winning 15 to the NBA's 9. The average margin of victory was 12.4 points for both leagues combined, down from 13.8 the previous year. For its part, the NBA snubbed its nose at the turnaround, attributing it to a lack of interest from its players. As previously noted, however, testament exists to the contrary, suggesting that, if anything, the intensity of the competition had increased.

Also on the increase was a notable gap in *style* of play. Big men continued to rule the NBA game from one generation to another: Mikan, Chamberlain, Abdul-Jabbar. While each was a tremendous individual talent in his own right, the trio's scoring techniques were similar: set up in the lane under the basket and wait for a teammate to pass the ball. Since dunking or stuffing the ball through the net remained illegal in the NBA, the score itself was predictable as well — a short jumper, a layup, or, in Abdul-Jabbar's case, a sweeping one-handed arch shot that broadcasters aptly dubbed the "sky hook."

That was not to say the league suffered from a lack of talent at other positions. Mega-stars like Jerry West, Oscar Robertson, and John Havlicek made huge contributions to the success of their clubs. But even a remarkable athlete such as Elgin Baylor, who had brought a whole new dimension to the game with his high-wire act, never managed to become the *focus* of the league. In the NBA, such status was reserved for the Goliaths of the game. Any GM in the league would have happily traded three Walt Fraziers for one Kareem Abdul-Jabbar.

The ABA had its own star center in 7'2" Artis Gilmore, but it was Erving's exciting, fast-paced style of play that defined the league. "I saw Elgin Baylor in his prime and I saw Connie Hawkins," said NBA great Zelmo Beaty. "Both of those guys could do some of the things that Julius later did, but he carried it a step beyond. No one could run and dunk and swoop down on the basket with the style of a young Julius Erving."[14] Things looked similar from a coach's standpoint. "I was in awe of what the guy could do," Kentucky's Hubie Brown admitted. "Nobody in the league could turn your own sellout crowd against you like Doctor J."[15]

The Doctor and the ABA was truly a match made in heaven. Crowds would have flocked to see Erving in either league, but the free-wheeling, open-court style of the ABA allowed him to showcase his talents to the max. While it would be unfair to say the ABA did not play defense, it was clearly an offensive-minded league. Over the previous three seasons, ABA teams had averaged a total of 114.2

points per game to the NBA's 110.1.[16] Fans came to see their team score, be it with jumpshots from 20-plus feet good for three points or length-of-the-court passes that resulted in breathtaking dunks that probably *should* have counted three.

As ABA owners knew full well, however, it took more than pizzazz and style to stay alive in the cutthroat world of professional basketball. The savvy that had allowed them to remain in business going on seven years was not limited to deferred salaries and pooled resources. The main reason the league survived where others had failed was its dedication to creative marketing. Most teams employed full-time marketing and sales directors. Giveaway promotions, then unheard of in the NBA, were commonplace among ABA clubs. Teams handed out free posters, hats, T-shirts, seat cushions, and the ever popular red, white, and blue balls. Tickets were provided to the media free of charge. Some clubs even offered free plane tickets to sports writers in exchange for a magazine or newspaper article featuring their team.

The San Diego franchise staged the ultimate promotion when it hired Chamberlain. Had the dual role of player and coach come to pass, it may very well have made the Conquistadors the golden boys of the ABA. But alas, Wilt's playing days ended via the Lakers' lawsuit, and there was not enough excitement in the coaching end of the job to hold his interest for long. By midseason, a once exuberant Chamberlain stopped attending practices. He began arriving late for the games themselves and, on occasion, never showed up at all. He did, however, find time to promote his new book, *Wilt: Just Like Any Other Seven-Foot Black Millionaire Who Lives Next Door*. Assistant coach Stan Albeck is generally credited with leading the team to a 37-47 record, good enough for the final playoff spot in the West. The Conquistadors lost to Utah in the semifinals 4-2, and Chamberlain's brief coaching career ended.

On the East Coast, Erving led his new team to a league best 55-29 record. The Nets breezed through the playoffs, losing only once in first two rounds before disposing of Utah in the Finals, four games to one. In addition to retaining his title as league scoring champ, the Doctor won the 1974 playoff and regular season MVP awards. Not surprisingly, the Nets led the league in attendance, pulling in an average of 8,923 fans per contest.[17]

In the NBA, Boston continued its title-hungry comeback, finishing atop the East with a 56-26 record, 7 full games ahead of the second place defending champion Knicks. The Celtics beat Atlanta four games to two in the first round of the playoffs before facing a shorthanded New York team in the Conference Finals. Injuries to big men Willis Reed and Dave DeBusscher made for easy pickings; the Celtics won the series 4-1 by an average of 13.7 ppg. In the West, Abdul-Jabbar was MVP as Milwaukee returned to the top of the league with a vengeance. The 59-23 Bucks rolled over the once mighty Lakers in five games and swept the rising Bulls in the Conference Finals.

The Bucks had the better record and thus home court advantage for the

Finals, but the series proved unusual in that each team could muster only a single victory on its home court through the first six games. Still, it was 3-3 heading into Game 7, and momentum was with the home-court Bucks following their double-overtime victory in Boston two nights earlier. But the Celtics blindsided their opponent with double- and triple-teams on Abdul-Jabbar, replacing the single-man coverage it had employed on the big man through the first six games. The surprise strategy made it more difficult for Kareem to score, while freeing up Cowens for easier shots. The frustrated Bucks fell behind early and never recovered, losing 87–102. A gleeful Celtics squad returned to Boston with championship number 12, its first since Russell had retired as player/coach in 1969.

The interleague All Star Game tentatively scheduled for May 18 in Providence, RI, was canceled for reasons unknown but probably related to the ongoing uncertainty surrounding the Oscar Robertson suit and increasing skepticism about the merger. As the off-season officially commenced, the biggest basketball news centered around the ABA and its signing of 6'11", 210-pound Moses Malone, an 18-year-old from Petersburg, Virginia.

Malone, named the country's top high school player the year before, had been swamped with offers of college scholarships from every area of the country during his senior year. The young man eventually signed a letter of intent with the University of Maryland, but changed his mind a week before he was scheduled to begin classes, opting instead to sign a seven-year, $3 million contract with the Utah Stars, making him the first player to jump directly from high school to the professional game.

Once the deal was announced, the NBA could do little but blink. The ABA had done it again, shocked and infuriated its rival while scoring a major coup. Merger or no, the ABA was sending a clear signal to the once dominant NBA: it would continue to look out for its own best interests, to hell with cultured traditions. The goal was no longer one of mere survival. The ABA was on a mission to win the hearts and minds of basketball fans by putting on the most exciting, entertaining game possible.

NBA owners wanted to do the same, but were divided insofar as how to go about it. Did they stay with the solid, defensive-minded style that had made their league successful for nearly 30 years? Or was the future of the pro game in the ABA's offensive, up-tempo approach featuring ever younger, athletic marvels who could defy the very rules of gravity itself?

The answer, of course, lay somewhere in between. The NBA's dilemma was how to arrive there before the ABA closed the gap.

LAST HURRAH

Despite the ABA's increasing popularity among fans, it still lacked *the* essential ingredient to compete in the hardcore world of professional sports: a major television contract. Today, the league's up-tempo, showy style would earn it a cable deal at the very least, but in the mid–1970s, national television outlets for sports consisted of the big three: CBS, NBC, and ABC. There were only so many time slots available, so many viewers to go around. The NBA, then in the midst of a three-year deal with CBS worth $27 million,[1] was *the* pro basketball league as far as network execs were concerned. Given that rumors of a pending merger persisted, it is understandable how networks were unwilling to make a deal with a league that could conceivably dissolve overnight.

Television executives weren't the only ones who lacked faith as the ABA headed into its eighth season. Although the league had scored a major coup by convincing a number of the NBA's top referees to switch leagues several years earlier, most had since returned to the more visible NBA. Rick Barry, who had played in the media capital of the country while with the Nets, was back in Oakland with the Warriors. The majority of ABA stars were courted by NBA clubs, while superstars such as Erving and McGinnis were wooed on a near daily basis. Players were tempted for a number reasons, most notably stability, more money — none of which was deferred — and higher visibility via national TV.

In the case of Carolina Cougar Billy Cunningham, the ABA's 1973 MVP, stability was the major factor that drove him back to the NBA 76ers for the 1974-75 season. Billy described his two years in the ABA as "the most enjoyable years of my pro career," and added, "I would have finished my career in the ABA, despite the crummy travel, if I had thought the league had a chance to survive."[2] Unfortunately for the Cougars, his defection caused a domino effect within the franchise. The team was sold during the summer and moved to St. Louis, where it would play as the Spirits. Coach Larry Brown, assistant Doug Moe, and GM Carl Sheer all left the team to work for the Denver Rockets, which would hence be known as the Nuggets. Former Cougars owner Tedd Munchak took over for Mike Storen as league commissioner.

Across the border in Virginia, Earl Foreman's cash from Erving's sale ran out, and he was forced to sell his beloved Squires. On the upside, the league convinced superstar George McGinnis to remain with the Indiana Pacers rather than jumping leagues to play for the Knicks. The victory left the ABA with three bone fide superstars— McGinnis, Gilmore, and Erving — and the potential for four with 19-year-old Moses Malone.

The NBA added the expansion Central Division New Orleans Jazz to the 1974-75 campaign, but lost two of its mega-stars, Jerry West and Oscar Robertson, to retirement. Meanwhile, the era of the dominant big man continued on course as UCLA star Bill Walton, the top pick in the 1974 draft, debuted with the Portland Trail Blazers.

The 6'11" redhead packed an impressive collegiate résumé, having averaged 20.3 points and 15.7 rebounds per game at UCLA while leading the Bruins to an 86-4 record. In each of his three varsity seasons, Bill was named the *Sporting News* College Player of the Year *and* a first team All American. When the Bruins won back-to-back NCAA titles in 1972 and 1973, he was Tournament MVP both times. Walton's finest moment came in the 1973 Finals against Memphis State, when he scored 44 points, connecting on 21 of 22 shots— a feat many critics laud as the best individual performance ever in a Final Four contest.

His illustrious achievements aside, Walton's personality presented a potential challenge to the NBA's public relations department. Pro-establishment had labeled him a radical for his antiwar views— views that had resulted in his arrest at a protest his junior year. Walton was anything but apologetic after the fact, releasing a statement that charged the then-current generation with screwing up the world. He was just trying to fix it. The Grateful Dead fan was a vegetarian before it was popular, and spoke often about seeking spiritual enlightenment.

Far more important to prospective NBA employers, however, were questions surrounding Walton's durability. By the time he arrived at UCLA, Bill had undergone knee surgery and suffered broken bones in his foot, ankle, and leg. A sore back and tendonitis in his knees plagued him throughout his collegiate career. Nonetheless, the Trail Blazers did not hesitate to nab the big redhead with the first overall pick in the 1974 draft. From the get-go, he was viewed as a franchise player. "There have been many great players in the game," Bill's UCLA coach, John Wooden, remarked, "but not many great team players. Walton is a very great team player."[3]

The initial void left by West and Robertson was felt by fans throughout the league, but on the upside, the decline of the Western Division's former powerhouses— the Bucks and Lakers— left a rare opening for young teams on the rise. The Seattle Supersonics, Chicago Bulls, and Kansas City–Omaha Kings were considered the most likely candidates, but none was as determined as Rick Barry's Golden State Warriors.

Basketball fans may have *thought* Barry had been around for decades because he had made news with so many different teams, lawsuits, and injuries, but in fact he was only 30 years old, in the prime of his career. And he was hungry for a title. Very hungry.

Unbeknownst to most critics, however, Golden State was not a one-man show. The franchise had a stellar leader in Coach Al Attles, who had been with the club, either as a player or coach, going on 15 years. The Warriors also featured a promising young center in Clifford Ray, acquired in September from the Bulls for durable but aging rebounding Goliath Nate Thurmond. The guard line of Butch Beard and Charlie Johnson was not on a par with Frazier–Monroe, but both were solid performers who got the job done. Still, it was the addition of former UCLA star, 6'6" rookie Keith Wilkes, that propelled the club to the next level.

Wilkes (who would soon convert to Islam and change his first name to Jamaal) was a kid who knew how to win. He had played with Walton at UCLA during the Bruins back-to-back NCAA Championships in 1972 and '73 and was present for most of the team's record 88-game winning streak, which had begun shortly before Walton's arrival. Wilkes was not a superstar in the making, and that was fine with Coach Attles, who felt one per team was enough. In addition to a solid all-around game, Wilkes brought with him an exemplary attitude, subscribing to the old-school theory that it was more important to win games than accumulate personal stats.

And with Wilkes, the Warriors *did* win games—a lot more than anyone expected. The team's 48-34 record was the best in the Western Conference. The newly energized Blazers finished 10 games back at 38-44. Chronic foot problems had limited Walton to 35 games.

In the East, it was an old-fashioned NBA battle of size and muscle between 60-game winners Boston and Washington. The latter, which had changed its name from the Capitols to the Bullets, was coached by K. C. Jones and featured two of the game's best power players in 6'9", 235-pound Elvin Hayes (12.2 rebounds and 23 ppg) and rebounding champ Wes Unseld (14.8 rpg). Aided by little Kevin Porter, a speedy 6'0" point guard who led the league in assists at eight per game, the club managed to beat the reigning champs 4-2 in the Conference Finals.

If the Bullets' victory over Boston was considered an upset, Golden State's march to the Finals was nothing short of extraordinary. The club had not been expected to get past Seattle, let alone the highly favored Chicago Bulls. But the overachieving Warriors disposed of both clubs and confidently marched on to the Championship series in Washington, where they shocked the sports world with a 4-0 sweep of the highly favored Bullets.

In the ABA, 19-year-old rookie sensation Moses Malone averaged 18.8 ppg and 14.6 rebounds, but it was not enough to propel the Utah Stars to another title. The team finished a disappointing 38-46 and lost to first-place Denver in the West's opening round of the playoffs. Former Providence standout Marvin

Barnes (24 ppg, 15.6 rebounds) edged out Malone for league Rookie of the Year, while Erving and McGinnis shared MVP. In the East, the Kentucky Colonels were led by an All Star trio of Dan Issel, Artis Gilmore, and Lou Dampier. The Hubie Brown–coached squad dominated the playoffs, losing only one game in each of its three playoff series to win the championship.

Winners and losers aside, the 1975 NBA Finals represented one of the most important milestones in the history of American professional sports. For the first time in a mainstream championship series, both opposing head coaches, K. C. Jones and Al Attles, were black. Interestingly, reports from the era suggest the majority of news outlets saw the red-letter event as no big deal. That in itself is testament to just how far basketball, and pro sports as a whole, had come in a few short years. In addition to Attles and Jones, black coaches led NBA teams in Detroit (Ray Scott), Seattle (Bill Russell), and Portland (Lenny Wilkens).

Still, the league had a long way to go before coaches reached racial parity with players. By 1975, the *New York Times* estimated NBA rosters were at least 75 percent black.[4] The percentage was even higher in the ABA, causing some journalists to speculate that should a merger occur, white fans might voice their disapproval at the box office, especially in regard to the game's dwindling number of white stars. There is no evidence to support such a theory, and in fact, the numbers rebuff it. Attendance figures for the 1974-75 season remained on the rise in both leagues. NBA attendance was up over 10 percent from the previous year, while the ABA showed an increase of more than 20 percent.[5] The latter suggested that regardless of race, basketball fans new to the pro game preferred the fast-paced style of the ABA.

The above assumption was not lost on the NBA's new commissioner, Larry O'Brien, who was selected by owners via a unanimous vote in April 1975 to replace retiring Walter Kennedy. O'Brien had a fascinating history, most notably in politics, where he had worked on the senatorial campaigns of John Kennedy in 1952 and 1958. He was at Kennedy's side during the Massachusetts Senator's presidential run, and went on to serve in the Kennedy Administration as an advisor to the president from 1961–65. O'Brien later directed the campaigns of Robert Kennedy, Lyndon Johnson, and Hubert Humphrey — all while serving as U.S. Postmaster General. He left the Postmaster position to take over as chairman of the Democratic National Committee in 1968–69 and again in 1970–73. The latter earned him a place in the national spotlight when his DNC office at the Watergate Hotel was burglarized in 1972.

League owners hoped O'Brien's political background would prove useful in solving their troubles with the pending merger and the never-ending Oscar Robertson suit.[6] It was a logical assumption, given O'Brien's congressional connections, but only time would tell whether his practiced negotiating skills would be enough to succeed where Walter Kennedy had failed.

In the interim, both leagues continued to operate as separate entities vying to become number one in the hearts and minds of pro basketball fans.

In the NBA, another blockbuster trade was in the works as the off-season got under way. The Milwaukee Bucks, winners of the Midwest Division for four straight years, had gone from a Finals appearance the previous season to missing the playoffs in 1975. Their freefall to last place at 38-44 was mainly attributed to the retirement of Oscar Robertson. Fans fully expected their team to regroup the next season, with Abdul-Jabbar leading the way.

The trouble was, Kareem did not want to lead the way, at least not in Milwaukee. Since his conversion to Islam, he felt out of place in small-market Milwaukee and the Midwest in general, an area that lacked the type of religious culture he was seeking to embrace. Following the 1974-75 season, the big man discussed his situation with the Bucks GM, Wayne Embry, and requested a trade to New York or Los Angeles. Embry was empathetic; as the first black general manager in the NBA, he knew a thing or two about feeling out of place. He told Kareem he would see what he could do. On June 16, 1975, Abdul-Jabbar was sent to the Lakers in exchange for a foursome of average players: Elmore Smith, Brian Winters, Dave Meyers, and Junior Bridgeman. The Lakers had a superstar center again, and the Bucks were a dynasty no more.

Kareem wasn't the only big name changing teams. George McGinnis, who had agreed to remain with the Indiana Pacers the previous season, bolted to the NBA over the summer, signing with Philadelphia. McGinnis's defection was the first of several major blows to strike the ABA during season nine. Shortly before the regular season tipped off, New York and Denver announced they had applied for membership in the NBA. The remaining ABA owners expressed outrage at the attempted defection. The Nets and Nuggets were the league's most lucrative teams; if the request were approved, the ABA would have little choice but to cease operations immediately. Commissioner O'Brien surely knew as much and wisely opted to continue ongoing negotiations with the ABA as a whole rather than promote further litigation.

Thus the ABA entered 1975-76 nearly intact from the previous year, short only the Memphis Sounds, which was supposed to have relocated to Baltimore but folded during training camp due to a lack of funds. The league announced it was scrapping its 30-second clock in favor of the NBA's long-standing 24-second rule — a move that suggested the merger talks remained alive and well. But as much as owners and players remained committed to staying in the game no matter what, eight seasons of operating in the red snapped at their heals. San Diego ran out of luck and money 11 games into the season. The Utah Stars followed five games later; Moses Malone was sold to the Spirits of St. Louis. The hapless Virginia Squires, barely a step from the grave, somehow managed to hang on.

By the time the All Star Game was played on January 26, 1976, the ABA's seven remaining franchises played in a single division league. The game itself differed from previous years in that the team with the best midseason record — which turned out to be the host Denver Nuggets— played against a mix of All

Stars from the other six clubs. Owners saw the game as their final chance to impress the NBA. With only seven teams left, there was little chance the ABA could survive beyond the current season, so it was now or never. Previous All Star Games had drawn well, but owners were far from confident, given their league's dwindling financial state, so they arranged for country superstars Glen Campbell and Charlie Rich to perform a two-hour pregame concert at McNichols Arena.

The concert may have contributed to the crowd of 17,798, but it would not be country music that fans would be talking about after the game that night. Nor would it be the contest itself, which the Nuggets won in exciting fashion, 144–138. Instead, the talk of the professional basketball world would center on the halftime show, a spicy little competition the league billed as a slam dunk contest.

The idea for the halftime show came about as a last-ditch effort by owners to convince the league's critics and the NBA that its players were something special, that they knew how to get fans excited, bring them out of their seats. The initial group of high-flyers was made up of George Gervin (6'7"), Artis Gilmore (7'2"), Larry Kenon (6'9"), David Thompson (6'4"), and Julius Erving (6'7"). Gervin, Gilmore, and Erving were natural choices, fixtures in the league. Forward Larry Kenon played alongside teammate George "Iceman" Gervin in San Antonio, and Nuggets guard David Thompson was a shoe-in for Rookie of the Year.

Thompson, who had snubbed the Atlanta Hawks in favor of playing for the Nuggets in Denver, was the most electrifying player to arrive in the ABA since Erving. Appropriately nicknamed the Skywalker, the quick, small forward out of North Carolina State possessed a golden shooting touch to go with his amazing 44-inch vertical leap. The back-to-back AP National Player of the Year led the ACC (Atlantic Coast Conference) Wolfpack to a 79-7 record over three varsity seasons, including a 30-1 stretch en route to the National Title in 1974. Thompson capped off the year by winning the NCAA's Tournament MVP. David continued to improve his senior year, winning more than a dozen individual honors, including the prestigious Naismith Award and *Sporting News* Player of the Year. He is among the most outstanding players in NCAA history and, by many accounts, the best player ever in the ACC.

Fans lucky enough to be at McNichols that night were treated to an awesome display of athleticism by the entire group, but there was no question the winner would come down to a choice between the home crowd favorite,

Opposite: The original Skywalker, David Thompson, joined the Nuggets during the ABA's final season (1975-76) and went on to play six more years in Denver and two in Seattle, delighting fans with his amazing hang time and jaw-dropping athleticism. Thompson owns bragging rights as the only player to win All Star Game MVP in the 1979 NBA game (Basketball Hall of Fame, Springfield, MA).

Thompson, or his Eastern rival, Dr. J. According to accounts of the day, Thompson's show included a two-handed jackknife reverse, a windmill cuff jam, and a 360-degree dunk — the first such maneuver to be caught on film. But Erving had several years of experience over the Skywalker, and it showed in his display. He began by standing under the basket with a ball in each hand, then jumped up, slamming both balls through the net simultaneously. The impressive move proved little more than a warm-up for his next attempt — a flying leap from the free throw line to the basket. (Young fans may equate the move with Michael Jordan, but it was Erving who first performed and perfected the feat.) "His Afro was big, and it was blowing," recalled ABA All Star Ron Boone. "He went up and threw that baby down and the crowd went crazy."[7]

The Doctor himself saw the move as risky, given how rims from the era were rigid, not the breakaway type used in today's game. "You had a rim that if you didn't get above it, and dunk the ball through the net right away, the rim would throw you to the ground," he recalled. Nonetheless, Erving couldn't pass up the opportunity to bring the fans out of their seats. "Here was my philosophy — dare to be great."[8] Suffice it to say, he was.

Regardless of what NBA execs may have said — or not said — following the spectacle in Denver, there is little question the slam dunk contest increased the stakes insofar as the merger was concerned. The dominant league was losing superstars at a much faster pace than it could replace them — a situation that intensified as long as its adversary remained in the game. While NBA owners could speculate as to the ABA's inevitable demise, they had no firm timetable to rely on. The league had already far surpassed expectations. Who was to say it wouldn't mount yet another unlikely comeback? Buzzer-beaters were rare, but they happened.

It was during this time of uncertainly that the NBA rid itself of a massive six-year migraine: the Oscar Robertson suit. The settlement, reached on February 3 during the NBA's All Star break, resolved many of the issues that stood in the way of a merger. Most important to players was the demise of the inequitable option clause that had kept them obligated to a team for an additional year after their contract expired. To compensate, the league instituted the right of first refusal, which allowed teams the chance to match any offer such a player received while shopping his free agent services to other clubs.

Another significant point concerned the college draft. Initially, the lawsuit had charged that the college draft was illegal because it forced a player to either sign with the team that drafted him or forfeit his right to play in the NBA for a period of two years. A compromise was reached cutting the time limit to one year; a player who had not signed a contract at that point was eligible to reenter the draft. The league also agreed to drop the hardship requirements for undergraduates who wanted to turn pro. The new rule went a step further, allowing any student whose high school class had graduated to apply for entry in the NBA draft as long as he renounced his college eligibility. Last, the league agreed to a monetary settlement of $4.3 million to be divided among the NBA's 479 players. The amount a player received was dependent upon how long he had been playing pro basketball prior to the settlement.

With the antitrust suit finally out of the way, a merger seemed imminent. In the interim, however, both leagues continued to operate independently as the season wound down.

Five of the remaining seven ABA teams made the playoffs. The reigning champion Kentucky Colonels beat Indiana in a first round mini-series but lost to the Nuggets in the semi-finals. The Nets beat San Antonio, setting up a best-case scenario for the league — a Denver vs. New York Finals, featuring two of its most exciting stars: slam dunkers David Thompson and Julius Erving.

A record crowd of 19,034 packed McNichols Arena for the May 1 opener, which Erving won on a last-second shot to give him a game-high 45 points. Three nights later, the Nuggets came away with a 127–121 win in front of 19,107 ecstatic fans; Erving was the high man again with 48. In New York, the Sky-walker edged out the Doctor for scoring honors with 32, but the Nets still won by 6 before a crowd of better than 12,000. Erving struck back in a sold-out (15,934) Game 4, scoring 34 points to help his team take a commanding 3-1 lead as the series headed back to Denver. But the Nuggets would not go quietly. Although the Doctor put on another eye-popping performance with 37 points, Denver sent their fans home happy with an 8-point win. It was back to another sold out house in New York for Game 6, where Thompson put on his best performance of the playoffs with 42 points. Alas, it was not enough to lift his team past the hometown Nets, which clinched the series with a 112–106 win after erasing a 22-point third quarter deficit.

Erving, who finished the game with 31 points and 19 rebounds, was Finals MVP.[9] For the series, he averaged 14.2 rebounds and 37.6 points on 60 percent shooting — all while being guarded by Denver's Bobby Jones, widely considered the best defensive forward in the league. "He was just ungodly," Nets coach Kevin Loughery recalled. "He wouldn't let us lose."[10]

David Thompson, meanwhile, had confirmed he was a force to be reckoned with. Appearing in 13 playoff games, the ABA Rookie of the Year played 39 minutes per contest, averaging 26.3 points, 6.4 rebounds, and 3 assists. "When you have an exciting talent like that on your team," fellow Nugget George Irvine remarked, "you know that your franchise is in great shape."[11] Indeed, the number of Nuggets season ticket holders had jumped from 2,200 to 6,000 following the Skywalker's addition. Denver's regular season attendance average of 13,000 was number one in the ABA and the fourth best in all of pro basketball.[12]

In the NBA, the defending champion Warriors proved they were not a fluke by capturing the West with a league-best 59-23 record. But there was a new Cinderella team on the march as the playoffs commenced — the surging Phoenix Suns. A young, athletic team led by former Celtics reserve Paul

Westphal, Phoenix won 10 of its final 13 games to finish 42-40, a game behind second-place Seattle. The offensive-minded club continued to roll in the playoffs, disposing of the Sonics in six games and the Warriors in seven to earn their first Finals appearance in franchise history.

In the East, few were surprised when Boston outlasted Buffalo and Cleveland to earn yet another trip to the Finals. The Celtics' frontline of John Havlicek, Paul Silas, and Dave Cowens was arguably the best in the league; each had been named to the NBA's All Defensive First Team while posting a combined scoring average of 44.7 ppg. A potent veteran backcourt of Jo Jo White (18.9 ppg) and former ABA scoring champ Charlie Scott (17.6) rounded out the club's starting five. Longtime Celtic Don Nelson provided leadership amid a group of young reserves that included 6'9", 225-pound Tom Boswell and the equally muscular 6'10", 235-pound Jim Ard. It was a Celtic team that epitomized the league's bump-and-grind power game that was appropriately headed by hoops fundamentalist Coach Tom Heinsohn.

In contrast, the Phoenix Suns were young and undersized. Westphal (20.5 ppg) was a trim, athletic 6'4" guard, equally adept at passing, scoring, and moving without the ball. At center was Rookie of the Year, 6'9", 210-pound Alvin Adams, an excellent scorer (19 ppg) who didn't hesitate to pass the ball to open teammates. The Suns had experience in the frontcourt with Curtis Perry and Garfield Heard, but featured another first-year player, Rickie Sobers (9.2 ppg), opposite Westphal in the backcourt. Coach John MacLeod was in only his third pro season, and new to playoff competition. Still, the upstart team was not all about youth. The roster featured veterans like Pat Riley, Dick Van Arsdale, and Keith Erickson, all players who knew how to win.

Nonetheless, predictions of a Boston sweep appeared on track when the Suns found themselves down 0-2. Add in the fact that Phoenix had not beaten the Celtics since December 1974, and Bean Town fans seemed justified in readying their celebration. But momentum changed dramatically when the Suns won the next two games at home for a 2-2 tie heading into Game 5 at Boston Garden. The resulting contest stands as one of the most thrilling playoff games in NBA history.

The Celtics took charge early and led 61–45 at halftime, but the Suns came roaring back, outscoring Boston 50–34 in the second half to force a 95-all tie at the end of regulation. Each team managed only six points in the first overtime period, but the Suns should have had an opportunity to make it seven when Paul Silas signaled for a Celtics timeout as the clock ran down. Boston had no timeouts left, a violation that should have resulted in a Suns free throw. But referee Richie Powers neglected to acknowledge Silas's signal. Time ran out, ending the first overtime with a disputed 101 deadlock.[13]

Both teams picked up their offense in the second overtime, scoring a total of 22 points, though again officials caused their share of controversy. With four seconds to go and the Suns up 110–109, Boston got the ball to Havlicek, who nailed a 15-foot banker from the left wing as time expired. The boisterous crowd erupted and fans ran onto the court, oblivious to Richie Powers, who was informing both coaches that a second still remained on the clock. Once word reached the frenzied crowd, numerous fights broke out on the floor. Irate fans, many of them drunk, began pummeling Phoenix players. A man got his hands on Powers and had to be pulled off by security and escorted from the building.

Once order was restored, Phoenix had one second to inbound the ball from under Boston's basket and score — a seemingly impossible task. But Coach MacLeod sprang a surprise by calling a timeout he knew the team did not have (a strategy that was later credited to Paul Westphal). This time the violation was acknowledged, resulting in a Boston free throw that put the Celtics up 112–110. Since NBA rules allowed the opposing team to inbound the ball at halfcourt after a made free throw, Phoenix now had a legitimate shot at extending the game. In what would come to be known as "the Shot Heard Round the World," the Suns' Garfield Heard caught the inbound pass from several feet beyond the top of the key and launched a high arching turnaround that hit nothing but net. The basket would have been a game-winner in the ABA, but since the NBA had yet to adapt to three-point field goal, the contest headed into overtime number three.

By this point both teams had lost key players to fouls and those remaining were exhausted. Westphal was still on the floor for Phoenix, however, as was his Celtics counterpoint, Jo Jo White. Each man led his respective club in scoring, but the game's final heroics would come from an unlikely source: Boston's seldom-used forward Glen McDonald. A first-round pick in 1974, McDonald made the most of his opportunity by scoring 6 points in the period, including the game's final basket, to lift the Celtics to a 128–126 victory. The 4 hour, 20 second marathon went down in the history books as the longest playoff game ever.

The deflated Suns never quite recovered. The Celtics took Game 6 in Phoenix, 87–80, to capture their 13th NBA title. Asked whether the thrill of playing in the finals ever got old, Havlicek responded, "Only if you lose."[14]

Winners and losers on a much larger scale were about to be determined as the league announced it had reached a merger agreement with the ABA, ending the latter's wildly unpredictable nine-year run.

A FIGHTING CHANCE

As the 1975-76 pro basketball season reached an official end, seven ABA teams remained: The Kentucky Colonels, Denver Nuggets, New York Nets, San Antonio Spurs, Spirits of St. Louis, Indiana Pacers, and Virginia Squires. The latter had barely muddled through the regular season without former owner Earl Foreman to cheer it on, and new ownership had neither the money nor desire to continue as merger talks pressed forward into the summer. Of the remaining six clubs, St. Louis and Kentucky remained question marks insofar as the NBA was concerned. St. Louis was on solid ground financially but had trouble averaging 3,500 fans. Talk of moving the Spirits to Hartford, Connecticut, was promptly stomped out by the NBA, who wanted no part of infringing on the Celtics' territory. The Kentucky Colonels presented a similar problem. Their proposed move to Cincinnati was met was skepticism, and rightly so as the Royals, even when led by the great Oscar Robertson, had failed to establish itself as a stronghold in the community. Besides, Ohio already had an NBA team in Cleveland.

Following several intense rounds of discussions, the NBA presented its final, take-it-or-leave-it offer: San Antonio, Denver, New York, and Indiana were in, Kentucky and St. Louis were out. The ABA was not happy with the ultimatum but saw the writing on the wall. "We wanted to get all six franchises in the league, but we had no real grounds to negotiate," merger committee member Roy Boe recalled. "We were dead on our feet and the NBA knew it."[1]

So why did the NBA care about those other four teams? If the league's ultimate goal was to acquire the ABA's top players, it had only to wait for its rival's formal demise, then conduct a special draft to absorb the Ervings and Gilmores into the fold. The fact was, not all established NBA clubs were on solid ground as the merger loomed. In its determination to beat the ABA at its own game, the league had grown far more quickly than it would have liked. Nine expansion teams had been added since the ABA's inception in 1967-68, nearly doubling the number of NBA franchises. And while league attendance continued to rise overall, up 9 percent from the previous year, Atlanta, Chicago, Detroit, and Houston were drawing fewer than 7,000 fans—more than 3,000 below the league average. It would prove little consolation to these struggling clubs should they be granted the top picks in any forthcoming dispersal draft, as they did not have the necessary funds to sign them.

Commissioner O'Brien realized that absorbing the ABA's stars on a piecemeal basis would almost certainly lead to less, not more, parity within the NBA. On the other hand, adding four new teams to the league would bring these same elite players into the fold while adding an influx of cash to all existing teams via the admission fees charged to the new clubs. Unlike adding four expansion franchises based on projected attendance, all four ABA teams were proven winners with an established fan following. It was a win-win situation for the NBA.

The situation was not as straightforward for the ABA. Accepting the NBA's offer meant abandoning two of its most loyal clubs. Kentucky had been part of the league since its onset in 1967-68. The same was true for the Spirits, which had previously played as the Houston Mavericks and Carolina Cougars. But the league knew it would not survive another season with only six teams. The best it could do was save four clubs and hope its legacy remained alive by planting seeds that would spread its style of play throughout the rest of the NBA.

The final deal, announced on June 17, 1976, called for the Indiana Pacers, San Antonio Spurs, Denver Nuggets, and New York Nets to pay the NBA $3.2 million each by September 15, 1976. The Nets were also required to compensate the New York Knicks an additional $4.8 million for infringing on their territory. Furthermore, all new teams—which would technically be referred to as "expansion" teams—would be excluded from the 1976 college draft, ineligible to participate in the upcoming dispersal draft of remaining ABA players, have no votes on the distribution of gate receipts for two years, and would not be allowed to share in the league's television revenues until the 1979-80 season.

There was more. To pacify St. Louis and Kentucky, the four accepted teams had to shell out $5.2 million to their former colleagues. The Colonels' owner, John Brown of Kentucky Fried Chicken fame, received an outright cash settlement of $3 million.[2] Brothers Ozzie and Danny Silna of the Spirits took a more futuristic approach. The Silnas asked for less cash upfront—$2.2 million—but insisted they receive 1/7 of a share of each new team's allotted television revenues (totaling 4/7 of a full share) when that part of the agreement kicked in. The stipulation was to remain in force for the life of the NBA.

The latter is often cited as the most lucrative deal negotiated in the history of professional sports. The Spirits never played an NBA game, yet their former owners continue to collect 4/7 of a share of NBA TV revenues to this day. At last count, ESPN estimated the most recent NBA contract nets the Silnas some $24 million per year.[3]

Several rule changes took effect as the new season began. The most noteworthy concerned positioning for the inbounds pass after timeouts. Normally, players inbounded the ball under the opposing team's basket after a score regardless of whether a timeout was used. In situations where only a few seconds remained on the clock, advancing the ball full court often resulted in Hail Mary, length-of-the-court passes that sailed out of bounds. In an attempt to make close games more exciting, the rule was amended to allow teams to advance the ball to half court following a timeout, but only during the final two minutes of the game.

Additionally, the "force out" rule, where an offensive player was "forced" out of bounds by a defender, was eliminated. At their discretion, officials would either call a foul on the defender or rule the offensive player had simply stepped out of bounds, in which case it was a turnover. The elbow foul, in effect since the 1961-62 season, was amended to include swinging of elbows and would be assessed regardless of whether contact occurred. Finally, the 24-second clock would be reset to 5 seconds if a defensive player had caused the ball to go out of bounds with less than 5 seconds remaining.

As would be expected, the NBA's first season as a 22-team league had its share of ups and downs. Average attendance for 1976-77 increased about 800 fans per game — not bad at first glance, but troublesome after noting those figures included major increases of 3,000 per game in Indianapolis and Phoenix, and 5,000 each in Denver and Chicago. The Nuggets owed their surge to the massive allure of the Skywalker, and the Bulls, who only a year before had seemed on the verge of collapse, had nabbed 7'2" Artis Gilmore in the dispersal draft, making them an instant playoff team. But New Orleans and Buffalo had lost more than 2,000 fans each while Atlanta and Detroit hovered at their previous year lows of 5,500 to 6,000. Of the struggling franchises, only the Houston Rockets had shown improvement, adding some 2,000 fans per game, thanks mainly to the addition of Moses Malone.

On the upside, two of the former ABA teams had strong debuts. Denver won the Midwest Division with a 50-32 record, 6 full games ahead of the Gilmore-revived Chicago Bulls, and the Spurs finished third in the Central at 44-38, good enough to qualify for a playoff berth. Postseason play had been restructured, expanding the number of playoff teams from 10 to 12, thus doubling the number of first-round series to four.

San Antonio lost 2-0 to the Celtics in the first round, but the surging Bill Walton–led Trail Blazers needed six games in the Conference semi-finals to dispose of David Thompson's Nuggets. The New York Nets would likely have made it to the postseason as well had its owners been able to resolve a contract dispute with Erving. Instead, the club sold the Doctor's rights to Philadelphia for $3 million only hours before the season began and struggled through a dismal 22-60 season, by far the worst in the league. The enriched 76ers, meanwhile, surged to the top of the Atlantic with a league-tying best record of 50-32.

Erving was no stranger to NBA fans by playoff time. He had dominated the nationally televised All Star Game in February with 30 points, 12 rebounds, and 4 steals to win the MVP award hands down. The 76ers also featured former

Pacers star George McGinnis. Together, the former ABA legends averaged 43 points per game. The additional one-two punch of Doug Collins (18.3 ppg) and Lloyd "World" Free (16.3 ppg) in the backcourt made Philadelphia one of the highest scoring teams in the league at 110.8 ppg (San Antonio was first at 114.2). But the Sixers were lacking a main ingredient: no dominant center. Second-year man Darrel Dawkins, the club's 1976 first-round draft pick, was not yet a force in the league and shared minutes with the undersized (6'9", 235 lbs.) Harvey Catchings.

In a league still dominated by big men and defense, Philadelphia's deficiency in the middle made their playoff road a difficult one. The club needed seven games to beat the Celtics in the semi-finals and six more to dispose of the much improved Houston Rockets to secure the East. In the West, it was the Blazers' strength in the middle — a nearly healthy Bill Walton — that propelled Portland to its first Finals appearance in the franchise's short seven-year history.

The 24-year-old redhead averaged a respectable 18.6 points in 62 regular season games for the Blazers on 53 percent field goal accuracy, but it was his defense that won games. Walton led his team in steals (66) and was number one in the league in rebounds (14.4) and blocked shots (3.25).[4] Joining Walton on the front line was one of the best power forwards in the league, 6'9", 215-pound Maurice Lucas, taken by the Blazers in the dispersal draft. Lucas led his team in scoring at 20.2 and pulled down 11.4 rebounds per game. The speedy backcourt of Lionel Hollins (14.7 ppg, 4.1 assists) and Dave Tardzik (10.3 ppg, 3.3 assists) fit perfectly into new head coach Jack Ramsay's team-orientated, pass-the-ball style that had produced a 234-72 record during his 11-year tenure at St. Joseph's College in Pennsylvania.

The Western Conference Finals featured former UCLA legends Bill Walton and Kareem Abdul-Jabbar in head-to-head playoff competition for the first time. The match-up had been expected to overshadow the Championship series, and delivered in some respects. Three of the four games were decided by five or fewer points, and Kareem left little question he deserved his fifth league MVP title, outplaying Walton in every contest. But the rest of the Lakers did not come through for new head coach Jerry West, thus it was the freckled redhead from San Diego who emerged the real winner. Portland dropped the Lakers in four straight and went on to meet Erving's 76ers in the Finals.

"Blazermania," as it was dubbed by fans and media alike, began to cool after Portland lost the first two games in Philadelphia. The final minutes of Game 2 were marred by an ugly brawl reminiscent of the early days of pro basketball; a stare-off led to an exchange of elbows, a grab-and-pull struggle for a rebound, and finally outright blows. The 76ers' Darrel Dawkins threw the first punch, which wound up connecting with teammate Doug Collins when intended target Bob Gross ducked. After Maurice Lucas retaliated with a nasty shot that hit Dawkins from behind, both benches emptied, coaches included, and the war was on. Fans rushed onto the floor, prompting security guards and officials to respond with force as they struggled to gain control. When order was finally restored, Lucas and Dawkins were ejected from the game, which the Sixers went on to win, 107–89. Lucas and Dawkins were fined $2500 by the league.

The Blazers regrouped at home to win Games 3 and 4 by an average of 27 points. The next two games were closer, but Portland won both to take its first NBA title, proving once again that size and power ruled in the world of professional basketball. Walton finished the deciding Game 6 with his best performance of the playoffs, posting totals of 20 points, 8 blocked shots, 7 assists and 23 rebounds on his way to Finals MVP. A disappointed Julius Erving had 40 points for the losers. The Blazers became the first team in the NBA's 31-year history to bounce back from a 0-2 Finals start to win four straight games.[5] Coach Ramsay heaped praise on his team after the win, calling them "the finest people I've ever coached."[6]

Throughout its duration, the ABA had done its best to promote athleticism over bulk and scoring over defense because owners and players genuinely believed that was the type of game basketball fans wanted to see. Slam dunks, length-of-the-court passes, and three-point shots. Brightly colored uniforms and flowing Afro hairstyles. A red, white, and blue ball. A league dedicated to flair, style, and spirit. The longevity of the ABA suggests it was right; the organization had no major television contract and most of its teams played in small market areas, yet it was able to survive nine full seasons.

Whether the NBA recognized the significance of this or not is open to debate, but the fact the league opted not to incorporate the three-point shot or play with a red, white, and blue ball once the merger was complete suggested it had no intention of changing its ways. If anything, the brawl during the 1976 Finals signaled a turning point in the opposite direction. The league was getting rougher, even more dependent on shoving, head slapping, and elbow swinging to determine its champion.

Two major incidents the following season severely damaged the NBA's reputation for years to come. During the opening game between the Lakers and Bucks on October 18, Abdul-Jabbar got in a struggle under the basket with the Bucks' Kent Benson. As the two big men jostled for position, Kareem took exception to Benson's flailing elbows and punched the rookie in the face. Kareem suffered a broken hand that kept him sidelined for the next two months. He was fined $5,000 by the NBA.

The October debacle proved but a warmup to the year's main event. Early in the third quarter of a tight December 9 contest at the Forum, a fight broke out between Lakers power forward Kermit Washington and Houston center Kevin Kunnert. Abdul-Jabbar, back in action and wiser for his October experience, grabbed Kunnert and tried to pull him away before things got out of hand. Meanwhile, Rockets star Rudy Tomjanovich, who had sprinted downcourt expecting to catch a fast break pass on the run, headed back upcourt with the same idea on his mind: break it up, let cooler heads prevail. But Washington broke free and landed a blow that knocked Kunnert to the floor.

When Rudy arrived a second later, Washington met him with a thunderous hard right. Tomjanovich fell backward, hit the back of his head on the floor, and lost consciousness. Blood oozed from his nose and mouth. "I'll never forget that sound," Kareem recalled. "I heard this crack, like a melon landing on concrete."[7] Rudy lay motionless for several minutes; most people in the building feared he was dead. Doctors later compared his injuries to someone being thrown through the windshield of an automobile at 50 mph.

Kermit Washington, already ejected from the game by officials for punching Kunnert, was physically removed from the floor by security.

Amazingly, Tomjanovich eventually regained consciousness and *walked* off the court with the help of Rockets trainer Dick Vandervoort. Back in the locker room, a dazed but furious Rudy had every intention of returning to the game. "If my nose is broken," he told Vandervoort, "hook me up with a mask."[8] Vandervoort called an ambulance. One of the Lakers' doctors arranged for a local head trauma specialist to meet Rudy at the hospital. X-rays taken at the emergency room showed the punch had actually moved the posterior part of Rudy's face an inch out of alignment. Spinal fluid was leaking from his brain. Doctors performed reconstructive surgery on his eye, jaw, and cheek.

The 29-year-old Tomjanovich missed the rest of the season but recovered from his injuries and returned to the Rockets the following year. Although he would never play a full 82-game schedule again, Rudy remained with the Rockets through the 1980-81 season, then went on to become one of the most successful coaches in the NBA. As for Kermit Washington, the league fined him $10,000 — the largest fine in sports history at the time — and suspended him for two months without pay. Shortly thereafter, he was traded to Boston, where he appeared in 32 games for the careening 32-50 Celtics. He spent the next season as a San Diego Clipper, and played three more years in Portland before retiring at the age of 30.

Ironically enough, Commissioner O'Brien had recently set up a committee to explore ways to curb the growing violence in the NBA; the group's first meeting had occurred the previous Monday. Among the ideas discussed was adding a third official. "The players are getting bigger, better, and stronger, and if that's happening then the officiating has to be upgraded," committee member Earl Monroe remarked to the *New York Times.* "They, by their actions, set the example for the tempo of the game." Detroit's Bob Lanier agreed. "The game has gotten too big for two men to handle. Flagrant things don't just happen, they build up. It's only when things get out of hand that people explode like that."[9]

Kareem had weighed in on the problem shortly after breaking his hand, though he felt the trouble was more a product of the NBA's style of play. "As

long as the league continues to view the game as a 'contact' sport, a philosophy which in my view is highly questionable, violent fouls will continue to go
undetected. This philosophy maximizes rather than minimizes the potential
for violent reaction. I've had to learn to play the game as a contact sport —
really, at the expense of playing basketball."[10]

Despite concerns, no immediate action was taken by the league. All told,
41 fistfights were reported during the 1977-78 season.[11] Media critics began comparing the NBA to the much bemoaned NHL. A mainstream editorial on the
subject appeared in the *New York Times.*

It didn't help the league's image that Kermit Washington seemed anything
but remorseful, instead presenting himself as a victim. "I see me being made a
villain all over the country. I see my future going up in an explosion. But on
the newsreels I never see Kunnert hitting me first, which he did ... I may never
play again. It's up to the dictator, O'Brien. I feel like I was walking out to my
car and somebody tried to mug me so I beat him up. Then the police came and
arrested me. So I have to go to prison."[12]

Supporters and lawyers for Washington's defense — he was being sued in
civil court by Tomjanovich and the Rockets— suggested he had been singled
out because of his race; Washington was black, Kunnert and Tomjanovic white.
While such an argument could not be dismissed out of hand, the severity of
Washington's case made it a poor barometer for such a study. Of the before-
mentioned 41 incidents, only Abdul-Jabbar and Tomjanovich suffered serious
injuries. Additionally, Washington had a history of fighting. He had flattened
Buffalo Braves forward John Shumate during a game the previous season and
gotten into an altercation with Celtics' Dave Cowens in another. So where did
the league draw the line, if in fact it drew a line at all? That was the question
haunting Commissioner O'Brien as the controversial 1977-78 season came to
an end.

Fortunately, the league got through the playoffs without a major incident
unraveling on national TV. Neither Philadelphia nor Portland made it back to
the Finals. The defending champion Blazers had gotten off to a roaring 50-10
start, but Walton went down with another foot injury in February and was out
for the rest of the season. Bill attempted a comeback in the playoffs by using a
pain-deadening injection and paid the ultimate price: a break in the navicular
bone above his ankle. Without him, the 58-24 Pacific Division champs lost in
six games to the fourth-place Seattle Sonics (47-35) in the semi-finals, though
Walton did receive a consolation prize by being named the regular season's
MVP. Philadelphia, also winners of its division with a 55-27 record, fell to the
surprising Washington Bullets (44-38) in the Eastern Finals. The Skywalker's
Denver Nuggets made it to the Western Finals but fell to Seattle in six games.

The Sonics–Bullets match-up lacked the superstar power of previous years,
but proved a highly competitive series. Washington was led by Elvin Hayes
and Wes Unseld, two of the NBA's most powerful inside players, and former

Milwaukee Bucks small forward Bobby Dandridge, in the prime of his career at age 30. Seattle had one of the game's best young backcourts with starters Gus Williams and Dennis Johnson and sixth man "Downtown" Freddy Brown coming off the bench. Guided by former player-coach Lenny Wilkens, the Sonics also featured veteran Paul Silas, rookie Jack Sikma, and rising star 7'1" Marvin Webster. The series went seven games and remained close throughout with the exception of Game 6, which the Bullets won 117–82. The Sonics returned home for Game 7, but the Bullets prevailed 105–99, becoming only the third team in NBA history to win a Game 7 Finals on the road. The Bullets' center, 6'7" Wes Unseld, was Finals MVP.

When the year-end numbers came in, it was obvious the ugliness of the regular season had taken a toll. Nationwide, NBA attendance for the year was down some 24,000 fans from the previous season, the first decline since 1961-62. Although the number was relatively small given the total attendance figure of 9,874,155, it was a warning sign owners could not afford to ignore, especially in the wake of rising operating costs. Average player salaries for the year had gone up $13,000 over the year before and were set to increase another $30,000 for the upcoming season. The good news was the league had already negotiated a new four-year contract with CBS worth $74 million, a hefty jump from its previous two-year, $21 million deal.[13]

But time was of the essence. Owners had to heal the wound before the league bled to death, so they slapped on a bandage and prayed it would hold long enough for them to realize a solution. As luck would have it, the answer was just around the corner, tearing up the college nets at Indiana and Michigan State.

SAVIORS

A significant event occurred following the NBA's disastrous 1977-78 season, and the repercussions had a much-needed positive impact on the league for years to come. The reeling Boston Celtics, owners of the number six pick in the 1978 college draft, used it to claim the rights to Larry Bird, an underclassman at Indiana State University. Boston hoped to convince Bird to don a Celtics uniform for the upcoming 1978-79 season but had made its pick knowing there was a strong chance he would remain at Indiana for his senior year. When Larry gave the word he was staying in school, Celtics management took a deep breath. One more year, and the title-heavy Celtics would very likely be on their way to dominance once again.

While no college pick can be considered a surefire success before his skills are tested in the pros, Bird came as close to foolproof as possible. During his three years at Indiana State, Larry led the Sycamores to an 81-13 record, including a 50-1 mark at home. Unlike the majority of truly dominate forces who preceded him in the NBA, the 6'9", 220-pound forward did not possess the height advantage of Chamberlain, Abdul-Jabbar, or Walton, the bulk of Elvin Hayes or Wes Unseld, nor the athleticism and agility of Elgin Baylor or Julius Erving. What he did have was a tireless work ethic and an obsessive desire to win. His philosophy was simple and to the point: "I've got a theory that if you give one hundred percent all of the time, somehow things will work out in the end."[1]

Bird grew up with his sister and four brothers in French Lick, a small town in the heart of Indiana farm country where money was sparse, bills overdue, and basketball a way of life. Larry's mother made her living as a waitress. His father, an alcoholic, was a laborer who toiled at numerous jobs amid frequent binges. Friday nights saw most of the community's 2,000 folks gathered in the gym at Springs Valley High School, watching their team play basketball. Larry sat out much of his sophomore year with a broken ankle, but he emerged as a star the following season, leading his squad to a 19-2 record. It wasn't long before word of Larry's talents spread beyond French Lick. As a senior, he averaged 30 points and 17 rebounds to become Spring Valley's all-time scoring leader and a target for scouts across the nation. Four thousand fans—nearly twice the population of French Lick — showed up to watch him play his final high school game.

The stage was set for Bird to play college ball for the Hoosiers under the guidance of the legendary Bobby Knight, but Larry had difficulty adjusting from small-town life to the big time and dropped out without ever having played a game. He wound up at Northwood Institute, a junior college located near his hometown, but that didn't last either. Larry spent the rest of the year putting his muscles to use as a garbage collector. He hit rock bottom at age 18 when his father lost his fight with the bottle and committed suicide.

Bird might have given up at that point. Instead, he traveled to Terre Haute and enrolled at Indiana State, determined to further his education and play basketball again. Although he concentrated more on academics his first year, Larry averaged his best collegiate numbers as a freshman — 32.8 points, 13.3 rebounds, and 4.4 assists — to lead the Sycamores to a 25-3 season.[2] Game attendance soared. Sales of season tickets tripled. Fellow students began to cut class on game days so they could stand in eight-hour lines to buy tickets.

Larry made the *Sporting News* All American First Team in 1978, the same year he was drafted by the Celtics. His decision to remain in school his senior year paid off with numerous national honors including *Sporting News* College Player of the Year and the prestigious Naismith and John R. Wooden Awards. His accumulative 30.3 ppg average made him the NCAA's fifth all-time leading scorer.[3]

Bird's individual accomplishments certainly warranted Boston's optimism insofar as the future of the Celtics was concerned, but it was his appearance in the 1979 NCAA Championship Game that would prove integral to the NBA itself. The game, a perennial favorite among sports fans, featured a much hyped match-up between Larry's 33-0 Sycamores and the 25-6 Michigan State Spartans.[4] Leading the Spartans was another prominent young talent by the name of Earvin "Magic" Johnson.

Johnson, in his sophomore year at Michigan State, brought his own impressive résumé to the big game: *Sporting News* All American First Team, All-America and All-Big Ten. While his individual numbers (17 points, 8.4 assists, and 7.3 rebounds per game) were not as impressive as Bird's, the 6'9" guard electrified crowds with his unfettered exuberance for the game and his amazing ability to pass the ball to open teammates with a variety of spectacular maneuvers. Putting his skills into perspective, Magic later said of himself: "I don't jump very high, but I jump high enough. I don't shoot very well, but I shoot well enough."[5] Well enough to be drafted number one overall by the Lakers in the 1979 college draft.

The sixth of 10 children, Earvin hailed from Lansing, Michigan, where he spent the majority of his childhood playing basketball at local schoolyards and Boys Clubs. He was often found practicing as early as 7:30 in the morning, and by his own admission, went to bed with a basketball cradled in his arms. His

Larry Bird's arrival in Boston returned the Celtics to the glory years. The tandem of Bird and Magic Johnson (front center) reignited the coast-to-coast rivalry with the Lakers, sticking the NBA with a much-needed shot of adrenalin. Bird led the Celtics to three championships and ten Atlantic Division titles during his 13-year career while averaging 24.3 points, 10 rebounds, and 6.3 assists (Steve Lipofsky Basketballphoto.com).

At 6'9", 255 pounds, Earvin "Magic" Johnson was the tallest point guard to ever play the game. Magic's tremendous talents and overall exuberance for the game helped propel the "Showtime" Lakers to five titles, the first coming in his rookie season (1979-80). Johnson's average of 11.2 assists per game remains tops in the NBA (Steve Lipofsky Basketballphoto.com).

mother was a school custodian and his father a factory laborer at General Motors. Earvin took a blue-collar approach to the game early on, developing skills that made other players around him better. Pistol Pete Maravich was one of his idols. By the time Johnson got to high school, his passing skills were so prolific he became known as Magic, a nickname his Seventh-Day Adventist mother was uncomfortable with because she considered it blasphemous. Fellow players, however, found it quite appropriate. "There have been times when he has thrown passes and I wasn't sure where he was going," future teammate Michael Cooper said. "Then one of our guys catches the ball and scores, and I run back up the floor convinced that he must've thrown it through somebody."[6]

But Magic was not only about passing. At the age of 15, he put the wow into Everett High School by recording a massive triple-double: 36 points, 16 rebounds, and 16 assists. During his senior year at Everett, he averaged 28.8 points and 16.8 rebounds while leading his 27-1 team to the state title. Earvin won numerous national awards as a prep star, including Associated Press, United Press All-State, and McDonald's All-American. Though he could have had his choice of universities, he enrolled in nearby Michigan State to remain near his family. He made an immediate impact on the basketball court, leading the Spartans to a 25-5 record and their first Big Ten championship in 19 years.

When comparing collegiate stats heading into the Big Game, it's easy to see why it was such a highly anticipated match-up. Johnson (17.1 ppg) scored less than Bird (28.6 ppg) but took about half as many shots. Each player shot about 84 percent from the foul line. Magic led in assists at 8.4 per game compared to 5.5 for Larry, while Bird had the edge in rebounding, 14.9 to 7.3. Steals for the season were equal at 75 each.[7]

As is often the case with such an anticipated event, the game itself failed to live up to its billing. The Spartans won rather easily in Salt Lake City that night, 75-64, ending Indiana's bid for an unbeaten season. Bird had a rare off-game, shooting only 7-21 from the floor and 5-8 at the line for a total of 19 points—his lowest output in five tournament contests. After the final buzzer sounded, he put a towel over his face to hide the tears.

Magic led the Spartans with 24 points on 8-15 shooting and 8-10 at the charity stripe, but he was not a one-man show. The Spartans' tough zone defense frustrated Bird from the opening tip. "There was no beating the Michigan State defense during this tournament," wrote Gordon White in the *New York Times*, "and there was little any team could do to stop the fast offense triggered by the magic of Johnson's passing."[8] In addition to Johnson, the Spartans got a stellar game from senior Greg Kelser (19 points, 8 rebounds, 9 assists) and Terry Donnelly (15 points on 5-5 shooting and 5-6 at the line).[9] Michigan shot .605 as a team to Indiana's .42.

"Everyone on our team had roles and performed very well," Kelser said in an interview with the *Tampa Tribune* years later. "I was a good player at

Michigan State before Earvin got there. And I was probably even a better player when he arrived. I think what Earvin taught us was how to be a champion."[10]

The game proved a winner for NBC, drawing an estimated 40 million viewers, the most ever for a college basketball game. The timing could not have been better for the slumping NBA, which had seen its attendance figures drop for the second straight year. Not only were Magic and Larry set to enter the league together for the upcoming 1979-80 season, they would be playing for long-standing rival franchises—Bird with the Celtics and Magic the Lakers. It was the stuff dreams were made of, at least for Commissioner O'Brien.

Hype surrounding collegiate mega-stars had helped revitalize the NBA before, most notably with Chamberlain, Abdul-Jabbar, and Walton. Each player eventually led his respective team to a championship, but none created anything close to a Russell-era dynasty. Chamberlain played eight seasons before securing a title with Philadelphia. Abdul-Jabbar delivered early in Milwaukee, but not until Oscar Robertson joined the line-up; the Lakers had yet to win a title during his tenure in L.A. Walton brought a championship to Portland his third season, but became estranged with the team for the way its doctors handled his injury during the 1978 playoffs and sat out the entire 1978-79 season. He was traded to the Clippers in May 1979, but reinjured the navicular bone in his foot during an exhibition and wound up playing only 14 games in 1979-80.[11]

Expectations for the Bird–Magic age differed greatly. Neither was a big man expected to dominate the game with a physical presence in the middle. Rather, they would arrive in the NBA as *complimentary* players, expected to make their existing teammates better. It had taken 30 years, but the essence of Dr. Naismith's game had finally found its way to the NBA.

Nearly as important to the league was the newcomers' style off the basketball court, as there was much more to the Larry–Magic story than statistics alone. Both had similar backgrounds: they grew up in large Midwestern families with meager, two-parent incomes. Nothing came easy for either, yet each was driven to his own sense of perfection. The two shared a simplistic philosophy in regard to achieving that goal: practice makes perfect. Finally, they chose to further their educations, learning the importance of structure and teamwork via the collegiate game. In a nutshell, Magic Johnson and Larry Bird epitomized everything the NBA *wanted* its league to represent.

Alas, nothing is ever perfect. While pro basketball had long abandoned race as an issue — by 1980, more than 80 percent of NBA players were black — it would be naive to assume the same was true of sports fans across the nation. Of the four major pro sports—basketball, football, baseball, and hockey—only basketball featured such a lopsided racial composition in favor of African Americans. Naysayers who feared such a disparity would cause repercussions at the box office pointed to the recent decrease in league attendance as proof their claim had merit. Some players fueled the argument themselves by siding with

Kermit Washington, suggesting he would not have been treated as harshly by the league for causing the injuries to Rudy Tomjanovich had both men been white.

Fans who chose to align themselves on either side of such issues were quick to stamp a racial emphasis on the Bird–Magic rivalry. Some went so far as to refer to Larry as "the Great White Hope," a reference to Jim Jeffries, the retired heavyweight champ coaxed out of retirement in 1910 by racist whites with the explicit hope he could defeat world title-holder Jack Johnson, an African American. As stated earlier, Johnson's victory incited a wave of racial violence, prompting some Congressmen to push for a ban on the sport. Boxing survived of course, but its image remained tarnished for many years.

Fortunately for the NBA, whatever racial overtones focused on Magic vs. Bird did not reflect negatively on the league. Most hoops fans, black and white, wanted to see Bird flourish with the Celtics and Magic revitalize the Lakers for the good of the game. Likewise, the NBA eagerly awaited the positive media attention its high-profile, cross-country rookies would generate. Publicity wise, the battered league needed all the help it could get. Cable television was still in its infancy. ESPN, billing itself as the Total Sports Network, launched in September 1979 and relied on college and amateur sports to fill its early programming schedule. The pro game remained dependent on network television, newspapers, and word of mouth to draw fans to arenas. As expected, Magic and Larry delivered on all fronts. Johnson's exuberant smile and Bird's diligent, blue-collar work ethic symbolized exactly the type of role models Commissioner O'Brien wanted to present to the general public so it would once again view the NBA as wholesome, family entertainment.

Naturally the addition of its two prize rookies remained the focus of the NBA's 1979-80 season, but the league also incorporated several new rules that had an immediate impact on the game. By far the most important of these was the three-point field goal. Owners had been going back and forth on the idea for years and remained divided as to whether it would add anything to the game short of desperation shots at the end of quarters. But others saw its obvious potential: a way to move scoring away from the basket, thus encouraging and rewarding less physical play. Another proposal that had remained on the fence for several years — adding a third official — was approved on a trial basis. In an attempt to increase local rivalries, schedules were realigned so that teams within the same division played each other more often.

The three-point shot did not live up to its hype that first year, at least insofar as shooting percentage was concerned, but Magic and Larry more than delivered on their end.

Boston saw the most dramatic improvement of any team in NBA history. Cellar dwellers the previous season at 29-53, it won the Atlantic Division with a league best 61-21 record, a 32-game jump.[12] Bird joined third-year man Cedric Maxwell and longtime veteran Dave Cowens on the Celtics frontline. The "small" rookie forward contributed 21.3 points, 4.5 assists, and 10.4 rebounds per game for the Celtics. The men in green swept Houston in the semifinals, winning by an average of 18.5 points per game, but ran out of gas when they got to the Conference Finals and fell to Philadelphia in five.

Although Los Angeles had never sunk to the abyss of its Boston rival, the acquisition of Abdul-Jabbar had not returned the Lakers to championship status either. Magic's arrival was expected to change that, and the 20-year-old from Michigan showed no sign of disappointing. The Lakers improved from 47-35 to 60-22 and disposed of their Western playoff opponents, Phoenix and Seattle, with consecutive 4-1 series victories. Kareem, finally playing with a talented passer again, won league MVP for the sixth time, surpassing Bill Russell's previous record of five. The Lakers had not made it to the Finals since Abdul-Jabbar's arrival in 1975-76. Its last appearance had been as defending champs in 1973, a series they lost 4-1 to the Knicks.

The 76ers squad that took Walton's Trail Blazers to six games in 1977 remained basically intact less George McGinnis, who had moved on to Denver. The high-flying Julius Erving (26.9 points, 7.4 rebounds, 4.6 assists) was still in near prime form at age 29, but the 76ers were hardly a one-man show. Darrel Dawkins and Caldwell Jones had matured into solid frontline players, averaging a combined 22 points and 20.6 rebounds per game, while former ABA defensive specialist Bobby Jones gave the team a lift off the bench. The 76ers also featured second-year Maurice Cheeks, who was fast evolving into one of the league's best point guards under the tutelage of Coach Billy Cunningham. (All Star guard Doug Collins was still on the team, but a knee injury kept him out of the playoffs.)

Likewise, L.A. was more than Kareem (24.8 points, 10.8 rebounds, 4.5 assists) and Magic (18 points, 7.2 rebounds, 7.3 assists). The club's supporting cast featured one of the game's top small forwards in Jamaal (formerly Keith) Wilkes, then in his third year with the Lakers. Norm Nixon started beside Magic in the backcourt, but Johnson often moved to power forward to make room for sixth man Michael Cooper. Together, the threesome averaged nearly 44 points and 18 assists per game. Veterans Spencer Haywood and Jim Chones helped Abdul-Jabbar upfront.

The much-anticipated series was a draw after four, with each club having secured a victory on its opponent's court. Game 5 in Los Angeles lived up to pregame hype with a nail-biter that saw the home team up by two as the third quarter wound down. But then the unexpected happened: Kareem twisted an ankle and headed for the locker room amid a suddenly hushed Forum crowd. Fans relaxed as he returned in the fourth quarter to score 14, giving him 40 points on the night, including the go-ahead basket with 33 seconds remaining on the clock.

Abdul-Jabbar's heroics proved costly, however; he was unavailable for Game 6 in Philadelphia two nights later. When Coach Westhead asked Magic to take over at center, a position Earvin had not played since high school, the rookie assured him it would be no problem. "Never fear," he told anxious teammates on the flight to Philly, "E.J. is here."[13]

No one gave the Lakers a chance on the opponents' court without Kareem — no one except a confident young rookie named Magic Johnson. Earvin switched from center to forward to guard throughout the game, depending on what the team needed at any particular time — a position he would later refer to as CFG Rover. When the final buzzer sounded, the Rover had scored a game-high 42 points, including 14 for 14 at the free throw line and 9 straight down the stretch to seal a 123–107 Laker win. "Amazing," Erving said of Magic's game. "Unreal."[14] An impressed Doug Collins added, "I knew he was good, but I never realized he was great."[15] Johnson played 47 of the game's 48 minutes. His line included 7 assists, 3 steals, a blocked shot, and 15 rebounds, earning him a spot in NBA history as the first rookie to win Finals MVP. His game that night is often referred to as the best single performance in NBA Finals history. After the game, a smiling Earvin said of his achievement: "If it weren't for the big fella, we wouldn't even be here."[16] Speaking directly into the camera, Magic encouraged Kareem, who had watched the game on television from his home in L.A., to go out and do a little dancing to celebrate.

And so it was a happy ending for the 1979-80 NBA season. Magic and Bird had supplied the initial breath of fresh air the embattled league had been gasping at for years. But experienced owners knew one successful season did not ensure a rebirth for professional basketball. As the league entered its fifth decade, the question on everyone's mind was, could it last?

GLORY DAYS

As the 1980s got under way, it was as if the NBA had received a new lease on life. The ugliness that had peaked with the Kermit Washington–Rudy Tomjanovich incident was a distant memory in most fans' eyes, relegated to the shadows of the Magic Johnson and Larry Bird show. The same media that had bombarded the NBA with merciless negative attacks was in Commissioner O'Brien's corner again, singing hallelujahs from coast to coast. Pro basketball was on the verge of a major breakout.

Alas, on the verge was where it remained. Despite the public's enthusiastic reaction to the league's newest stars, such interest did not translate into a ratings surge for CBS. The 1980 Lakers–Philadelphia series posted a disappointing 8.0 percent in the Nielsen ratings, up a mere .8 from the superstar-less Seattle–Washington Finals the previous year.[1] Given how ratings for the 1979 NCAA Championship Game had exceeded all expectations, CBS's situation was perplexing. Doubts as to whether Johnson and Bird could be instant impact players on the professional court had been laid to rest early in the season. Bird's Celtics were the most improved team in league history, and Magic's Lakers were in the Finals. Johnson's enthusiastic, from-the-heart smile was the stuff cereal box covers were made for.

So why weren't viewers tuning in? Numerous arguments could be explored, but the most obvious was a lack of marketing. When comparing the lowest rated Finals in league history, the 1980 series ranks a dismal third.[2] All six games were televised by CBS, but not one was shown in prime time. This when the league had such high-caliber stars as Abdul-Jabbar, Magic, and Dr. J gracing its courts. Although Erving may have been slightly past his prime, he could still draw his share of oohs and aahs while soaring through the air toward the hoop. Thirty-three-year-old Abdul-Jabbar remained the most dominant player in the game, having won his sixth league MVP, a new record, and Magic was, well, *magic*. Established NBA fans knew all of this, of course. And perhaps that was Commissioner O'Brien's thinking: it was unnecessary to promote the 1980 Finals because everybody knew what a great series it would be.

But the fact was that everyone *didn't* know. And neither O'Brien nor CBS executives took it upon themselves to enlighten Joe Public. Aside from a few 30-second ads scattered throughout the network's regular, primetime schedule, little was done to publicize the games in a way that would make average viewers, aka nonfans, curious enough to tune in — especially given how evening games would be shown via *tape delay* at 11:30 p.m.

The NBA's television season had come a long way since 1953-54, when DuMont paid $39,000 for the rights to show 13 games. CBS was in the midst of a four-year, $74 million deal. Additionally, the beginning of the Bird–Magic era had kicked off the league's first cable venture, a three-year contract with the USA Network worth $1.5 million.[3] USA, formerly known as the Madison Square Garden Network, was no stranger to sports programming or innovation; it was one of the first national networks to broadcast via satellite.

Bottom line, the league had all the marketing tools necessary to make the NBA a primetime player in the world of professional sports, yet it failed to utilize them to full potential. Perhaps owners should have taken a cue from their former adversaries; for more than a decade, ABA owners had kept their league operating on a shoestring budget. Be it wild-colored uniforms, high-flying slam dunk contests, or eye-catching red, white, and blue balls, the ABA had always realized the importance of marketing its product. Free tickets, promotional give-aways, and media events such as the hugely successful slam dunk contest at halftime during the 1976 All Star Game had dominated the league's fan-friendly era.

Most NBA owners believed the need for such acts of desperation, if indeed there had ever been any, had passed with the dissolution of the ABA. Following a two-year decline, attendance during Magic and Bird's inaugural season had risen about 2 percent across the board; hardly numbers to brag about, but it did suggest fans were willing to give the league another chance. So confident were owners that their newest superstar duo would prove a fix-all for the NBA that they nixed their experiment with three officials and returned to two for the upcoming 1980-81 season. Several small rules changes also took effect in what marked the league's 35th anniversary. The 24-second clock would no longer be reset following a technical foul on the offensive team; 20-second "injury" timeouts were eliminated; one regular 20-second timeout per half was added; red lights were installed on backboards and synchronized with the game horn to signal the end of quarters.

Lest there be any doubt the NBA had no intention of mirroring the ABA's flamboyant image, players would now be forbidden from wearing jewelry of any kind on court (which the league cited as a safety issue), and the staple leather game ball would undergo a color change from basic brown to dull orange.

The league's strategy to rely solely on the Bird and Magic show hit a snag in year two when the Lakers point man suffered a cartilage tear in his knee and wound up missing much of the regular season. Johnson returned in time for the playoffs, but the Lakers never reached peak form, losing to Moses Malone's Houston Rockets in the first round.

Luckily for the league, it was quite a different story in the East, where Bird's Celtics had made big changes in the off-season. GM Red Auerbach had acquired seven-foot veteran center Robert Parish in a trade with Golden State and drafted power forward Kevin McHale, giving the Celtics one of the best frontlines in the game. Boston tied Philadelphia's league best 62-20 regular season record and went on to beat the 76ers in the Conference Finals in a tight seven-game series before going on to squash the Rockets in the Finals, four games to two. If there was a downside for Bird, it was his failure to duplicate Magic's feat of winning Finals MVP, an honor that went to the Celtics' starting power forward Cedric Maxwell. Larry had his share of trouble against his Houston counterpart, Robert Reid, posting consecutive subpar scoring efforts in Games 3, 4, and 5 (8, 8, and 12 points, respectively), but none of that mattered in the end. "We're the champions," Bird said in the locker room after winning Game 6.[4] The champions for an NBA record 14 times.

Title score: Magic one, Bird one. What made the rivalry between the two stars all the more compelling was the fact that it was not the result of a phony competition dreamed up by the league to sell tickets, it was the *real deal*. Not since Russell–Chamberlain had the NBA had two such ferocious competitors who lived to play ball against each other. The fact that Bird and Magic played different positions and thus were not directly matched up against each other, except for an occasional switch on defense, did nothing to diminish the drama.

"When the new schedule would come out each year, I'd grab it and circle the Boston games," Magic later related. "To me it was The Two and the other 80 (games). During the season I'd check out Larry's line first thing. If he had a triple double, I knew what I'd want that night. But what would get me would be his big ones—say, when he had 20 rebounds. I'd say, 'I'd better get me 20 assists tonight.'" Bird: "The first thing I would do every morning during the season was look at the box scores to see what Magic did. I didn't care about anything else."[5]

Naturally, the rivalry encompassed both teams as well as the sports-minded population of their respective cities, a factor that would be more than enough to carry the NBA to ratings stardom in today's age of ferocious 24-hour media coverage and multimillion-dollar advertising campaigns. But such was not the case in the early '80s. While a few athletes had product endorsement deals, it was not the norm for players to earn more from those contracts than they did for playing the game. Julius Erving was among the first big name NBA players to land a shoe deal. "Dr. J's" were manufactured by Converse in 1981, but the company did little to promote them to the general public. Even when Converse added Bird and Magic to the list, no one within the business seemed to realize what they had. Company execs reportedly told Johnson not to expect too much publicity out of the deal because "a player will never sell shoes."[6]

Converse would soon learn how wrong it was.

Bird and company finished the year with a league-best 63 wins, but lost to the 76ers in the Conference Finals. In the West, Magic's 57-25 Lakers, enriched by the addition of three-time scoring champ Bob McAdoo, swept playoff opponents Phoenix and San Antonio to set up a Finals rematch with Philadelphia. The Lakers prevailed in six, giving new head coach Pat Riley his first NBA title from the bench.[7] Magic won his second Finals MVP in as many tries.

Score: Magic two, Bird one.

Attendance had declined again for the 1981-82 season, making the NBA ever more dependent on television revenues to survive. Fortunately, things looked good on that end. Despite the low Finals ratings, CBS renewed its contract for another four years to the tune of a whopping $91.9 million — up $17.9 million from the previous deal.[8] Rising star ESPN, fast becoming the largest draw on standard cable TV, jumped into the fray with a two-year contract. Coupled with a renewal from the USA Network, the league would reap an additional $11 million from its cable contracts over the next two years.[9]

It would need every penny. Average player salaries had reached $246,000 heading into the 1982-83 season.[10] In addition, the league was shelling out some $80 to $90 million in deferred payments to former players as stipulated by the last collective bargaining agreement. The league's weakest teams, San Diego, Cleveland, and Kansas City, were on the verge of collapse. The Clippers, in the midst of the disastrous Bill Walton trade repercussions, pulled in a league-low 4,344 fans per contest, more than 6,200 below the league average of 10,567.[11] Overall, 17 of the league's 23 teams were in the red.[12]

The Players Union, now headed by Bob Lanier, was not oblivious to the situation. Neither side wanted to see NBA players out of work. So, as the media fueled rumors of a possible player strike midway through the season, Lanier and Commissioner O'Brien sat down together and negotiated a new, groundbreaking three-year agreement that gave both sides something to smile about. Owners got a salary cap in exchange for a guarantee that players would receive 53 percent to 57 percent of the league's gross revenues. The percentage would include gate receipts as well as radio and TV revenues from all preseason, regular, and postseason games. Players would receive an addition $500,000 in licensing revenue and a further guarantee that the league would retain a minimum of 253 players regardless of whether all current teams remained in operation.[13]

The new deal averted the negative publicity that would have accompanied a strike, allowing the 1982-83 season to end on a positive note. In on-court activity, Bird's Celtics had trouble with Philadelphia for the second straight year, finishing a full nine games behind the 76ers in the Atlantic Division and losing to Milwaukee 0-4 in the second round. Meanwhile Erving's squad, frustrated by its failure to win a title in three tries, had finally snared the missing piece by luring free agent center Moses Malone away from Houston during the off-season. The one-two superstar punch of Erving (21.4 points, 6.8 rebounds) and Malone (24.5 points, 15.3 rebounds) propelled the talented Sixers to a league-best 65-17 record heading into the playoffs.

In the West, Magic's Lakers had improved as well with the addition of number one draft pick James Worthy, a smooth 6'9" forward out of North Carolina.[14] Worthy helped L.A. win its third Pacific Division title in four years, but broke his leg in the final week of the regular season, leaving the team riddled with injuries as it headed into postseason play. Neither point guard Norm Nixon nor high-scoring reserve Bob McAdoo was at full strength for the playoffs. Nonetheless, the Lakers made it out of the West, beating the Spurs in six games to earn another trip to the Finals.

But it was Philadelphia's year. The 76ers lost only one game en route to the Finals and swept the short-handed Lakers in four straight to capture their first title in the Erving era. Moses Malone won both the regular season and Finals MVP. Bobby Jones was named Sixth Man of the Year, and the Doctor added a much-deserved Walter Kennedy Citizenship Award to his first NBA title. Like Bird and Magic, Erving represented the type of presence and the character the league wanted to be about. "I've always tried to tell myself that the work itself is the thing, that win, lose, or draw, the work is really what counts.... As hard as it was to make myself believe that sometimes, it was the only thing I had to cling to each year — that every game, every night, I did the best I could."[15]

So too had Commissioner O'Brien, who retired midway through the 1983-84 season. The league gave him quite a stylish sendoff with the introduction of All Star Saturday at Denver's McNichols Arena on January 28. The day's proceedings featured a contest between former NBA legends in the Schick Legends Classic, and, straight from the archives of the ABA's last hurrah, a slam dunk contest. Ironically, McNichols had also played host to the ABA affair in 1976, which had come down to a two-way duel between Julius Erving and the Nuggets' hometown Skywalker, David Thompson. Erving won that one, and remained the favorite going into the 1984 competition. Thompson, who had moved on to Seattle, did not compete.

Joining the Doctor for the NBA's dunking debut were Dominique Wilkins (Hawks), Darrel Griffith (Jazz), Larry Nance (Suns), Clyde Drexler (Trail Blazers), Michael Cooper (Lakers), Orlando Woolridge (Bulls), Ralph Sampson (Rockets), and Edgar Jones (Spurs). The event consisted of three levels with each player required to make three dunks per round. A panel of judges rated the dunks, which were worth from 1 to 50 points each. The 33-year-old Erving made it to the finals but lost out to the Suns' third-year man, Larry Nance, despite posting a perfect score of 50 with his last dunk.[16]

Erving scored a game-high 34 points the next afternoon in the All Star Game, leading the East to a 154–145 overtime victory, but it was the Pistons' young point guard, 22-year-old Isiah Thomas, who took home the MVP with 15 assists and 21 points. Magic broke his own assist record from the previous year's game, recording an astounding 22 assists in the West's loss.[17]

Three days later, Commissioner O'Brien's retirement became official. His successor, 41-year-old David Stern, brought with him a longtime history with the NBA, having first served as an outside counsel to the league in 1966 while working at the Proksauer Rose law firm in New York. The Columbia Law School graduate took over as the NBA's General Counsel two years later, and became the league's executive vice president in 1980. Stern's legal training was of paramount interest to owners, and understandably so, given the state of the league. "The '70s and '80s were places where there was a lot of confrontation in sports," the Commissioner recalled during an interview years later. "If you look across the landscape, everything seemed to be about confrontation, litigation and the like. The relationships between the teams and the leagues, between the players and the leagues, between the leagues and the cities ... there was a lot of agitation."[18]

Asked whether his lack of an extensive basketball background had been a hurdle, Stern responded:

> I think that, today, if the consultants came down and deconstructed the industry, they would say that it's now no different than any other CEO. You've got to understand the league, the structure, the referees, etc., but the president of (General Motors) is not necessarily an engineer that knows how to construct cars. But he better damn well know people that can and have a big interest in them. Obviously everyone would tell you that the car is at the core of GM's business.... But, to me, the most important part (of my job) is to make sure you protect the game, that you don't change it radically and try to keep it away from bad influences.[19]

The latter would prove Stern's biggest challenge. He tackled the issue quickly by instilling a groundbreaking antidrug policy — the first in all of professional sports. Under the guidelines, any player who tested positive for illegal substances during a drug screen would be expelled from the NBA, his contract legally voided. Exceptions were made if a player came forward and admitted his problem, in which case the league paid for treatment.

Drugs played a key role in Seattle's decision to waive Skywalker David Thompson at the end of the 1984 season. The former All Star, a shadow of himself at age 29, had battled alcohol and cocaine addictions throughout most of his professional career. "I had the ability to be one of the greatest basketball players in the history of the game, and I blew it,"[20] he later admitted. Substance abuse was also the downfall of one of the era's top point guards, John Lucas, who had been one of few points ever drafted number one (1976). "Our society went through a craze in the late '70s and early '80s that said that drugs were not addictive, and I was caught up in that," Lucas acknowledged, "only to find out how damaging it is to a person. Our League was terribly impacted until it got cleaned up, for which David Stern deserves a lot of credit."[21] Not all affected players joined Lucas's chorus, but the policy quickly became the envy of other professional sports leagues.

Stern's on-court tenure also began with a bang insofar as postseason play was concerned. Sensing the need for further exposure during what many considered the NBA's "real" season, Stern expanded the number of teams that made the playoffs from 12 to 16. The new format extended the first-round best-of-three mini-series, which had been faulted for allowing inferior teams to advance on a fluke, to best of fives. The realignment also called for division winners, previously afforded a first-round bye, to participate in every round. The latter was a brilliant marketing move as it afforded the league additional exposure for its elite teams. Twenty-seven more first-round games were played than the previous year, all of which translated into extra box office receipts. The second, third, and fourth (Finals) rounds remained best-of-seven series, but generated greater interest because more fans had been drawn into first-round play.

The new commissioner could not have dreamed of a better welcoming gift than the 1984 Finals: Lakers vs. Celtics. Five years had passed since basketball fans watched Bird and Magic compete against each other in the 1979 NCAA Championship game, but the rivalry in each player's respective camps remained alive and well. Although Bird had edged out his challenger for Rookie of the Year in 1980, Magic had two NBA titles to Bird's one and two Finals MVPs to Bird's none. Suffice it to say, the two Lakers–Celtics regular season games were among the most anticipated of the year for players and fans alike. Stern realized the opportunity to watch two such competitive stars battle for an NBA title was a hoops dream come true. "When you have the Number 1 and Number 2 teams meeting in a championship, that's terrific," he said. "And when you have the tradition of Boston and L.A. and the great stars these two teams have, it's almost more than we should be permitted to hope for."[22]

To call it a match for the ages did not overstate. The two clubs had last met during the 1969 Finals, a heated, seven-game affair that saw Boston win by two points on the Lakers home court. Since then, each team had won three titles. Although no active players from the 1969 series were present on either roster, historical connections remained. The head coaches were former players— Pat Riley for the Lakers and K. C. Jones for Boston. Red Auerbach still ran the Celtics front office, and Jerry West called the shots for the Lakers.

Suffice it to say, there was no love lost between the two franchises, their cities, or their fans. "Hatred would be a strong word," James Worthy said, reminiscing about the rivalry. "We really respected each other.... We knew we were equally talented and we knew that we balanced each other out on the floor, and there had to be an edge."[23] Whether that edge would prove to be Magic or Bird was the question on most people's minds as the series got under way.

The Celtics held home-court advantage with 62 regular season wins to the Lakers' 54, but Los Angeles came into the series on a roll, having racked up an 11-3 playoff record. Boston coach K. C. Jones told anyone who would listen that the Lakers were the more talented team, but the fact was both rosters were amazingly deep. Laker superstars Kareem, Magic, and Worthy were complimented by the likes of Byron Scott, Michael Cooper, Bob McAdoo, and Jamaal Wilkes. Bird shared the spotlight with Cedric Maxwell, Robert Parish, Kevin McHale, Dennis Johnson, Gerald Henderson, and Danny Ainge. All would play pivotal roles as the series progressed.

Despite all the hype surrounding Bird and Magic, Game 1 in Boston Garden belonged to the Lakers captain, 37-year-old Abdul-Jabbar. Having battled a migraine earlier in the day, Kareem bounced back to deliver a stellar performance of 32 points, 5 assists, 8 rebounds, and 2 blocks en route to a 115–109 Lakers victory. Game 2 looked to be heading toward a similar outcome with Worthy leading the charge; Bird's counterpart hit for 29 points on 11 of 12 shooting to give the Lakers a come-from-behind two-point lead with 18 seconds to play. McHale missed two free throws that would have tied the game, but Irish luck won out when Worthy threw an ill-advised pass on the next play that resulted in a Celtics steal and layup by Gerald Henderson. Riding momentum, Boston prevailed in overtime, 124–121.

At a packed Forum three days later, Magic's triple-double set the tone for the afternoon. Johnson had 14 points, 11 rebounds, and a Finals record 21 assists while leading his team to an impressive 137–104 win. Afterward, a disgusted Larry Bird said the Celtics had played like a bunch of sissies. "I know the heart and soul of this team, and today the heart wasn't there, that's for sure. I can't believe a team like this would let L.A. come out and push us around like they did."[24] When asked what his team needed to bounce back in Game 4, Larry quipped, "Twelve heart transplants."[25]

Bird's blunt remarks changed the dynamics of the series, beginning with Game 4. While Larry's individual performance of 29 points and 21 rebounds did its share of damage, it was the Celtics' response to their leader's sissy remark that stole the series' momentum. The tone was set in the second quarter, when Kevin McHale clotheslined Lakers forward Kurt Rambis on a breakaway layin. The game grew more physical from that point, and the Celtics eventually won it in overtime, knotting the series at two-all.

Game 5 returned to Boston, which was in the midst of a 90-degree heat wave. The temperature inside the non-air conditioned Garden was a stuffy 97 degrees at tip-off. The Lakers had oxygen tanks on the sidelines. Referee Hugh Evans left the game at halftime suffering from dehydration. Kareem would later describe the playing conditions as akin to "running in mud."[26] Bird, on the other hand, didn't understand what all the fuss was about. "We used to play in conditions like that back home all summer. The heat just loosened me up."[27] Indeed, while his teammates cooled off on the bench with a portable fan, Larry stung the Lakers for 34 points and 17 rebounds en route to a 121–103 victory and 3-2 lead heading back to L.A.

The Celtics started strong in Game 6 and held a four-point lead at the start of the final 12 minutes, but the Lakers pulled away in the stretch and coasted to a 119–108 win. Fittingly, the first Magic–Bird championship would be decided by a single game.

Eighteen years had passed since the last Lakers–Celtics Game 7 match-up at Boston Garden. The Celtics had prevailed in that one 95-93, giving coach Red Auerbach a fitting sendoff as he moved to the front office. Boston fans were confident in their team's ability to get the job done again, and with good reason: the Celtics had never lost a Game 7 in the championship round — at home or on the road. Laker fans, meanwhile, were hopeful 1984 would be the year their club would finally get the monkey of its back. Seven times the Lakers had met the Celtics in the Finals, and seven times it had lost, three of those losses coming in the deciding seventh game.

It is unlikely Commissioner Stern would have dared to dream of such a finale to wrap up his inaugural season. "It's like the opening of a great play," Jerry West told reporters. "Everyone's waiting to see it."[28] In Bean Town, fans were so keyed up that the Lakers needed a police escort from their hotel to Boston Garden. It didn't get any easier once the game was under way. The Celtics, led by Cedric Maxwell's pregame promise to carry the team on his back, took it to the visitors from the opening tip. A tough inside game and suffocating defense on Magic put the Lakers down by 14 points in the second half, but Kareem and company refused to fold. With less than two minutes left in the fourth quarter, the Lakers were within three and had possession of the ball. Magic spotted Worthy under the basket, but before he could get off the pass, Maxwell slapped the ball free. The Celtics recovered. Dennis Johnson was fouled and nailed both free throws to give the Celtics a five-point lead. Another Boston steal led to two Bird free throws. When the red light came on, the scoreboard read 111–102 Celtics, and Boston had its 15th NBA title.

True to his word, Maxwell delivered a stellar performance with 8 rebounds, 8 assists, and 24 points. Dennis Johnson, who had harassed Magic at every turn for the fourth straight game, finished with 22, including 12 for 12 at the free throw line. Magic had a game-high 15 assists to go with 16 points, but turned the ball over 7 times. Kareem led the Lakers with 29 points.[29] Over the series, the Lakers outscored the Celtics 823–806, making 51.4 percent of its shots for a new NBA Finals record. In contrast, Boston connected on only 44.2 percent of its shots, but won the rebounding battle, 337–301.[30]

Bird had 12 rebounds and 20 points in the deciding game. For the series, he averaged 27.4 points, 14 rebounds, 2 steals, and 3.2 assists — good enough to win his first Finals MVP. Magic's corresponding numbers came in at 18.1 points, 7.7 rebounds, and 13.6 assists. Just as some had questioned whether Abdul-Jabbar should have been the 1982 series MVP instead of Magic, many felt the Celtics would not have won the series without Dennis Johnson's steady defense on Magic during the last four games. Nonetheless, Bird had played the entire series without one subpar game, posting subsequent totals of 24, 27, 30, 29, 34,

28, and 20 points. Dennis Johnson had two below average performances back-to-back in Games 2 and 3 — 10 points and 2 assists, and 4 points and 1 assist, respectively.[31]

"We worked hard for this," Bird said in the locker room afterwards. "Anybody gonna say we didn't earn it?"[32]

"The best team won," Kareem admitted.[33]

In reality, it was the entire league that came out a winner. Some 40 million viewers had tuned in to watch Game 7, which was broadcast by CBS in prime time with no tape delay. The show finished with a 19.3 Nielsen rating, the best ever for an NBA game.[34]

Commissioner Stern seemed like the right man for the right job at the right time. After decades of instability, pro basketball was on a steady rise. Attendance surpassed 10 million for the first time in league history. The Lakers–Celtics rivalry was back and would only get better as Magic and Bird continued to improve.

Of course NBA owners had seen good times before, only to have them fade into a hazy sunset. The reality was that the league needed more than two good teams and two superstars to solidify its position in the world of professional sports. Fortunately, help was on the way via a 21-year-old Tar Heel by the name of Michael Jordan.

THE GREATEST SHOW ON EARTH

The 1984 college draft proved one of the most talent-laden in NBA history. Nigerian-born Hakeem Olajuwon, a seven-footer from the University of Houston, became the first foreign player to be drafted number one when he was selected by the Rockets. In a move that would prompt thousands of what-ifs for years to come, the Portland Trail Blazers opted for big man Sam Bowie at number two, allowing the next team — the Chicago Bulls — to claim Michael Jordan with the third pick. Forward-center Sam Perkins, a teammate of Jordan's at North Carolina, was drafted fourth by the Dallas Mavericks. The Philadelphia 76ers selected Charles Barkley with number five. Going to the Utah Jazz at number 16 was John Stockton. All would have lengthy, productive careers in the NBA. Most would reach All Star status. One would soar to heights never before witnessed in the world of sports — professional or otherwise.

All of that would take time, of course. Fortunately, thanks to Bird, Magic, and Stern, it was time the league could well afford. Heading into the 1984-85 season, owners had much to feel good about. The television medium had finally begun to pay dividends. The Lakers–Celtics Finals had been a ratings hit for CBS in prime time, and the league still had two years left on the lucrative deal. No sooner had the $11 million contact with USA–ESPN expired than cable's newest star on the block, Turner Broadcasting Systems (TBS) came knocking with a two-year $20 million agreement.[1] Basketball, once the laughingstock of the professional sports world, was suddenly the envy of its peers.

From a talent standpoint, the league was growing beyond the Bird and Magic Show. Isiah Thomas, a multitalented 6'1" point guard in his fourth year with the Pistons, was the East's answer to Magic Johnson. Thomas had orchestrated the East's comeback win in overtime at the 1984 All Star Game, scoring all 21 of his points in the second half while dishing out 15 assists. The Portland Trail Blazers' second-year guard Clyde Drexler was exciting northwest fans with his athletic, showy play to the tune of 17.2 points, 6 rebounds, and 5.5 assists per game. Down in Houston, 1984 Rookie of the Year Ralph Sampson, by far the league's tallest player at 7'4", continued to improve as he shared the frontcourt with the Rockets' second consecutive number one draft pick, Ola-juwon. The "Twin Towers" as the two became known, averaged a combined 42.7 points and 22.3 rebounds for the season. In New York, sharp shooter Bernard King helped Knicks fans through another dismal season by scoring a league-best 32.9 points per game.

While all these players contributed to the NBA's growing popularity, the buzz of the 1984-85 regular season was centered in Chicago, where Bulls fans had begun to grasp the potential of their team's latest first-round draft pick from North Carolina.

Michael Jeffrey Jordan, the fourth child of Delores and James, was born in Brooklyn on February 17, 1963, but the family moved to Wilmington, North Carolina, a few years later so it was Tar Heel country Michael called home.[2] His father worked for General Electric, and his mother was employed by a local bank.

As with most boys growing up in the pre-video game days, Michael and his brothers spent countless hours outside playing sports. Michael shared a deep passion for baseball with his father; together, they dreamed of Michael playing in the major leagues someday. But it was on the basketball court where the talents of James's youngest son would be discovered. Michael honed his early skills by playing one-on-one against his taller, bulkier brother Larry, and used the lopsided losses as motivation to improve.

Young Jordan received further incentive during his sophomore year at Laney High School when he was cut from the varsity basketball squad. "When-ever I was working out and got tired and figured I ought to stop, I'd close my eyes and see that list in the locker room without my name on it," he revealed years later, "and that usually got me going again."[3] Jordan's determination, paired with a four-inch growth spurt, did the trick the following year. He made the varsity squad and played well enough that he was invited to attend the Five-Star Basketball Camp in Pittsburgh over the summer.[4] The organization's claim, "To eat, breathe and live basketball there is only one place to be!" proved on the mark for the 17-year-old Jordan, who would later refer to it as "the turn-ing point in my life."[5]

Jordan's play improved enough during his senior year at Laney to earn him All American honors and a scholarship from the University of North Car-olina, where he would play under the tutelage of the legendary Dean Smith. Jordan was inserted into the starting line-up from the get-go—only one of 10 freshmen ever afforded such an honor under Smith's tenure.[6] Playing alongside such talented Tar Heels as upperclassmen Sam Perkins and James Worthy, Michael often became lost in the crowd. Still, he more than pulled his weight during the team's NCAA Finals appearance against Georgetown, scoring 16 points, including the go-ahead basket to give the Tar Heels a 63-62 win for the school's third national title.

Few will argue that His Airness was the best basketball player ever, but Michael Jordan was about more than basketball. In addition to his enormous on-court accomplishments, MJ transcended sports and race to become the most popular and recognizable figure of his time (Steve Lipofsky Basketballphoto.com).

Michael finished the season as the 1982 Atlantic Coast Conference (ACC) Rookie of the Year, the first of many national awards. His reputation as a last-minute savior in big games continued through his sophomore and junior years, earning him back-to-back *Sporting News* National Player of the Year, first-team All ACC, and All American. During his three years at North Carolina, Michael averaged 17.7 points and 5 rebounds from the two-guard spot.[7]

As an amateur, Jordan topped all scorers for the men's basketball team at the 1983 Pan American Games in Venezuela,[8] averaging 17.3 points while leading the United States to an 8-0 record and its third consecutive gold medal.[9] He duplicated the effort the following summer in Los Angeles, leading the 1984 Olympic team to an undefeated 8-0 record while averaging 17.1 ppg. Joining Michael on that Bobby Knight–coached squad were future NBA greats Patrick Ewing, Sam Perkins, Chris Mullin, and Alvin Robertson. The 1984 Games marked the first time basketball had been played as an Olympic sport on U.S. soil, and American athletes did Dr. Naismith proud; the United States became the first country to win both the men's and women's basketball tournaments in the same Olympiad.[10]

Eager to step up the level of his competition, Jordan passed on his senior year at North Carolina to join the Bulls. One of the first things that impressed him about Coach Kevin Loughery's training camp was that players were allowed to *sit* during practice. "You never, ever sat down in one of Dean's [Smith] and you sure never sat during one of Bobby's [Knight]," Michael told Terry Boers, a sports reporter for the *Chicago Sun-Times*.[11] Assistant coach Bill Blair found it amazing that Michael could get his entire hand above the backboard square, but comparisons to the high-flying Dr. J were off target, according to Loughery. "The way he plays is like Jerry West," Loughery said. "He has the same movements, particularly on defense."[12]

While Jordan's defensive abilities would soon become apparent, it was his offensive skills that earned the rookie a spot as a starter in the All Star Game on February 10, and an invitation to participate in the league's second All Star Saturday. Not surprisingly, the slam dunk contest proved Michael's forte. The previous year's finalists, Dr. J and Larry Nance, were eliminated in the semifinals, setting up a Michael Jordan–Dominique Wilkins finale. Jordan became the early favorite when he landed a perfect 50 on his third dunk in the semifinal round, but Dominique returned the favor in the finals, slamming down *two* perfect dunks to beat the rookie by a final round total of 147 to 136.[13]

After 30-plus years of disappointment and frustration, the NBA had finally found a place in the hearts and minds of basketball fans. The All Star Game in Indianapolis on February 10, the first under the marketing genius of David Stern, drew 43,146 fans to Hoosier Dome — the largest crowd in NBA history. And they got what they paid for: 48 minutes of competitive ball among the most talented players in the league. Ralph Sampson dominated the contest with 24 points and 10 rebounds. The Spurs' George Gervin, nicknamed the "Ice Man" for his ability to knock down shots under pressure, was a close second with 23 points. Magic added 21 points and dished out a game-high 15 assists en route to a 140–129 win, the West's first victory since 1979. Magic's counterpart, Isiah Thomas, led the losers with 5 assists and 22 points. Bird chipped in 21 points and 8 rebounds.

While Jordan managed only 7 points in 22 minutes of action in his All Star debut, he bounced back two nights later with a remarkable 49-point performance against the Pistons to set a Bulls single-game rookie record. He was named to the NBA's All Rookie and Second teams and won Rookie of the Year going away with season averages of 28.2 points—third in the league behind Bernard King (32.9) and Larry Bird (28.7)—5.9 assists, and 6.5 rebounds. As a team, the Bulls improved from 27-55 the previous year to 38-45, and made the playoffs for the first time in four years. Jordan played 42.8 minutes per game in the club's first round loss to the Bucks while scoring an average of 29.3 points.

Once Jordan was out of the picture, the remainder of the postseason evolved as expected: a rematch between the Celtics and Lakers in the Finals.

The Bird and Magic Show, nearing the end of its sixth season, was in peak form heading into the series. Both players had been named to the NBA's All First Team for the third consecutive year. (It was Bird's sixth consecutive appearance.) Larry's regular season averages of 28.7 points, 6.6 assists, and 10.5 rebounds were his best to date, earning him his second successive MVP award. Although Magic's assists were off slightly from the previous season, he continued to improve as a shooter, making a career-best 56.1 percent from the field and 84 percent from the free throw line. The Celtics finished the regular season with a league-high 63 wins. The Lakers were right behind with 62. Neither club had any real competition on the road to the Finals; Boston was 11-4 in playoff competition heading into the rematch, the Lakers even better at 11-2.

The heat was on the Lakers as Game 1 got under way in Boston Garden on Memorial Day. The Celtics clicked in every gear en route to an embarrassing 148-114 rout of its West Coast rivals. "It doesn't feel good," Magic admitted afterward. "They were just tremendous. If you're looking for a perfect game, they played it."[14] Insofar as series momentum was concerned, however, it was not that all five Celtics starters scored in double figures, nor that Boston reserve Scott Wedman shot a perfect 11-for-11, including four 3-pointers. The statistic that would fuel the rest of the series was Abdul-Jabbar's line at the end of the game: 3 rebounds, 12 points, and 1 assist.

Kareem was no longer in his prime at age 38, but he had remained a force during the regular season, posting averages of 22 points and 7.9 rebounds. Following the Lakers' loss in Game 1, however, critics began writing his epitaph en masse. At film sessions the next day, Abdul-Jabbar personally apologized to each of his teammates for his performance and promised it would not happen again. Coach Pat Riley would later refer to the Game 1 debacle, dubbed the Memorial Day Massacre by the media, as "a blessing in disguise."[15]

True to his word, Kareem came out strong in Game 2, grabbing seven rebounds in the first quarter alone. By the end of the game, he had amassed 30 points, 17 rebounds, 8 assists, and 4 blocked shots. Final score: 109–102, Lakers. Magic posted a game-high 13 assists to go with 14 points. Bird topped the Celtics with 30 points and 12 boards. Wedman was a nonfactor with four points, including 0-2 from three-point range.

The series moved to L.A. for Game 3, where the Lakers would have a chance to wrap things up, thanks to the league's decision to return the series to a 2-3-2 format for the first time since 1955. Play turned more physical in Game 3 as the Celtics were out-rebounded by 12 amid a flurry of elbows and body jabs. "They [Celtics] expected us to crawl in a hole, but we're not going to,"[16] L.A.'s assistant coach Dave Wohl said after the Lakers crushed Boston 136–111. Kareem turned in another stellar performance with 26 points and 14 rebounds.

Boston fought back in Game 4, fueled by strong offensive performances from Bird (26 points), McHale (28 points), and Dennis Johnson (27 points). Still, it took a last-second jumper by DJ to give the visitors a 107–105 win. Game 5 was another close affair until midway through the second quarter, when the Lakers went on a 20-7 run. Boston could get no closer than 4 points the rest of the way, losing 111–120. Kareem led all scorers with 36. Magic and Worthy added 26 and 33, respectively. Magic and Dennis Johnson each registered 17 assists.

Game 6 returned to Boston Garden, where the Celtics hoped to tie the series and force another winner-take-all Game 7. But Abdul-Jabbar wanted nothing to do with that scenario. Despite missing most of the second quarter with foul trouble, Kareem scored 29 points on 13-for-21 shooting to lead the Lakers to a 111–100 win on the infamous parquet floor. Worthy added 28, and Magic finished with a triple-double—14 points, 10 rebounds, and 14 assists. Bird, who had played with a sore finger and elbow for most of the series, hoisted 29 shots but connected on only 12 for a total of 28 points. McHale had his best game of the series with 32 points and 16 rebounds, but fouled out midway through the fourth quarter.

And so finally, after eight consecutive failures, the Lakers knew how it felt to beat the Celtics in the Finals. "This is the start of the Laker mystique," Coach Riley said afterward. "We broke the dynasty."[17] The fact that Boston had never lost a title series at home before made it all the sweeter for Los Angeles—and no one was more disgusted about that than Larry Bird. "I didn't play to my standard. I missed too many shots. When you lose, you're a failure. Your goal is to win a championship, and if you don't win it, you're a failure."[18]

Abdul-Jabbar was named Finals MVP. Despite his poor outing in Game 1, the 16-year veteran center averaged 25.7 points, 9 rebounds, and 5.2 assists for the series.[19] So much for epitaphs. "He defies logic," Riley said. "He's the most unique and durable athlete of our time, the best you'll ever see."[20]

Few dared to question that assessment, especially in the aftermath of the

Lakers' most recent triumph. As a championship contender, Los Angeles appeared to be set for the foreseeable future. Although Abdul-Jabbar was in the twilight of his career, Magic was in his prime at age 26 and continued to improve on the offensive end. Worthy (25) and Byron Scott (24) were already seasoned veterans. The 29-year-old Michael Cooper, a regular member of the NBA All Defensive Team, remained one of the best sixth men in the league. The loss of Jamaal Wilkes and Bob McAdoo, both of whom had retired, was offset by rookie A. C. Green and the arrival of longtime veteran Maurice Lucas.

Despite Bird's assessment of the Celtics being losers, they remained a strong, veteran team heading into the second half of the 1980s. Larry was three years older than Magic, but the league's back-to-back MVP was playing the best ball of his career. Five-year man Danny Ainge, 26, was coming into his own as a scorer, especially from three-point range. The Sixth Man of the Year, 28-year-old Kevin McHale, continued to improve on both ends of the court. Dennis Johnson (31) and Robert Parish (32) remained solid performers.

But Red Auerbach, ever the competitor, was not content to stand pat. While Parish was one of the premier big men in the league, he had been consistently outplayed in the finals by the 38-year-old Abdul-Jabbar. McHale normally slid from power forward to the middle when Parish went to the bench, as 6'11" Greg Kite, the Celtics first-round pick in 1983, had not lived up to expectations. The team needed help in the middle if it were to beat the Lakers again.

Enter the long-forgotten redhead from San Diego, Bill Walton. Since his trade from Portland to the Clippers in 1979, Bill had made a slow but steady comeback after undergoing radical surgery in 1982. Doctors speculated that lowering his left arch would expose his bones to less stress when running and jumping—and they were right. After sitting out the entire 1981-82 season, Walton played one game a week for the Clippers during the 1982-83 campaign, 55 games the next year, and 67 in 1984-85, the team's inaugural year in Los Angeles. During the latter, Walton averaged a steady 10 points and 9 rebounds without sustaining a major injury. Auerbach realized it was a gamble, but he rolled the dice; power forward Cedric Maxwell and a first-round draft pick went to the Clippers in exchange for the much-maligned center.

Meanwhile in Chicago, the Michael Jordan–revitalized Bulls entered the 1985-86 season anticipating more than a first-round playoff appearance as their Rookie of the Year took his skills to the next level.

So obvious was Jordan's talent that Nike, daring to ignore Converse's philosophy that basketball stars could not sell shoes, had signed the former Tar Heel to a five-year, $2.5 million deal shortly after he was selected in the 1984 draft.[21] Appropriately named "Air Jordan," the high-top sneaker featured the Bulls' red and white colors and was adorned with the famous Nike swoosh on the sides. Michael wore the shoes for much of his first season, most notably during his appearance in the nationally televised 1985 All Star Game. The following month, Nike released a commercial version of the shoe for general sale that included a silhouette of Jordan flying through the air on his way to a dunk. The insignia, dubbed "The Jump Man," is considered one of the most brilliant marketing strategies in history. Sales for 1985 alone totaled $130 million.[22]

As it turned out, Nike would have a much better year than its budding superstar spokesperson. A mere 3 games into his sophomore season, Jordan broke a bone in his foot and missed the next 64 games. He was still voted onto the starting All Star squad, but was unable to play in the game, let alone participate in the slam dunk contest. Also notably absent from the competition was 35-year-old Dr. J. While fans surely missed two of the contest's most popular entries, they were treated to what would become one of the most talked-about showdowns ever between defending champion Dominique Wilkins and freshman entry Anthony "Spud" Webb.

Webb was drafted by Detroit in the fourth round but failed to make the team because his 5'7", 135-pound frame was considered too small for NBA competition. But the scrappy little point guard got a tryout with the Hawks, and found a spot playing alongside Doc Rivers in the backcourt. Naturally, Webb's size made him a crowd favorite in the slam dunk contest. Fans roared their approval as the shortest active player in the NBA advanced to the finals against teammate and reigning champion 6'7" Dominique Wilkins. Spud shocked Wilkins by posting two perfect scores in the deciding round to beat him 100–98.

Prior to the 1986 slam fest, All Star Saturday in Dallas launched the premier of an event that would eventually become even more popular with fans than the dunk competition: the three-point shootout. Eight of the league's best long-distance shooters were invited to participate. Players were given 60 seconds to sink a total of 25 shots from five specified areas behind the three-point line. The first four baskets in each set counted one point each, and the fifth — identified by the ABA's signature red, white, and blue colors — was worth two.

Bird, one of the league's best shooters from behind the line, was among the original group of contestants. Larry got off to a slow start in the first round, causing fans to get behind the Bucks' Craig Hodges, who dazzled the crowd by scoring an NBA-record 25 points in the semi-finals. But, as was usually the case on game day, Larry hit the shots when they mattered. A confident Bird smothered Hodges in the finals, 22–12, to become the contest's first champion.

Although the three-point shot had been around since Bird's rookie year (1979-80), it had taken a while to gain popularity during game play, especially from a coaching perspective. In its season debut, only 15 players managed to connect on 25 or more of the long-range baskets, sinking 720 of 2,066 attempts. In 1985-86, 20 players made at least 25, taking 2,361 shots while making 848. Of those, Bird had attempted the most at 194, and connected on 82 for a respectable 42 percent — fourth best in the league. Trent Tucker of the Knicks

(41 of 91 shots) and Hodges (73 of 162) were tied for first place at 45 percent. Houston's John Lucas was the league's least accurate long-distance shooter that year, making 48 of 146 shots for 30.8 percent.

While there was no question the long distance bomb had caught fire with fans, its impact on the NBA's offense in general was difficult to measure. Since the three's inception, team scoring had increased from 108.5 points per game to 110.2. But field goal percentage had also gone up during the same period, from 46.9 percent to 49.5 percent.[23] Given that the majority of players shot a lower percentage from long distance, the field goal percentage increase suggested players had become more accurate overall.

One thing was obvious: while coaches continually stressed the importance of good defense, it was offensive-minded players who became stars in the league, and it was those stars who drew fans to the arenas. In the season prior to the arrival of Bird and Magic, average NBA attendance stood at 10,947 fans per game. By 1985-86, that number had jumped to 11,893, an increase of 946.[24] While that figure does not appear significant at first glance, it is important to remember the league had 23 teams playing 82 games each for a total of 1,886 regular season games, thus the 946 represented an overall increase of 1,340,733 paying customers in one season alone. Estimating the cost of an average NBA ticket at $11.50, that translated into an additional $15,418,430 revenue at the gate.

Meanwhile, the number of franchises struggling to meet their payrolls had dropped dramatically over the past few years. No franchise averaged fewer than 8,000 fans per game for the 1985-86 season, and only seven drew fewer than 10,000. Even clubs that had always drawn well were seeing their numbers soar. Boston had grown from 10,193 fans in the season before Bird's arrival to 14,892 in 1985-86. Attendance at Lakers games had risen 5,055 over the same period. In Chicago, the once lowly Bulls had posted an increase of 5,552 per game during Michael Jordan's first season alone — an astonishing jump of 87 percent.[25]

It was an amazing comeback for an organization that had been all but written off by financial experts only three years earlier. "There are so many screwy things going on in that league that its initials ought to stand for National Basketball Folly," Frederick Klein had suggested in a 1982 issue of the *Wall Street Journal*. "That all 23 teams which started last season also finished it was considered something of a surprise. If it happens again this year, it will be a miracle."[26]

To Commissioner Stern, the "miracle" was simply business as usual. "There's a narrower swing between the top and bottom teams,"[27] he noted when explaining the league's turnaround at the gate.

Someone should have warned Magic and the Lakers about the league's new-found parity. Following another banner year, the 62-20 defending champs hit a brick wall in Houston, a.k.a. the Twin Towers. The Lakers took Game 1 of the Western Conference Finals in the Forum 119–107, but dropped the next four, including a last-second 112–114 loss at home. "We beat them the first game and thought it was gong to be a cakewalk," Magic's backcourt mate Byron Scott admitted. "Then they caught up and got us in Houston and we never recovered."[28]

Jordan faced similar disappointment in Chicago. After spending the majority of the season on the injured list, he returned to duplicate his heroics of the previous year, propelling his club to a late-season recovery and a second consecutive playoff berth. But the Bulls were no match for the determined, reenergized Celtics. Despite a thrilling 63-point outburst by Jordan in Game 2's double overtime contest (a new NBA playoff record), Boston swept the series in three, winning by an average of nearly 14 points per game. Chicago fans had much to feel hopeful about regarding the future, however; their superstar guard had averaged 5.7 assists, 6.3 rebounds, and 43.7 points on 50 percent shooting for the series.[29]

As for the Celtics, the Walton experiment had proven a rousing success. Bill appeared in 80 of the team's regular season games, a career high. The rejuvenated 34-year-old logged 19.3 minutes per game in his backup role, averaging 7.6 points, 6.8 rebounds, and 2.1 assists—good enough to snare the league's Sixth Man of the Year award. Larry Bird, not yet ready to close the curtain on the Bird and Magic Show, captured his third consecutive MVP with averages of 25.8 points and 9.8 rebounds while leading his team to a 67-15 season, the best in Celtics history.[30] Remarkably, the club dropped only one game at home, a 103–121 loss to the Trail Blazers on December 6. After disposing of Jordan's Bulls, the Celtics beat Dominique and the Atlanta Hawks 4-1 in the semi-finals and crushed the Milwaukee Bucks 4-0 in the Conference Finals.

In the West, Houston swept the newly relocated (from Kansas City) Sacramento Kings in the first round, but needed six games to defeat Denver before disposing of the Lakers in the Western Finals. In addition to big men Sampson (18.9 points, 11.1 rebounds) and Olajuwon (23.5 points, 11.5 rebounds), the Rockets featured point guard John Lucas (15.5 points, 8.8 assists), two-guard Lewis Lloyd (16.9 points, 4 rebounds), small forward Robert Reid (12 points), and sixth man Rodney McCray (10.2 points), making for a total of six players who averaged double figures. Houston coach Bill Fitch was in his fourth season with the Rockets. Fitch had led the Celtics to a 242-86 record over four seasons, but was fired by Auerbach after the club was swept by Milwaukee in the 1983 Eastern semi-finals. Needless to say, he was eager for a little revenge.

But the men in green were a team on a mission — to reclaim the NBA Championship — and had no intention of allowing anyone or anything to stand in their way, including the Twin Towers from Texas. Bird and company defended their home court honorably, easily winning Games 1 and 2 in Boston Garden by an average of 17 points. But Houston would not go quietly. Refueled by the home cooking of a friendly crowd, the Rockets pulled out a 106–104 win in Game 3, led by Ralph Sampson's 24 points and 22 rebounds. Bird provided the heroics in Game 4, nailing a late three-pointer to break a 101 tie. Walton grabbed an offensive rebound a few plays later and jammed it home, sealing the Celtics victory. Game 5 was marred by an ugly second quarter brawl that saw both benches empty. When the smoke cleared, Ralph Sampson and Celtics reserve Jerry Sichting were ejected. The Rockets responded with a 20-8 run and never looked back, posting an easy 111–96 win. Olajuwon set a new NBA record for a playoff game with 8 blocked shots to go along with 32 points and 14 rebounds.[31] As the series returned to Boston for Game 6, it was the Celtics who wanted no part of an all-or-nothing Game 7. Bird had his best outing of the series with 29 points, 11 rebounds, 12 assists, and 3 steals. McHale added 29 points, 10 rebounds, and 4 blocked shots while holding Ralph Sampson to 8 points. Final score: Celtics 119, Rockets 97.

Hakeem Olajuwon, who had swatted away 19 shots in the series while averaging 24.7 points and 11.8 rebounds, said of Bird, "He's the greatest player I've ever seen."[32] Added teammate Jim Peterson, "I saw him take on five guys by himself. He's the best. At times, he doesn't seem to need teammates."[33] Larry won the Finals MVP hands down, but he continued to look ahead. "My goal is to win as many championships as possible," he said, adding that he planned to improve his game over the summer. "I've got some things to work on. I'm not real comfortable with my moves to the basket. By next fall, I want four or five moves I can go to. If I do that, I think I'll be unstoppable."[34]

In leading the Celtics to their 16th NBA title, Bird drew even with Magic in the championship race. Each player had three rings and two Finals MVP awards to show for his seven seasons in the league. Larry led in regular season MVPs, however, three to none. Any suggestion the discrepancy was based on race seemed unfounded, given how 23 of the 30 MVPs awarded since 1956 belonged to African Americans. The difference lay in each player's respective job description. While Bird was an excellent passer, his first option was to get himself in a position to score. As the point guard, Johnson's major task was to deliver the ball to teammates so *they* could score. It was no coincidence Abdul-Jabbar won league MVP in Magic's rookie year, nor that Larry was the only Celtic to accomplish the feat since his arrival in Boston. As with an overwhelming majority of MVP recipients, Bird's game was geared toward offense. Previous winners from 1956 to 2005 include only four MVPs who averaged less than 20 points per game: Bill Russell (five-time winner), Wes Unseld, Bill Walton, and Steve Nash. Twenty-six averaged better than 25 points, and 12 had 30 or more.

Magic fans who wanted more kudos for their hero could soon take heart, however, as the face of the Lakers was about to change. Meanwhile in the East, a strong Midwestern headwind was picking up steam as it swept toward Boston Garden.

THE GOOD, THE BAD, AND THE GLOBAL

Despite the absence of Michael Jordan on the court for much of 1985-86, NBA attendance rose nearly three-quarters of a million to an all-time high of 11,214,888.[1] Thanks to the latest collective bargaining agreement that allowed players to share in up to 53 percent of league revenue, owners were not the only beneficiaries of the upswing in gate and TV receipts. In 1986-87, the average NBA player made $450,000 for the season, an increase of $100,000 over 1984-85. Magic was the highest paid star at $2.5 million per year.[2]

Still reeling from his team's loss to Houston the previous May, Johnson took it upon himself to squash pundits' claims that the Lakers' best years with the Magic man were over. L.A.'s point guard delivered his best overall season to date, averaging 23.9 points, 12.2 assists, and 6.3 rebounds while leading his club to a league-best 65 wins. Magic's increased scoring came about via a decision by Coach Riley to switch the club's emphasis away from its aging center in favor of a faster paced offense centered on Magic and James Worthy.

Meanwhile in the East, Bird's Celtics had their work cut out for them if they were to repeat as NBA champs. The club lost its first-round draft choice, Len Bias, a promising talent out of Maryland, to a cocaine overdose days after selecting him with the second overall pick. Bill Walton missed most of the season with an ankle injury suffered during training camp in October. Danny Ainge, Scott Wedman, and Sam Vincent also missed numerous games to injury, forcing the Celtics starters to play mega-minutes. Still, Boston remained the odds-on favorite to win it all, thanks to its relentless workhorse, Larry Bird. "I'll do whatever it takes for us to win the championship again," he told the *New York Times*, "even if it takes practicing five hours a day. No team has repeated since 1969. It would be nice to get the monkey off our backs."[3]

The monkey would be clinging to those green jerseys like a rabid bat if Michael Jordan had anything to say about it. Fully healthy again, His Airness stormed through the 1986-87 season averaging 37.1 points per contest, including a stretch of nine straight games where he scored 40 or more.[4] At All Star

Saturday, he dazzled fans in Seattle's Kingdome, beating Portland's Jerome Kersey in the dunk contest 146–140. Michael scored only 11 points in the East's All Star Game defeat, but exploded for 58 against the Nets later that month. Putting Bird and company on notice as the playoffs neared, Jordan poured in 61 points in Atlanta on April 16, including a NBA record 23 straight points. Not since Chamberlain had any player logged more than 3,000 points in a single season. Jordan made the All-NBA First Team but was not named to the All-Defensive First or Second Team despite being the first player in the league to log 100 blocked shots and 200 steals in a single season.

The problem for Chicago was that basketball remained a team sport, especially in the playoffs. Jordan averaged 35.7 points, 7 rebounds, and 6 assists in the Bulls' first-round series against Boston, but it was not enough to propel his team to a single victory in the 1987 playoffs. The injury-riddled Celtics got a lift off the bench from Bill Walton, who had returned to active status during the final weeks of the regular season. Sam Vincent and Danny Ainge were healthy again, though key reserve Scott Wedman was not.

Bird's weary squad needed all seven games to beat Milwaukee in the semifinal round, and the road proved just as difficult in Detroit, where Isiah Thomas led the Pistons to a 3–3 tie in the Eastern Conference Finals, including two blowout victories in Detroit, before losing Game 7 in Boston Garden, 114–117.

In the West, the Houston Rockets made an early playoff exit in the semifinals, losing in six games to a revitalized Seattle Sonics team. Meanwhile, Magic and the Lakers breezed past opponents with ease, bolstered by the addition of veteran forward/center Mychal Thompson, acquired in a midseason trade with the Spurs. After sweeping Denver in the first round, L.A. disposed of the Warriors in five games and swept Seattle in the Conference Finals. For the third time in four years, Bird and Magic would meet in the NBA Finals.

This time, it was Johnson's squad who held home court, and it took full advantage, winning the first two games by an average of 16 points. Magic led the new fast break "Showtime" offense with 24.5 points and 16.5 assists. Michael Cooper set a playoff record in Game 2 by sinking six of seven three-point shots. The Celtics remained hampered by injuries. Wedman was out, Walton had never reached full strength, and McHale was playing on a bad ankle. But that was no excuse, according to K. C. Jones, who described the Lakers' running game as "a thing of beauty."[5] Bird was simply disgusted. "We had no fast break. When we got a rebound, we'd hold it and show everybody we got a rebound."[6]

The Celtics fought back in Game 3, but it took a superb defensive performance by seldom used backup center Greg Kite to pull out a 109–103 win. Los Angeles fell behind by 16 points in the third quarter of Game 4, but came back to win it 107–106 on a last-second running hook shot by Magic. The loss marked only the fourth time in 98 games that the guys in green had lost at Boston Garden. "We made the mistakes," Larry said after the loss, "so we have nobody to blame but ourselves."[7] The Lakers had momentum and a chance to wrap up the series in Game 5, but Boston was not ready to throw in the towel. Bird's club bounced back with plus-20-point scoring from all five starters en route to a 123–108 win. McHale, whose ankle injury had been diagnosed as a hairline fracture, was particularly impressive with 22 points and 14 rebounds. Ainge shot a blistering five-for-six from three-point range. "They [3-pointers] have a way of knocking opponents out," K. C. Jones admitted.[8]

The series returned to Los Angeles for Game 6, where the Lakers used a 30–12 scoring burst in the third quarter to put the series away. Bird had his worst outing of the Finals, scoring only 16 points in the 93–106 loss. He attributed the Lakers' win to the acquisition of Mychal Thompson, who averaged 16.3 points in the final three games. "They made changes and we didn't," Bird said. "They have a really great basketball team." Of his own play, Larry said, "I have to get a little stronger, stay in shape this summer. I'm getting a little older, and next year, I've got to use my abilities a little better."[9]

It was the Lakers' fourth title of the 1980s, its tenth overall, and the fifth since the franchise had moved from Minneapolis to L.A. Magic, already named the regular season's Most Valuable Player, picked up his third Finals MVP, posting averages of 26.2 points, 13 assists, and 8 rebounds. Johnson was the first guard since Oscar Robertson in 1964 to win the regular season MVP, and only the third in NBA history. (Bob Cousy was the first, winning in 1957.)

Both Magic and Bird made the All-NBA First Team for the fifth consecutive season, but the separation of power between the two rivals would soon begin.

Overall, 1986-87 was another great year for Stern's NBA, with the lone exception of a simmering media-related disaster ignited by comments from Isiah Thomas after his team lost to Boston in the Conference Finals. Thomas, angered by the media's constant praise of Larry Bird and reeling from a disappointing Game 7 defeat at the Garden, told reporters: "I think Larry Bird is a very, very good basketball player. An exceptional talent, but I'd have to agree with Rodman. If Bird was black, he'd be just another good guy." Isiah was referring to an earlier remark by rookie teammate Dennis Rodman that Bird had won three consecutive MVPs because he was white. The next day, Thomas tried to clarify his position, saying his commentary was not an affront against Bird in particular, but "the perpetuation of stereotypes about blacks" in general. "When Bird makes a great play," Thomas said, "it's due to his thinking, and his work habits. It's all planned out by him. It's not the case for blacks. All we do is run and jump. We never practice or give a thought to how we play. It's like I came dribbling out of my mother's womb."[10] What Thomas, winner of the league's J. Walter Kennedy Citizenship Award, was really objecting to was the general societal perception that all blacks were born "athletic," while their white counterpoints were not, thus owing their success in the game to superior intelligence.

The accusation was not without merit. It had become the norm for many broadcasters to refer to black players as "athletes," though the term was rarely used when speaking of whites. Unfortunately for Thomas, he picked the wrong player to use as an example. During Bird's three-year tenor as league MVP, he had averaged 26.2 points on 50 percent shooting, 10.1 rebounds, and 6.7 assists. His team had played in the championship each of those three years and won twice. He had single-handedly captured a number of those games on last-second heroics. To suggest Larry Bird had not earned a place among the greatest NBA players ever was nonsense, and it served only to undermine the legitimacy of Thomas's charge.

The flare-up over the issue brought the league's most difficult challenge to the surface: how to sell a predominately black league to a corporate America that remained overwhelmingly white. From a public relations standpoint, the NBA could say in all sincerity that race was no longer an issue at the box office; fans came to see their favorite players and teams compete. Overall attendance was determined by two major factors: a franchise's current win-loss record and the presence — or lack thereof — of star caliber players on the roster.

While Commissioner Stern was elated with those developments, he knew full well the NBA could not continue to thrive on television and attendance revenues alone. Even the newly integrated salary cap would not stop the recent trend of escalating salaries and operating costs. To keep pace, there was no question the league had to come up with additional sources of income. Marketing NBA products, including its stars, was the obvious direction to take; the question was how to convince white corporate executives to hire African American sports personalities as major sponsors.

The idea was not without precedent. Former Buffalo Bills running back O. J. Simpson had proven extremely popular with the media and general public, as had tennis great Arthur Ashe. In most cases, however, athletes — black or white — were not considered primetime candidates for product endorsements. "Athletes who think they're going to become professional endorsers are mistaken," warned Olympic swimmer and gold medalist Mark Spitz. "It's like the centerfold in *Playboy*; there's always another pretty face."[11] But Stern could take heart in the fact that of the few athletes considered to have major appeal, the *Wall Street Journal* listed basketball stars at the top of the list. According to Vangue Hayes, in charge of casting for advertising giant J. Walter Thompson, image was the key. Advertisers wanted "people who have a wholesome life, who aren't connected with drugs, and have charisma and honesty."[12]

Fortunately for the NBA, Michael Jordan possessed all of those qualities and more. As such, he was a man in demand. According to the *New York Times*, Jordan's profits from endorsements and personal appearances in 1986 alone totaled more than three times his annual NBA salary of $600,000.[13] Thanks to its Air Jordan line, Nike surpassed its closest competitors, Reebok and Converse, to become the frontrunner in athletic footwear. Meanwhile, Jordan's success at the company led to major deals with McDonald's, Coca-Cola, and

Chevrolet. The Bulls star had become so popular that marketing agents described him as transcending race — exactly the terminology David Stern wanted to hear.

Jordan's successful relationship with international corporations opened up yet another striking possibility to the commissioner: marketing the NBA abroad. Early steps were taken toward that end in October 1987, when the league paired with FIBA to promote the McDonald's Open, an international round-robin basketball tournament. The first competition, held in Milwaukee, featured the reigning European champion, Italy's Tracer Milan, against the Milwaukee Bucks. The top scorer on the Italian club was none other than former three-time NBA scoring champion Bob McAdoo. "We could play with a good college team," McAdoo said of his squad when asked about the difference in talent level between European leagues and the NBA. The Italians were smaller, he said, and didn't have the "intensity" of NBA players.[14] But the Bucks' less than dominant 123–111 victory left the losers feeling the gap might not be so wide after all. "C'est fou," said a French journalist when asked what Europeans would think of the score.[15] English translation: It is crazy.

American dominance on the amateur level could no longer be taken for granted either. Earlier that summer, the U.S. basketball team dropped the gold medal game to Brazil at the Pan American Games in Indianapolis. At the Junior World Championships in Italy, another U.S. team coached by Larry Brown suffered two defeats at the hands of a Yugoslavian squad that included future NBA players Vlade Divac and Toni Kukoc. In a sign of things to come, Kukoc sank 11 of 12 shots from behind the three-point line.

European players were not alone in their fondness for the long-distance weapon. The three was becoming increasingly popular with NBA players as well. During its initiation in 1979-80, only 28 players had attempted 50 or more shots, with the top 5 launching a total of 974. In 1987-88, 61 players took 50 or more threes, with the top 5 attempting 1,424. Accuracy over that same period rose gradually from 28 percent to 32 percent.[16]

The three was not a big part of Michael Jordan's repertoire in his fourth year — he took 53 shots from downtown and made only 7 — but His Airness still averaged 35 points per game in 1987-88. That was two points shy of his average the previous year but still higher than any other player since Rick Barry in 1966-67. Bulls management, finally having accepted that its star guard could not win a title on his own, had added two talented rookies to its roster over the summer: Power forward Horace Grant and swingman Scottie Pippen. Along with third-year power man Charles Oakley and his 13 rebounds per game, a team was beginning to take shape. A midseason deal with Seattle brought in veteran guard and former Boston Celtic Sam Vincent, who fit nicely alongside Jordan in the backcourt. Michael remained the heart of the Bulls' scoring, of course, leading the team in 81 of its 82 regular season contests, including 18 games where he scored 40 or more.

Chicago played host to the 1988 All Star festivities, and Jordan treated the hometown crowd to quite a weekend. On Saturday, he battled Dominique Wilkins in the final round of the slam dunk contest in a thrilling display that featured *four* perfect scores, two by each player. Jordan squeezed out a 2-point win and followed it up with a 40-point performance in the All Star Game on Sunday, leading the East to a 138–133 victory while collecting his first All Star MVP. Chicago finished the season 50-32, its best record since 1973-74. Jordan won league MVP, along with numerous other awards including All-NBA First Team, All Defensive Team, and Defensive Player of the Year. The Bulls made it out of the opening round of the playoffs for the first time in seven years, beating Cleveland 3-2, but the young team was undermatched against the experienced Pistons in the semi-finals and lost four games to one. Jordan averaged 36.3 points, 4.7 assists, and 7.1 rebounds in 10 playoff games.

The Pistons moved on to meet the Celtics in the Eastern Finals for the second consecutive year. In addition to Thomas (19.5 points, 8.4 assists), the defensive-minded club included veteran bruisers Bill Laimbeer (13.5 points, 10.1 rebounds) and Rick Mahorn (10.7 points, 8.4 rebounds), and second year frontliners John Sally (8.5 points, 4.9 rebounds) and Dennis Rodman (11.6 points, 8.7 rebounds). Small forward Adrian Dantley, a bit past his prime but still effective, led the team in scoring at 20 ppg. Guards Joe Dumars (14.2 points, 4.4 assists) and Vinnie Johnson (12.2 points, 3.3 assists) played equally well with Thomas or each other in the backcourt. The Pistons were led by 57-year-old Chuck Daly, a player's coach best known for his ability to blend diverse personalities.

Age proved the major factor in the series. Of the Pistons' main contributors, Dantley was the oldest at 31, while Boston had only one starter — Danny Ainge — under 30. Detroit also had a younger, deeper bench, allowing its starters to rest more frequently. The result was a 4-2 victory for Detroit, with two of those wins coming in Boston Garden. Within hours, critics were writing the club's epitaph. "An era in the Boston Celtics' history ended tonight," Sam Goldaper wrote in the *New York Times*.[17] "They were humbled by a young, aggressive team that made the Celtics look even older than their years," Peter Alfano noted the following day.[18]

In the West, the Lakers finished the year with a league-best 62-20 record. But like Boston, the team's age had begun to show, especially in the middle, where 40-year-old Abdul-Jabbar still manned the starting center spot. The Lakers easily swept first-round opponent San Antonio, but needed all seven games to get past Utah and Dallas before moving on to the finals against Detroit. L.A. was under intense media pressure to become the first team to win back-to-back titles since the 1969 Celtics, especially in the wake of Coach Riley's promise following his team's 1987 victory that the team would do just that.

In the opening game of the Finals on June 7, Thomas shocked his good friend Magic by stealing home court advantage with a 105–93 victory at the

Auerbach, Bird and Russell: generational cornerstones of the most successful professional sports franchise in history (Steve Lipofsky Basketballphoto.com).

Forum. The Lakers came roaring back in Game 2, led by Worthy's 26 points and 10 rebounds. Magic, playing with the flu, added 11 assists, 23 points, and 7 rebounds. Byron Scott chipped in 24 points in a contest that saw Lakers starters outscore their counterparts 100 to 65 in the 12-point win. Los Angeles took charge as the series moved to the Pontiac Silverdome, where a crowd of 39,188 saw the Lakers use a 31-to-14 scoring run to take a 2-1 lead in the series. Johnson, still battling the flu, scored 18 points and dished out a game-high 14 assists.

A disgusted Coach Daly had seen enough of the Magic Show. Daly instructed his troops to take their offense straight at Johnson in Game 4, hoping to get the Lakers point man in foul trouble. The strategy worked. Magic was able to play only 34 minutes as the Pistons evened the series with a 111–86 rout. The Lakers' attempt to return the physical play in Game 5 resulted in a 10-point loss and a 2-3 deficit heading back to Los Angeles.

In Game 6, the home team survived a 43-point outburst by Isiah Thomas, including 25 points in the third quarter, to slip away with a 1-point win.[19] Thomas sprained his ankle late in the third but insisted on finishing the game. The injury limited his effectiveness two nights later, but Detroit managed to stay close throughout with key rebounding and pressure defense. Thomas, who played sparingly in the second half, had a chance to tie the game with three seconds to play but tripped before getting off a shot. Final score: Lakers 108, Detroit 105.

James Worthy, who had his first career triple-double with 36 points, 10 rebounds, and 16 assists in the deciding game, was the series MVP. "It's a great honor," he said of the award, "but individual honors come with the success of the team."[20] The victory marked the first time in six tries that the Lakers won a Game 7 in the championship series. They were also the first franchise to play three consecutive seven-game series en route to the title. "This was the toughest playoff I've ever been through," Magic said after the win.[21]

And that was the point, of course; tough was what the Pistons were all about. Bill Laimbeer, Detroit's 6'11", 260-pound center, was one of the least liked players in the league because of his physical style of play. Power forward Rick Mahorn (6'10", 240 pounds) had a similar reputation. Second-year man Dennis Rodman, a rebounding and defensive specialist, was well on his way to achieving the same. "A lot of people say that we win ugly, but the way we play we make teams play bad," Adrian Dantley had remarked after the Pistons' Game 1 victory in Los Angeles.[22]

While Dantley may have had a point regarding his own team's success, Commissioner Stern and NBA owners had to look at the bigger picture. For decades, the NBA had fallen behind the college game in popularity because of the pro's bump-and-grind, elbow-flailing, inside game. Only when the ABA came along with its upbeat, run-and-gun style of play did mainstream fans discover that professional basketball could actually be *fun* to watch. The influx of the rogue league's top stars such as high-wire acts Julius Erving and David Thompson had breathed new life into the NBA and kept it going long enough for Bird and Magic to arrive. But with Larry and Ervin set to enter their 10th seasons and their respective teams aging rapidly — the Celtics were the oldest team in the league in 1988, the Lakers the second oldest — it was unrealistic to expect them to carry the league into the '90s. Erving had already retired, and with him, fans' fond memories of the ABA.

Michael Jordan was exciting fans in similar fashion to Dr. J, but his team was not in the same class as the up-and-coming Pistons — at least not yet. Meanwhile, big men continued to dominate the top picks in the college draft: Sam Bowie, Patrick Ewing, Benoit Benjamin, Brad Daugherty, David Robinson, Rik Smits, Danny Manning, Chris Washburn. Only Ewing and Robertson proved good enough to build a team around, yet all were at least number three picks. Most teams carried at least one seven-footer on their roster, and many had two. It was as if outside shooters and assist men had become an afterthought. John Stockton, who would go on to become the greatest assist man in the history of the NBA, was taken with the 16th pick. Reggie Miller, one of the most prolific scorers and best clutch men ever, was drafted 11th. Mark Price, the six-foot point guard often credited with saving the Cleveland franchise from ruin, was not drafted until the *second round*.

From an image standpoint, the success of Detroit's "Bad Boys" (as the Pistons were dubbed by the media), threatened to set a dangerous precedent for the league as it neared its sixth decade of play. Fortunately, Stern saw the warning signs and took the necessary steps to alter course. The Bad Boys may have been on the verge of becoming the new powerhouse in the East insofar as win-loss records went, but it was the face of Nike's jumpman, His Airness, that would come to represent the NBA on city billboards and television screens from coast to coast — and not only in the United States.

Stern could not have been happier that companies such as McDonald's and Coca-Cola were in the process of making Jordan an international celebrity. "The truth is, we never promoted Michael Jordan," the commissioner related in an interview years later. "His sponsors did, so we didn't have to. We never sat in a room and said, 'Michael is our savior, so let's make sure everyone pushes him.' Other people did that for us."[23] Small wonder. A Jordan signature basketball marketed by Wilson made the company $7 million in 1988 alone.[24] That same year, General Mills ran a photo of Michael flying through the air, basketball in hand, on the cover of its Wheaties box. Jordan was also doing charity spots for the Special Olympics and the Ronald McDonald House. An executive with Marketing Evaluation, responsible for assigning recognition values to athletes, gave His Airness the highest possible mark, saying that the Bulls basketball star had become more "lovable" than Walter Cronkite.[25]

Like Jordan's agents, Stern was thinking global. The Olympics seemed a natural conduit. A couple of months before the 1988 Summer Games got under way in Seoul, the commissioner sent the Atlanta Hawks to the Soviet Union to participate in a basketball exhibition featuring the Soviet's Olympic team. A few weeks later at the Civic Center in Rhode Island, the NBA sponsored a pickup game between the U.S. Olympians and a group of NBA stars including Jordan, Magic, Bird, Isiah Thomas and Patrick Ewing. The game was won by the Olympians, 90–82.

Stern did an excellent job of riding the wave. The NBA had already generated a good amount of publicity heading into the summer amid speculation the International Olympic Committee might soon allow NBA players to compete. The idea had been floating around since the 1972 Games in Munich, when the Soviet team had shocked the United States by winning the gold. The argument revolved around the fact that other countries spent years readying their teams for the Olympics while U.S. teams were composed of various collegiates assembled on the run. The 1988 team was headed by legendary Georgetown coach John Thompson. "It's a tremendous honor for a player to be able to represent his country," Thompson said when asked his feelings on the idea, "but at the same point, we have to become realistic. There can't be one definition of a professional in this country and one definition in another. We need to use professional players against professional players."[26]

Somewhere deep behind the walls of the commissioner's NBA office in New York, David Stern was nodding and smiling.

There was little for U.S. basketball fans to smile about the following month in Seoul, as Thompson's squad fell to the Soviets in the semi-final round, 82–76. It was no consolation that the U.S. team had accumulated a 6-0 record prior to meeting the Russians; the loss meant the team would not even compete for the gold, let alone bring it home — a first since the sport had been introduced at the Games in 1936. Additionally, unlike the disputed loss in 1972, there was no question the Soviets had the superior team.

Critics cited the lack of a superstar on Thompson's squad as the main reason for the loss. If future Spur David Robinson took exception to that theory, he kept it to himself.[27] In addition to Robinson, the 1988 Olympic team featured a number of players who would go on to have long, distinguished careers in the NBA, among them Dan Majerle, Danny Manning, Mitch Richmond, and Hersey Hawkins. Still, critics had a point when comparing the team to the 1984 Olympians, which had included some serious powerhouse talent in Jordan, Ewing, Chris Mullin, Sam Perkins, and Alvin Robertson.

Ironically, the performance of the 1988 Olympians, who finished the Games with a 78–49 thrashing of Australia to earn the bronze medal, would serve as a catalyst to ensure American dominance at the 1992 Olympics the likes of which no one — with the possible exception of Commissioner Stern — would have dared to dream of.

Meanwhile, the Commish had his work cut out for him at home. The sting of America's Olympic defeat was not likely to fade quickly from the hearts and minds of U.S. basketball fans anytime soon, especially with the McDonald's Open only weeks away. The Boston Celtics would be representing the NBA at that international tournament, which would take place in front of a pro–European crowd in Madrid rather than the previous year's friendly confines of Milwaukee, Wisconsin. The recent playoffs had confirmed what pundits had been suggesting for quite some time; Boston was not the same team that had beaten Houston in the Finals two years earlier. Whether Bird and company would ease fans' humiliation brought on by the Olympians' mediocre performance or add to it was the hundred thousand dollar question floating across the airwaves as the league prepared to kick off its 1988-89 season.

INTERMISSION

NBA teams had been making global appearances, referred to as "goodwill trips" by the league, for over a decade. The most notable had occurred in 1979 when the Washington Bullets traveled to China. But those games were little more than exhibitions put on by what were then the best basketball players in the world. America's historical dominance on the professional level remained a concern to some FIBA committee members, who ultimately voted against allowing NBA players to compete in the 1988 Summer Games. But that did not stop David Stern and FIBA Secretary General Boris Stankovic from exploring future options. Both were curious as to how FIBA's international rules would fare against the NBA's style in actual game play—thus the McDonald's Open was born.

The decision to move the games to Madrid for the 1988 tournament marked the first official NBA-sponsored basketball event held outside the United States. The sport's global popularity on a pro level had spread substantially, aided by the arrival of former NBA players who migrated to Europe in order to continue their careers. Naturally, those players also impacted the style of their European teammates. Bottom line—as the first McDonald's Open had proven a year earlier—vast U.S. superiority was no longer a given.

Fortunately for the NBA and its fans, Bird and company still proved capable of beating lesser opponents, which included most every team but the Lakers and Pistons. The Celtics were joined in the tournament by a team of Yugoslavians, Scavolini Pesaro of Italy, and Spain's own Real Madrid. Boston overwhelmed Yugoslavia in the semi-finals 113–85, led by Larry Bird's 27 points. Madrid proved a tougher match-up in front of its home crowd, but the Bird man netted a game-high 29 and the Celtics prevailed 111–96.[1]

Victorious Boston returned to the States intent on proving it still belonged among the league's elite teams. Its prowess was short-lived, however, when only six games into the schedule Bird announced he was having surgery on his feet to remove bone spurs and would miss the rest of the 1988-89 season. The loss was a devastating blow to new head coach Jimmy Rogers, who had taken over for K. C. Jones before the start of the season.[2]

The story of the Celtics' early demise, at least on a national front, was overshadowed by the debut of two new franchises—the NBA's first addition since the Dallas Mavericks had joined the league in 1980-81. The Miami Heat entered the Midwestern Division and the Charlotte Hornets were added to the Atlantic. Teams in Minnesota and Orlando were slated to join the schedule the following season. The bold move reflected Stern's optimism that smaller cities could successfully play host to NBA teams. It was working so well in Sacramento and Milwaukee that both clubs opened the season in larger arenas, and the Utah Jazz was in negotiations to expand the Salt Palace by nearly 6,000 seats.

Existing owners were pleased with the expansion, especially from the financial end. Each new club was charged an entrance fee of $32.5 million. The cash would be evenly divided among the 23 veteran franchises, amounting to a bonus of $5.6 million per club.[3] Pundits warned they would need every penny, especially in wake of the league's latest contract with the players association reached the previous April. The deal was expected to double players' salaries within six years, meaning that by 1993 the average NBA player would make $1 million per season. League revenues were not projected to increase nearly that fast, but Stern remained confident in the NBA's ability to surpass expectations.

The commissioner had reason to be optimistic. National TV contracts with CBS and cable giant TBS would net the league $142.5 million over the next two years.[4] Combined deals with local stations reflected similar numbers. And television was no longer the only major source of outside revenue. Under Stern's guidance, the league's marketing department had grown from a two-person operation to a full-time staff that traveled around the country pushing fancy catalogs of officially licensed NBA merchandise. Fans could buy everything from hats and jackets and T-shirts to keychains and coffee mugs. In 1989 alone, such products generated an astounding $525 million in retail sales—a 50 percent increase over the previous year.[5]

On the hardwood, lest there have been any doubt, the 1988-89 season proved just how important Larry Bird was to the Celtics. Boston managed to win only 42 games without their main man, and was swept by Detroit in the first round of the playoffs, losing by an average of 10.7 points per game.

Magic's aging squad fared much better. Spurred on by the announcement that Abdul-Jabbar would retire after the season — his 20th — the defending champion Lakers finished with the best record in the West at 57-25. L.A. waltzed through the playoffs, sweeping Portland, Seattle, and Phoenix for a perfect 11-0 record heading into the finals, the first time an NBA team had accomplished such a feat. Magic won his second league MVP.

Meanwhile in the East, Isiah Thomas's Pistons were 7-0 going into the Conference Finals, where they met up with a very determined Michael Jordan. His Airness was coming off his best all-around season to date with averages of 32.5 points, 8 assists, 8 rebounds, and 2.89 steals. The Bulls' 4-2 victory over

New York in the second round marked only the third time in franchise history that Chicago had advanced to the Conference Finals, and Jordan had no intention of stopping there. The Bulls star guard led his team to a surprising 2-1 lead against Detroit, highlighted by a 46-point performance in Game 3 that included the game-winning shot with three seconds to play.

The Pistons got serious from that point, opting to incorporate Dennis Rodman's advice after losing Game 1. "We'll go out there and break some arms, break some legs,"[6] he was quoted in the *New York Times*. No actual bones were broken, but Scottie Pippen, fast becoming the Bulls' second leading man, suffered an ankle injury late in Game 2 that affected his play for the rest of the series. "You will not see a pretty game throughout the rest of the series," Pistons coach Daly said after the win. "They'll all be knock-down, drag-out affairs."[7] Daly's prediction played out in Game 6, when Laimbeer clobbered Pippen with an elbow less than a minute into the game. The Bulls forward lost consciousness momentarily and was taken to the hospital for observation. He did not return. Detroit won the game and the series.

The Pistons' victory set up a Finals rematch with the Lakers, who were eager to continue their playoff-making history with a sweep of Detroit, sending Kareem to retirement with a third consecutive ring. But Los Angeles had to open the series in Detroit without the services of two-guard Byron Scott, who tore a hamstring in practice prior to Game 1. Showing no mercy, Detroit's guard line of Thomas, Dumars, and Vinnie Johnson combined for 65 points in a 109–97 win. The Lakers' woes continued in Game 2. With the score tied at 75 late in the third quarter, Magic went down with a hamstring pull and had to leave the game. The Lakers stayed close the rest of the way without him, but fell 105–108. Magic could play only a few minutes in Game 3, and watched from the bench as his club lost another close one, 110–114. No team had ever come back from a 0-3 deficit in the Finals, and the Lakers—still without Magic or Scott—did not prove an exception. Detroit completed the 4-0 sweep with a 105–97 win for its first NBA title. "We won because we had a greater will to win than anyone else in the league this year," Finals MVP Joe Dumars said after the game. "It's an unbelievable feeling."[8]

Commissioner Stern was all smiles as he presented the trophy, but inwardly he had to be concerned for his league whose latest champion featured "Bad Boys" T-shirts with cross and skull insignias on the front. Furthermore, the Pistons' actual style of play — its overly physical tactics aside — emphasized defense over scoring, much as the NBA had done prior to incorporating the up-tempo ABA into its fold. Detroit had allowed only 92.9 points per game in the postseason, the lowest playoff total in NBA history.[9] Only once in the first five games of the Bulls–Pistons series had either team reached 100 points, and that was with the game's top scorer putting up numbers over his season average. Coaches and players could respect tenacious defense, but fans attended games, or watched them on TV, to see their favorite team score points.

Luckily for Stern and his NBA, Michael Jordan was happy to oblige. Despite the Bulls' loss to Detroit in the Eastern Finals, it was obvious Chicago was a club on the rise. The acquisition of 7'1" veteran center Bill Cartwright from the Knicks for Charles Oakley prior to the start of the season had given the Bulls a legitimate presence in the middle, and three-point shooting specialist Craig Hodges, acquired from Phoenix, provided a lift off the bench. Starters Scottie Pippen, Horace Grant, and John Paxton had developed into very solid contributors.

Considering the above additions, Bulls owner Jerry Krause had expected his team to improve on its 50-32 showing from the year before. Instead, it finished the regular season 47-35, 16 full games behind division winner Detroit. Thus, despite his club's strong showing in the '89 playoffs, Krause fired head coach Doug Collins during the off-season and replaced him with assistant coach Phil Jackson.

Like Collins, Jackson had numerous years of playing experience in the NBA, including 10 straight years with the Knicks. His coaching career began as a player-coach assistant with the Nets in 1978. Phil ended his playing career in 1980, but remained with New Jersey as an assistant coach, and later worked as a TV analyst for Nets broadcasts.[10] In 1982, Jackson took over as head coach of the Albany Patroons of the Continental Basketball Association (previously known as the Eastern League). He led the Patroons to the CBA title in 1984, and was the league's 1985 Coach of the Year.

Jackson joined the Bulls as an assistant to Collins in 1987. When he took over as head coach two years later, his first priority was to dump the isolated plays Collins had used to feature Jordan in favor of a triangle offense designed to involve all five players on the court. Jordan initially resisted the new style offense, which emphasized crisp passing and constant movement by players with or without the ball, but once His Airness adjusted, he and the Bulls became instant contenders.

Jordan's star power was more important to the NBA than ever during 1989-90, the league's first season in 20 years without Kareem Abdul-Jabbar. Wilt Chamberlain, who could do nothing but sit by helplessly as Kareem eclipsed most of his NBA records, had publicly suggested Abdul-Jabbar should have retired at least five years earlier. But Wilt's opinion did not reflect the majority. While it was obvious Number 33 was no longer the powerhouse he had once been, basketball fans still appreciated the opportunity to watch one of the greatest sports legends of all time in action on the court.

"To watch Kareem Abdul-Jabbar these past few months was not just to observe a geriatric marvel with a skyhook but also to witness a quarter of a century of American history romping past," wrote sports columnist George Vecsey.[11] Indeed, Abdul-Jabbar was bigger than basketball, and his absence would be mourned from Los Angeles to Milwaukee to New York. "With dignity and grace, Kareem went from being 'The Franchise' to a supporting player,"

Kareem Abdul-Jabbar was the first player to log 20 years in the NBA and is considered by many to be the best center ever to play the game. He holds NBA career records
for most minutes played (57,446), most points scored (38,387), most field goals made
(15,837) and most field goals attempted (28,307). He won his first championship in
Milwaukee, and later teamed with Magic to bring five titles to the Lakers (Steve Lipofsky Basketballphoto.com).

noted the June 19 editorial in the *New York Times*.[12] "But the record was already made and his place in history sealed. From now on, when basketball greats are compared, Kareem will be the standard." And what a standard it was. Six MVPs, six championships, two Finals MVPs, 18 All Star appearances. All told, Kareem played in 1,815 NBA contests, including regular season, All Star Games, and 18 years' worth of playoffs. During that period he amassed a grand total of 44,149 points—a record that has yet to be eclipsed.

The league still had several high-profile big men, most notably New York's Patrick Ewing and Hakeem Olajuwon in Houston, but neither had proven franchise makers on the level of Abdul-Jabbar. Houston's other "tower," Ralph Sampson, had developed knee problems during his fourth season with the Rockets. He was traded to the Warriors midway through '87–88, and later moved on to Sacramento and Washington. Sampson retired in 1991–92 at age 31, having played an average of 34 games per season over his last five years. David Robinson was just beginning his career in San Antonio as a 24-year-old rookie. Longtime veteran All Star Moses Malone had failed to make anything special happen in Atlanta since signing with the Hawks as a free agent in 1988–89, despite a number of quality teammates that included Dominique Wilkins, Doc Rivers, Kevin Willis, and Spud Webb. Forwards Karl Malone of the Jazz and the 76ers' Charles Barkley were among the league's up-and-coming dominant players, but lacked the supporting casts to make a Kareem-like impact on the league.

The Abdul-Jabbar–less Lakers filled the void in the middle with Mychal Thompson and first-round draft pick, seven-foot rookie Vlade Divac. The Serbian-born Divac had played on the Yugoslavian national team that had beaten Larry Brown's squad at the 1987 Junior World Championships in Italy, and won the silver medal at the 1988 Summer Olympics.

Divac was among the first foreigners to jump directly to the NBA without the buffer of an American university. In 1985, the Phoenix Suns had drafted Georgi Glouchkov, a 6'8", 235-pound center from Bulgaria, but he played only one season in the NBA. Glouchkov could not speak English, and his translator was hard of hearing—a combination that proved too much for Coach MacLeod. "By the time I'd repeat what I needed him to interpret for Georgi during a time-out," the coach recalled, "we'd have to go back on the floor."[13] The Glouchkov experiment gave owners and coaches pause for thought, but failed to stop the practice. In 1986, Portland used the second of its first-round picks on Arvydas Sabonis, a bulky, 7'3" Lithuanian, and took Croatian Drazen Petrovic, a guard, in round three. That same year, Atlanta chose Ukrainian Alexander Volkov in the sixth. All three would eventually play in the NBA, but several years passed before any of them reported to their respective teams.

Fortunately for the Lakers, Divac arrived on schedule and proved a quick study. A translator helped ease the language barrier, and a patient Magic Johnson provided an abundance of on- and off-court tutelage. Divac played in all

82 games for the Lakers his first year, averaging 8.5 points and 7.2 rebounds per game.[14] Together with Thompson's 10.1 points and 6.4 rebounds, Los Angeles got by well enough in the middle. The team still had its championship core of Worthy, Magic, Scott, and Cooper. The previous season's addition of veteran Orlando Woolridge, and the continued improvement of defensive and rebounding specialist A. C. Green propelled the Lakers to a league-best 63-19 record. Magic was named MVP for the second straight season — his third in the last four years — pulling him even with Larry Bird in the Most Valuable Player race.

Although the Bird man was back for the Celtics, age was more of a factor than ever for his veteran squad. Boston won 10 more games than it had the previous season, but competition in the East had vastly improved with the influx of youthful talent. The Celtics core of Bird, Parish, DJ, and McHale averaged 34 years of age between them. Third-year guard Reggie Lewis was developing into a quality player, but the Celtics lacked depth. Sixth man Jim Paxton led the bench scoring with a paltry 6.4 ppg. Boston finished second behind Charles Barkley's Philadelphia 76ers in the Atlantic, but fell to Patrick Ewing and his Knicks, three games to two, in the first round of the playoffs.

Detroit swept first-round opponent Indiana and lost only once to the Knicks in the semi-finals en route to its fourth straight Conference Finals appearance. In Chicago, the Bulls finished Jackson's debut with the second-best record in the East at 55-27, 4 games behind the defending champion Pistons. Jordan and company lost a single game to Milwaukee and one to Philadelphia on their way to a Conference Finals rematch with Detroit. The Bulls stretched the series to seven games, but lost the finale on the Pistons' home court, 74–93.

The Lakers looked to be on the way to another Finals appearance with an easy 3-1 victory over the Rockets in the opening round, but were surprised by a hot Phoenix Suns squad in round two. Six players on the Suns averaged in double figures, led by power forward Tom Chambers's 27.2. Third-year point guard Kevin Johnson added 22.5 points and 11.4 assists. Phoenix's up-tempo, run-and-gun style proved too much for Magic's aging Lakers; Los Angeles fell in five games. Coach Riley was so shocked by his team's performance that he resigned to take a broadcasting position with NBC. As was the case in the East, the Western Conference was experiencing an influx of young, gifted athletes.

The Portland Trail Blazers had one of the league's most exciting players in 6'7" "Clyde the Glide" Drexler, in the prime of his career at age 28. Partnered in the backcourt with the high-flying Drexler (23.3 points, 6.9 rebounds, 5.9 assists) was veteran point man Terry Porter (17 points, 8 assists). The Blazers also had one of the league's best frontlines in forwards Buck Williams (13.6 points, 9.8 rebounds) and Jerome Kersey (16 points, 8.4 rebounds), and seven-foot center Kevin Duckworth (16.2 points, 6.2 rebounds). Coming off the bench were rookie forward Cliff Robinson — a surprisingly talented second-round pick — and Croatian guard Drazen Petrovic.

Portland's depth proved too much for upstart Phoenix; the Blazers took the series in five games and advanced to meet the Pistons in the Finals. Blazers fans were encouraged when their team lost the opening game in Detroit by only six points, then went on to squeak out a one-point overtime victory in Game 2, but the celebration fell short when Portland returned home and proceeded to lose three straight games and the series in front of its home crowd. The Bad Boys were champions for the second straight year, and were quickly proclaimed the team of the '90s.

Somewhere in Chicago, the Bulls' number 23 was shaking his head and smiling.

THE GREATEST SHOW
ON EARTH, II

As the NBA prepared for its seventh season with Michael Jordan, critics took pleasure in dwelling on the negative; prolific scorer that he was, His Airness had failed to deliver the ultimate prize to Chicago—an NBA Championship. No one was more aware of that shortcoming than Jordan himself. From Stern's standpoint, however, it mattered little. The lack of a ring had not stopped MJ from becoming the most recognizable and popular figure in the NBA, if not of all professional sports.

A group of innovative Nike commercials pairing the Bulls' number 23 with independent filmmaker Spike Lee had surpassed all expectations—for advertisers, Jordan, and the NBA. The grainy, black-and-white ads promoted Jordan's more personal, human side, making him all the more appealing to the general public. One of the most popular of the series featured the Mars Blackman character (Lee) facing off against Jordan on the court. When Mars failed to perform at Jordan's level, he attributed MJ's superior game to his Air Jordan shoes. The catch phrase, "It's Gotta Be the Shoes," quickly became one of the most memorable in advertising history.

Selling products via endorsements was one thing, pundits argued, winning an NBA title was quite another. Jordan naysayers were quick to point out that no team had won it all with the league's scoring champ on its roster since the 1971 Milwaukee Bucks, led by Abdul-Jabbar. Basketball was supposed to be a team sport, after all. Such was the way in Detroit, the home of back-to-back NBA championships. The Pistons had no dominant superstar, just a group of hardworking, do-whatever-it-takes blue-collar players who got the job done. So what if it wasn't pretty? While basketball purists may have agreed with such an analogy, the majority of NBA fans—and advertisers—did not. Clubs that featured superstars drew better than those that did not, regardless of where they finished in the standings. As long as Michael Jordan was on the roster, the Bulls did not have to win a championship in Chicago to sell out the house.

Jordan, however, was intent on proving he could do both. The Bad Boys welcomed the challenge of proving otherwise, while Bird and Magic ran interference, neither quite ready to relinquish the torch that had reignited a dying league some 12 years earlier.

But the nineties would prove a decade of change. Larry and Magic each began 1990-91 under the direction of a new head coach. In Boston, former Celtic Chris Ford took over for Jimmy Rogers. And for the first time in seven years, the guys in green would be without the steady hands of Dennis Johnson, who had retired at the age of 35. In DJ's place, Ford instilled a fast-paced offense featuring a young backcourt of Reggie Lewis, Brian Shaw, and rookie sub Dee Brown. Combined with the veteran experience of McHale, Parish, and Bird, the Celtics got off to a surprising 29-5 start. But Boston's good fortune took a nosedive in midseason when Bird began to develop back problems. The three-time MVP, playing in pain for much of the year, averaged the second-lowest numbers of his career with 19.4 points and 8.5 rebounds in 60 regular season games.[1]

In L.A., new head coach Mike Dunleavy put the emphasis on defense, a ploy that netted an uncharacteristic 2-5 start out of the gate. But Lakers fans needn't have worried. Over the summer, GM Jerry West had made a key acquisition in free agent Sam Perkins. A six-year veteran from Dallas, Perkins added experience, size, and scoring to the Lakers frontline. By midseason, the club was playing like a title contender again, at one point running off a streak of 16 consecutive wins. On April 15, Magic reached a personal milestone when he dished out his 9,888th assist, surpassing Oscar Robertson's NBA record.

Meanwhile in Detroit, the champion Pistons found the going tougher than expected in their bid for a third consecutive title. Although the team retained its winning core of Isiah Thomas, Joe Dumars, Bill Laimbeer, Dennis Rodman, Mark Aguirre, James Edwards, and John Salley, the 29-year-old Thomas was able to play only 48 games due to midseason surgery on his wrist. As with Boston and L.A., age had become a factor in Detroit. "As they try for a third consecutive National Basketball Association championship, they aren't bad the way they once were, and they certainly are no longer boys," wrote Joe Lapointe in the *New York Times.* "With many miles on these wheels, the tires are showing more thread than tread."[2] Detroit finished the second half of the season 22-19 heading into the playoffs.

As the competition battled injuries, Michael Jordan and company coasted through the regular season with no starter missing more than four games. After going a respectable 20-9 out of the gate, the Bulls posted 30 wins against only 7 losses from January through mid–March, including a streak of 11 straight wins and 20 of 21. Jordan capped off the year by winning his second regular season MVP.

Bird and Thomas were back by the time the playoffs got underway. Still, their respective clubs each needed five games to get out of the first round before playing each other in the semi finals. The Celtics took an early 2-1 lead in the series before losing the next three, including the deciding Game 6 in overtime at Detroit. The Bird man, still battling persistent back pain, averaged a career playoff low 17.1 points and 7.2 rebounds in 10 postseason contests. Across the shores of Lake Michigan, the red-hot Bulls swept the Knicks in round one and lost only once to Barkley's 76ers en route to another Conference Finals match-up against Detroit.

For the first time in four years, Pistons fans would not be attending an NBA Finals game, at least not in Detroit. The Bulls breezed past their former nemesis in four straight, winning by an average of 11.5 points. It was not pretty. "The Detroit Pistons finished the NBA playoffs like defending chumps instead of defending champs," wrote Ira Berkow in the *New York Times*. "The Pistons went out kicking and whining. Literally kicking at their opponents, the Bulls, who were as classy as the Pistons were crass." Berkow went on to describe several nasty incidents, among them Rodman kicking Pippen in the head as Scottie lay on the floor trying to call a timeout, and James Edwards pulling Jordan down by his ankle as MJ soared through the air. The coup de grace came near the end of the game with Detroit trailing by 25 points. Players on the Pistons bench, led by Isiah Thomas, left the court before the game ended. "It was a miserable display of sportsmanship, but it was consistent with their play during the game," Berkow concluded. "It was one of the ugliest examples of basketball in memory."[3]

No doubt David Stern and the majority of owners breathed a sigh of relief at the outcome of the series. Phil Jackson managed to address the topic in a noncontroversial manner by dismissing Detroit's conduct as "frustration," then coyly pointing out his squad would leave a different mark on the Finals. "It's time to move on to another style of play. We're a lot like L.A., and I think that's good basketball to watch."[4]

Magic could not have agreed more. Johnson led his Lakers to another 3-0 sweep of the Rockets and disposed of Golden State 4-1 before meeting the division-winning Blazers in the Conference Finals. Portland was favored in the series but lost in six games, sending Los Angeles to the Finals for the ninth time in Magic's illustrious 12-year NBA career.

And so it was another dream Finals for Stern's NBA; the game's top scorer and reigning MVP against the league's all-time assist leader and previous year's MVP. "This is like the early days when it was me and Larry Bird, and everyone wanted to see a serious showdown between the two best in the game," Magic said of his impending match-up with MJ. "I went against Larry in his high time and now I get to go against Michael in his high time. Everyone's happy. The fans are happy. The media's happy. The league is happy. The network's happy. Michael is happy and I'm happy."[5]

Game 1 in Chicago was a hotly contested affair that more than surpassed expectations. Neither team led by more than seven points. Jordan lived up to his MVP status in front of the sold-out home crowd, scoring a game-high 36 points. Between baskets, he dished out 12 assists and grabbed 8 rebounds. For his part, Magic fought off double-teams by Jordan and Scottie Pippen for most of the game, and still turned in a solid performance with 19 points, 10 rebounds, and 11 assists. Assist number 11—a cross-court pass to Sam Perkins—resulted in a three-pointer that put the Lakers ahead 92–91. After Jordan missed a 17-footer on the next play, the Bulls fouled Byron Scott on the rebound. Scott made only one of two free throws, but the Bulls had no timeouts left, forcing Pippen to heave a hail Mary as the clock ran out. He missed. Final score: Lakers 93, Bulls 91. "If every game of the series is like this, it will be remembered for years," proclaimed the next day account in the *New York Times*.[6]

Alas, the same could not be said of Game 2. The Bulls made 50 of 81 field goal attempts—a Finals record 61.7 percent—in a 107–86 blowout. MJ deferred more to teammates during the contest, but still netted a game-high 33 points, including a stretch of 13 straight baskets. The series shifted to Los Angeles for Game 3, where everyone expected the savvy Lakers to take control. Instead, the Bulls escaped with a surprising 104–96 overtime win. Jordan scored 6 of his team's 12 points in the extra period. Chicago won the game on the glass, grabbing 24 offensive rebounds to the Lakers' 8. L.A.'s overall rebounding total of 29 set a new low for a Finals game.

By this point it was obvious the Bulls had learned something about defense from their Eastern Conference foes in Detroit. L.A. shot a dismal 36.6 percent from the field in Game 4. The Lakers made only five field goals in the entire second quarter, seven in the third. Byron Scott was held scoreless for the game. The Lakers finished with 82 points to the Bulls' 97. Los Angeles was averaging only 89.3 points per contest in the series, compared with a 108.2 average in their previous 14 playoff games. The club had yet to reach 100 points. Adding to the home team's woes, Worthy reinjured an ankle that had given him problems in the Portland series and Byron Scott hurt his shoulder. Neither would play in Game 5.

Magic's squad had faced impossible situations before, thus Johnson was not about to walk onto the court in Game 5 waving a white towel. His confidence proved contagious. Despite the loss of two starters, the Lakers led 49–48 at halftime. Rookie backup center Elden Campbell led all scorers with 21. L.A. kept it close in the second half as Magic registered his 30th career triple-double (16 points, 11 rebounds, 20 assists). The score was tied at 93 with under four minutes to play when Jordan's backcourt mate, John Paxton, got hot. Paxton pumped in 10 quick points to propel the Bulls to a 108–101 win and their first ever NBA Championship.

"We played as hard as we could," Magic said, "but they made every big shot. We still feel good. We're a proud bunch of guys, and we gave it our best shot." Afterward, a gracious Johnson went into the Bulls locker room to congratulate Jordan and his teammates for a job well done. "You hear so much talk about him [Jordan] as an individual player, but he's proved everyone wrong with this championship. It's gonna taste sweet."[7]

It did. Normally unemotional during interviews, Jordan broke down after the win, shedding tears of joy in front of the cameras. "We shocked a lot of people, I know, but we earned it," he said of the trophy. "We deserved it. We took it — no one gave it to us. That's what I'm proudest about. We took it, and we took it as a team."[8] Still, Jordan was the unanimous choice for Finals MVP, having averaged 31.2 points, 11.4 assists, 6.6 rebounds, and 2.8 steals. His Airness joined Kareem as only the second player in NBA history to win regular season MVP, league scoring title, and Finals MVP in the same year.[9]

Overshadowed in the Lakers' loss was the excellent play by Johnson and second-year man Vlade Divac. The 31-year-old Magic logged two triple-doubles in the series and set a five-game Finals assist record with 62. Divac, who had posted respectable sophomore numbers of 11.2 points and 8.1 rebounds during the regular season, elevated his play in the Finals, averaging 18.2 points and 8.8 rebounds in five games against the Bulls.

But the story of the season remained Michael Jordan. Gone were all the predictions from a year earlier that Detroit was the undisputed team of the '90s. Overnight, the Bad Boys' skull and cross insignias disappeared into the shadow of Nike's Jump Man. Critics, won over by the Bulls' domination of the Pistons in the Eastern Finals and the Lakers in the Championship, openly speculated on how many titles Jordan would bring to the Windy City. Given the Bulls had only four players over 30, the team's future looked amazingly bright.

So too did David Stern's NBA. Owners could not have dreamed up a better league spokesperson if they had submitted a wish list to God himself. Jordan was a champion in every respect, having won titles at North Carolina, the Olympics, and now the NBA. Personality-wise, he was the humble but charming guy next door, the type of fellow parents dreamed their daughters would bring home for dinner. Advertisers absolutely loved him. And not just in America. Jordan's management group, ProServ, was overwhelmed with phone calls from marketing reps as far away as Japan inquiring about using His Airness in their commercials. In Italy, a Jordan basketball highlights video was one of the hottest items on the market. Even players such as Divac and Toni Kukoc, shining sports heroes in their respective countries of Yugoslavia and Croatia, trailed Number 23 in popularity among their fellow countrymen.

There was no rationale to suggest either Jordan or the NBA had peaked in popularity, or would do so anytime soon. In addition to its MVP, the league abounded with runners up, both old and new. Although Bird had shown signs of slowing, Magic remained at the top of his game. "I've watched basketball come from the bottom to the top," Johnson said during his Finals match-up with Michael. "We've surpassed a lot of sports that were killing us because we've got so many marquee players."[10] The list — a mixture of young and old — continued to grow. Charles Barkley, Patrick Ewing, Isiah Thomas, James Worthy, Hakeem Olajuwon, Karl Malone, John Stockton, Dominique Wilkins, Chris Mullin, Reggie Miller.

Under the guidance of Commissioner Stern, the National Basketball Association had become an impressive, sturdy ship ready to float its noble wares abroad. Confident owners predicted nothing but blue skies ahead. Luckily for the game's players and fans, Captain Stern was keeping watch on the deck as the inevitable iceberg crept into view.

PROMISED LAND

The 1991-92 season began amid a wave of optimism. Due in large part to Jordan's popularity, television revenues had soared beyond imagination. The league was in the second of a four-year deal with NBA worth an astounding $601 million, an increase of nearly 250 percent over its previous four-year contract with CBS. Similar numbers were reflected in the newest cable deal. TNT, which had paid a total of $50 million for the 1988-89 and 1989-90 seasons, had upped the booty to $275 million for four years.[1] Despite the addition of four expansion franchises during the past two seasons, average attendance for 1990-91 stood at 15,245 — the second-highest on record. No team averaged fewer than 10,000 fans.[2]

Although the Summer Olympics in Barcelona was still a year away, anticipation among hoops fans had been climbing since April 7, 1989, when FIBA voted 56–13 in favor of allowing "open competition." The vote gave NBA players the green light to participate in the 1992 Games, though the final 12-man roster would include at least one collegiate to be chosen after the college season ended in March. Pistons coach Chuck Daly signed on to lead the squad.

The selection committee released the names of its first 10 invitees on September 21.[3] As expected, Jordan, Bird, and Magic headed the list. The big three were joined by Patrick Ewing, Charles Barkley, Karl Malone, Scottie Pippen, David Robinson, Chris Mullin, and John Stockton. Some critics questioned the choice of Stockton over Isiah Thomas, suggesting it was done to appease Jordan. Rumors that Jordan and Thomas did not like each other had existed for years, beginning with MJ's first All Star Game in 1985, when a supposed "freeze-out" by the East's point guard, Thomas, kept Jordan from stealing the show. A comparison of then-recent stats between the two, however, showed Stockton with an obvious lead.

The players were officially introduced on a primetime special aired by NBC that same evening. Produced by NBA Entertainment, the show was financed via commercials by USA Basketball sponsors such as McDonald's and Coca-Cola. Popular network announcers Marv Albert and Bob Costas hosted the hour-long broadcast, which included features about the just-named NBA players and USA Basketball. The program also took a look at the upcoming Tournament of the Americas to be held in Portland from June 27 to July 5.

As the NBA's regular season kicked off in November, the talk of the basketball world returned to Jordan and his Bulls and whether or not they would repeat as champions. A mere week later, pundits were questioning whether the league itself would survive the decade.

The drastic turn of events occurred on November 7 when Magic Johnson shocked the Lakers, the NBA, and the world by announcing he had been infected by HIV and was retiring from professional basketball, effective immediately. The 32-year-old Johnson added that while he felt fine physically — he had tested positive for the virus that caused AIDS, not the disease itself — doctors feared continued athletic competition would harm his immune system. Speaking of his future, Magic said he planned to use his celebrity status to help educate the public about the dreaded disease. While Johnson did not specifically mention how he had contracted the virus, he emphasized it was important for young people to understand the risk of unprotected sex. "I think sometimes we think, well, only gay people can get it — 'it's not going to happen to me.' And here I am saying that it can happen to anybody, even me, Magic Johnson."[4] Commissioner Stern, present for Johnson's news conference at the Forum, said the league would work with Magic in his AIDS-related education efforts.

So much for clear skies and smooth sailing. Once the initial shock of Magic's news wore off, the inevitable questions arose. How badly would the nature of his illness hurt the sports world? How would fans, especially children, react to their beloved basketball hero admitting he had engaged in promiscuous behavior? Would his pregnant bride, longtime girlfriend Earletha "Cookie" Kelly, divorce him? Was the unborn child in danger? Would the damage be limited to Johnson and his family, or spread throughout the entire NBA?

The talking heads of course predicted the worse — that advertisers would drop Magic overnight. And it did seem a logical course of action. The very nature of AIDS was in direct conflict with the public's perception of a hero, which Johnson certainly was to many. But his decision to go public and accept responsibility for his behavior went a long way toward salvaging his nice guy image. Most companies who had inked the Lakers star to endorsement deals — and there were many — decided to take a wait-and-see approach. While Magic did not rival Jordan's income for pitching products, he was the fourth most popular sports personality among advertisers, earning an estimated $10 million in 1991.[3] In addition to athletic giants Converse and Spalding, Magic had deals with Pepsi, Nintendo, Target Stores, Kentucky Fried Chicken, Nestlé, and CBS-Fox Video. He was also a spokesperson for such major charity organizations as Muscular Dystrophy, the United Negro College Fund, and the American Heart Association.

A few companies whose contracts with Johnson were set to expire within the coming year opted to lie low, but others took the opposite approach. Converse launched a public service campaign centering on the dangers of AIDS titled "Magic's Athletes Against AIDS." Target Stores moved forward with their planned electronics ad campaign featuring Johnson under the slogan, "Electronics, Like Magic."

Fans showed their support by voting Magic onto the starting squad of the All Star Game despite his inactive status. A few players took exception, but a poll conducted by eight major newspapers across the country revealed that of the 132 players in the NBA, 96 thought Johnson should play in the game. The others either had no comment (25) or thought Magic should not participate (8) in actual game play.[6]

Privately, some colleagues admitted they had health concerns about playing with Johnson. Cuts and scrapes were part of the game, and HIV *could* be transmitted through blood-on-blood contact. But the likelihood that two players would sustain open wounds, then have their blood from those wounds come in direct contact with each other simultaneously was minuscule. Those odds dropped even further, given the nature of All Star Games, which were hardly physical, grind-and-slap affairs under the basket. "Magic would never play if he thought he was endangering anyone's life, or doing harm to his own," Johnson's agent, Lon Rosen, said of the debate. "But doctors have assured him that it's okay to play in the game."[7]

Miraculously, David Stern had done it again. Thanks to the commissioner's support of Magic's newfound cause, what most thought would be a public relations disaster for the NBA instead became a public service AIDS awareness campaign, allowing the league to go about the business of basketball.

No team was more businesslike than the champion Bulls. Chicago got off to a red-hot 21–4 start and never looked back. Jordan, who began the season by scoring 40 or more points in three of the Bulls' first four games, appeared on track toward another MVP year. Future Olympian Scottie Pippen came into his own as a star as well, surpassing the 5,000-point mark on Christmas Day in a game against the Celtics.

Boston, all but written off by critics when the season began, managed to survive what would prove a very difficult year. Although Bird had opted for surgery over the summer, his back continued to give him problems. And trouble begat trouble. Teammate Brian Shaw alleged Larry's on-again off-again game day status was stifling the development of the club's younger players. Shaw's insight got him traded to Miami for Sherman Douglas 17 games into the season. Sophomore point guard Dee Brown missed most of 1991-92 recovering from knee surgery, and Kevin McHale's production was down nearly five points per game from the previous year. Nonetheless, the Celtics managed to keep their heads above water in the weak Atlantic Division, where only one other team — Patrick Ewing's Knicks — would post a winning record.

In the West, the Lakers gave fans reason for hope by responding to Magic's retirement with a nine-game winning streak, but it would not be L.A.'s year.

Divac had back surgery early in December. Worthy hurt his knee in March, and Perkins went down with a shoulder injury a short time later. With the Lakers on injured reserve as the season wound down, Portland, Golden State, and Phoenix battled it out for the Pacific Division crown. Across the mountains in Utah, USA teammates John Stockton and Karl Malone kept the Jazz ahead of its nearest rival, David Robinson's injury-riddled Spurs.

Magic's participation in the All Star Game in Orlando on February 9 provided the depleted league with a welcome burst of midseason energy. Critics who had suggested he would be an out-of-shape, unconditioned shadow of himself had some major crow to eat once the final buzzer had sounded. Johnson finished the game with 25 points, 9 assists, and 5 rebounds in 26 minutes en route to his second All Star MVP. Jordan led the losing East with 18 points and 5 assists.[8] Magic's performance fueled earlier rumors that he might return to the Lakers for the playoffs. Johnson said that wasn't likely, but emphasized he had every intention of competing in the upcoming Olympics. "People with this virus can live on," he said. "That's the message.... Life doesn't stop because something happens to you."[9]

Life in Lakerland may not have stopped, but the battery was running mighty low. Without its Magic man, Los Angeles fizzled quickly in postseason play, falling in four games to the Pacific Champion Blazers. Up-tempo Portland dumped Phoenix 4–1, then beat the Jazz in six for the Western Conference title and its second trip to the Finals in three years.

In the East, a deep New York team led by a healthy Patrick Ewing edged the fading Pistons in the first round, 3–2. Meanwhile Coach Lenny Wilkens's steadily improving Cavaliers, led by All Stars Mark Price and Brad Daugherty, wrestled a defiant Celtics team to the ground in seven games. But the real playoff surprise was the Bulls–Knicks semi-final series, which began with a shocking five-point New York win in Game 1 at Chicago Stadium. When all was said and done, it took a 42-point performance by His Airness in Game 7 to finally put the gritty Knicks away. When Cleveland won Game 2 of the Conference Finals by 26 points on the Bulls' home court to even that series at 1–1, critics began to question whether Jordan's Bulls might be a one-time wonder. Speculation continued, even as the defending champs wrapped up the series in Game 6 and moved on to the Finals.

Portland had its own Michael Jordan of sorts in Clyde the Glide Drexler, who had recently been added to Team USA. Drexler's game was a bit less showy than Jordan's, but he was every bit as instrumental in his team's success. "If there is anyone in this game who comes close to Michael in terms of talent, it's Clyde Drexler," Phil Jackson noted as the preseries hype got under way. "Basketball aficionados think his game is absolutely terrific."[10] Nonetheless, there was a stark difference between the two when comparing end results. Jordan was a proven winner, having led his teams to championships at North Carolina, the Olympics, and with the Bulls. Drexler's University of Houston team had made it to the Final Four twice during his tenure, but never won. He led the Blazers to the NBA Finals in 1990, only to lose in five games to Detroit. Most recently, he had put on an impressive display at the All Star Game with 22 points, 9 rebounds, and 6 assists. Yet it was Magic who took home the MVP.

Clyde was ready to break the trend. "We've been here before," he said. "Now we want to win it. That's the ultimate thrill. Nothing else will do."[11] Like Jordan's Bulls, the Blazers were not a one-man team. Playing with Drexler in the backcourt were veteran guards Terry Porter and Danny Ainge. Upfront, the Blazers featured a tough combo of Kevin Duckworth, Jerome Kersey, Buck Williams, and Clifford Robinson. Rick Adelman was in his fifth season as head coach.

A short series seemed likely when Portland suffered a 122–89 thrashing in Game 1, but the Blazers regrouped with an overtime win two nights later. Chicago stormed back in Game 3, but it was 2-2 heading into Game 5, leading pundits to question the toughness of Jordan and his Bulls. Michael responded with games of 46 and 33 points to Drexler's 30 and 24.[12] The Bulls took the series 4–2, including a 15-point come-from-behind win in the fourth quarter of Game 6. Jordan, winner of his sixth consecutive scoring title and second straight regular season MVP, became the first player to win back-to-back Finals MVPs. His Finals scoring average of 35.8 was the highest ever recorded for a player on the winning team.

Jordan had little time to savor his accomplishments. Team USA members were scheduled to report to training camp in La Jolla, California, on June 21, a mere seven days after the Bulls were crowned NBA champs. Numerous questions remained regarding the final makeup of the team. Topping the list was the health status of Bird and Magic. Larry had missed nearly half the season with back trouble, including the final eight games of the regular season and six playoff contests. His last notable performance had come in Game 6 of the Eastern semi-finals against Cleveland, when his 16 points and 14 assists propelled the Celtics to a 122–91 rout of the Cavaliers. But he managed only 12 points in Game 7, a 104–122 blowout in Cleveland. "This is a bad feeling, to lose this way," he said afterward. "But what can you do about it now?"[13] No doubt Bird was as unhappy as the Celtics with his playoff performance. Larry had averaged only 11.3 points, 4.5 rebounds, and 5.3 assists in four playoff games.

Reservations about Magic revolved more around his conditioning, or possible lack thereof, than his actual HIV status. Johnson had not played at a professional level since the All Star Game in February. Skeptics, including some on the Olympic Committee itself, questioned whether he would really have the stamina to play major minutes in Barcelona.

Answers were expected over the next several days, when Johnson and the rest of Team USA scrimmaged against a group of top collegiates. The list included such future NBA stars as Shaquille O'Neal, Chris Webber, Grant Hill, Alonzo Mourning, and Jim Jackson. The fact that most would have been headed to the Olympics in previous years was not lost on the young, talented prospects. "We definitely feel that if they hadn't changed the rules all of us would have had a chance to represent our country," Grant Hill admitted. "But it's out of our control."[14] Christian Laettner was the lone amateur to make the team. Laettner, a 6'11" forward out of Duke, was the third pick in the '92 college draft, behind Shaquille O'Neal and Alonzo Mourning.

Following a week of scrimmages, Team USA moved north to Portland for the Tournament of the Americas. By now, questions surrounding Magic's ability to keep pace had been laid to rest. "Magic was as well conditioned as anyone here," Coach Daly proclaimed. "I saw no flaws in his ability to play whatsoever."[15] Jordan concurred, saying he had noticed no dropoff in Johnson's game.

Of the 10 nations chosen to participate in the Olympic qualifying tournament, only the top four would advance to the Games in Barcelona. Among the countries competing for those spots were Cuba, Canada, Brazil, Puerto Rico, Argentina, and Panama. Cuba was the first to fall against the Americans, losing by 79 points in a game where Jordan scored only 6. Starting for Coach Daly were Magic and Jordan in the backcourt, Bird and Charles Barkley upfront, and David Robinson in the middle. After the rout, Barkley said in defense of the blowout: "Who do we let up with? We have no scrubs."[16]

Indeed. Team USA, appropriately dubbed the Dream Team by the media, beat its next five opponents—Canada, Panama, Argentina, Puerto Rico, and Venezuela—by an average of 46 points. Overall, the United States averaged 121.1 points per game on 63 percent shooting. Seven players averaged in double figures, led by Barkley's 16.3. The other qualifying teams were, in order of their respective records, Venezuela, Brazil, and Puerto Rico.[17]

Several U.S. players were battling injuries as the actual Games approached. John Stockton had fractured his right fibula during a collision with Jordan; Patrick Ewing was nursing a dislocated finger; Drexler had aggravated a previous injury to his knee; and Bird's back continued to torment him. The media speculated about possible replacements, but when the July 15 deadline for submitting a final roster arrived, no changes were made to Team USA. "No one is thinking about that [withdrawing]," Patrick Ewing said. "When you get a chance to play for your country, it's an honor."[18]

From Portland, the team moved on to Monte Carlo, where players spent one last week training for the Games. The European media was waiting en masse to cover the event. The *New York Times* reported no fewer than 170 press credentials had been issued to the scheduled practices. Why all the fuss for a team that had a virtual lock on the gold medal before the Olympics ever got under way? Certainly part of the draw was the celebrity status of Jordan, Magic, and Bird, who were no less than living legends in the international sports world. But what really made the team special was its attitude. "This is the most competitive team ever assembled," Magic said. "There's talent. But it's more than that. We compete."[19]

Compete may have been an understatement. Given its depth, Team USA certainly could have coasted through the warm-up games in Portland and still won every game by a sizable margin. But the players were not looking to coast. Each and every man on Team USA had a clear goal in mind: to avenge the United States' embarrassing loss to the Soviets in 1988. To reclaim the gold. To secure America's rightful spot at the top of the basketball world. And no mercy would be shown in the process. "Semi passivism is garbage," the usually soft-spoken David Robinson said of the team's determination to play its best. "If you're going to war, send your best troops and support them."[20]

The United States opened with a 116–48 demolition of Angola, and made no apologies afterward. Barkley led all scorers with 24. Jordan was high man the following night against Croatia, scoring 21 in the 103–70 win. It was Bird's turn to shine in the team's next outing; Larry was able to ignore his sore back long enough to score 19 points in the team's 111–68 victory over Germany. Barkley was back to dominating form in a 127–83 rout of Brazil; Sir Charles set a U.S. single-game Olympic scoring record with 30 points. The team wrapped up its pool play with a 122–81 win over Spain to advance to the quarterfinals.

Reserve Chris Mullin led the way with 21 points in a 115–77 victory over Puerto Rico, setting up a semi-finals contest against Lithuania. Obviously it had not escaped Coach Daly's group that the Lithuanian squad featured four of the top scorers from the 1988 Soviet gold medal team; the Americans responded with their most lopsided thrashing of the quarterfinals, 127–76. Croatia's 6-1 record afforded them the sole honor of facing Team USA a second time as it advanced to the Finals, but the outcome was never in doubt. Michael Jordan took game-high honors with 22 points. As John Stockton dribbled out the clock, his Croatian counterpart pleaded with him not to add to the final margin. Stockton obliged, content with a 117–85 gold medal win and possession of the game ball, which he refused to surrender after the buzzer sounded. A souvenir to remember the experience of a lifetime.

"The feeling was just tremendous," Magic said of the medal presentation afterward. "It was the most awesome feeling I ever had for winning anything, especially when the national anthem was played. Goose bumps came all over my body."[21]

The final stats were every bit as dominating as expected. Team USA won by an average of 44 ppg — second only to the 1956 team led by Bill Russell, which had blasted its opposition by an average of 53. Charles Barkley scored a total of 144 points, the most by any Olympian in an eight game span of competition. Jordan was second with 119.[22] "You will see another team of professionals," Coach Daly acknowledged, "but I don't think you'll see another team like this."[23]

Advertising gurus had reached a similar conclusion heading into the Games; U.S. Basketball was represented by 13 sponsors and 23 official licensees.

Corporate execs had spared no expense touting their company's fortunate association with the historic event. Kraft spent several million dollars on promotional posters and baseball caps to advertise its role as an Olympian food provider, while Skybox International invested some $7 million pushing its trading cards.[24] Licensees held exclusive rights to sell a wide range of Team USA memorabilia, everything from paperweights and alarm clocks to pricy team uniform gear.

Naturally, the vast amount of dollars involved made it impossible to keep everyone happy. Many Dream Team players had existing contracts with athletic companies heading into the Olympics, raising numerous conflict of interest concerns. Michael Jordan and several other members of the Dream Team represented Nike. Magic was still aligned with Converse, the "official" shoe of USA Basketball, and Coach Daly was obligated to Reebok. For weeks, pundits speculated on how the gold medal ceremony would be affected if, as it was rumored, Jordan would refuse to appear on stage dressed in the team's "official" Reebok garb due to his exclusive Nike deal. In the end, he wound up draping an American flag over the Reebok logo on his uniform — a decision that caused a number of critics to question his patriotism.

Despite an occasional road bump, however, the Barcelona Games were a huge success on almost every front. NBC exceeded numbers guaranteed to advertisers with 18.2 ratings and a 32 share during its prime time broadcasts.[25] Critical reviews were mainly positive, though the network took some heat for televising the more prestigious events, including the Dream Team's gold medal game, via tape delay so it could be presented in prime time. The Olympics attracted some 25 million American viewers at any one time, while more than a billion people watched at least one part of the 17-day event.[26]

Stern's NBA came out a clear winner as well. The Dream Team had surpassed all expectations while completing its mission, and no player had sustained a serious injury during competition as some league GMs had feared. Lest there have been any doubt regarding America's basketball supremacy from an international standpoint, it ended in Barcelona. "They're so good that these other teams can't beat them even in their dreams," Heavyweight Champion Evander Holyfield proclaimed.[27] While some Stateside critics had cried foul over the Dream Team's dominance at the Games, the international reaction remained upbeat. "It is interesting to note that while the Dream Team has been the subject of sniffs from the parsons of U.S. sports reporting, in Europe the response has been overwhelmingly positive," the *Wall Street Journal* reported in its August 6, 1992, issue. "Jordan, Johnson, Bird et al. rise above the national identity, as Europe's announcers root for an ever more dramatic display of basketball artistry." Even Team USA's opponents appreciated the scope of talent they were up against. "I was impressed with the way Mr. Jordan and Mr. Daly pronounced our names," Croatia's coach said after losing to the United States by 33 points. "They know about us. That is very important to us. That means we are something in the world of basketball."[28]

As far as 1992's Team USA was concerned, there was no disputing its members represented the most talented group of basketball players ever assembled. But to say without a doubt that all future Olympic gold medals in basketball would belong to America was foolishly premature. The international talent pool had been steadily improving since the shocking loss to the Soviets in 1972. If Americans thought their team's embarrassing third place finish at the 1988 Games in Seoul was a fluke, they had only to listen to Magic tell it like it was. "You better believe these guys can play," he said of Dream Team's competition. "I'm telling you that now. All the people complaining better look over at Croatia and Lithuania. You send that college team and it's going to be a problem, that's for real."[29]

Ironically, the thrashing defeats suffered by Dream Team's competition hastened the inevitable narrowing of the talent gap between the United States and Europe. Italy's Phillips Milan coach Mike D'Antoni, a former ABA and NBA player, said the Games had been a great motivator. "Up to now, they [Europeans] have only been able to imagine how good the NBA players are because the ones we get over here are either at the beginning or end of their careers. This will give them a close up view of what they have to do."[30]

Following the gold medal ceremony, Dream Team players returned home, shook hands, and went their separate ways. Within a month, most would return to their respective teams and go about the business of pursuing an NBA title. Whether former saviors Magic Johnson and Larry Bird would be among them, however had yet to be determined. Prior to the Jordan era, the idea the NBA might lose two of its premier, beloved players during the same season would have sent critics racing to write its epitaph in the morning paper. But thanks to the immeasurable popularity of His Airness and the performance of the Dream Team, a spirit of optimism reverberated throughout the league.

Notably absent from the party were the Los Angeles Lakers and Boston Celtics. Each had witnessed life on the court without its respective star, and the results had not been pretty. L.A. was eliminated in the first round of the playoffs, Boston in the semi-finals. No one expected rival owners to shed tears at either club's misfortune, but as businessmen, it behooved them to consider the long-term repercussions. Jordan's Bulls were a contemporary ratings magnet, but what of the rest of the league? Detroit, touted as the "team of the nineties" only a few years earlier, was already down for the count and in the process of rebuilding. New York could never quite get over the Conference Finals hump, even with Patrick Ewing leading the way. Out West, Clyde Drexler was in his 10th season with the Blazers and had yet to deliver a title. John Stockton and Karl Malone needed help in Utah. Back-to-back injuries to Hakeem Olajuwon left pundits speculating about Houston's future. The Spurs were improving with David Robinson, but had yet to make it past the conference semifinals. And while the outlook in Phoenix had suddenly brightened with the off-season addition of Charles Barkley, critics continued to question whether the outspoken, controversial star could deliver a championship. (Barkley requested a trade after Philly failed to make the playoffs in 1991-92.)

Larry Bird and Magic Johnson, meanwhile, had provided stability and championships for more than a decade, as had their predecessors before them: Cousy, Russell, Havlicek, Baylor, West, Abdul-Jabbar. The Celtics and Lakers had been the cornerstones of the NBA for as long as fans could remember. Regardless of what transpired during the regular season, come playoff time, they expected to see either Los Angeles or Boston — preferably both — competing into June.

No one could dispute the fact Jordan was the reigning king of the modern era heading into 1992-93. Whether fans were prepared to accept his Chicago Bulls as the new NBA dynasty, however, was quite another matter. Ideally, a slow transition would take place so the basketball world had time to adjust.

Of course few things in life are actually ideal.

THE DARK AGE

Webster's defines a *dynasty* as "a family or group that maintains great power, wealth, or position for many years." No NBA team fit that description better than the Boston Celtics. For decades, the franchise had managed to draft and sign numerous quality players, meld their talents, and develop consistently winning teams. Young players were brought along slowly, groomed to take over as starters when the time was right. Most recent case in point: Reggie Lewis for Danny Ainge. Lewis was a natural leader with a likable personality and top-notch talent. Similarly, Dee Brown was growing into an adequate replacement for Dennis Johnson, with some help from Brian Shaw. But the Celtics' long-time strength — its impermeable frontline — was another story. Designated replacements for Parish (39 years old), McHale (35), and Bird (35) had never arrived, forcing the longtime veterans to remain on the court for too many minutes, too many games, too many years.

Bird was the first warrior to raise the white flag when he announced his retirement shortly after returning from Barcelona. "I played as hard as I could," he said during a news conference on August 19. "I wasn't going to let an injury stop me from diving on the floor to try to do everything that I was capable of doing to win a basketball game, and that's all I wanted to be remembered for."[1] The 12-time All Star left the game as the 11th best scorer in NBA history, having amassed 21,791 points. "I thought about staying one or two more years," he admitted, "but I knew I wouldn't be able to give it my best."[2] The Celtics announced Bird would remain on the payroll as an assistant to the vice president.

Upon hearing the news, Magic said, "Larry was the only player in the league that I feared, and he was the smartest player I ever played against. I always enjoyed competing against him because he brought out the best in me."[3] Commissioner Stern promptly gave credit where it was due. "Quite simply, Larry Bird has helped to define the way a generation of basketball fans has come to view and appreciate the NBA. In the future, great players will be judged against the standards he has set, but there will never be another Larry Bird."[4]

Nor would there ever be another Magic Johnson.

Like Bird, Magic had been the subject of nonstop speculation throughout the summer. Would he, or would he not, "un-retire?" His Olympic performance had shattered critics' claims that his HIV status would affect the level of his game. Magic was still Magic. And basketball remained the core of his being. "For as long as I can remember, my life has been about basketball," he wrote in his 1992 autobiography, *My Life*. "About being part of a team. About winning. As soon as I realized that I had God-given talent to play this game, I was determined to take it as far as I could."[5]

Clearly, Johnson wanted to return to the game he so loved. But would the world allow it? While it seems a near certainty there were other HIV-positive players in professional sports at the time, none had publicly admitted it. Their reluctance was understandable. Magic's immense popularity had helped him buck the negative response, but it was unlikely others would be as fortunate. The mention of HIV remained socially unacceptable in the mainstream public — a point that was not lost on the first Bush administration. Following Magic's disclosure in November 1991, the president had assembled a committee to develop a national consensus on what should be done to fight the disease. But nothing had been accomplished in the 10 months since, despite Johnson's high-profile presence on the board. In June, members had publicly complained the White House continually rejected or refused to act on any of their recommendations. Magic became so disgusted with the lack of progress he resigned in late September. "I cannot in good conscience continue to serve on a commission whose important work is so utterly ignored by your Administration,"[6] he said in a public statement to President Bush. The president had no direct comment in response.

A few days later, Magic decided to lead by example. "Life itself is a risk," he said at a September 29 news conference at the Forum. "If I was concerned about that, I wouldn't be up here." He said he had decided to return to the Lakers for the 1992-93 season and see how his health fared. The Lakers happily accommodated him with a one-year contract extension worth $14.6 million, making him the highest paid athlete in all of professional sports. As always, Commissioner Stern remained supportive. "Since the day that Magic announced that he had tested H.I.V. positive, our principal concern has been his personal well-being. We have conferred with his doctors, who have advised that they are comfortable with Magic's decision to return to active competition. We are pleased that he feels well enough to return."[7]

Initially, players and coaches throughout the league reacted in similar fashion. Larry Bird told him to go for it. Lakers teammates were anxious to reunite with their All Star floor leader. Former Coach Pat Riley, who had moved on to the Knicks, wished him the best. "This is another great day in the life of Magic Johnson," Riley said. "He will give the fans what they've missed."[8]

But the closer the season opener got, the less supportive the basketball community became. No one had spoken out publicly against the idea of playing on the same court with Magic, yet behind the scenes, players were expressing concern. What if Magic elbowed them in the mouth and blood or fluid was exchanged? Could doctors say without a doubt the virus would not be transmitted? In a word, no. Little was known about the disease at the time, and as stated earlier, the less the better as far as politicians were concerned.

Things came to a head in late October when Magic's Olympian teammate Karl Malone spoke out after a preseason game at Madison Square Garden. In the locker room, Malone pointed to numerous cuts and bruises on his body. "I get these every night, every game. They can't tell you that you're not at risk, and you can't tell me there's one guy in the NBA who hasn't thought about it.... The Dream Team was a concept that everybody loved, but now we're back to reality."[9] Dominique Wilkins's brother, Gerald, then with the Cleveland Cavaliers, concurred. "Everybody's talking about it. Some people are scared. This could be dangerous to us all, but you're dealing with Magic Johnson, so people are handling it with white gloves. They're not going to say how they really feel."[10]

Some players remained steadfast in their support. Among the most outspoken was another of Magic's teammates in Barcelona. "I was with him all summer and never once thought about it," Charles Barkley said. "Never. Never. Never." Doc Rivers, in his first season with the Knicks, dispelled the idea that the game itself might be altered if Johnson played due to defenders backing off to avoid contact. "We're going to play the same. If Magic comes down the lane and needs to be knocked down, then he'll be knocked down."[11]

As it turned out, Johnson was blindsided by an unexpected enemy: the male ego. Rumors had begun to circulate among players that Magic lied about how he had contracted the virus, and that in fact he was gay or bisexual. At the core of the rumor mill was none other than Magic's former best friend, Isiah Thomas. Thomas denied having started the rumors, but his possible involvement made the issue front-page news on supermarket tabloids across the globe. Faced with the prospect of dispelling such gossip on a daily basis, in addition to coping with the stress of his health during a rigorous 82-game schedule, Magic re-retired on the second of November, four days before the Lakers were set to play their first game of the regular season. "It has become obvious that the various controversies surrounding my return are taking away from both basketball as a sport and the larger issue of living with H.I.V., for me and the many people affected,"[12] Johnson said in a prepared statement released to the media.

Through no fault of his own, Commissioner Stern had finally met a foe he could not defeat. "A professional sports league with a long history of being at the fore of social issues could not, finally, hold up against the weight and power of AIDS,"[13] editorialist Harvey Araton concluded. "Now the NBA will have to live without Johnson and Larry Bird on TV and build even more around Michael Jordan, Charles Barkley, Patrick Ewing and younger stars like Shaquille

O'Neal," the *New York Times* reflected in a November 3 editorial. TNT analyst Hubie Brown addressed the new state of reality by challenging players directly. "Now it's up to the new stars to step out and become leaders in their own right."[14]

Jordan was happy to oblige, averaging 32.6 ppg as he led Chicago to its fourth straight 50-plus win season and another division title. Barkley did his part in Phoenix as well. The Suns improved from a respectable 53-29 in 1991-92 to a league-best 62-20 under the guidance of Sir Charles (25.6 points, 12.2 rebounds, 5.4 assists), silencing Barkley's critics and earning the "Round Mound of Rebound" his first league MVP. The most dramatic improvement record-wise came in Orlando, where 7-1 Rookie of the Year Shaquille O'Neal (23.4 points 13.9 rebounds) led the Magic to its first .500 record at 41-41, an astounding 20 more wins than it had posted in 1991-92. Meanwhile up the coast in New York, Patrick Ewing (24.2 points, 12.1 rebounds) finally delivered an Atlantic Division title and an Eastern best 60-22 record.

Suffice it to say, the league's new would-be leaders had delivered.

Hopes ran high in New York as the playoffs got under way. The Knicks lost only twice en route to the Eastern Conference Finals, and, boasting a healthy Ewing and home court advantage, took a 2-0 lead against longtime nemesis Chicago. But Jordan would not be denied. The Bulls won the next four games and another trip to the Finals, where they would attempt to become the first team since the 1966 Celtics to win three consecutive NBA titles.

Barkley's Suns needed overtime in Game 5 to get past the Lakers in round one, six games to dispose of Robinson's Spurs, and all seven games of the Western Conference Finals to beat a strong Seattle team led by the league's newest dynamic duo, Gary Payton and Shawn Kemp. But the Suns' hard-fought victories made for a determined Phoenix team with momentum and home court advantage heading into the Finals.

The Suns' hopes plummeted after they became the first team in NBA history to drop the first two games of a championship series at home. Sir Charles matched Jordan's 42 points in Game 2, but it was not enough to offset a triple-double by Pippen and a playoff career-high 24-point night by Horace Grant. For disappointed fans who had booed point guard Kevin Johnson during the loss, Barkley offered up his usual dose of frank advice: "If you're not going to be here with good times and bad times, we don't want you there. And I'm not concerned if they don't like it. They know where to find me."[15]

Next-day accounts of the Suns' demise proved premature. Phoenix fought its heart out in Game 3, escaping with a 129–121 triple-overtime win. Several records were set in the marathon, including most combined three-point shots made in a Finals game (14), and most threes made by any one team (Phoenix, 9). Kevin Johnson set a new record in minutes played with 62, while teammate Dan Majerle tied the Finals record with six made threes. The Bulls rebounded in Game 4 with a 111–105 win, but the Suns took Game 5 by 10 points and

Controversy followed Charles Barkley for the majority of his career, but he was a flamboyant, hard-nosed player who gave his all every time he set foot on the court. A eleven-time All Star, "The Chuckster" averaged 22.1 points, 11.7 rebounds, and 3.9 assists in 16 seasons. He is currently employed as an analyst for TNT (Steve Lipofsky Basketballphoto.com).

headed back to Phoenix with a chance to even things up in front of a rejuvenated home crowd.

Fans got their money's worth in a hotly contested Game 6. With Chicago leading 87–79 at the end of three, Phoenix went on a defense tear, holding the Bulls scoreless through the first six minutes of the quarter. The Suns were up by four with 2:23 to play in the game, but neither team scored again until Jordan struck with a coast-to-coast basket at the 38-second mark. Majerle launched an air ball in response as the 24-second clock expired. The Bulls inbounded the ball with everyone expecting that Jordan — the only Bull to score in the period — would take the final shot. But Horace Grant found John Paxton open at the 3-point line, and Paxton nailed a 25-footer to put the Bulls up 99–98 with 3.9 seconds left. Grant swatted away Kevin Johnson's last-second runner in the lane to seal the win.

Jordan was named Finals MVP for the third straight year, a new NBA record.[16] His Airness posted a Finals' record 41 ppg average in the series to go along with 8.5 assists, 6.3 rebounds, and 2.05 steals. Pippen added 20.8 points, 9.8 boards, and 7.7 assists. Barkley led the Suns with 27.3 points, 13 rebounds, and 5.7 assists. "It has to mean something to win three in a row," Jordan said afterward. "There's so much parity in this league. That makes for a heck of an argument by anyone's standards. We feel we must be considered one of the best teams ever."[17]

One thing was certain: the Bulls were among the most popular sports teams ever. The 1993 Suns–Bulls series set a record with a 17.3 share on NBC, meaning almost 17 million households had tuned in to watch the games.[18] Internationally, the series had been broadcast in 100 countries, from Guam to China to Greenland.[19] And retailers were absolutely giddy with the result. In 1991 and 1992, licensed merchants had cashed in on the Bulls and Jordan to the tune of $45 million within 10 days of the Bulls' victories in the Finals.[20] Projected sales for 1993 were off the charts as Chicago's NBA "three-peat" and "3-peat" merchandise hit stores.[21] The league's vice president of marketing, Bill Marshall, confirmed the Bulls had been the NBA's top selling team for licensed merchandise for several years running, and that he expected "to do significantly more," following the Bulls' third consecutive title.[22]

So much for fears the league might collapse after back-to-back losses of Larry Bird and Magic Johnson. The NBA had weathered the storm and owners saw nothing but impervious, deep blue skies ahead. Michael Jordan, a mere 31 years old, was in the prime of his career. Fellow superstars had accepted their leadership roles. Young stars were on the rise. New four-year deals with NBC and TNT worth in excess of $1 billion were in the bag. Global marketing was growing by leaps and bounds. The NBA had fought the battles, survived the wars, and emerged the undisputed king of the professional sports world.

Or so it seemed to those on the outside. Had someone dared to interrupt the celebration to ask Commissioner Stern, he would have told them, with a cautious shake of his head and an apprehensive smile, just how quickly an unexpected tornado could swoop down.

Several funnel clouds had already been sighted. A few months earlier, the Celtics' captain, fifth-year man Reggie Lewis, had collapsed in a playoff game between the Celtics and the Charlotte Hornets on April 29. Boston's leading scorer spent a week in the hospital, was diagnosed with cardiac abnormalities, and missed the rest of the playoffs. Doctors disagreed on whether the 27-year-old Lewis would be able to resume his career. A team of cardiac specialists initially determined he suffered from cardiomyopathy, a condition that causes damage to an area of the heart tissue. When informed he would have to retire, Lewis requested a second opinion. The latter group diagnosed him as having a nonfatal fainting condition, and said it would be possible for him to resume his career.

Meanwhile across the state line in New Jersey, the league's most prominent European player, Drazen Petrovic, had announced he was leaving the Nets and the NBA after the season. Petrovic cited concerns with the Nets' inability to keep quality players on the roster, but media reports claimed he was deserting the NBA because he had lined up a huge deal with a European team. The popular Croatian averaged better than 22 ppg, and was considered one of the best outside shooters in the league. Overseas, he was often referred to as the European Michael Jordan.

Petrovic's motives became moot on June 7 when the 28-year-old crashed his car into the back of a truck while traveling in Germany. Petrovic and his girlfriend were killed instantly. Commenting on the tragedy, Commissioner Stern said Petrovic's loss would be felt throughout the league, and that he had opened the door for other international players to compete in the NBA. Speaking at a news conference in New Jersey, Nets coach Chuck Daly said, "I guess this points to the fact of how precious life is."[23]

Daly's remark would prove hauntingly eerie. On July 27, Reggie Lewis was in the midst of deciding whether he would return to the Boston Celtics or retire when he collapsed again, this time while shooting baskets at the Celtics training center in Waltham, Massachusetts. He was rushed to the hospital, but doctors were unable to revive him. The cause of death was listed as a heart attack.

Remarkably, the Grim Reaper was not finished yet. In North Carolina, events had begun to unfold that would pierce the entire sports world to its very core.

On July 22, Michael Jordan's father, James Jordan, had driven from his home in Charlotte some 200 miles to Wilmington to attend the funeral of Willie Kemp, an old friend and co-worker from his days at General Electric. After the service, James spent several hours visiting with Kemp's widow, Azella, and her friend, Carolyn Robinson. According to later accounts, she and Jordan left Azella's about 9:00 p.m. and went to Carolyn's home, where the two had dinner together. Around midnight, Jordan told Robinson that despite the late hour, he had to be on his way as he was planning to leave for Chicago the following day.

Nearly two weeks later on August 3, a fisherman discovered a badly decomposed body floating in a creek near McColl, South Carolina. An autopsy was performed. The cause of death was listed as a single gunshot wound to the chest. Police had no missing person report on file that might have matched the victim. Dental records were secured, and the man's body — as of yet unidentified — was cremated.

Two days later, police found a vandalized, red Lexus 400-SC in a wooded area off Highway 24 near Fayetteville. The vehicle's windows had been smashed, its license plates, rims, and tires removed. No blood was found in the car, nor was there any sign a struggle had taken place. Police sent the vehicle identification number to Lexus, and the company was able to match the car to its owner: James P. Jordan, father of Michael Jordan. Beginning to put two and two together, police ordered copies of James Jordan's dental records and compared them with those of the body found near the state border. They were a match.

As if the tragedy were not enough in itself, some members of the media speculated James Jordan's murder was connected to his son's supposed underworld gambling connections — a scandal that had broken several months earlier. The allegations stemmed from a book written by Richard Esquinas, a San Diego businessman who claimed Michael owed him $1.25 million in golf bets. The book saw release only a few days after Michael and his father were seen together gambling in Atlantic City during the Bulls' Eastern Finals series against the Knicks in May. The NBA was looking into the matter at the time of the elder Jordan's death.

Adding to the rumor mill was the fact that no one in Jordan's family had reported James missing since he had last been seen by Robinson on July 22. But family members, including his wife, Deloris, said it was normal for Jordan to go off on his own, driving from one city to the next, without calling to check in for weeks at a time.

On August 15, two 18-year-old North Carolina men, both of whom possessed extensive criminal backgrounds, were charged in Jordan's murder. Police determined the 56-year-old Jordan had been sleeping in his car at a rest stop about 3:30 a.m. when he was robbed and shot in the chest. Once the killers realized who their victim was, they pulled his body from the Lexus and dumped it in a swamp, hoping to cover their tracks. End of story. No malicious gambling connections. No anticelebrity hate crime. Just another random act of senseless violence.

"During this tragic ordeal, the vast majority of the media reports approached the situation with dignity, sensitivity and respect for human decency," Jordan said in a statement released on August 19. "Unfortunately, a few engaged in baseless speculation and sensationalism. These few should cause us all to pause and examine our consciences and our basic human values. My dad taught me to carry myself with love and respect for all. The wisdom of his principles will help me rise above any thoughtless insensitivity and unfounded speculation. With the help of God's strength, I will find the inner peace to carry on in Dad's way."[24]

Mulling over what that way might be, Michael reached a decision some six weeks later. "I've always stressed to people that when I lose the sense of motivation, it's time for me to move on," he said during an internationally televised news conference at the Bulls practice facility in Deerfield on October 7. "I've reached the pinnacle and I've achieve a lot in a short period. I don't have anything else to prove." Reacting to speculation that his father's death had influenced his decision to retire, Jordan said he had already been leaning in that direction. "What my father's death made me realize is how short life is, and how it can be taken from you in a minute."[25] He added that he planned to spend more time with his family and get back to as much of a normal lifestyle as possible, though when pressed, he did not rule out the possibility he would un-retire. "Who knows? That's an option that will never close."[26]

Naturally, everyone who was anyone had something to say about Jordan's retirement: NBA players, coaches, and owners; fellow celebrities and sports figures; fans; journalists; economists. None, however, came close to President Clinton's eloquent observation. "We will miss him, here and all around America, in every small town backyard and paved city lot where kids play one-on-one and dream of being like Mike."[27]

While David Stern, Bulls owner Jerry Reinsdorf, and the rest of the NBA could cling to the faint hope His Airness would miss "being like Mike"[28] as well and return a year or two up the road, the league had to cope with the reality of the moment. Michael Jordan was gone. Bird and Magic were gone. Drazen Petrovic and Reggie Lewis were gone. The Celtics–Lakers rivalry was history for the foreseeable future, and America's new favorite team, the Chicago Bulls, had gone from elite to ordinary in the blink of an eye.

Meanwhile, a new crisis for Stern and company was sizzling on the back burner. Hornets forward Larry Johnson, the number one pick in the 1991 draft, received a contract extension despite the fact he had four years remaining on his current deal that would have paid him $3.9 million annually. As a sophomore with the Hornets, Johnson had averaged 21.2 points and 10.5 rebounds; decent numbers for a frontline player, but certainly not extraordinary. Yet Charlotte owner George Shinn thought it imperative to lock up Johnson's services for the long term, thus he offered his star a new 12-year deal worth an astounding $84 million. "David Stern laughed when I told him about it," Shinn admitted. "He said, 'George, you're going to give him twice the price we charged you for the franchise.'"[29]

Chances were, Stern hadn't laughed very hard. A week after Johnson's deal was announced, Anfernee Hardaway, a 6'7" guard who had yet to play a professional game, signed a 13-year deal with the Orlando Magic worth $45 million on expectations he would be the new Magic Johnson. The agreement included a $20 million loan, bumping the total to an astounding $65 million. Fellow rookie Chris Webber, the first pick in the 1993 draft, inked his name to a 15-year, $75 million contract with Golden State, while Philadelphia gave the number two pick, 7'5" center Shawn Bradley, $44 million over eight years.[30]

The danger was obvious. "What they are doing," Sacramento Kings GM Jerry Reynolds pointed out, "is paying for superstars and obviously not all these guys going to be."[31] Former Lakers coach Mike Dunleavy, who had moved on to the Bucks, put it more bluntly. "Teams are playing Russian roulette, giving $60–$70–$80 million contracts to players who haven't really proved themselves. I'm shocked by these contracts, and some of them are going to be mistakes. I don't see how teams are going to survive under the salary cap if they do turn out to be mistakes."[32]

Such potential mistakes could be traced, at least in part, to the Larry Bird exception that had been in effect since 1983. Essentially, the rule allowed a team to sign its own existing free agents for any amount it wished, regardless of whether that amount put it over the NBA's current salary cap. The only stipulation was that the player had been with his current team for at least three years. Boston had concocted the idea and was the first to take advantage by signing Bird to a new seven-year deal worth $12.6 million before his contract expired. By nixing Bird's potential free agency, the Celtics never faced the prospect of losing him to a higher bidder. More recently, teams had begun to stretch the rule by acquiring soon-to-be free agents who had been with another club for the required three years, then signing them to contract extensions.

In yet another exploitation of the so-called soft cap, teams such as Orlando and Golden State were offering their rookies ridiculously long term deals because it allowed them to stay within the cap while still acquiring a high draft pick they otherwise would not have been able to afford. The contracts called for less money during a player's initial year or two, then escalated drastically. Hardaway's contract with the Magic, for instance, paid him $1.6 million the first year — substantially less than he would have gotten had he signed a two- or three-year deal. The borderline practice was risky, however, because should the player fail to live up to expectations, the team would be stuck with him — and his huge salary — for a number of years.

On the basketball court itself, the league faced a different type of potential implosion: a return to the old school-power game that had sent fans rushing to the exits in the pre–Bird and Magic era. With Jordan gone, the league's premier veterans were Charles Barkley, Patrick Ewing, Karl Malone, David Robinson, and Hakeem Olajuwon. The most popular newcomers, at least insofar as NBA marketing went, were Shaquille O'Neal and Alonzo Mourning. The Knicks, the club most expected to capitalize on Jordan's exit in the championship quest, featured a string of defensive players — Ewing, Charles Oakley,

Hakeem "The Dream" Olajuwon, a University of Houston alumnus, became the first foreign-born player to be drafted number one when he was selected by Houston in 1984. The native Nigerian was one of the best and most durable centers in NBA history, averaging 21.8 points and 11.1 rebounds during his 18 years in the league (Steve Lipofsky Basketballphoto.com).

John Starks, Anthony Mason, Derik Harper. "Defense is going to be the key," Barkley said as the '93-94 season approached. "You can tell by the way we're training that we're emphasizing defense more. I think that, sooner or later, the Western Conference is going to change that myth that that's the difference between the East and the West."[33] Charles and company took their defensive game to Munich in late October, where they beat Buckler of Bologna 112–90 in the annual McDonald's Open. Barkley was voted the tournament's MVP.[34]

The '93-94 regular season proved a bust for the rebuilding Lakers (33-49) and Celtics (32-50), but Chicago surprised fans with a 55-27 record, then pushed the Knicks to seven games in the semi-finals before fading. New York went on to beat Indiana in the Eastern Finals for its first championship series appearance since 1973. In the West, the Seattle Supersonics surged to a league-best 63 wins and were the running favorite to win it all under charismatic head coach George Karl, tough-nosed point guard Gary Payton, and high-flying power forward Shawn Kemp. But the Sonics fell apart in the first round against Denver, becoming the first number one seed to lose a playoff series to a number eight team. The Suns' chance to return to the Finals was stamped out by a determined Rockets team in the semi-finals. Houston needed seven games to dispose of Barkley's crew, but whipped the Jazz in the Western Finals 4-1.

New York vs. Houston provided exactly what critics had predicted: a defensive, low-scoring match-up of elite inside power players. For the first time since the introduction of the shot clock in 1954-55, neither team broke 100 points in any of the seven games. The Knicks averaged 86.9 points, the Rockets 86.1. New York took a 3-2 lead in the series, but lost Game 6, 84–86, when Olajuwon — league MVP and Defensive Player of the Year — blocked his fourth shot of the game. Houston wrapped things up with a 90–84 win in Game 7 for its first NBA title. Hakeem "the Dream" added Finals MVP to his 1994 résumé. The 10-year veteran had led the Rockets with 26.9 points, 9.1 rebounds, and 3.6 assists in the series. Ewing had averaged 18.9 points, 12.4 rebounds, and 1.7 assists.

Talent-wise, the Rockets were for real. Playing alongside Olajuwon in the front court were veteran power forward Otis Thorpe (14 points, 10.6 rebounds) and second-year man Robert Horry (9.9 points, 54. rebounds, 2.9 assists). The Rockets had one of the most experienced guard tandems in the league with Vernon Maxwell (13.6 points, 5.1 assists) and Kenny Smith (11.6 points, 4.2 assists). Rookie Sam Cassell and Mario Ellie provided floor leadership and firepower off the bench. The question was, did anyone outside the greater Houston area care? Olajuwon was truly a great center along the lines of Chamberlain and Abdul-Jabbar, but he did not possess Magic's smile, Bird's coyness, or Jordan's charisma — traits marketers looked for in a marquee sports star. Olajuwon's teammates were role players along the lines of the former champion Detroit Pistons. And the club did not play in a major media outlet.

While it was far too soon for epitaphs, initial response did not bode well for the Jordan-less NBA. The 1994 Rockets–Knicks series posted a meager 12.4 share — NBC's lowest rated championship since 1986, when, ironically, the Celtics defeated the Houston Rockets.[35] Off court, the league and the NBPA (National Basketball Player's Association) failed to meet the June 23 deadline for a new collective bargaining agreement, spewing shockwaves of uncertainty across the league. The NBPA insisted that the salary cap, the college draft, and the Right of First Refusal violated antitrust laws, and were demanding they be expelled from any future contracts. The NBA said it didn't think so, and filed a lawsuit in federal court.

Meanwhile, critics geared up to spend the summer as they had many others — speculating on the possible demise of the NBA. If no agreement was reached prior to the start of training camp, it was conceivable that Commissioner Stern would face a scenario much worse than no Michael Jordan: no NBA games in 1994-95.

STAYING ALIVE

Given the level of disparity between the two sides as the 1994-95 season approached, neither a lockout by owners nor a players' strike could be ruled out. The initial court ruling on July 18, handed down by U.S. District Court Judge Kevin Duffy, went in favor of the NBA. Duffy ruled that the issues players claimed were antitrust violations— restricted free agency, the salary cap, and the college draft —fell under the guidelines of a nonstatutory labor exemption because the union had already agreed to include them in the previous collective bargaining agreement. The NBPA filed an immediate appeal. The two sides began arguing their cases in a Manhattan Federal Appeals Court in late September.

As players and owners considered their options, they had numerous examples to draw from. Major League Baseball players were in the midst of a summer strike; players had walked off the job on August 14, infuriating sports enthusiasts from New York to Chicago to San Diego. Angry fans saw the players as a bunch of spoiled, greedy millionaires who got to play a game for their livelihood, and owners as whiny liars who claimed they were going broke because their players made too much money. Things were just as ugly in the National Hockey League, where players were in the midst of a lockout with no end in sight. Meanwhile in the NFL, both sides were grumbling about the newly established salary cap.

Stern had always considered his league above such squabbles, and the latest crises proved no exception. "We expect to prevail in this case," he said of the appeal. "We've told the players we have to make a deal."[1] Both sides suspected Stern was right, but neither was willing to cry uncle before the Appeals Court weighed in. It did not appear that ruling would come in time for the November 4 tip-off, but the commissioner saw to it that cooler heads prevailed; owners and players agreed they would begin the season without a new contract in place.

No doubt both sides were happy to see the off-season come to an end. In addition to the lawsuit against the players' union, the NBA and Chicago Bulls owner Jerry Reinsdorf were fighting over television broadcasting rights,

Timberwolves ownership was attempting to move its team to New Orleans without league approval, and Portland was ignoring salary cap restrictions regarding free agent signings.

Still, all was not dark clouds and thunderstorms in the early, post–Jordan era. The NBA saw attendance rise to an all-time high of 17,984,014 for 1993-94, an increase of 205,719 from the previous season.[2] Even disheartened Bulls fans remained loyal; Chicago averaged an additional four fans per game through its first non–MJ season. Most owners remained optimistic about the future, especially in lieu of the league's latest expansion plans. The Vancouver Grizzlies and Toronto Raptors were slated to join the schedule for 1995-96, giving the league its first international members.[3]

From a marketing standpoint, Jordan remained a visible athlete, albeit for a different sport. Following his retirement from basketball, speculation arose that Michael might turn his passionate golf hobby into a new career. Instead, he decided to chase the lifelong dream he had shared with his dad: playing Major League Baseball. The White Sox gave him a tryout in 1994 that led to a position with the team's Double A affiliate, the Birmingham Barons. The Sox hoped to call Jordan up to the majors by midseason, but that scenario never unfolded. While His Airness was the king of the hardwood, he did not possess the skills to play Major League Baseball. Michael hit only .202 for the season while striking out 114 times in 436 at-bats. He also committed 11 errors—the most of any outfielder in the Southern League.[4]

Jordan's washout on the baseball diamond had NBA fans buzzing as the 1994-95 season tipped off. Helping to fuel the rumor that His Airness might return was his performance in a charity game held at Chicago Stadium on September 9. Jordan scored 52 points in the contest, connecting on 24 of 48 shots.[5] Afterward, he insisted he planned to stay the course with his baseball dream.

Nonetheless, rumors persisted throughout the NBA season. By early March, word out of Chicago was that Jordan would return to the Bulls in time for the playoff run. Jordan made it official on March 18 with a statement that read, in part, "I'm back."[6] Much to the delight of marketers, the Bulls announced that since they had retired Michael's number 23 jersey back in November, he would change to 45. The possibilities were endless: jerseys, hats, T-shirts, jackets, mugs, key rings. Anything and everything that could be stamped with the number 45 was likely to sell out, regardless of the price attached. Sponsors who had stuck with Jordan were absolutely giddy. And execs at NBC were no longer crying in their milk. A season and a half into their new four-year deal, the network finally had Michael Jordan on its schedule.

The Bulls were three games over .500 when Jordan rejoined the team. NBC wasted no time returning His Airness to the spotlight, broadcasting the March 19 Bulls–Pacers Sunday afternoon match-up nationally, a game it had originally slated for regional coverage. A 15-minute warm-up show not previously scheduled was penciled in. Chicago lost the game 103–96 in overtime. MJ finished with a lackluster 19 points in 43 minutes on 7-for-28 shooting. "Either I was too short with my shots, or I was too long," he said, adding that he had played a "bad game." When asked why he had returned, Jordan replied, "For the love of the game. Because I started to miss it more and more."[3] The game fetched an impressive 13.4 overnight rating, NBC's highest NBA game to date. In the same time slot a year earlier, the network drew a dismal 2.2. Both games had gone head-to-head with NCAA tournament games on rival CBS. The latter saw its ratings dip from 6.1 in 1994 to 3.2 opposite the return of Jordan.[8]

Of course not *everyone* had missed Michael. Ewing saw his team's chance to reach the Finals slip a few notches overnight. The same was true for Shaquille O'Neal's vastly improved Orlando Magic and Reggie Miller's Indiana Pacers. In Utah, Karl Malone and John Stockton could have lived without Jordan's return just fine. Ditto for Seattle's Gary Payton and Shawn Kemp, and for Sir Charles and Kevin Johnson in Phoenix.

The champion Rockets, however, were on a mission to prove they belonged at the top of the heap, Michael Jordan or no Michael Jordan. Skeptics who had dubbed the Rockets a one-hit wonder — and there were many — looked to be on track as Houston got off to a slow start. But a midseason trade that sent rebounder Otis Thorpe to Portland for Clyde Drexler kicked Olajuwon's club into high gear. The Rockets finished the season at 47-35, 10th best in the league, but racked up wins when it mattered — in the playoffs. Houston did not have home court advantage in any of its playoff series, but managed to dispose of Karl Malone and company at Utah in round one, three games to two, Barkley's Suns in the semi-finals, four games to three, and league MVP David Robinson's Spurs in six.

Phil Jackson's club went 13-4 with Jordan on the roster to finish third in the Central Division at 47-35. Michael averaged 26.9 points over those 17 games. Meanwhile in Orlando, back-to-back first-round picks Shaq O'Neal and Penny Hardaway led the Magic to an Eastern Conference best 57 wins. Orlando finished off the Celtics 3-1 in the first round of the playoffs before moving on to face Jordan's Bulls in the semi-finals. But Chicago was not the same team that Michael had taken to the Finals two years earlier. Bill Cartwright and Horace Grant had moved on, leaving the Bulls short on muscle and rebounding. As a result, they were unable to stop O'Neal in the paint, and lost the series to the Magic in six. Jordan wrapped up the post-season with a 31.5 ppg average in 10 playoff contests.

The Knicks lost in the semi-finals again, this time to the up-and-coming Indiana Pacers. The Magic needed all seven games to stop Reggie Miller's club before moving on to meet the Rockets in the Finals, where Orlando jumped out to a 20-point lead in Game 1 before losing in overtime, 118–120. Kenny Smith was the hero of the day for Houston, scoring five consecutive three-pointers in the third quarter and seven overall, both NBA Finals records.

The Magic fell behind early in Game 2 and never recovered, losing 106–117.

The victory made seven straight for the Rockets on the road, another Finals record. The defending champions finished things off back home in Houston, winning 106–103 in Game 3 and 113–101 in Game 4. Olajuwon joined Jordan as the only other player to win consecutive Finals MVPs, having averaged 32.8 points, 11.8 rebounds, and 5.5 assists for the series. O'Neal had been nearly as impressive for the Magic with 28 points, 12.5 rebounds, and 6.3 assists.[9]

The Rockets joined Los Angeles, Boston, Detroit, and Chicago as the only teams to successfully defend an NBA title, and the first to do so via a Finals sweep. It was also the only club to beat four teams with 50 or more regular season wins (Jazz 60, Suns 59, Spurs 62, Magic 57) en route to the crown. Unlike the 1994 Finals where the Rockets had struggled to score 90 points per game, the defending champs averaged 114 against the Magic, a swing of 28 points. "The Rockets sensed a lack of respect across the nation last year, but this playoff performance should secure them a fond place in history," Clifton Brown proclaimed in the *New York Times* on June 15.

While it was possible Houston had proven itself to NBA fans, advertisers remained another story. Despite Olajuwon's impressive performance in back-to-back Finals, he was not a hot property off the basketball court. Hakeem's agent said his client had been in the running for a huge Sprite deal but lost out to co–Rookie of the Year Grant Hill because execs thought Hill had more youth appeal.[10] Another problem for Olajuwon was his Nigerian homeland. Sponsors preferred Americans, according to Marty Blackman of Blackman & Raber, a company that matched advertisers with athletes. Blackman added that it wasn't a matter of racial prejudice, just a fact.[11] Hakeem's off-court endorsements had totaled about $2 million in 1994, compared to $13.5 million for Shaq, and $31 million for Jordan, the latter of which had yet to take into account Michael's return to the NBA.[12]

Jordan erased any doubts regarding that return after the playoffs, saying he was back for the foreseeable future. That, of course, providing a new collective bargaining agreement was reached in the off-season. Hockey owners had finally ended their lockout in February, preserving a shortened NHL season, but opening day of spring training came and went without a Major League Baseball deal. On April 2, disgruntled owners finally accepted the players' last-minute offer, ending a 234-day work stoppage, the longest in the history of professional sports.

Negotiations between the NBA and the players union had continued throughout the season to no avail. Meanwhile, a rift between the players and their union leader, Simon Gourdine, had taken hold. Some players, spurred on by their agents, accused Gourdine of failing to keep them informed of what was being said between the two parties behind closed doors. The disagreement eventually resulted in players circulating a petition that amounted to a vote of no confidence against Gourdine. Agents and players were most concerned about the possibility of a luxury tax being included in the new collective bargaining agreement. The tax, which had been a losing issue for owners in the baseball strike, would be assessed to teams who exceeded the salary cap by resigning their own free agents to lengthy, exorbitant contracts. Players saw it as an attempt to water down the Larry Bird exception.

Stern was caught in the middle. If the union no longer represented the players, how could negotiations continue? Until things were sorted out, the NBA said it had no choice but to impose a league-wide lockout, effective July 1. "We believe this work stoppage could have been avoided had certain agents restrained themselves from trying to dictate union policy for our players," Gourdine said in a statement released to the press. Those players opposed to Gourdine's leadership, including such giants as Jordan, Ewing, and Pippen, contended the lockout violated antitrust laws and was therefore illegal. Stern countered that the players had made decisions based on "incorrect legal advice of some very significant magnitude" which would "ultimately be borne out by the courts and by the losses that both we and our players are going to suffer from this work stoppage."[13]

The work stoppage applied to all off-season operations, of which there were many. All summer league games, practices, and tryouts were canceled. Teams could not negotiate player contracts or trades. Practice and training facilities were shut down.

With the future of the NBA literally on hold for the first time in history, Stern and Gourdine took their case directly to a group of 25 players, none of whom were firmly aligned with the union decertification movement. The two sides came to an agreement on a new six-year contract in the late hours of August 8. The players got what they wanted most, a continuation of the Larry Bird exception, and owners got their long-awaited cap on rookie salaries. The deal was formally approved by player representatives, of which each team had one, on September 13. The agreement came in the wake of a league-wide vote by players to stand behind their union, 226-134.[4] Owners ratified the deal, 24-5, shortly thereafter.[15]

To critics' amazement, Commissioner Stern had done it again. While neither side had gotten everything it wanted, the NBA season opened on schedule November 3, sparing fans, owners, and players the ugliness that had tarnished baseball and hockey.

On the court, Jordan returned to his old number 23, and his Bulls wasted no time returning to the top of the heap. Chicago, which had added an inside presence via volatile rebounding maniac Dennis Rodman, entered February with a stunning 40-3 record, including a streak of 17 straights wins.

The 1995-96 season proved quite a "magic" one for the Lakers as well. While the team was still rebuilding, it had accumulated a pretty talented back-court with Nick Van Exel and Eddie Jones, and a frontline that featured Vlade Divac, Elden Campbell and Cedric Ceballos. Midway through the season on January 29, the club made a stunning announcement: it was activating 36-year-old Earvin Johnson. Coach Del Harris said Johnson would serve as the team's sixth man and play the position of "point forward."

While the news came as a surprise to most of the league, Magic had been considering a return since the previous summer, after assurances from David Stern that he would still be welcome. "The guys have educated themselves, and when you educate yourself, you don't have to think all those crazy thoughts,"[16] Johnson said, commenting on his HIV status that had cut short his comeback four years earlier. A few players still expressed reservations about playing with Johnson, but the outspoken Karl Malone was no longer among them. "It's great for him, if that's what he wants to do," Malone said. "It's great for basketball."[17]

It was pretty good for the Lakers, too. In his first game back, Magic played 27 minutes and barely missed a triple-double with 19 points, 10 assists, and 8 rebounds in LA's 128–118 win over Golden State.[18] TNT altered its schedule to televise the game, which reaped a 4.4 Nielsen rating — the network's highest ever for a regular season game shown in a late evening (7:30 p.m. Pacific) times-lot.[19] That record was wiped out just three nights later when Johnson's Lakers vs. Jordan's Bulls drew a 7.1.[20]

Magic played in 32 regular season games, averaging 14.6 points, 6.9 assists, and 5.7 rebounds: above average numbers for a sixth man, yet all was not rosy within the Lakers organization regarding his return. Some teammates were jealous of lost playing time, others felt Magic's game simply did not fit with the new, younger Lakers. For his part, Magic felt he should be more involved in leading the offense, as the point guard rather than point forward. There were differences off the court as well. Johnson did not appreciate rap music blaring full volume in the locker room and on the team bus. "Not that I don't like rap music," he said, "but they boom it."[21] It was, of course, a generational thing. Magic was 36 years old, soon to be 37. During the four-plus years he had been away, the game's culture had evolved with that of its players, and those players were getting younger every year.

For Jordan, adaptation came easier. He was only 32, and had been away from the game less than two years. Still, he did have to make adjustments, most notably on the basketball court. Michael took far more jump shots than he had prior to his retirement. And while he could still fly through the air toward the hoop, it was not always with the greatest of ease. No matter. Jordan's ability to accept his limitations and adapt to them only added to his appeal. More than ever, kids wanted to "be like Mike." And no wonder. The older, wiser Jordan led his Bulls to an incredible 72-10 season, shattering the 1971-72 Lakers' record of 69-13. Chicago lost only twice at home and won a record 33 games on the road. His Airness led the Bulls, and the league, with 30.4 ppg to earn his eighth scoring title. Chicago continued its demolition derby in the playoffs, rolling over Miami 3-0, New York 4-1, and Orlando 4-0 en route to the Finals. Jordan, who had captured his second All Star Game MVP back in February, added a fourth regular season MVP to his trophy collection.

In the West, Magic's Lakers won 53 games, but managed only a single playoff victory in the first round against the reigning champion Rockets. Talk of a three-peat in Houston ended abruptly in the semi-finals, where the Rockets were swept by George Karl's Sonics in four straight. Seattle then edged Utah in a tough seven-game series to earn a shot at another title.

The Rockets' dominance against the Lakers might have seemed less glaring had the champs gone on to win another title. Losing to a club which then dropped its next series in four straight, however, gave critics free rein; perhaps there *was* something to the theory the team was better without Magic Johnson. There were arguments on both sides, of course, but all that mattered was what Johnson himself concluded: it was time for him to re-retire. Given that he would become a free agent in July, many speculated he would resurface with a different team. But Magic insisted his decision was final. He said Los Angeles was home, and he planned to remain with the Lakers organization in one capacity or another.

NBC had desperately wanted a Jordan–Magic match-up in the Finals, but would take a Bulls–Sonics series over Houston–New York any day. Things looked bleak for Seattle fans when the highly favored Bulls jumped to an early 3-0 lead, but the Sonics, led by Shawn Kemp's inside power game and the tenacious play of Gary Payton (Defensive Player of the Year), regrouped to make a series of it. Stellar passing from backup point guard Nate McMillan (slowed by injuries), timely three-point shooting from Hersey Hawkins and Sam Perkins, and steady play from veteran swingman Detlef Schrempf forced a Game 6 in Chicago. The Sonics lost 75–87, but NBC came out a winner on the night, scoring an impressive 20.9 in the Nielsen, an increase of nearly 7 points from the Rockets–Knicks Game 6 two years earlier.[22]

Jordan led all scorers in the series with 27.3, down several points from his regular season average but good enough to earn his fourth Finals MVP. Michael joined Willis Reed (1970) as the only players to capture all three MVPs in the same season. Despite Jordan's individual efforts, the league recognized Chicago's accomplishments as a team effort. Pippen joined Michael on the All NBA First Team and the All Defensive Team, Sixth Man of the Year went to Croatian Toni Kukoc, and Phil Jackson, who had been overlooked during the Bulls' three-peat reign, was finally named Coach of the Year.

Labor issues concerning television revenues surfaced briefly during the off-season, but were settled before the issue generated headlines, leaving teams free to go about their summer business, most of which included a barrage of free agent signings.

Media-wise, the NBA was more than happy to take a back seat to Dream Team II, and the 1996 Summer Games in Atlanta. Returning for an encore were original Dream Teamers Karl Malone, John Stockton, Charles Barkley, Scottie Pippen, and David Robinson. New to Olympic action were Shaq O'Neal, Gary Payton, Mitch Richmond, Hakeem Olajuwon, Reggie Miller, Penny Hardaway, and Grant Hill. The group provided a nice mixture of youth and experience for head coach Lenny Wilkens, in his 24th season as a coach and his third with Atlanta. Wilkens had made recent news by passing Red Auerbach to become the most winning coach in the NBA.

Like its predecessor, Dream Team II delivered a perfect 8-0 record and the gold medal, the 11th for USA men's basketball. Overall, the United States had bettered its opponents by an average of 31.75 points — impressive until viewed side-by-side with the 1992 team average of 44. As Magic had warned in Barcelona, foreign teams *were* improving, and more quickly than anyone had imagined. In the gold medal game against Yugoslavia — a team shorthanded because of the Balkan War — the United States led by a meager five points with 11 minutes to play in the game. The Americans were able to take control with a 19–3 spurt, but there were moments when the outcome had actually seemed in doubt. In earlier games, Lithuania played Team USA to a tie late in the first half, and Argentina found itself within two points at half-time.

The United States had the Olympic Committee, David Stern, and the NBA to thank for narrowing the gap. In its quest to promote the game overseas via satellite TV, exhibition games, tournaments, and clinics, America had given the rest of the world a blueprint to achieve equality. "It took a long time for us to catch up to the college level," noted Australian Andrew Gaze. "Now we're on a path to be on equal footing with the very best in the world."[23]

Coach Phil Jackson won six championships in Chicago and three more in Los Angeles, tying him with Red Auerbach for the most NBA titles as head coach. He is currently in the midst of a three-year deal with the Lakers (Steve Lipofsky Basketballphoto.com).

Indeed, some had already achieved that mark,

and the list was growing. The NBA opened 1996-97 with 24 players of foreign origin scattered throughout the league.[24] Among the most recognizable were Hakeem Olajuwon (Nigeria), Vlade Divac (Serbia), Toni Kukoc (Croatia), Dikembe Mutombo (Democratic Republic of the Congo), Detlef Schrempf (Germany), Patrick Ewing (Jamaica), and Arvydas Sabonis (Lithuania). In June, a record six foreigners had been selected in the first round of the draft: Peja Stojakovic, Steve Nash, Efthimi Rentzias, Martin Muursepp, Vitaly Potapenko, and Zydrunas Ilgauskas.

As Magic had learned during his comeback, the face of professional basketball was changing on another front: its players were getting younger. Much younger. Fourteen underclassmen were chosen in the first round of the June draft, including *nine* of the first ten picks. Even more astounding, five teenagers—players who had never dribbled a ball during a college game let alone played in a national collegiate tournament—were first-round picks. Kobe Bryant, chosen by Charlotte with the 13th pick, was only 17 years old.

Given the increased global popularity of Naismith's game, the influx of foreign players had to be viewed as a positive development. The more countries represented within the league, the greater overall interest generated abroad, and the more likely basketball would overtake soccer as the number one international sport.

Whether the youth movement would be as constructive was debatable. Certainly a young man talented enough to enter the league as a teenager was a tremendous athlete, far and above his peers. But as history had proven, it took a great *team*—five players working together—to make a champion. The Celtics and Lakers had not built their dynasties by acquiring the most individually talented players available and tossing them together on the court. They did it by combining youth with experience, offense with defense, passing with scoring. The younger the player, the less likely it was that he would possess the full package, let alone know how to use it.

There was also the maturity factor to consider. Was a teenager who had never lived away from home or attended college equipped to handle the pressures that accompanied a multimillion-dollar paycheck? How would he deal with the sudden adulation—or jealousy—that accompanied his fame? Was he ready to go from being the star of his high school team to a bench player in the pros? How could he develop a sense of camaraderie with teammates when he was not old enough to join them in a nightclub or casino?

The NBA was left to ponder those essential questions and many more as it prepared to celebrate its 50th year of operation as a professional basketball league.[25] Thankfully for Commissioner Stern and league owners, fans and critics opted to debate simpler issues, namely, whether Jordan's Bulls would be able to duplicate—or better—their 72-win season.

THE MONEY TREE

Spurred on by a summer crop of 165 veteran free agents, owners ushered in the league's 50th year by opening their wallets as never before. Topping the list of available treasures was none other than Michael Jordan. The second tier included such big name talents as Shaquille O'Neal, Reggie Miller, Gary Payton, and Alonzo Mourning. Jordan was expected to remain in Chicago, though it was deemed likely his salary, expected to be in the $18 to $25 million range for a one-year deal,[1] would be used as a free market gauge.

By the time the wheeling and dealing came to an end, the league had undergone some major personnel changes. All Star defensive specialist Dikembe Mutombo moved from Denver to Atlanta. New York lured two guard Allan Houston away from Detroit, and acquired power forward Larry Johnson — and his huge contract — in a trade with Charlotte. High-flying Dominique Wilkins, still a major scoring threat at age 37, joined David Robinson's club in San Antonio. And Charles Barkley, unable to win a title during his four years with Phoenix, was traded to Houston for Robert Horry, Sam Cassell, Mark Bryant, and Chucky Brown.

The Rockets–Suns trade emphasized a growing strategy employed by zealous owners in their neverending search for ways around the salary cap — a cap they themselves insisted on. Owners remained adamant a limit on team salaries was necessary to keep the league from going broke, yet whenever the opportunity arose to snare a big-name player, they did everything in their power to find a way to sign him regardless of the cost. In essence, what they really wanted was a limit on what the *competition* could spend.

The cap was supposed to create parity throughout the league by making it impossible for one team to sign all the best players — a common problem in Major League Baseball. Ironically, what the cap had done was to preserve the status quo among the elite while making it very difficult for average teams to reach the next level. A club looking to acquire a franchise player via the free agent market had to adjust its roster by cutting or trading some of its existing players to make room under the cap before it could present the courted star with a competitive offer.

Trades were just as difficult. In cases like the Barkley deal, where one super-star was not exchanged for another, several mid-range players had to be included so the salary numbers came out even.[2] But teams had become creative, using that caveat to their advantage. In Phoenix's case, all four players it got from the Rockets would be free agents after the season. If the Suns opted not to re-sign any of them, it would be able to use their combined salaries to pursue other options while having rid itself of Sir Charles's bulky paycheck prior to the expi-ration of his contract. Optionally, it could re-sign any or all of those players to new deals without having to worry about staying within the cap.

Those owners who saw the big picture realized such loopholes could even-tually lead to the same type of interleague wrangling that had occurred prior to the formation of the NBA, when leagues bid against each other until both went out of business. Obviously, the salary cap had to be retained, so the ques-tion was how to do so without disrupting the relatively calm waters that were flowing between players and management.

As the potential for disaster floated beneath the surface, both sides turned their attention to the 1996-97 season and how the numerous personnel changes would affect the balance of power. No one could argue that free agency had shifted that balance from East to West with 24-year-old Shaquille O'Neal mov-ing from Orlando to Los Angeles. (Owners had given up the right of first refusal in the last collective bargaining agreement.) The Lakers made room for O'Neal's record seven-year, $121 million contract by sending Vlade Divac to Charlotte for the Hornets' number one draft pick,[3] Kobe Bryant, and moving Anthony Peeler and George Lynch to the Vancouver Grizzlies. The acquisition of O'Neal so excited Lakers GM Jerry West that he compared it with the birth of his chil-dren.

Meanwhile up in Seattle, the Sonics gambled that 7'1" Jim McIlvaine would help guide them back to the Finals. Although the former Washington Bullet had averaged a paltry 2 points and 2.4 rebounds per game over his first two seasons, the Sonics inked him to an astonishing seven-year, $35 million deal.[4] Keeping its feisty point guard also proved costly. Payton got a new seven-year contract worth $85 million.[5] The numbers leaked to the media, and All Star Shawn Kemp became so upset he demanded his contract be renegotiated. The Sonics' refusal to do so caused a rift between management and its budding superstar that would never be resolved.

There was no rift in Chicago, where Jordan — the recipient of a one-year $30 million contract that made him the highest paid athlete in professional sports— led his Bulls to a league-best 69-13 record. But times were beyond rough in Bean Town. The young, depleted Celtics, devoid of any superstar, posted a franchise low 15 wins, one game ahead of last place Vancouver. In the West, a midseason injury to O'Neal put a damper on the Lakers' promising 37-13 start. L.A. finished the season 56-26, a game behind Pacific Division winner Seattle, which continued to be plagued by off court distractions surrounding

Kemp. It was strictly on-court business in Utah, however, as the aging veteran duo of Malone (33) and Stockton (34) led the Jazz to a franchise best 64 wins.

The regular season would be remembered best for a poignant Golden Anniversary tribute held during halftime of the All Star Game in Cleveland as the league took time out to honor its 50 greatest players to date. The list included such historic giants as Bob Cousy, Wilt Chamberlain, Bill Russell, and Oscar Robertson — groundbreaking heroes who had a noticeable affect on the new generation of stars chosen to represent their league. "I think most of the younger guys were in awe," noted All Star Glen Rice. Indeed, many admitted they couldn't take their eyes off the screen during the ceremony. But the walk down memory lane left others — namely fans and critics — wondering if the next generation would be able to carry the torch into the twenty-first century. Jordan's return had bought the league some time, but even His Airness would not be able to defy the laws of physics forever. "I hope guys still have the love for the game we had," Magic commented during the festivities. "This type of weekend is why you play."[6]

No one had to remind the 34-year-old Jordan of that. Michael became the first player to record a triple-double at the All Star Game, contributing 14 points, 11 assists, and 11 rebounds while leading the East to an exciting 132–120 comeback victory. But MVP honors went to Charlotte's high-scoring forward, Glen Rice, who lit up the net for a record 20 points in the third quarter. He finished the game with 26, including four 3-pointers.

Rice, the third best scorer in the league (26.8 ppg), led Charlotte to a franchise high 54 wins — up 13 from the previous season. The jump was particularly impressive given it was made under a rookie head coach — former Celtics great Dave Cowens — and without super forward Larry Johnson. The Hornets were one of many teams that saw their regular season standings rise via free agents and/or trades. Still, it mattered little in the playoffs. Charlotte was swept by New York in the first round, and Ewing's pricy, revamped Knicks washed out in the semi-finals again, losing in seven games to the up-and-coming Miami Heat. The champs had no trouble duplicating their run of the previous year, losing only twice — once each to Atlanta and Miami — en route to the Finals.

In the West, beleaguered Seattle struggled past the Barkley-less Suns in five before falling to Sir Charles's new Rockets in a thrilling seven-game series. Meanwhile, Shaq's much-hyped Lakers could muster only one win against the surging Jazz in its semi-final match-up, leaving Houston and Utah to battle it out in the Conference Finals. The Jazz prevailed in six, sending Stockton and league MVP Karl Malone to their first Finals appearance.

As with all teams that made it to the Championship series, the Jazz was more than a two-man show. Joining the dynamic duo in the starting lineup were crafty two-guard Jeff Hornacek (14.5 points, 4.4 assists), three-point specialist Byron Russell (10.8 points, 4.1 rebounds), and 7'2" shot-blocking center Greg Ostertag. Twelve-year veteran Antoine Carr and youngsters Shandon

Anderson and Howard Eisley contributed strong minutes off the bench. Utah was led by head coach Jerry Sloan, a hardnosed, no-nonsense type who demanded a player's best effort each and every time he set foot on the court.

The series was hyped as a battle between MVPs and delivered as such from the tip-off. In what had proven a tight Game 1 throughout, Karl Malone went to the free throw line with 9.2 seconds left to play and the score tied at 82. To the delight of the frenzied crowd, he missed both shots and the home team's MVP responded with a 20-foot jumper at the buzzer for an 84–82 win. Malone shot 6-for-20 in Game 2, and Stockton had a frustrating night as well, collecting seven assists and four turnovers. His Airness took advantage to the tune of 38 points, 13 rebounds, and 9 assists, and the Bulls headed West with a 2-0 lead. The Jazz delighted their home fans with a 104–93 coast-to-coast win in Game 3. Malone was in MVP form with 37 points, 10 rebounds, and 4 steals. Game 4 was much closer most of the way, but the Jazz rallied with a 12–2 scoring burst in the final few minutes to even the series at 2-2. The Bulls fell behind early in Game 5, but MJ, playing with the flu, led Chicago's comeback. Jordan scored 17 points in the second quarter and 15 in the fourth, including the deciding 3-pointer with 25 seconds to play. Michael finished with 38 points and the Bulls took a 3-2 lead back to Chicago.

Alas, as many of the league's modern superstars had already learned, a championship that ran through the Windy City had an impenetrable roadblock. The Jazz, hampered by a poor performance at the free throw line, lost 86–90 in front of a jubilant Bulls crowd. Malone and Stockton joined an impressive group of almost-rans that included Patrick Ewing, Charles Barkley, Kevin Johnson, Reggie Miller, Dominique Wilkins, Gary Payton, Shawn Kemp, Mark Price, Brad Daugherty, Chris Mullin, Alonzo Mourning, and Tim Hardaway. Many critics argued that list would have included Hakeem Olajuwon and Clyde Drexler as well, had they gone up against Michael's Bulls in the Finals.

Jordan capped another tremendous season by winning his fifth Finals MVP in as many tries, and topped the league in scoring at 29.6, his ninth first-place finish. When all was said and done, there were too many awards to list, and little point in doing so. The Bulls' Number 23 sat well atop the heap of the professional game, begging the question, how much was enough? Jordan had hinted several times during the season that he might be playing his final year. But when asked whether the bottle of victory champagne he was holding after securing his fifth title represented a full career, Michael replied, "No. When it gets to six, it's going to be bigger."[7]

So much for parity.

As talking heads flooded the off-season airwaves with inevitable predictions of a second Bulls three-peat, the NBA kept on court action flowing via the launch of its women's league, the WNBA. The eight-team league, in the planning stages since April 1996, tipped off on June 21 with clubs in New York, Houston, Cleveland, Charlotte, Los Angeles, Phoenix, Sacramento, and Utah.

The former made up the Eastern Conference, the latter the West. The schedule consisted of 28 regular season games and 3 playoff contests—two semifinal games and a championship. Playoffs were one-game, winner-take-all events. The Houston Comets won the first WNBA title on August 30, beating the New York Liberty 65–51.[8]

The WNBA proved a strong partner in its debut, drawing in excess of a million fans to arenas across the country. Additionally, some 50 million viewers watched games on NBC, ESPN, and Lifetime.[9] But the face of professional basketball remained 34-year-old Michael Jordan, be it on or off the court. And that was just fine with Commissioner Stern. The league had the most famous athlete in the world, still playing near the top of his game. The more Jordan dominated the headlines, the less the league had to worry about debating its problems—namely out-of-control player salaries—in public domain.

It was obvious the salary issue had reached crisis stage. Ever since Charlotte cracked open the bank with the Larry Johnson deal, money had been gushing like water through the sinking *Titanic.* Jordan signed another one-year deal with Chicago for $33 million—more than $6 million *over* the league's then-current team cap of $26.9. The amount seemed astronomical, until compared with other deals. Kevin Garnett, a stilt of raw talent at 21 years of age, signed a 6-year deal with the Timberwolves worth $126 million. Ewing, nearing the end of his career, got a four-year deal from the Knicks for $68 million. Shaq was entering the second year of his seven-year, $120 million contract.[10] In Cleveland, ownership desperate for a superstar of its own brought disgruntled Shawn Kemp to town via a three-way deal with Seattle and Milwaukee. Despite the fact that Kemp's contract ran through 2003, the Cavaliers gave him a new seven-year deal that would pay him an annual salary of $15 million. In comparison, the highest paid player in all of Major League Baseball—the sport without a salary cap—was the Mets' Mike Piazza, whose new seven-year contract paid him $13 million per year.[11]

Owners knew if the trend was allowed to continue, their league—once the envy of the professional sports world—would be in disarray well before the collective bargaining agreement expired in 2001. So again they turned to their $6 million man, David Stern,[12] to correct the ill-advised course they themselves had set.[13]

The commissioner would earn every penny in 1997-98. In addition to the growing labor dispute, the year was host to one of the league's ugliest incidents in its 51-year history. On December 1, Warriors All Star guard Latrell Sprewell assaulted his coach, P. J. Carlesimo, during a heated practice session. Reportedly reacting to criticism, Sprewell threatened to kill Carlesimo, then proceeded to punch and choke his coach until shocked teammates pulled him away. Sprewell was escorted from the building, but returned a short while later and landed another punch before storming out. The Warriors responded by voiding the remainder of his $32 million contract on the grounds that he had failed to "conform to standards of good citizenship and good moral character," as stipulated by Section 16 in the Uniform Player Contract.[14]

A few days later, Stern announced Sprewell would be suspended by the NBA for an entire year without pay — the league's harshest penalty ever. The commissioner said the severity was warranted by Sprewell's decision to return for another go-round at Carlesimo, which constituted a premeditated attack.

Nearly as shocking as the violence itself was the response of the player's union, which insisted the punishment was too severe. As the case awaited arbitration, Sprewell showed his lack of remorse by suing the Warriors and the league under the guise of racial discrimination. In March, arbitrator John D. Feerick ruled that while Sprewell had acted badly, he had not violated the "moral turpitude" clause. The Warriors were ordered to reinstate his contract, and his suspension was reduced to 68 games. In accordance with the collective bargaining agreement, Feerick's decision was final.

Aside from the Sprewell disruption, the season played out much as expected. Scottie Pippen sat out the early part of the year after undergoing toe surgery, but the Bulls still won 62 games. Even a surprisingly determined Indiana Pacers team led by rookie coach Larry Bird could not crash the blockade in Chicago come playoff time. Reggie Miller's crew fell 3-4 in the Conference Finals, setting up the likely scenario of a second three-peat for the Bulls. Along the way, MJ collected All Star Game MVP number three, his tenth scoring title, and another regular season MVP, his fifth.[15]

Out West, Stockton missed the early part of the season because of knee surgery, but Malone kept his club on course to tie Chicago for a league-best 62 wins. More important, the Jazz swept the Bulls 2-0, assuring home court advantage in the playoffs. Seattle won 61 games without the services of Kemp, whose slot had been adequately filled by Vin Baker (19.2 points, 8 rebounds). The Lakers' young nucleus of O'Neal (28.3 points, 11.4 rebounds), Eddie Jones (16.9 points) and Kobe Bryant (15.4 points) matched Seattle's record, while down in San Antonio, another youngster — seven-foot Rookie of the Year Tim Duncan (21.2 points, 11.9 rebounds) — joined David Robinson (21.6 points, 10 rebounds) in the Twin Towers revisited to post a 56-win season for the Spurs. The Lakers trounced the Sonics in the semi-finals 4-1, but a determined Jazz squad would not be denied. Utah dumped Houston, San Antonio, and Los Angeles to earn a second shot at the Bulls.

MJ and company were happy to oblige. Lest anyone forget, it was playoff time, and Phil Jackson's club knew how to win on the road. The Jazz fell in six games again, this time in front of its stunned home crowd, which watched Michael steal the ball from Malone, then hit the game-winning shot, an 18-foot jumper, with 5.4 seconds to play. His Airness finished the game with a series high 45 points, and left town with his sixth Finals MVP trophy in hand — three more than any other NBA player.

Was the champagne bottle full enough yet? Perhaps. A lot depended on

Phil Jackson and Scottie Pippen. Jordan had vowed throughout the season that he would not return to the Bulls without both of them onboard.

Behind the scenes, owners had more pressing matters to discuss than the odds of a "four-peat" in Chicago. Convinced something had to be done to stop the escalating salary madness, they voted 27–2 to take advantage of a three-year-out clause in the collective bargaining agreement that allowed them to reopen negotiations if player salaries exceeded 51.8 percent of basketball-related income.[16] The percentage had already reached 57 and was climbing fast. Players, of course, were quite happy with the way things were, and so a stalemate resulted in another league-imposed lockout for the summer.

Owners wanted to link player salaries to a percentage of the cap, ensuring that no player could make more than 30 percent of his respective team's total payroll. The players union insisted the league had plenty of cash to go around, especially given the huge escalation in television revenues over the past few years. The league was in the final year of its four-year contract with the NBA worth $892 million, up 48 percent from the previous four-year deal. Cable revenues were up 37 percent. Unlike the summer lockout of 1995, neither side spoke optimistically about a settlement prior to the start of the season.

The picture wasn't very optimistic in Chicago, either. Phil Jackson, whose relationship with Bulls owner Jerry Reinsdorf had deteriorated to the point of no return, said he would not come back for a 10th season under any circumstances. The lockout kept Chicago from negotiating a new deal with Pippen. Jordan would not tip his hand, though his agent hinted at the possibility Michael might return if Scottie did.

All wheeling and dealing remained on hold as the lockout continued into September. Training and rookie camps were postponed. When an October 12 exhibition game in Tel Aviv featuring the Miami Heat and Israel's Maccabi Elite was called off, it marked the first time the NBA had lost a game to a labor dispute. Both sides dug in their heels. The exhibition season, 114 preseason games worth an estimated $35 to $40 million in ticket sales,[17] was scratched. Still, owners and players reiterated they were in it for the long haul. The first two weeks of the regular season were officially canceled.

As had been the case during the baseball strike, fans found it hard to sympathize with millionaire owners who claimed they were going broke paying their players outrageous salaries. Players were viewed with similar disdain. A judge had dismissed Sprewell's discrimination lawsuit in July as baseless, but fans remained disgusted with his behavior and the union that had stood behind him. Players whining about lost wages did not endear themselves to the masses, either. Celtics point guard Kenny Anderson was raked over the media coals for complaining he might have to sell one of his eight luxury cars to make ends meet if the lockout continued.

But continue it did. The rest of November was axed, then all of December. Stern asserted that agents who represented some of the most well-paid players in the league were stalling negotiations in order to preserve a system that currently favored the elite while shortchanging those in the middle. Several midrange players spoke up in support of the commissioner's position, but for the most part, the union kept its members in check as it continued to push for a bigger piece of the revenue pie.

Fed up with the lack of progress, Stern called for a vote in early January: either the players demanded their union return to the table and get a deal done or he would declare the season officially over. The players—many without paychecks since July—blinked. Following a lengthy 11th-hour session, a new six-year deal, with owners' option for a seventh, was hammered out. The union settled for 55 percent of shared revenue during the final three years of the deal rather than the 64 percent they had originally demanded, though no limit would apply during the first three. For their part, owners received something no other professional sports league afforded: a maximum salary provision. Existing contracts would not be affected, but all future deals would have an annual ceiling of $9 to $14 million, depending on how long the player had been in the league. Additionally, salaries could increase no more than 10 percent per year during the length of the contract. Free agents could re-up with their teams for 105 percent of their previous salaries. Other issues addressed in the deal included retooling of rookie pay scales, a tightening code of player conduct, increased drug testing, and a ban on marijuana.

Although the union fell short of much it had promised to deliver during the six-month standoff, the majority of players were satisfied and anxious to get back to work. An abbreviated 50-game schedule began on February 5, with a full playoff schedule expected to stretch toward the end of June.

Nearly lost amidst the labor dispute was a trade that sent Mitch Richmond and Otis Thorpe from Sacramento to Washington in exchange for budding superstar Chris Webber (20 points, 13 rebounds, 4.1 assists), a move that would affect the balance of power in the West for years to come. Joining Webber on the Kings was fellow newcomer Vlade Divac (14.3 points, 10 rebounds, 4.4 assists), acquired via free agency, and Sacramento's first-round draft picks from the previous two seasons, point guard Jason Williams (12.8 points, 6 assists) and Yugoslavian Peja Stojakovic (8.4 points, 3 rebounds). The Kings finished the condensed season 27-23 under new head coach Rick Adelman, the franchise's first winning record since it had moved to Sacramento, and its best since 1982-83. Jubilant fans sensed a bright new day had dawned in Arco Arena.

Much to the disappointment of basketball fans in Chicago—and millions of others across the globe—a new day had dawned in the Windy City as well, and it wasn't very bright. Scottie Pippen moved to Houston in a sign-and-trade deal. Teammates Steve Kerr and Luc Longley left town under similar circumstances. All told, only four players from the Bulls' 1998 Championship team returned: Ron Harper, Toni Kukoc, Randy Brown, and Keith Booth. Little known Tim Floyd, the former head coach at Iowa State and a personal friend of Bulls VP Jerry Krause, replaced Zen master Phil Jackson on the bench. More notable than all of the aforementioned combined was the absence of Number 23. Jordan announced his re-retirement on January 14, saying he no longer felt a passion for playing in the NBA. "This is the perfect time for me to walk away from the game," he concluded. "And I'm at peace with that."[18]

Perhaps Michael saw the writing on the wall. This was not the feel-good league Magic and Larry had resurrected 20 years earlier. Johnson's showtime Lakers had given way to the power game of Shaquille O'Neal, and Bird's savvy, hard-working Celtics were but a string of championship banners on the wall. Jordan's freestyle, high-wire act which had swooped in to save the league from the Bad Boys had evolved into a contest of manhood propelled by in-your-face slam dunks. Teams that played together and stayed together were a relic of the past. "The days of having three stars are gone," a prominent sports agent told Harvey Araton of the *New York Times*. "It's two stars and then managing well enough to surround them with the right role players."[19] Two stars, maybe. Provided their main concern was winning. Shawn Kemp had decided $107 million was more important than playing on a championship caliber team.[20] The game's newest would-be stars seemed of similar mindset. Only three of the league's 13 lottery picks from 1995 had remained with the team that had drafted them, and two of those — Kevin Garnett and Bryant Reeves — had signed astronomical contracts that would keep their clubs from surrounding them with quality role players, let alone another star.

While players were busy bolstering their egos and bank accounts, fans were tuning out. Team scoring had fallen off from 110.8 ppg in Jordan's rookie year to 91.6 for '98-99, the lowest average in 45 years.[21] Ticket prices had kept pace with rising salaries, putting the NBA out of reach for many families. The average seat ranged from a low of $26 in Toronto to a high of $79 in New York.[22] To attend a baseball game in the same cities, tickets cost $17 and $23, respectively.[23] Football charged from $34 (St. Louis) to $65 (Tampa Bay),[24] and hockey $26 (Calgary) to $59 (New York).[25] Meanwhile, the day of the sports star as role model had gone the way of the $5 ticket. Kids wanted to "be like Mike" for his $33 million salary, not his hang time. And more and more of those kids were making their dream come true without the benefit of a college education. The maturity factor aside, the influx of so much raw talent had begun to take a toll on the quality of play. Athleticism had taken precedence over skill in a league already diluted because of the NBA's rapid expansion.

If the league had yet to notice, the 1999 Finals provided a shrill wakeup call.

The series represented the first time an eighth seed made it all the way to the championship round. The fact New York was able to do so without the services of its captain Patrick Ewing, who went down in the second game of the Eastern Finals with an Achilles tendon injury, made the club's fairytale finish all the more amazing. New York had retooled its roster again, trading

John Starks, Chris Mills, and Terry Cummings to the Warriors for the bemoaned Latrell Sprewell, and sending veteran Charles Oakley to Toronto for promising young center Marcus Camby. The overhaul looked like another bust when the Knicks finished the abbreviated season 27-23, but the team came together in the playoffs. New York squeezed past top seed Miami 3-2 in the first round on a last-second shot by Allan Houston, swept Atlanta in four games, and beat Reggie Miller's crew in the Eastern Finals, 4-2.

In the West, Seattle, Phoenix, and Houston dropped out of contention, MVP Karl Malone and his Jazz got upended by a resurgent Portland team, and the new Twin Towers of San Antonio finally found their way. Thriving under the steady leadership of head coach Gregg Popovich, the Spurs lost only one game to Minnesota before sweeping the Lakers and Blazers en route to the franchise's first Finals appearance in its 23-year history. The Towers were surrounded by a compliment of savvy veterans including Sean Elliott, Mario Ellie, Steve Kerr, Avery Johnson, and Jerome Kersey — all players who knew how to win. In addition, the club featured two excellent young role players in Antonio Daniels and Malik Rose.

New York's Cinderella season wilted quickly in the suffocating defense of the Texas heat. The Knicks scored a Finals low 10 points in the second quarter of Game 1, losing 77–89, and failed to break 20 points in any quarter of Game 2. The Spurs' 80–67 win was its 12th straight playoff victory, a new NBA record. Alan Houston's 34 points in Game 3 propelled New York to an 89–81 win at the Garden, but the Spurs won the next game 96–89 behind the rebounding of Duncan and Robinson, who combined to grab 35 boards — one more than the entire Knicks team. A hotly contested Game 5 showcased great individual performances by Duncan (31 points, 9 rebounds) and Sprewell (35 points, 10 rebounds), including a stretch during the third and fourth quarters where the two accounted for 28 of the 29 points scored. In the end, however, it was defense that decided the game and the series. New York was held scoreless for the final 3:12, preserving a 78–77 San Antonio win. Duncan was the series MVP.

If owners had expected New York's Cinderella season to rekindle the flame of disgruntled basketball fans, they were sorely disappointed. The five-game series drew a Nielsen of 11.3, the lowest rated Finals since Houston vs. Boston in 1981, a series that had not even been broadcast in prime time.[26] While it is reasonable to blame the labor dispute and the departure of Jordan for part of the fallout, there was definitely broader cause for concern. After reaching an all-time high of 17,252 fans per game in 1995-96, the numbers had begun to creep downward. The shortened 1998-99 season saw a 2.2 percent drop in average attendance over the previous year, accounting for 379 fewer fans per game.[27]

Marketers, who had certainly done their part to help catapult the NBA into the global arena, recognized the drift. Reebok severed ties with Shaquille O'Neal and his annual $3 million paycheck after determining the big man was not the heir apparent to Jordan after all. The company's list of NBA endorsement stars, once in excess of 100, was down to 40. Converse, the unfortunate recipient of Sprewell's endorsement services, dumped him and the under-performing Larry Johnson. Younger stars such as Grant Hill and Allen Iverson remained in demand, contributing to cautious optimism. Smaller companies such as K-Swiss and New Balance were shying away from pro sports stars all together. Even mainstay Nike, which had proven basketball stars *could* sell shoes, saw its first quarterly loss in 13 years. "There's been an over saturation of athletes associated with signature product," the VP of marketing for Fila explained. "It's too much of a good thing, like the stock market correcting itself. Whether it's athletes' off court behavior or people unhappy with the business of sports, people are tired of it and they vote at retail."[28]

Whether owners would count those ballots was one of many questions floating about the league as it prepared to cross into the new millennium. Fans, critics, and the NBA could agree on one thing, however: no answer was more important than how the league handled the loss of its two-time savior, Michael Jordan, especially given that his heir-to-be had failed to arrive by tip-off.

THE AIR APPARENTS

Although the league expected 1999-2000 to be a rebuilding season, owners remained optimistic about its MJ-less future. Several young players had emerged as possible successors to Jordan, though none was yet ready to lace up his shoes. The most promising prospects, at least insofar as the media hype was concerned, were Vince Carter, Tracy McGrady, and Kobe Bryant. All were true fan pleasers on the basketball court: tremendous young athletes capable of performing breathtaking feats. Whether they could become leaders who made their teammates better, however, had yet to be determined.

Of the trio, only Carter had college hoops experience, having played three years at — ironically enough — Jordan's alma mater, North Carolina. Carter was chosen by Golden State with the fifth pick in 1998 and shipped to Toronto in a draft-day deal. Also playing for the Raptors was Carter's distant cousin, Tracy McGrady, drafted ninth by the Raptors in 1997. Carter was 23 years old when the '99-2000 season began. McGrady was 20, and Bryant, who had arrived in Los Angeles via the Divac trade in 1996, was 21.

Bryant was the only All Star in the group. Kobe played 22 minutes in the 1998 game and led the West in scoring with 18 points.[1] The previous year, his rookie season, he made his national debut in the slam dunk contest and proved by far the best of what was considered a relatively thin group of dunking talent. (Other contestants included Chris Carr, Michael Finley, Ray Allen, Bob Sura, and Darvin Ham.) During his first three years with the Lakers, Kobe increased his scoring steadily, from 7.6 in his rookie year to 19.9 during the shortened '98-99 season. Over the same time, his rebounds jumped from 1.9 to 5.3, his assists from 1.3 to 3.8. His minutes increased accordingly, from 16 per game as a rookie to 38 in '98-99.

McGrady was entering his third season. Over his first two years, his scoring rose from 7 points to 9.3, his rebounds 4.2 to 5.7, and assists 1.5 to 2.3 while playing an average of 20 minutes per game. Carter had only the shortened 50-game season under his belt but his stats were impressive: 18.3 points, 5.7 rebounds, and 3 assists. Those numbers reflected a starter's playing time of 35 minutes. Carter won Rookie of the Year hands down in 1999 — an honor neither Bryant nor McGrady could add to their résumés.

Not coincidentally, all three would-be heirs to the throne were of similar build and played small forward, guard, or swingman. The 6'7" Carter weighed 215; Bryant was 6'6" and 200 pounds; McGrady 6'8" and 210. During Michael's playing days, he was listed at 6'6", 195.

Small forwards and guards are generally considered the most athletic players on the court and often lead their teams in scoring. Four-time All Star Grant Hill, once thought to be in the running for Jordan's crown, was a 6'8", 225-pound small forward. The 27-year-old Piston remained one of the league's more popular players, but his game was far less showy than that of Carter, Bryant, or McGrady. Hill averaged a steady 21 points, 7 rebounds, and 6 assists — numbers that had varied little during his five years in the league. But Hill's time to cash in was fading. Detroit had made the playoffs only twice since his arrival, and both occasions had resulted in first-round losses to Atlanta.

It was too soon to judge McGrady, Carter, and Bryant in similar fashion. The Raptors had been in existence only since 1995-96. McGrady had been with the team two years, Carter one. Kobe had seen playoff action in each of his first three seasons, but the Lakers were a playoff team prior to his arrival. And his arrival had coincided with that of Shaquille O'Neal.

No one could carry Jordan's torch, of course, without sharing his appeal to the masses outside the sports arena. Landing a major shoe contract was but an appetizer. The NBA's popularity could not have risen to such global proportions in so short a time span without the aid of MJ's handsome face and alluring on-screen personality, his endorsements of mainstream products from McDonald's fries to GM automobiles.

No company was more aware of that fact than Reebok. The athletic corporation had gambled mightily that the imposing 7'1", 320-pound Shaquille O'Neal would take over where Jordan had left off on the marketing front. "We will use Shaq to catapult to leadership throughout the world," the company's chairman, Paul Fireman, announced after signing O'Neal during his rookie year with the Magic.[2] Alas, it had never come to pass. "Even when basketball sales were very good at Reebok, Shaq shoes didn't sell very well," John Horan, the publisher of *Sporting Goods Intelligence*, an industry newsletter, confided.[3] But O'Neal had certainly delivered *on* the court, transforming Orlando from cellar dweller to title contender.

Ironically, the very qualities that made O'Neal so desirable on the floor worked against him in the endorsement arena. He was so huge, so overpowering, that average consumers were unable to identify with him. Kids could easily envision themselves being like Mike — jumping, twisting, turning, and flying through the air toward the hoop. Few 10-year-olds could imagine themselves as a 320-pound behemoth who powered his way to the basket with two or three defenders hanging on his back.

Nonetheless, the big man's presence on the Lakers made the team one of the hottest sports properties on national TV, and the added exposure definitely gave Bryant a leg up over his competition. Carter and McGrady played on a losing team, and network execs did not like losing teams. The Lakers secured yet another advantage before the start of the 1999-2000 season when Phil Jackson took over as head coach. Jackson instituted the triangle offense he had used so successfully in Chicago, a move that arguably played more to O'Neal's strengths than Bryant's. But it was the end result that mattered: Jackson made the team a contender again. L.A. finished the season with a league-best 67 wins, 11 more than the second-place Indiana Pacers.

Toronto had a respectable season at 45-37, and Carter had a great year individually. He and teammate McGrady competed against each other in the slam dunk contest, which was back after a two-year hiatus.[4] Carter won in impressive fashion, collecting three perfect scores. The most amazing involved a bounce pass delivered by teammate McGrady. Carter scooped up the ball off the bounce, passed it between his legs while in flight toward the hoop, and slammed it through with a one-handed jam. McGrady scored one perfect 50 in the first round, but fell off in the finals, coming in a distant third behind Carter and Houston Rockets rookie Steve Francis.

Comparisons between Carter and MJ soared following the dunk contest, especially given Michael's decision to return to the NBA as President of Basketball Operations for the Washington Wizards several weeks earlier. Jordan's obvious desire to remain active in the league sparked the inevitable rumors that he was contemplating another return to the court. While His Airness insisted he was content to remain behind the scenes, the possibility of him un-retiring again, regardless of how remote, slowed the rise of a probable successor, whether Carter, Bryant, or McGrady.

NBC, halfway through its four-year, $1.6 billion contract with the NBA, had no intention of waiting on MJ. Following Carter's performance at All Star Weekend, the network shifted its schedule to feature the Raptors in a nationwide Sunday afternoon broadcast on February 27, the first game of a planned tripleheader. The broadcast included a short pre-game promo feature on Vince, aka "Skywalker," complete with baby pictures. Carter's name was mentioned 165 times during the actual game broadcast, and cameras zeroed in on him 105 times during live action and replays.[5] Amidst all the hype, Vince managed to deliver an outstanding 43 minutes, finishing with 9 rebounds, 3 steals, and a career-high 51 points in the Raptors' exciting 103–102 win over Phoenix. Teammate McGrady had 15 points, 5 rebounds and 4 steals in 35 minutes.[6]

Ratings-wise, the game pulled in a disappointing 3.4 — the lowest of the tripleheader games. But those numbers were deceiving. NBC was not permitted to add Canadian stations into the mix, essentially removing any benefit the network received from Carter's home market in Toronto—a potential booty of 2.3 million households. By contrast, games featured in the second and third timeslots benefited from their respective team's home market. The Knicks–76ers and Jazz–Blazers regional games pulled in a combined 4.6, with each game drawing larger audiences in its home base. In the nightcap, the Rockets–Lakers and Spurs–Timberwolves topped the day with 4.8. Still, the overall numbers gave NBC reason for concern. Its combined tripleheader rating of 4.2 represented a 25 percent drop from the same period the previous season.[7]

If Carter fell short of network expectations, it was not for lack of effort. Between February 5 and March 22, Air Canada, as he had been dubbed by local fans, scored 20 points or more in 23 straight games. He was the Raptors' leading scorer in 65 of team's 82 regular season contests.[8] Nonetheless, doubts remained. Could Vince dominate in similar fashion to MJ once the playoffs got under way? Few players better understood Carter's situation than former runner-up Grant Hill. "You come after the greatest, there's no way you'll ever live up to it," Hill said of the Air Apparent hype. "None of us could be Michael. None of us ever will."[9]

San Antonio Spurs big man Tim Duncan could certainly relate. Despite his tremendous basketball skills, he played the wrong position and lacked the pizzazz to be like Mike. Nonetheless, the mild-mannered seven-footer from the U.S. Virgin Islands was on track to become one of the league's best power forwards ever. Unlike most young players of his talent level, Duncan had played four college seasons at Wake Forest prior to entering the draft. The experience left him well schooled in the game's fundamentals and in performing in pressure situations. In his third season with the Spurs, Tim surpassed veteran teammate David Robinson to lead the defending champs in rebounding (12.4) and scoring (23.2). On an individual basis, Tim shared the 2000 All Star Game MVP with Shaq and made the All NBA First and All Defensive First teams.

Duncan and his defending champion Spurs looked poised to win back-to-back titles until Tim suffered a late season knee injury. Without him, San Antonio won only one game against Phoenix in the first round of the playoffs. Meanwhile, Chris Webber (24.5 points, 10.5 rebounds) and the free-wheeling Sacramento Kings took the Lakers to five before succumbing in their first round of what signaled a new and exciting Western rivalry. Shaq and Kobe's group disposed of Phoenix 4-1 in the next round, but needed all seven games to subdue a feisty Blazers team — bolstered by the addition of Scottie Pippen — in the Western Finals.

In the East, an ankle injury to Grant Hill helped Miami complete a first-round sweep of Detroit. New York disposed of Air Canada's crew in similar fashion. Carter averaged 19.3 points in the series, down more than 6 ppg from the regular season, while McGrady increased his scoring slightly, from 15.4 to 16.7. Following its sweep of the Raptors, New York faced off against the Heat in what had become one of the league's most bitter rivalries. Ewing's club escaped with a one-point win on the road in Game 7, but fell to Reggie Miller's Pacers 2-4 in the Eastern Finals.

After countless disappointments during the Jordan era, 34-year-old Reggie Miller, in his 14th season with Indiana, finally had a shot at the title. Miller remained one of the league's most overlooked players on the marketing end. Reggie was an alumnus of UCLA, where he trailed only Abdul-Jabbar in all-time points scored with 2,095.[10] During his first pro season, he broke Bird's rookie record for 3-pointers, finishing the year with 61. The lanky, 6'7" guard was most famous for his ability to make big shots near the end of games, a period often referred to as "Miller Time." But Reggie was not enough to lift the small market Pacers beyond mediocrity until 1994, when Indiana played New York in the conference finals. The team had been up and down since that point, though Miller remained a legitimate star, at least on the basketball court.

Unfortunately for Reggie and his fans, his long-awaited Finals debut turned into a nightmare. Miller made only 1 field goal in 16 tries as his Pacers fell in Game 1, 104–87. Shaq led L.A. with 43 points, 19 rebounds, and 4 assists. Kobe added 14 points and 5 assists. The Pacers tried to exploit O'Neal's poor free throw shooting ability in Game 2, sending him to the line for an NBA record 39 attempts. Shaq made only 18 of those, but finished with a game high 40 points and 24 rebounds—enough to put the Lakers up 2-0 as the series headed East.

The Pacers responded in front of their home fans with a 100–91 win, though the Lakers played without Bryant, who had sprained his ankle in Game 2. Reggie tied Shaq for game-high honors with 33. Kobe returned for Game 4 to score 28 points, including the game-winner — a tip-in off a missed basket by Brian Shaw with 5.9 seconds to play. Miller had nailed six-of-eight from behind the arc, but missed the potential game-winning three at the buzzer. Game 5 was Pacers coach Larry Bird's swan song in Indiana, and his emotional team responded by gift-wrapping a 33-point win.[11] The Pacers hung tough in L.A. throughout Game 6, but the Lakers pulled out a 116–111 win for their 12th NBA title. Shaq, who had averaged a phenomenal 38 points and 16.7 rebounds in the series, added Finals MVP to his regular season and co–All Star Game MVPs.

While O'Neal established himself as the most dominant player in the game, Bryant took the lead in the Jordan heir apparent race by virtue of visibility. In March, he appeared on the cover of *Forbes* under the headline "The New Stars of Money." His spectacular, over-the-top game-winning tip-in at the end of Game 4 in the Finals drew instant comparisons to MJ's famous late-game heroics. The media dubbed him a leader, wise beyond his years.

Meanwhile, Vince and Tracy, still feeling the sting of a first round sweep, could do little but watch from the sidelines. As Carter dropped to runner-up, McGrady fell through the crack. Any media hype he received was geared toward the theory he made a great one-two punch for Carter, as Pippen had done for MJ. Such talk did little to entice McGrady into a long-term association with Cousin Vince in Toronto. The Raptors had made steady improvement, but remained years away from serious contention. From a marketing standpoint,

Toronto was a world away from the spotlights of Hollywood and Broadway. McGrady wanted a chance to show he could lead a team to the Finals, and the Orlando Magic, still smarting from the loss of O'Neal, was overjoyed to present him with the opportunity. McGrady would pair with All Star Grant Hill, another disenchanted free agent snapped up by Orlando. Each was given a seven-year, $93 million deal.[12]

Carter joined the Olympians in Sydney that summer, but he was a late addition. Tim Duncan and Grant Hill were scratched due to late season injuries, and Shaq had declined a request to join the team, as had teammate Kobe Bryant. Carter joined Kevin Garnett, Gary Payton, Ray Allen, Antonio McDyess, Vin Baker, Allan Houston, Jason Kidd, Alonzo Mourning, Steve Smith, and Shareef Abdul-Rahim — a solid yet unspectacular group.

The 2000 team was still good enough to take home the gold, but the USA's margin of victory continued to shrink. In the first round, Team USA beat Lithuania by only nine points, the narrowest victory since the arrival of NBA players in 1992. When the two teams met again in the semi-finals, the United States squeaked out an 85–83 win. The Americans led throughout the gold medal game against France but were unable to pull away until the final minutes, winning 85–75. The United States averaged a modest 95 points per game in its eight-game sweep. Carter was the team's top scorer at 14.8.[13]

The league entered 2000-01 hopeful that either Carter or Bryant would emerge as a clear favorite in the Jordan successor sweepstakes, but NBA fans remained noncommittal. Each player was developing a strong fan base in his own right, but nothing that compared with the popularity of Jordan. Advertisers, however, had made their choice. The new Michael Jordan was neither Kobe nor Vince, but a handsome, personable young *golfer* named Tiger Woods.

THE YOUNG AND
THE RESTLESS

Like Jordan, Woods had something special about him that appealed to the masses, in and out side of the sports world. But Eldrick "Tiger" (named in honor of a Vietnam war comrade of his father) differed from MJ — and most other sports stars with multimillion-dollar endorsement contracts — in that he did not have to worry about how well his team played, or in what city it was located. Golf was all about individual stats, and Woods came up gold. At 24, he was the youngest player to complete a career grand slam, and only the second player ever to win three pro majors in one year. "Other golfers want to win," his father said. "Tiger expects to win. And he doesn't accept second because second stinks."[1]

The multiethnic Woods was every advertiser's dream: A young, handsome, charismatic, sports star who knew how to win. Former PGA Player of the Year Paul Azinger called him a "Michael Jordan in long pants."[2] Marketing execs were of similar mindset. When 21-year-old Woods turned pro in 1996, Nike was waiting with a $40 million contract. Buick, American Express, and game giant Electronic Arts got on board the money train shortly thereafter. In the spring of 2000, Woods signed a contract extension with Nike in excess of $105 million.[3] Bob Williams, the president of Burns Sports Celebrity Service in Chicago, proclaimed Tiger the number one active athlete in the world. "Jordan is still No. 1 overall," Williams added, "but the gap is closing quickly."[4]

Gap or no, NBA owners realized the post–Jordan slump went beyond the lack of a new marketing giant. TV ratings had yet to recover — and that included both college and NBA broadcasts. Some former players blamed the growing number of prep school players jumping directly to the pros. Abdul-Jabbar, working as an assistant with the Clippers, called it the "dumbing-down" of the game. "Young guys are trying to learn the fundamentals in the pros. But there is no time for teaching in the pros!"[5] Jerry West took things a step further, calling for a 20-year age limit. "In the long run, the most important thing is to preserve the integrity of the game rather than continue to add players who need so much more work and so much more care."[6]

Losing the top prep school players to the NBA was also affecting the college game in negative fashion by robbing it of potential stars. School rivalries featuring players who became familiar to fans over the course of several years were relics of the past. If the top-ranked prep stars opted for college, it was rarely for more than a year or two. Most jumped directly to the NBA because greedy agents or team execs desperate for the next Jordan dangled contracts potentially worth millions of dollars in front of their eyes.

Naturally, little was said about what would happen should these prospects fail to catch on with an NBA club, that by signing on the dotted line, they were squandering the opportunity for a free education that would prepare them for alternate careers should they fail to perform at the level necessary to make it in the pros. Scores of young men raised in poverty and surrounded by urban crime had begun to view the NBA as a likely savior for them and their families. Yet for every one who made it, there were tens of thousands who never came close to realizing their dream. "You have to think about the players who fall through the cracks," said four-time All Star Ray Allen, "[those] who aren't as successful and end up not getting a college education or being able to see what that whole experience is like."[7] Grant Hill agreed, recalling the experience of former teammate Korleone Young, a prep player drafted by the Pistons in the second round in 1998. Young's pro career lasted all of three games, during which he played a total of 15 minutes. "He would have benefited by going to school and developing," Grant said.[8]

Ironically, the few who proved good enough to make the leap were causing problems on another front: public relations. Resentment among fans had already set in during the lockout, when multimillionaires had whined about having to stretch their budgets to make ends meet. Now teenagers who had never set foot inside a college gym were collecting more money in a year than most fans made in their lifetimes. While a select few earned their paychecks, most proved works in progress. And, unlike their college-educated counterparts, they were paid handsomely as they learned. Jonathan Bender, the fifth overall pick in the 1999 draft at age 19, was averaging 3.3 points for the Pacers in his second season. Even those with major potential needed several years to develop into solid contributors. Kevin Garnett was among the league's highest paid players at age 24, but the 6-year veteran had yet to lead his team beyond first-round playoff competition. Budding superstar Jermaine O'Neal spent four years as a Blazers reserve before he became a starter in Indiana.

For better or worse, the youth movement had clearly arrived, and it was having a profound effect on the culture of sports. Hip hop music, born in the inner cities during the 1970s, had slowly dethroned rap and classic rock to become the mainstream sound of the NBA. While critics denounced its often racy lyrics as glorified brutality that encouraged violence, supporters claimed it reflected the hopelessness that encompassed poverty by portraying an accurate view of what modern civilization had become. Many of those supporters were divided when it came to the partnership of hip hop and the NBA, however; although some felt the league made a great ambassador, others saw its wealthy, famous stars as hypocrites who had forsaken their roots. Regardless, the music had spurred an entire culture rich with personal expression, not unlike the days of the ABA with its dyed Afros and bright, multicolored clothes. In the age of hip hop, it was tightly braided hairstyles and multiple body tattoos.

Naysayers cited any or all of the above as they peered into their crystal balls, predicting the doom of the NBA. But the facts told quite another story. Attendance for the 1999-2000 season had risen slightly from the lockout year, up 132 fans per game.[9] And although television ratings *were* down, the face of sports was fast evolving into the digital age via the Internet and pay-per-view satellite TV, diminishing the importance of the network Nielsens. November 2000 marked the first anniversary of NBA-TV, the league's 24-hour pay cable station. The network, which billed itself as "all basketball all the time," offered everything from basketball-themed movies and replays of classic games to real-time scores and live game updates. For an additional $169, hardcore fans could purchase NBA League Pass on satellite or digital cable, a package that included coverage of almost every regular season game on the schedule. The league's website at NBA.com was among the top five trafficked sports sites on the Internet, having averaged more than 800,000 visitors per *day* during the 2000 Finals.[10] The website also linked fans to a newly revamped NBA online store where they could purchase official NBA gear featuring their favorite teams and players, regardless of whether they lived in Manhattan or Singapore.

The revolution was not confined to the digital arena. Advertising within those mediums helped push old-fashioned marketing venues to a new level. The NBA operated a state-of-the art retail store on Fifth Avenue in New York, featuring the same authentic gear available from its Internet site. Fans vacationing in Orlando could stop by NBA City at Universal Studios Plaza for a burger and fries at the league's theme-based restaurant. The bistro featured a rich array of historic photographs and video clips, as well as an interactive game center and, of course, a merchandise shop featuring the latest in official NBA gear.

Bottom line, predictions of the NBA's demise were vastly premature. The same went for the epitaph of runner-up number three in the Jordan replacement sweepstakes, Carter's cousin, Tracy. Playing in his debut season with the Magic, "T-Mac" posted the biggest offensive improvement of the three would-be kings, increasing his production from 15.4 to 26.8 points per game — good enough for seventh best in the league and the 2001 NBA's Most Improved Player award. Meanwhile up in Tracy's former playground, the Raptors won two more games without him to finish at 47-35. Air Canada upped his scoring a couple of points to 27.6, fifth best in the league. Kobe Bryant was fourth at 28.5.

Unfortunately for Michael Jordan, his new club was anything but improved. Washington won only 19 games under the front office guidance of His Airness—10 fewer than the previous season. Ironically, only Chicago had a worse record in the East, finishing the year at 15-67. Across the way in New York, the Knicks played without their imposing center for the first time in 16 years. Ewing, in the last year of his $60 million contract, was traded to Seattle in a multiteam deal that netted four draft picks and six midrange players. The Knicks washed out in the first round of the playoffs without him, but the real story in the East was the rebirth of the Philadelphia 76ers, led by the league's top scorer, Allen Iverson.

At 6 feet, 165 pounds, Iverson was one of the smallest players in the NBA and one of the most dynamic. The 25-year-old guard averaged 31.1 points in 2000-01, the highest regular season scoring average since Jordan's 32.6 in 1993. He also topped the league in steals, snatching 2.51 per game. The former Georgetown standout, aka "The Answer," had led the Sixers in scoring since joining the team in 1996-97, and consistently finished among the league's top assist men. At the 2001 All Star Game in Washington, he led the East to a thrilling 111–110 comeback win, scoring 15 of his game high 25 in the fourth quarter en route to MVP.

What Iverson lacked in size he made up for in pure energy and devotion to winning. "I see traits of me in him in terms of his competitive nature,"[11] Jordan said. Had it not been for several off-court incidents, Iverson may very well have been in the running for the heir apparent race despite his lack of hang time. But Allen had a storied background, stemming from all-too-familiar circumstances: inner city poverty and a broken home. He'd had several run-ins with the law, and had established a habit of arriving late for practice. Additionally, he was among the first NBA players to popularize cornrows and body tattoos—an image that had yet to be embraced by corporate America. Prior to the start of the 2000-01 season, he came under fire for a rap CD that bashed gays, women, and blacks. Iverson eventually issued an apology, but the damage had been done. As good as he was on the basketball court, Iverson did not represent The Answer sponsors had in mind for Jordan's successor.

But that did not stop the feisty guard from leading his team to an Eastern-best 56 wins. Among Iverson's supporting cast were point guard Eric Snow, Defensive Player of the Year Dikembe Mutombo, former Bull Toni Kukoc, and solid swingman Aaron McKie. Head coach Larry Brown, in the midst of his 20th NBA season, was in his fifth year with Philadelphia.

Tim Duncan's Spurs were the best regular season team in the West and the league, finishing the year at 58-24, but the Lakers and Kings were breathing down their necks with 56 and 55 wins, respectively. All told, 10 teams finished the 2000-01 season with 50 or more wins and only 6 had fewer than 30, making a strong case for management's claim the salary cap was doing its part to promote parity within the league.

In the Eastern playoffs, Carter's Raptors advanced to the second round for the first time in franchise history and forced the surging 76ers to seven games before bowing out with a one-point loss. Carter averaged 27.3 points in postseason play, slightly off his regular season output of 27.6, but much improved from the 6-point drop-off the previous year. Down in sunny Orlando, the playoff fate of the Magic rested heavily on Cousin Tracy's shoulders. Grant Hill's ankle hadn't healed as expected, forcing the six-time All Star to miss 78 regular season games and the entire playoffs. McGrady responded to the challenge by scoring nearly 34 ppg in the Magic's first-round series against the Bucks, but it was not enough to defeat a resurgent Milwaukee team led by the high-scoring trio of Ray Allen (22 points), Sam Cassell (18.2), and Glen Robinson (22). The Bucks, headed by former Seattle coach George Karl, pushed the Conference Finals to seven games before succumbing to Iverson's 76ers. Philadelphia was heading back to the Finals for the first time since the 1983 team led by Moses Malone and Julius Erving had swept the Lakers in four straight.

Out west, Kevin Garnett's Timberwolves fell in the first round again, losing 1-3 to Duncan's Spurs. San Antonio easily disposed of Dallas in the semifinals 4-1, but Tim's hope for another title ran into a brick wall covered with the size 22 shoeprints of Shaquille O'Neal. The Spurs were swept by the Lakers in the Western Finals, losing by an average of more than 22 points per game. But San Antonio was not the only Western victim to fall so quickly. Phil Jackson's club entered the Finals with a perfect 11-0 postseason record.

Allen Iverson showed Lakers fans why he was league MVP in Game 1, netting 48 points in the Sixers' shocking 107–101 overtime win at Staples Center in L.A. The Answer averaged 32.5 points over the next four games, but it was not enough to combat a determined O'Neal. The Lakers took the series in five to post a 15-1 NBA playoff best-ever record. Shaq (33 points and 15.5 rebounds) won his second consecutive Finals MVP.

Bryant's postseason stats of 29.4 points, 7.3 rebounds, and 6 assists represented his best all around showing to date. His continued improvement, paired with Shaq's overpowering dominance, fueled talk of a probable Lakers three-peat in 2002. As such, Kobe remained the frontrunner in the Jordan replacement sweepstakes until September 25, when the Wizards announced the original was returning to the court.

Speculation on why Jordan decided to un-retire again varied among the talking heads. Some attributed it to ego, others to his insatiable desire to remain a part of the game. Even Michael himself offered mixed messages.

I am returning as a player to the game I love because during the last year and a half, as a member of the Washington Wizards' management, I enjoyed working with our players, and sharing my own experience as a player. When I left the game, I left something on the floor. When I retired last time, I didn't say I was ready to quit the game. It's an itch that still needs to be scratched here, and I don't want that itch to bother me for the rest of my life.... It's all about challenges and going out and seeing if I can achieve something. America is supposed to be free will and choosing what you want to do. That's all I'm doing.... I'm just trying to play the game of basketball.[12]

Assisting MJ on his return flight was none other than Doug Collins, Jordan's former and first NBA coach. Collins gave up his popular broadcasting position with TNT to take the Wizards coaching job at Jordan's request. Rumors that Charles Barkley, who had called it a career after the 1999-2000 season due to chronic knee problems, would also un-retire to join his friend on the court proved premature. Barkley toyed with the idea, but remained at TNT, where he and Kenny Smith joined host Ernie Johnson on the network's increasingly popular postgame show, *Inside the NBA*.

Without Sir Charles, Jordan was by far the Wizards' elder statesman at 38. Only four other players on the team were 30 years or older: Christian Laettner (32), Popeye Jones (31), Chris Whitney (30), and Hubert Davis (31). Of those, only Laettner and Jones saw regular minutes. The remaining Wizards averaged 23 years of age and possessed a grand total of 12 years of NBA experience among them. Four were rookies, including the top draft pick of 2001, 19-year-old Kwame Brown — the first of a record four prep players chosen in the top 10.[13] A 6'11", 243-pound forward out of Glynn Academy in Brunswick, Georgia, Kwame was the first high school player to be drafted number one, and the youngest in NBA history.

Jordan's age and the fact that he had been away from the game for three years may have given critics reason for pause as the season got under way, but network television execs were floating on cloud nine. TNT's October 30 opening night broadcast of the Wizards–Knicks game posted a 3.3 rating, up 106 percent from the previous year's tip-off— the best showing for an NBA opening night game since cable had entered the fray in 1994.[14] The number was all the more impressive given the broadcast competed directly with Game 3 of the World Series. Unfortunately for His Airness, his team high 19 points, 6 assists, and 4 steals were not enough to prevent a 91–93 loss to New York. "I guess the biggest difference is I'm a little older than I was the last time I shot the ball," Jordan told reporters after shooting a lackluster 7-for-21 from the field. "My game's a little bit different. My teammates are a little bit different. Obviously, the outcome tonight was a little different than I wanted."[15]

And so it would be for much of the season. MJ averaged a very respectable 22.9 points, 5.7 rebounds, and 5.2 assists, but his body was showing its age. Bad knees and numerous other injuries limited him to 60 games and a field goal percentage of .416, the second lowest of his career. Michael was voted an All Star for the 13th time, but he scored only 8 points on 4-for-13 shooting in 22 minutes of play as the East lost on its home turf in Philadelphia, 120–135. Topping Jordan's highlight reel was an attempted break-away dunk that banged off the back of the rim as the sold-out crowd of 19,581 looked on in disbelief.

Ironically, the game's MVP was top Airness runner-up Kobe Bryant, whose game high 31 points was the best individual showing at an All Star Game since Jordan's 40 in 1988. The Lakers star played 30 minutes, shot 12-for-25 from the field and 7-for-7 at the line, grabbed 5 rebounds, and dished out 5 assists — all amidst a heavy shower of boos from the local crowd. Kobe had played his high school ball at nearby Lower Merion, but rather than view him as the hometown boy made good, fans saw him as a traitor who had helped propel the Lakers to a 4-1 victory in the 2001 Finals. Locals wanted desperately to cheer for their NBA hometown guy, especially with Iverson donning a Number 6 jersey in honor of former Sixers superstar Dr. J. Unfortunately, Allen had one of his worst outings ever, scoring only five points in 25 minutes as the West dominated the game from start to finish.

The lone bright star for the East was the performance of third runner-up, Tracy McGrady. T-Mac had 4 steals, 3 rebounds, and 4 assists to go with 24 points, including a breathtaking dunk that was clearly the play of the game. McGrady dribbled upcourt amid heavy defense, tossed the ball off the backboard from the free throw line, caught it coming off the glass, and threw it down with a reverse dunk. Tracy had expected to reunite with former teammate Cousin Vince on the Eastern squad, but Carter — the top vote-getter in fan balloting for the third straight year — had to sit out the game with a quadriceps strain.

As it turned out, Iverson's lackluster performance at the All Star Game proved hauntingly prophetic for 76ers fans. While The Answer had another great year individually — he was the league's top scorer for the second straight year, averaging 31.4 ppg — the season did not go well for the defending Eastern Champions. Various injuries to Iverson, Aaron McKie, Eric Snow, and newcomer Derrick Coleman kept Larry Brown's club from reaching its full potential. The Sixers finished the year a disappointing 43-39, and were ousted in the first round by an all too familiar opponent: the Boston Celtics.

Bean Town, meanwhile, was abuzz with talk of its revitalized men in green, who were out to prove there *was* life after Larry Bird, even if had taken a decade for rebirth. Leading the charge was fourth-year man, Paul Pierce, a 6'6" shooting guard out of Kansas. Drafted by Boston with the 10th pick in 1998, Piece had increased his offensive output from 16.5 as a rookie to 26.5 in 2001-02, third best in the league. The 24-year-old was also Boston's second-best rebounder with 6.9, and third in assists at 3.2. The Celtics featured another rising star in 6'8" forward Antoine Walker, the team's first-round pick in 1996. Walker and Pierce were joined by a solid group of veterans that included Kenny Anderson, Eric Williams, Rodney Rogers, Tony Delk, Erick Strickland, and Tony Battie. Jim O'Brien was in his second year as head coach.

Boston finished the regular season at 49-33, the first time it had won more than 40 games since Bird's 1991-92 finale. Pierce proved he could deliver under pressure in the deciding Game 5 against the Sixers, when he pumped in 46 points, including 8-of-10 from three-point range. His total of 151 points in the five-game series broke Bird's record of 122. The Celtics went on to defeat the Pistons 4-1 in the next round before falling to the Nets 2-4 in the Conference Finals.

New Jersey, appearing in the Finals for the first time in franchise history, was led by point guard Jason Kidd, who had been acquired in a trade with Phoenix for Stephon Marbury. The eight-year veteran consistently placed among the league's top assist men, but averaged less than 15 ppg. In fact, the Nets had no player who averaged 15 points. Leading the team was second-year man Kenyon Martin with 14.9. As a team, the Nets ranked 18th in offense at 96.2 ppg. Defensively, however, it was second-best team in the league, giving up only 92. New Jersey was among the youngest teams in the NBA with an average player age of 25.9. Reserve guard Lucious Harris was the club's elder statesman at 31. Former Lakers guard Byron Scott was in his second year as the Nets head coach.

Out West, the big story was not Tim Duncan's first MVP season nor the Lakers' quest for a three-peat, rather the emergence of the title-hungry Sacramento Kings. The combination of All Star big men Chris Webber (24.5 points, 10.1 rebounds, 4.8 assists) and former Laker Vlade Divac (11.1 points, 8.4 rebounds, 3.8 assists) gave the club one of the best passing frontlines in the league. Yugoslavian small forward Peja Stojakovic (21.2 points, 5.3 rebounds, 2.5 assists), in his fourth season, was fast developing into one of the league's deadliest outside shooters. Point guard Mike Bibby (13.7 points, 5 assists) blended well with his defensive-minded backcourt mate, Doug Christie (12 points, 4.2 assists, 4.6 rebounds, 1.95 steals), while sixth man Bobby Jackson (11.1 points, 3.1 rebounds, 2 assists) added spark and firepower off the bench. Twelve-year veteran coach Rick Adelman was in his fourth year with the Kings. Sacramento— second in the league in offense at 104.6 ppg — posted a franchise-best 61-21 record en route to its first Pacific Division crown.[16]

In the Midwest Division, Kevin Garnett (21.2 points, 12.1 rebounds, 5.2 assists) led his Timberwolves to another 50-win season only to disappoint yet again at playoff time. Minnesota fell 0-3 to Dallas— the sixth year in a row the team had failed to advance beyond the first round. The Kings lost only one game in each of its first two playoff series against Utah and Dallas en route to the Conference Finals, while down in L.A., the Lakers followed up its Portland sweep with a 4-1 trouncing of the Spurs, sending Tim Duncan and his MVP trophy home to Texas for another extended summer vacation.

For the third year in the row, Sacramento would meet the Lakers in post-season play, this time in the Western Conference Finals. The seven-game duel proved one of the most hard-fought, thrilling series in recent NBA history. Sacramento was up two games to one and looked on its way to taking a commanding 3-1 lead in the closing seconds of Game 4 until Robert Horry nailed a 3-pointer at the buzzer for a 100–99 Lakers win. The Kings held on for a 92–91 win in Game 5 to retain home court advantage, but the defending champs took

Game 6 on their home floor, 106–102. Sacramento fought its heart out in Game 7, but the Lakers prevailed on the Kings' court in overtime, 112–106.

"I think it's safe to say we don't like them much, and they don't like us,"[17] Lakers forward Rick Fox said after the win. Indeed, the California rivalry had become everything the NBA could hope for, and ratings were no exception. The game drew an overnighter of 16.9 — up 66 percent from the previous year's deciding Game 7 Eastern Finals match up between the Sixers and Bucks. Game 6, which had aired on Friday night, pulled in 13.5, the highest overnight rating for a playoff game — excluding the Finals — since the Portland–Lakers Game 7 in 2000.[18]

The Lakers–Kings Western Finals would have been a difficult act to follow for the best of title series, and, alas, the Lakers–Nets proved anything but memorable. Los Angeles easily prevailed in four games, joining the Boston Celtics and the Chicago Bulls as the only franchises in NBA history to win three or more consecutive titles. The lopsided show drew an average rating of 10.2, the lowest number for a Finals series since 1982, when the games were moved to the live, primetime format.[19]

While interest from television viewers in the States may have been waning, NBA broadcasts continued to gain popularity overseas. The 2002 Finals were available in 36 languages and 205 countries, drawing an estimated 2.5 billion viewers.[20] And no wonder. Basketball fans around the world had much to cheer about. The 2002 Rookie of the Year was not Kwame Brown or Tyson Chandler — American prep stars who had gone one and two in the 2001 draft — but the number three pick, Pau Gasol, a 21-year-old 7-foot forward from Spain.

Gasol was the first foreign player who had not attended an American university to win the award, and one of a record three to make the All Rookie First Team, joining Tony Parker (France) of the Spurs and Utah's Andrei Kirilenko (Russia). Two more imports from Yugoslavia — the Sonics' Vladimir Radmanovic and Detroit's Zeljko Rebraca — made the All Second Rookie squad. Previously, a *total* of three such foreigners (those who had not attended college in the United States) had made the All Rookie First Team: Cleveland's Zydrunas Ilgauskas (1998), Arvydas Sabonis of the Blazers (1996), and then–Laker Vlade Divac (1990).

As Europeans celebrated their long-awaited coup, NBA fans in the People's Republic of China were preparing a gala for their favorite star on the Shanghai Sharks: the number one pick in the 2002 NBA draft, 7'6" Yao Ming.

THE GLOBAL REVOLUTION

Born in Shanghai, China, on September 12, 1980, Yao Ming appeared destined to follow in the footsteps of his tall, athletic parents; his father, Yao Zhi Yuan, stands 6'7", and his mother, Fang Feng Di, 6'3". Fang was once the captain of China's National Team, while Yao's father played for the Shanghai Sharks, a local professional club. Yao, jokingly nicknamed the "Little Giant," began learning organized basketball at the Youth Sports School in China when he was nine. Three years later, his parents sent him to Shanghai's Provincial Sports Academy, where he worked diligently on developing his game for several hours every day. He joined the Shanghai Youth Team a couple of years later.

Needless to say, word of the Little Giant spread quickly to the States. The 17-year-old's performance at Nike's All American Camp in Paris led to a U.S. visit where he and fellow Sharks teammate Lui Weil played with an elite AAU junior squad before traveling to Indianapolis to attend the prestigious Nike All American camp. In a field that boasted the top 200 teenage players in America, coaches and recruiters ranked Ming the second-best center.[1]

Playing on China's National Team in the 2000 Olympics, Ming had led his country with a .639 field goal percentage, averaging 10.5 points, 6 rebounds, and 2.2 blocks. His performance at Sydney fueled rumors that he would enter the 2001 NBA draft, but unlike most international players, it was not simply a matter of Yao signing on the dotted line. Permission from the Chinese government and the Sharks had to be secured before such a move could even be considered. The situation was further complicated by several zealous sports agents fighting over who had signed Ming to what and when. In the end, Yao's name was left off the list. He remained with the Sharks for the 2001-02 season and won his second straight MVP, posting averages of 29.7 points, 18.5 rebounds, and 4.8 blocks. The Sharks went on to win their first championship; Ming averaged a phenomenal 41 points and 21 rebounds in the best-of-five series.[2]

Ming's obvious potential for greatness—and China's desire to play host to the 2008 Olympic Games—softened the government's view. Yao was allowed to enter his name in the 2002 draft, though several stipulations would apply prior to his being able to sign an actual NBA contract: a transfer fee would be paid to the Sharks, a percentage of his NBA salary would be handed over to various Chinese sporting agencies, and the CBA (Chinese Basketball Association) would be allowed to call him back to China for international competition whenever it wished.

Critics remained skeptical that Ming would ever be allowed to play in the NBA, but the Houston Rockets selected him with their number one pick, making him the first international league player ever chosen number one overall. "This is now a new start in my basketball life," the 21-year-old Yao said, speaking through an interpreter during a postdraft interview. "This is a new league in front of me for me to play, so it will be a new challenge for me. I know there will be a lot of difficulties in front of me, but I'm confident that I will learn from the NBA and improve myself and improve Chinese basketball in the future."[3]

Yao was one of a record six international players selected in the first round of the 2002 NBA draft. The others, in order of their selection, were: Nikoloz Tskitishvili, a 7-foot center from Georgia (#5, Denver), Nene Hilario, a 6'11" forward out of Brazil (#7, New York), Bostjan Nachbar, a 6'9" forward from Slovenia (#15, Houston), Jiri Welsch, a 6'7" guard from the Czech Republic (#16, Philadelphia), and Nenad Krstic, a 7-foot center from Yugoslavia (#24, New Jersey). In a stark reversal of recent trends, only *one* prep star was selected in the first round: Amare Stoudemire, a 6'10" forward from Orlando (#9, Phoenix). Eight more foreigners were chosen in the second round, compared with zero high school players.

To suggest teams had deemed the prep star frenzy a failure was premature, but clearly a caution sign had been raised. Owners shelling out millions of dollars to inexperienced rookies expected to see at least some return for their money in the here and now. The top four high school players chosen in 2001 (Kwame Brown #1, Tyson Chandler #2, Eddy Curry #4, and DeSagana Diop #8) had posted a combined average of 4.7 points and 3.3 rebounds in their rookie year. Currie topped the group with 6.7 points and 3.8 rebounds. The three foreigners selected (Pau Gasol #3, Vladimir Radmanovic #12, Tony Parker #28) averaged 11.2 points and 5.1 rebounds. Rookie of the Year Gasol led the trio with 17.6 points and 8.9 rebounds.

As Magic had pointed out during the 1992 Olympics, these guys could play. Regarding their current and would-be American counterparts who expected a leg up because of their native homeland, former champion Pistons and Dream Team coach Chuck Daly had a few words of warning: "They better pay attention to what's happening.... They're [foreign players] willing to practice many, many hours on shooting. Our people are not. We have great athletes who don't have the skill of shooting the basketball."[4]

While pure shooting had yet to become a lost art, there were signs the game was moving in that direction. Prolific scorers like Bryant, McGrady, Pierce, and Iverson consistently finished among the league leaders in scoring, but all were volume shooters, taking far more shots than they made. Of the 11 guards who made the top 20 in scoring during the 2001-02 regular season, Bryant led the pack with 47 percent accuracy. Iverson brought up the rear at just under 40 percent. Together, the 11 combined for a field goal percentage of 44 percent. Ten years earlier, in 1991-92, 13 of the top 20 scorers were guards. That group shot a combined 49 percent. Six players made better than half their shots, led by the Warriors' Chris Mullin, who shot an impressive .524. The top scoring guards of 1981-82 also averaged 49 percent, though only six made the list. As the Bird and Magic Show reformed the face of the NBA, offensive-minded small forwards were at their peak. Nine made the top 20 scorers in 1981-82. Together, they averaged 23.2 points on 52 percent shooting.[5]

China's Yao Ming (7'5", 296 pounds) became the first international player drafted number one overall (Houston, 2002) to jump directly from his home country to the NBA. He is fast becoming the global marketing face of the league.

The decline in field goal percentage was reflected in team scoring as a whole. From 1957-58 through 1992-93, NBA clubs had posted an average of 110.2 points per game. During that 36-year span, only twice had that average failed to better 105 points: in 1974-75 (102.6 points) and 1975-76 (104.5). Beginning with the 1993-94 season, however, offensive production began to decrease on an annual basis. The low point came during the 1998-99 lockout season, when clubs scored an average of 91.6 points, the lowest total since 1953-54, the last season played without the 24-second shot clock. Averages for 2000-01 stood at 94.8, with players connecting on 44 percent of their field goals—the worst, excluding the 50-game lockout season, in 33 years.

The league was not anxious to acknowledge its decreased scoring was a concern, but owners had approved several major rules changes in 2001-02 in an attempt to jumpstart the stagnate offensive. Hand checking, previously prohibited, was allowed as long as refs determined it did not impede the offensive player's progress; the 10-second count to advance the ball across the midcourt line was reduced to eight; a three-second defense rule was added; the illegal (zone) defense was eliminated. The hand checking rule appeared to favor the defense, though in theory, the fewer fouls called, the faster the game. Teams were forced to start their offensive more quickly under the eight-second count, but the change also increased the chance of backcourt turnovers via multiplayer traps. The three-second defensive rule, which had actually been part of the old illegal defense, was intended to prevent defenders from clogging up the paint — an increasingly common strategy employed by coaches to stop easy inside scores by opponents, especially layups. Under the rule, a defender had to be within close proximity of an offensive player while in the paint or he was whistled for a technical foul. The league hoped that more stringent enforcement of the rule, while at the same time permitting a perimeter zone defense, would cut down on rough fouls under the basket.

Nixing the illegal defense rule that had long separated the college and international game from the NBA was expected to have more far-reaching effects, and critics were sharply split on whether it was good or bad for the NBA. Under the old rule, a player could guard only one man exclusively unless he left to double the offensive player with the ball; players who left to double a man without the ball were called for illegal defense, resulting in a technical foul.[6] The new rule allowed players to gang up on *any* offensive player, a move opponents feared would effectively stifle scoring outbursts by the game's best one-on-one players and make it more difficult for big men like Shaq and Duncan to set up in the post.

"The pro offense will be reduced to 15 passes and a 23-foot jumper," Dave D'Alessandro of *Sporting News* predicted. "And since most guys who shoot jumpers hit them about 40 or 42 percent of the time, it would be nice if someone explained how this might translate into a more exciting game."[7] Others were more optimistic. "The new rules will force a change," argued *Basketball Digest*'s Brett Ballantini, "and not for the worst."[8] Critics who weighed in with Ballantini anticipated the new rules would force one-on-one players to buy into a team game, while improving the game's fundamentals: cutting and passing, setting picks — and making midrange open jump shots, a skill that was fast becoming lost amid the wave of three-point bombs and brassy power dunks.

While it was premature to predict which side would eventually claim victory, early results were not promising. Point production rose marginally in 2001-02, up to 95.4, but field goal accuracy remained a dismal 44 percent across the league. By the halfway point of 2002-03, those numbers had dipped to 91.5 points on slightly less than 43 percent shooting.[9]

As had been the case for most of his career, Michael Jordan, who turned 40 on February 17, remained ahead of the pack. MJ had struggled during his first season with the Wizards, posting the second-lowest percentage of his career

(.416), but he regained his shooting touch in 2002-03, finishing the year at .445. His season highlight came just a few days after his birthday, when he torched the Nets for 43 points on 18-for-36 shooting. Alas, the one-two punch of His Airness (20 points) and Jerry Stackhouse (21.5 points) was not enough to propel the 37-45 Wizards into the playoffs. Michael hung up his shoes for good after the regular season finale against Philadelphia on April 16, ending a disappointing year that had been riddled with in-team fighting and finger-pointing. "Now I guess it hits me that I'm not going to be in uniform anymore, and that's not a terrible feeling. It's something that I've come to grips with, and it's time. This is the final retirement."[10]

Jordan's critics, those who had said he ought to have stayed off the court because he could no longer be great *every* night out, would finally be silenced. But he left them with some numbers to think about as he headed into the sunset. During 2002-03, he led the Wizards in scoring 36 times and was the top assist man 25 nights. He logged 40 or more points in 3 games, 30 or more points in 9 games, and 20 or more points in 42 games. As George Kimball of the *Boston Herald* aptly put it, "The final benchmark should be this: When Jordan retires again this month, he will leave the NBA in better hands than it was the last time he walked out the door. Wasn't that sort of the point of this whole exercise in the first place?"[11]

No one had reason to answer that question with a resounding yes more than Wizards owner Abe Pollin. Although his dream of making Washington a title contender with MJ had not materialized, the Wizards had sold out every home game for the past two seasons, drawing an average of 20,335 fans—an increase of 5,017 fans per game over the two seasons prior to Jordan's arrival. With an average NBA ticket costing roughly $52, that translated into an extra $21,392,488 in ticket revenue alone — not bad, especially when taking into account that Jordan was on the payroll for the league's minimum salary (around $1 million per year). While it was true that Michael's input insofar as drafts and trades had yet to produce a playoff team, the same could be said for most young clubs. But the days when owners left basketball decisions to basketball people and waited patiently for their team to develop had vanished beneath the reality of guaranteed contracts worth tens of millions of dollars. The name of the game was to win and win fast. Or lose and pay the price.

Even Michael Jordan was not immune; his expected return as president of Basketball Operations for the Wizards was nullified in early May via a pink slip from Pollin. "I am shocked by this decision and by the callous refusal to offer me any justification for it," Jordan said afterward. "I want to thank the fans for the support I received during my 3½ years here. I have never backed down from a challenge, and I'm disappointed that I wasn't given the opportunity to make this franchise one of proud tradition. I will never forget the outpouring of affection I received from the fans."[12] Pollin released a statement saying that while he did not question Michael's desire to win, management had decided to go in another direction.

"He's still considered the greatest player to ever play the game of basketball," former Wizards teammate Richard Hamilton said of the news. "I don't think anybody can take that away from him."[13] Indeed. Jordan led the league in scoring a record 10 times during his 15-year career. He left the game with a scoring average of 30.12, putting him in a virtual tie with Chamberlain as the best in NBA history. His total points scored — 32,292 — ranks third behind Abdul-Jabbar (38,387) and Karl Malone (36,928). The five-time MVP won six championships and was Finals MVP in every one of them. He was voted an All Star 14 times, named the game's MVP in three of those, and won the slam dunk contest twice. He scored 50 points or more in 37 games, including 5 over 60. He owns the highest scoring average of an NBA Finals (1993, 41 ppg), and the best career playoff average (33.4 ppg). Reflecting on the illustrious career of His Airness, former NBA coach and popular TNT/ABC broadcaster Hubie Brown observed, "I think the quality that sets him apart from other players is that he set the bar of excellence at such a high level that in our immediate future, his status is unlikely to ever be challenged."[14]

Jordan was one of three NBA legends to play his final season in 2002-03. Out west in Utah, 41-year-old John Stockton ended a remarkable 18-year run with the Jazz — every one of which had resulted in postseason play. The 10-time All Star left the game atop the all-time assist list with 15,806. His 10.5 assists per game remains second only to Magic's 11.2 career average. The Jazz and its aging Stockton-Malone duo had not advanced beyond first-round playoff competition in several years, however, and 2003 proved no exception. Utah was ousted 4-1 by the Pacific Division Champion Sacramento Kings, ending Stockton's quest for an NBA title. "I'm sure there are people that have won championships that haven't had to work very hard at it, and we worked very hard and haven't done it," Stockton acknowledged. "Yet I feel a lot of reward out of the effort that it took to compete for that."[15]

Meanwhile in San Antonio, the Midwest Champion Spurs were attempting to send the game's other retiree, 14-year veteran David Robinson — also a 10-time All Star — to his rocking chair with another ring. Although his scoring role had diminished since the arrival of teammate Tim Duncan in 1997-98, Robinson's regular season career stats of 21.1 points (.518 field goal percentage) and 10.6 rebounds assured him a place among the league's best-ever big men. Nicknamed "the Admiral" for his service in the navy, the 37-year-old Robinson remained one of the most admired and well-liked players in all of professional sports — except, perhaps in Los Angeles, where fans saw their chance for a fourth consecutive NBA title ruined when their Lakers lost 4-2 to the Spurs in the Western semifinals.

L.A. wasn't the only California city in mourning. Sacramento's bid to redeem itself for the heartbreaking Game 7 loss to the Lakers in the 2002 Western Finals fell short when it lost to the Dallas Mavericks in Game 7 of the other Western semi-finals. With its two most feared opponents out of the race, San

Antonio, led by regular season MVP Tim Duncan (23.3 points, 12.9 rebounds, 3.9 assists), finished off its Dallas neighbors 4-2 en route to a Finals match-up against the back-to-back Eastern Conference Champion New Jersey Nets.

Following a tough, first-round 4-2 win over the Milwaukee Bucks, the Nets swept Boston and Detroit to earn its second straight Finals appearance. Jason Kidd had the best offensive year of his career, averaging a team-high 18.7 points while dishing out 8.9 assists. Teammates Kenyon Martin (16.7 points, 8.3 rebounds), Richard Jefferson (15.5 points, 6.4 rebounds), Kerry Kittles (13 points), and Lucious Harris (10.3 points) all made substantial contributions. But the Nets remained among the lowest scoring teams in the league at 95.4. Pitted against one of the West's best defensive teams in the Spurs, the match-up failed to generate much excitement among viewers outside of the local New Jersey and San Antonio markets.

The Spurs' 101–89 victory in Game 1 proved the only time either team scored 100 points in the series. New Jersey averaged 80.6 points in Games 2 through 6, compared to 85.2 for the Spurs. Field goal percentage was even more dismal: 43.1 percent for the Spurs and 37 percent for the Nets. The latter barely escaped the all-time NBA low of 35.5 percent set by the 1958 Celtics. With San Antonio up 42–34 at halftime in Game 5, former NBA great Bill Walton, working as a commentator for ABC, looked into the cameras and asked the obvious: "Where has the shooting gone? Can't anyone make a shot anymore?"[16] It didn't help matters that 7 of the 17 players who saw major playing time in the series had three or fewer years of NBA experience. "It's nice to have young players serve as the future of the league," wrote Sean Deveney of *Sporting News*, "but it's not very nice when those players are forced to be the present, too."[17] Viewers agreed, at least those watching on ABC. The six-game series shown in prime time registered a 6.5 Nielsen, eclipsing the previous Finals low of 6.7 for Houston-Boston in 1981.[18]

Fortunately for the NBA, it no longer relied on America's Nielsens to survive. Of the $900 million the league generated in annual TV revenue, nearly 15 percent came from the NBA's 148 non–U.S. television partners. Games could be seen in 212 countries. The champion Spurs were quite popular abroad, especially in the Virgin Islands, France, and Argentina, the respective homelands of Tim Duncan, starting point guard Tony Parker and rookie Manu Ginobili. And while Yao Ming (13.5 points, 8.2 rebounds) had not single-handedly catapulted the Rockets back into the playoffs during his debut, he was so popular among Asian fans that he was voted onto the starting All Star squad over Shaq. In Yao's homeland, hundreds of millions of viewers watched their hero during the regular season.[19] The Rockets–Lakers game on January 17 drew the second highest ratings for an NBA game broadcast on cable. The Rockets won the game 108–104. Yao had 10 points and 10 rebounds; Shaq scored 31 points and pulled down 13 rebounds.

Television was only a small part of the picture. Some 40 percent of fans who logged onto the league's website at NBA.com did so from outside the United States—and many visited the online store as well as other sites that offered NBA items for sale. International fans accounted for 20 percent of all NBA merchandise sold in 2003.[20]

Yao Ming was proving quite a global commodity for the league. Despite his limited English, he possessed numerous qualities that made him an early hit among marketers. The good-natured, smiling giant was already pitching such big-name products as Apple computers and Visa credit cards. As long as the Rockets continued to improve with Yao, the Little Giant had a future as the global poster boy of the NBA.

On the domestic front, that poster boy window was inching shut for Kobe, Tracy, and Vince, all of whom had been in the league long enough to be observed by the masses on and off the court. Kobe had three NBA titles to show for his seven years in the league, but was lambasted in the media as a loner, unable to get along with his coach or teammates, especially co-superstar and franchise-maker Shaquille O'Neal. Tracy and Vince, neither of whom had adequate help on his respective team to become a contender, were criticized either for shooting too much or not enough, depending on the outcome of the season.

But if three doors had closed, a new one had opened. As the league bid Jordan adieu for the final time, there were whispers of the *true* second coming of His Airness via the number one pick in the 2003 draft—19-year-old LeBron James, a prep school standout from St. Vincent–St. Mary's High School in Akron, Ohio.

A New Foundation

Unlike Vince, Tracy, or Kobe, LeBron James was not promoted as a prodigy with superstar potential, rather the real deal upfront. The 6'8", 240-pound swingman won virtually every national honor available to high school players including the coveted John R. Wooden and Morgan Wooten Awards, and was the *Parade Magazine*, Gatorade, and *USA Today* Player of the Year in both his junior and senior years.

Described as a mixture of Jordan and Magic, LeBron was a great ball handler and passer who could run up the court with the quickest of defenders, hit open jumpers, or jam it home with a variety of impressive dunks. No player entering the draft had been so hyped since the arrival of Abdul-Jabbar in 1969; numerous sellout crowds in excess of 20,000 had turned out to see him play in high school All Star Games. Aside from James's obvious talent, what really separated the new would-be heir from previous runners up was the Big C: charisma. "From the moment he enters a room, or a gym, like Michael Jordan or Paul Newman, he is the center of attention," noted Taylor Bell of the *Chicago Sun Times*. "He is magnetic with a smile as big as a hoop. And, despite so much media scrutiny, he has developed a charming personality that doesn't come equipped with a sharp edge or a sarcastic tone."[1]

Somewhere in his New York office, with the door locked and the shades pulled down, David Stern was jumping up and down, clapping his hands, and smiling like a little boy about to blow out his birthday candles. And suit-and-tie executives at Nike were doing handstands and cartwheels. The athletic giant, which had been in a bidding war with Adidas and Reebok over the future NBA superstar for months, locked up his endorsement services in May — prior to the NBA draft — with a multiyear deal worth over $90 million. The amount was believed to be the highest for an initial endorsement contract for anyone, anywhere.

Skeptics predicted it was too much for any human being to live up to, let alone an unproven youngster who had yet to score his first professional hoop. Folks in the city of Cleveland, however, begged to differ. One day after the

The next Michael Jordan? Too soon to say, but early returns on Cleveland's LeBron James (right), the 2004 Rookie of the Year (shown here at a 2003 summer league game) are promising. The 6'8" guard averaged 27.2 points, 7.4 rebounds, and 7.2 assists in his second year with the Cavaliers (Steve Lipofsky Basketballphoto.com).

Cavaliers hit the draft lottery jackpot, securing the rights to the overall number one pick, fans began lining up outside Gund Arena, checkbooks in hand.

LeBron's status as the top pick was never in doubt, but the 2003 draft offered several other promising young players, most specifically Darko Milicic, a 7-footer from Serbia-Montenegro (Detroit, #2), Carmelo Anthony, a 6'8" forward out of Syracuse (Denver, #3), Chris Bosh, a 6'10" forward from Georgia Tech (Toronto, #4), and Marquette's Dwyane Wade, a 6'4" guard (Miami, #5). Continuing the recent trend, eight international players— a new record — were selected in the first round, compared with four high schoolers. Still, the movement toward youth over seasoned experience could not be denied; not one of the top four players was 20 years old when his rookie season got under way.

One team was determined to buck the trend. The Lakers, still steaming from their 2003 playoff ouster by the champion Spurs that had interrupted what might have been a quadruple title, went free agent shopping over the summer. Regardless of where it finished at season's end, the team was a mainstay in the gossip columns thanks to its Hollywood location, high profile coach, and public bickering among teammates, most notably its two superstars, Kobe and Shaq. Owner Jerry Buss wanted a chance at one more title from his high-priced duo before Kobe's upcoming free agency had a chance to interfere. Management was convinced that task would entail adding some stable veteran help — a problem, given the Lakers were already well over the salary cap.

Enter the collective bargaining agreement, which allows teams to go over the cap once every two years via the minimum and mid-level exceptions. As luck would have it, two of the league's most experienced players at their respective positions, Karl Malone and Gary Payton, just happened to be free agents. Pals off the court, Malone and Payton opted to team up with the Lakers for millions less than they would have received from other teams in the hopes of winning a championship. Payton signed for the mid-level ($4.9 million), Malone the minimum ($1.5).

Anticipation may have been riding high in Los Angeles, but elsewhere, NBA fans saw little reason to rejoice as the 2003-04 season unfolded. The defensive-oriented Spurs and Nets remained the name of the game, especially in the East, where New Jersey won the Atlantic Division with a paltry 47 wins. Amazingly, the Nets' average of 90.3 ppg was only the *fifth* lowest average in the league. Toronto brought up the rear at 85.4. The Central Division Champion Pacers, winners of the best record in the NBA at 61-21, managed a mere 91.4 ppg. Only two other Eastern teams, Detroit (54-28) and Miami (42-40), finished the season with winning records. As a group, the East averaged 91.6 ppg on 43 percent shooting.

Teams in the West scored 95.3 ppg on 45 percent, and only four had losing records. Minnesota tied Sacramento for the best field goal percentage at .462. The Timberwolves, led by first-time league MVP Kevin Garnett (24.2 points, 13.9 rebounds, 5 assists), finished atop the Midwest Division at 58-24. The revamped Lakers (56-26) edged the Kings by a game in the Pacific. Remarkably, every club in the Midwest division finished with a winning record, even the Utah Jazz (42-40), which had lost the cornerstones of its franchise in Malone and Stockton. The Spurs, forced to make do with one Twin Tower, finished a game behind Minnesota, scoring an average of 91.4, fourth lowest in the West.

In Houston, Yao's Rockets, led by the defensive-minded former Knicks head coach Jeff Van Gundy, improved to 45-37. Ming improved his numbers to 17.5 points (.522 FG percent) and 9 rebounds.

Thanks to the addition of LeBron James (20.9 points, 5.5 rebounds, 5.9 assists), attendance at Cleveland's Gund Arena jumped from 11,497 fans per game in 2002-03 to 18,497 in 2003-04. Although LeBron was not enough to propel the Cavaliers into the playoffs, the budding superstar won Rookie of the Year over stiff competition from Carmelo Anthony (21 points, 6.1 rebounds, 2.8 assists) and Dwyane Wade (16.2 points, 4 rebounds, 4.5 assists). Anthony and the Nuggets edged into the playoffs but were ousted by the Timberwolves in the first round; the Wolves' 4-1 victory in the series marked the first time the 15-year-old franchise had advanced beyond the first round. Wade, the oldest (23) and most experienced of the top five picks with three years of college play under his belt, led the Heat deep into the second round of the playoffs before bowing to the Pacers in six. Dwyane elevated his stats to 18 points, 4 rebounds, and 5.6 assists in 13 playoff games. The second player chosen in the draft, Darko Milicic, played little under head coach Larry Brown in Detroit, appearing in only 34 games. Number four Chris Bosh, playing in 75 games for Toronto, averaged 11.5 points and 7.4 rebounds. Although teammate Vince Carter had another stellar year (22.5 points, 4.8 rebounds, and 4.8 assists), the Raptors failed to make the playoffs for the third season in a row.

The brightest story of the 2003-04 season — Garnett's MVP and his Wolves' long-awaited escape from playoff futility — took a back seat to the league's biggest miscue: the failure of the revamped Lakers to live up to preseason hype. With its notable off-season additions, L.A. began the year with four future Hall of Famers in the starting lineup: newcomers Payton and Malone, Shaq, and Kobe. With veterans such as Rick Fox, Derek Fisher, Horace Grant, and Byron Russell coming off the bench, the Lakers appeared the team to beat. Some critics went so far as to predict the club might break the 72-win record set by Jordan's 1995-96 Chicago Bulls.

Things rarely go according to plan, of course, especially in professional sports. Although the Lakers started out hot, winning 20 of their first 25 games, Gary Payton was the only one of the so-called fab four who played in all 82 regular season games. Former starter Rick Fox, still hampered by a foot injury suffered the previous season, played in only 34 games and was a shadow of his former self. Thirty-eight-year-old Horace Grant was limited to 55 games. Shaq and Kobe suffered numerous injuries, playing in 67 and 65 games, respectively. But the team's biggest disappoint came on December 21, when Karl Malone sprained his right knee during a game against Phoenix. The injury kept Malone — one the most resilient players in the league throughout his long career — out of the lineup for 39 games.

The Lakers managed to stay in the hunt for the Pacific Division title nonetheless, thanks to the coaching of Phil Jackson, the steady play of Payton

(14.6 points, 4.2 rebounds, 5.5 assists), and the late season heroics of Kobe Bryant (24 points, 5.5 rebounds, 5.1 assists). The Lakers entered the playoffs having won 14 of 17 games, including a stunning double-overtime victory in Portland on April 14 in which Bryant made a last-second shot to send the game into overtime, and another to win it. The victory gave Los Angeles the Pacific Division title by a game over Sacramento, which had led its rivals by as many as four games only a month before.

L.A. started its playoff run by beating Yao Ming's Rockets 4-1, setting up a much anticipated semifinal contest against the Spurs. Duncan's club took a commanding 2-0 lead but then fell apart, allowing the Lakers to even the series at 2-2. The often pivotal Game 5 produced one of the most memorable finishes in league history. Trailing 70–71 in front of an anxious home crowd, Tim Duncan nailed a three-point shot while falling away to give his team the lead with .04 seconds to play. The shot looked to be the game winner, but L.A. still had time for a quick catch-and-shoot. Following a couple of timeouts, Payton inbounded the ball to a wide open Derek Fisher, who launched a jumper from behind the arc that hit nothing but net. Final score: Lakers 74, Spurs 73. The defending champions never recovered. The Lakers took Game 6 easily, 88–76, and moved on to face a hungry, energized Kevin Garnett.

Desperate to escape another early playoff exit, Wolves management, led by former Celtics legend Kevin McHale, had followed the Lakers' off-season lead by shoring up veteran help. Sam Cassell (19.8 points, 7.3 assists) and Latrell Sprewell (16.8 points, 3.5 assists) became the club's new starting backcourt.[2] The club also added Michael Olowokandi (6.5 points, 5.7 rebounds), a young, underperforming 7-footer from the Clippers, to replace free agent Rasho Nesterovic in the middle. As with the Lakers, the Wolves suffered numerous injuries during the regular season. Starting forward Wally Szczerbiak played in only 28 games, backup point guard Troy Hudson was limited to 29, and Olowokandi appeared in 43.

As the Lakers were busy shocking the Spurs, the Wolves were engaged in a hotly contested seven-game series with the Kings. Sacramento had recovered from its disastrous late season slump to beat Dallas in round one, but came up three points short in Game 7 at Minnesota. The Wolves had home court advantage in the Western Finals, but the Lakers snatched it back in Game 1 with a 97–88 win. Garnett's crew held court in Game 2, but lost both games in Los Angeles. A two-point Timberwolves win in Game 5 kept the series alive, but the Lakers took care of business at the Staples Center, winning the series in Game 6, 96–90.

In the East, the Nets blanked the Knicks 4-0 before falling to the Pistons in a tough seven-game series. Game 1 produced the lowest scoring playoff half in NBA history with Detroit up 37-25. The Pistons finished with 78 points to the Nets' 56. The latter was the second lowest point total ever for an NBA playoff game. (Utah remains number one with 54 points scored against the Bulls in the 1998 Finals.) New Jersey made only 19 of 70 shots in the game for a field goal percentage of .271. The only time either team reached 100 points was Game 5, a triple-overtime affair won by the Nets, 127–120.[3] In other Eastern action, Reggie Miller's Pacers swept Paul Pierce and the Celtics, then beat Miami in six to advance to the Conference Finals. Detroit ended the Pacers' season with a 69–65 win in Game 6. Indiana averaged 72.7 points in the series, Detroit 75.2.

The win sent the Pistons back to the Finals for the first time since the Bad Boys era, when Isiah Thomas had led the team to back-to-back titles in 1989 and 1990. While those clubs had prided themselves on defense, they had still posted regular season averages of 106.6 and 104.3 ppg respectively, about 15 points higher than their 2004 counterparts. The Lakers brought a 98.2 scoring average to the Finals, some 12 points fewer than its 1989-90 team. As had been the case with the Bad Boys, no Detroit player averaged 20 points; Richard Hamilton led the 2004 Pistons with 17.6. Kobe topped the Lakers with a 24; Shaq added 21.5.

The Lakers were highly favored heading into the Finals, but injuries, team squabbling, contract disruptions, and an off-court incident involving Kobe Bryant finally took its toll on Phil Jackson's weary club.[4] After splitting the first two games in L.A., the Lakers collapsed, losing the next three by an average of 13.7 points. The defense-oriented Pistons averaged 90.8 ppg in the series, slightly above their regular season average of 90.1. The Lakers, meanwhile, fell more than *16 points* shy of their season average, scoring a meager 81.8 ppg.

Numerous excuses could be offered for L.A.'s demise, some of them valid, but one thing was undeniable: the NBA had become a youthful, defense-orientated league. While veteran leadership remained an important commodity, it had to be peppered with young legs and strong, athletic bodies able to sustain a rigorous, bump-and-grind schedule that included 82 regular season contests and as many as 28 playoff games. Winning a championship had become more a matter of having the last rather than the best men standing when the final buzzer sounded, especially in the hard-nosed Eastern Conference. Describing the action during the Pistons–Pacers Eastern Final, Dana Gauruder wrote in the *Daily Oakland Press*: "Going head-to-head against crafty veteran Reggie Miller, Richard Hamilton knew he would face clutch-and-grab tactics in this series. The Pacers upped the physical ante in Game 4 with jarring picks and hard knocks. Hamilton got floored twice in the first six minutes while chasing Miller around screens. On the second one, Ron Artest nailed him with a forearm. Jermaine O'Neal also went out of his way to keep his path obstructed, an illegal tactic that is rarely called by officials."[5]

The more physical the play, the greater chance of injury; the older the player, the greater the risk, and the longer the recovery time. Starters for the 2004 Lakers averaged 31.6 years of age compared to the Pistons' 27. No starter for Detroit was 30 years old. Kobe was the lone member of the fab four who was under 30. Although Malone and Payton represented two of the toughest, most durable players in the league, neither proved much of a factor against Detroit as the series progressed. Payton averaged 4.2 points and 4.4 assists in the five-game series, down from 8.8 points and 5.5 assists in the three series leading up to the Finals. Malone, who reinjured his knee in Game 2, averaged 5 points and 7.3 rebounds in four games. He did not play in the deciding Game 5. (He had averaged 13.3 points and 9.2 rebounds in the earlier series.) Kobe and Shaq were the only Lakers to score in double figures in every game. And only once, in Game 5, did *any* other Lakers post double-figures (Medvendenko 10, Fisher 10). The Pistons also had two regular double figure scorers— Billups and Hamilton — but at least one other Piston scored in double figures in every game, and it was not always the same player. L.A.'s bench played 411 minutes in the series and logged a total of 90 points. Detroit's bench scored 73 points in 261 minutes. The superstar-less Pistons were able to beat the Lakers not on superior talent but a greater abundance of residual energy.

Bottom line, for the second year in a row, the NBA crowned a team whose prowess was tough, in-your-face defense. While that may have brought a smile to the face of basketball purists, the trend was not welcome news for the league, its sponsors, or network TV. Although ABC pulled an 11.5 Nielsen for the five-game series— a big improvement over the 6.5 generated by the Spurs–Nets in 2003 — the numbers were more likely a reflection of the Lakers and its fab four lineup than the series itself. Generally speaking, L.A. was a team that many fans outside of Los Angeles loved to hate — a situation that attracted viewers, whether they were rooting for or against. But what if the Finals had pitted the defending champion Spurs against the Pistons? Would anyone have bothered to tune in?

Jittery network execs could only hope they would never have to find out.

RENOVATION

"Who would have thought the college game would feature more offense than the pros?" mused Pete Alfano, a staff writer for the *Fort Worth Star Telegram*, in a column on the 2004 NBA Finals. "Remember, Connecticut defeated Georgia Tech, 82–73, to win this season's NCAA championship. And there are eight fewer minutes, a 35-second shot clock and far less talented players on college rosters.... NBA players are probably the best athletes in the world. They can do everything it appears, but shoot a basketball, which is still the object of the game."[1] Alfano went on to note that in the 65 postseason games played as of June 13, the 100-point mark had been reached only 21 times, which translates into a meager 32 percent.

Despite their lack of pizzazz, the Pistons *did* soundly beat the Lakers and their fab four to become the 2004 NBA champs—a fact the Associated Press called "methodical and shocking."[2] Moreover, they did it Naismith style: tenacious defense, hard work, and togetherness. "Their shift is over, but the Pistons' championship work continues to be a testament to what sacrifice, effort, and teamwork can do," noted the *Detroit News* in an editorial. "They did play, as Coach Brown likes to say, the right way." Hall of Famer and former Knick Bill Bradley likened Brown's club to the 1973 championship Knicks, a team with five players who averaged double figures but none among the league's top 10 scorers. "The Pistons reminded NBA fans once again that the game of basketball is not about individual showmanship. People come to see teams play as teams and win.... They [Pistons] are young, determined and, most important, play together as a team."[3]

Things were not so together in Hollywood, where Lakers owner Jerry Buss wasted no time pulling the plug on his veteran, mega-star experiment. Within days of the team's 1-4 defeat in the Finals, Phil Jackson, who had guided the Lakers to the Finals four of the past five years and won three of them, was told to hit the road. Shortly thereafter, Shaq publicly requested a trade. The Lakers complied, sending him to Miami for Lamar Odom, Caron Butler, and Brian Grant — three solid but unspectacular players. Bryant, blamed by pundits and fans for the departure of Shaq and Jackson, spent several weeks shopping his services as a free agent before signing a new seven-year deal with the Lakers. Karl Malone remained coy throughout the summer, hinting he might retire. And Gary Payton, not a fan of the team's meticulous triangle offense, was traded to Boston along with Rick Fox for Celtics reserves Chucky Atkins, Chris Mihm, and Jumaine Jones.[4] The Lakers also lost popular sixth man Derek Fisher to the Warriors via free agency, and Horace Grant retired.

So much for the fab four and its Hollywood hype. And so much for the league's favorite one-two superstar punch of Kobe and Shaq. The two would now be viewed in the media as mortal enemies, showcased like foes in a heavyweight title match.

Outside the greater city of Los Angeles, Shaq's relocation to the East was cause for celebration throughout the West, most notably in Houston, where Yao had a chance to emerge as the top big man in the conference. The Rockets aided his cause by shipping its starting backcourt of Steve Francis and Cuttino Mobley, along with backup center Kelvin Cato, to Orlando in exchange for Tracy McGrady, Juwan Howard, Tyronn Lue, and Reece Gaines. The Suns won top prize in the free agent sweepstakes, luring point guard Steve Nash away from the Mavericks. Once the blockbuster moves were complete, the off-season proved relatively quiet. The collective bargaining agreement did not expire for another year; there was no LeBron James in the 2004 draft; the Lakers' fab four were history; and Phil Jackson was writing a book. That left Team USA and the Summer Games in Athens—hoops news that was not of a particularly happy nature, at least for American fans.

About the only thing the 2004 squad shared with its 1992 Dream Team ancestors was an affiliation with the NBA. The days of the league's top stars doubling as Olympians had been dwindling since 1996. Numerous excuses were offered, namely the potential for injury—a pretext rejected by original Dream Team members, several of whom had insisted on playing with existing injuries. Of course at that time, the average NBA salary was $1.2 million, with David Robinson earning a league-best $5.72 million.[5] In 2004-05, the average player made $4.92 million, an increase of more than 400 percent. Shaq topped the list with an eye-popping salary of $30,466,072.[6] Suffice it to say, a lofty investment to put at risk.

The only two proven superstars on the 2004 Olympic roster were Allen Iverson and Tim Duncan. Midlevel veterans Stephon Marbury, Shawn Marion, and Lamar Odom were joined by rising stars Carlos Boozer, Amare Stoudemire, and Richard Jefferson. The remaining members reflected the NBA's commitment to its youth movement: 2003 rookie sensations LeBron, Carmelo, and Dwyane, and one of the top picks of the 2004 draft, Emeka Okafor. Not coincidentally, the team was led by two of the game's best defensive-minded coaches: Larry Brown and his assistant and close friend, Spurs coach Greg Popovich.

On August 15, the U.S. opened competition against Puerto Rico, a team it had beaten three straight times by an average of 23 points at the Olympic

Qualifiers in 2003 and by 25 points in an exhibition game only 16 days earlier. Duncan had an MVP outing with 15 points, 16 rebounds, 2 blocked shots, 4 assists, and 5 steals, but Team USA, which shot a miserable 34.7 percent from the field, fell behind early and never recovered, losing 73–92. The United States won its next two games against Greece (77–71) and Australia (89–79), but a 90–94 loss to Lithuania unveiled the writing on the wall: Team USA was vulnerable. A lopsided win against Angola (89–53) gave the Americans a feeble 3-2 record heading into quarterfinal play against unbeaten (5-0) Spain. Stephon Marbury put on an offensive show in that one, netting an Olympic record 31 points including six 3-pointers. As a team, the United States shot an amazing 54.5 percent from behind the arc, making 12-of-22 threes en route to a 102–94 win.[2]

The United States played Argentina in the semi-finals, a game that pitted Tim Duncan and Coach Popovich against fellow Spur Manu Ginobili. Duncan played sparingly because of foul trouble, and his teammates could not connect from the outside, an all too familiar scenario that resulted in a shocking 81–89 loss. So much for American dominance and respect abroad. "When the buzzer sounded," Alan Crosby of the *London Independent* reported, "the booing only stopped when the team left the court."[8]

Some of that animosity could be attributed to the partisan crowd; fewer Americans attended the Games than in previous years because of the terrorism scare triggered by September 11, 2001. Furthermore, the United States was in the midst of a very unpopular war in Iraq. Still, Team USA hardly performed up to the high standards expected of NBA players, making only 44 percent of its shots from two-point range and 27 percent from three, compared to 57 percent and 50 percent for Argentina.[9] Marbury was the top scorer for the United States with 18 points. Ginobili led the winners with 29 on 9-of-13 shooting. "It's our first time in the final of the Olympics and I'm proud to be a member of this team," Ginobili said. "We proved to the world that we are a very tough team and we made it against an NBA team."[19] Argentina went on to beat Italy 84–69 to take home the gold.

Team USA managed to defeat Lithuania 104–96 in the bronze medal game to end on a semi-positive note, though it was hard to downplay the fact that its 5-3 record represented more losses than all of its predecessors combined. When it was over, Larry Brown stated the obvious: "We have to re-examine what kind of team we send because basketball all over the world has gotten better."[11]

Talent wasn't the only matter that needed to be addressed. The 2004 team was sharply criticized in the media, at home and abroad, for displaying a lack of character and team commitment — an assessment that had begun to permeate much of the NBA. "The only thing worse than the average NBA attitude these days are the excuses for it," sports columnist Bill Plaschke wrote in *Sporting News*. "Though the NBA's actual games continue to function like a tightly wound clock, the league's moral compass is spinning out of control." Plaschke put the blame squarely on society's doorstep. "This is about the privileged subculture that has become youth basketball. Good players are pampered and pimped from the time they are in elementary school. By the time they reach their destination, what the league has gained in energy and excitement has been lost in maturity."[12] And all of that from an article published in December 1997. Some six years later, a former player turned scout told *Basketball Digest*: "Our product is dehydrated beyond any recognition right now. And it comes down to more than just that these players are no Michael, Magic, or Bird. It's that they have no character. But how could they have any? Where would they learn it?"[13]

The issue came front and center a few weeks into the 2004-05 season when a brawl erupted during the waning seconds of a November 19 Pistons–Pacers game at the Palace in Auburn Hills. With Indiana up 97–82, Detroit's Ben Wallace was fouled hard by Ron Artest. Wallace retaliated by shoving Artest, and within seconds, both benches emptied. As coaches, refs, and security guards attempted to restore order, Artest was hit by a plastic beverage cup thrown from the stands. Enraged, he charged into the crowd, assaulting several fans. When the patrons responded in kind, Artest's teammate Stephen Jackson joined the action.

Several Pistons, including the short-tempered Rasheed Wallace, tried to stop the fight, but the melee continued to build steam. An angry fan went down onto the court to confront Artest, who promptly knocked him to the floor. When he got up, he was met by Artest's teammate Jermaine O'Neal, who punched him in the face. The officials called the game with 45.9 seconds left on the clock. As the Pacers made their way to the locker room, Pistons fans yelled obscenities and bombarded them with popcorn, beer, and ice. One even hurled a metal chair which reportedly struck a player, a Palace usher, and a police officer.

Bill Walton, part of ESPN's crew working the game as the scene unfolded, repeatedly commented that he could not believe what he was seeing. A shellshocked Larry Brown called it the "ugliest thing I've ever seen as a coach or a player."[14] Pacers coach Rick Carlisle went so far as to say he had feared for his life.[15] Given how it was a national broadcast, the melee was shown coast to coast within minutes, and replayed for weeks on end.

In a written statement, Commissioner Stern called the players' actions "shocking, repulsive and inexcusable — a humiliation for everyone associated with the NBA."[16] Swift punishments were doled out. For the visiting Pacers, Ron Artest, arguably the most volatile player in the league, was suspended for the remainder of the season.[17] Stephen Jackson was suspended 30 games, Jermaine O'Neal 25, Anthony Johnson 5, and Reggie Miller 1. Detroit's Ben Wallace received a six-game suspension for shoving Artest after he was fouled, and teammates Chauncey Billups, Derrick Coleman, and Elden Campbell lost one game each for leaving the bench when the fight broke out.

The Auburn Hills police department and the Oakland County prosecutor's office announced they would conduct a full investigation and file criminal charges — against players and fans — where appropriate.

General consensus among the media was that the punishment fit the crime, though some suggested the fans were at least partly to blame. A few commentators, as well as a number of players, active and retired, went so far as to say the players had a right to defend themselves. Stern would have none of that argument. "The penalties issued today deal only with one aspect of this incident," he said after announcing the suspensions, "that of player misconduct. The actions of the players involved wildly exceeded the professionalism and self-control that should fairly be expected from NBA players. We must affirm that the NBA will strive to exemplify the best that can be offered by professional sports, and not allow our sport to be debased by what seem to be declining expectations for behavior of fans and athletes alike."[18]

Player's Union director Billy Hunter, however, deemed the suspensions far too severe and filed for review. On December 22, an arbitrator upheld all the suspensions but O'Neal's, which was reduced from 25 to 15 games. The league challenged that ruling in federal court, claiming the collective bargaining agreement (CBA) afforded the commissioner full control as to what punishments would be handed out to players. But on December 30, Judge George

NBA Commissioner David Stern, considered by many to be the most influential and savvy executive in professional sports, has presided over the league since 1984 (Steve Lipofsky Basketballphoto.com).

B. Daniels agreed with the arbitrator. Daniels said the CBA was specific in that it limited Stern's power to "on court" incidents. Because the action on November 19 had spilled into the stands, the judge said that stipulation no longer applied.

As shocking as the incident was, it did not break completely new ground. During a Blazers–Rockets game at Portland in 1995, Houston's Vernon Maxwell had charged some 12 rows into the seats and punched a heckler during a third quarter timeout. He was fined $20,000 and suspended for 10 games. The

Rockets released him that June. More recently in Major League Baseball, Texas Rangers relief pitcher Frank Francisco was suspended for 15 games for throwing a chair into the seats during a game at Oakland on September 13, 2004. The chair hit two fans in the head, breaking one's nose.

Much space could be allocated regarding whether obnoxious fans should be allowed to verbally provoke players at sporting events. But blame is not at issue here, character is. And on that end, the astute Bill Walton will have the final word. "This is the NBA, professional basketball. It is supposed to be about fun. It is supposed to be about going to an event to have a good time. As I consider what got us to this place, I'm reminded of the strategically placed poster that I have on my office wall. It's got a big, beautiful eagle soaring above a majestic scene. The caption reads: 'An eye for an eye makes the whole world blind.' And now, more than ever, is a time for everyone to see."[19]

Thanks to Stern's integrity, people did see, and the NBA did not suffer the repercussions it might have. And while the possibility of another summer lockout dangled in the wind, general consensus was the league and the players' union would come to terms prior to the July 1 deadline. Neither side wanted to duplicate the aftereffects of the 1999 lockout, let alone the NHL stalemate that had caused the cancellation of the entire 2004-05 season.

That sense of cooperation was reflected on the hardwood, where the remainder of the season played out with relative calm. ABC's much-publicized Kobe vs. Shaq match-up on Christmas Day was preceded by Detroit at Indiana — the first meeting between the two clubs since the melee. Both games proved entertaining and violence-free. At Indiana, the players shook hands before the game and distributed holiday gifts to children in the crowd. The Pacers won the game 98–93. At Staples Center in L.A., Kobe and Shaq exchanged a brief greeting before tip-off, then let their games do the talking. The Heat prevailed in an overtime thriller, 104–102.

The league's effort to reconnect with its fans had actually begun prior to the start of the season via a major realignment process. The addition of the expansion Charlotte Bobcats gave the NBA 30 teams, which owners opted to split into six more localized divisions. The Western Conference, previously comprised of the Midwest and Pacific, was divided into the Pacific, Northwest, and Southwest divisions. The East added a new Southeast division to its Atlantic and Central spots. The playoffs were also restructured, with division winners no longer assured home court advantage over clubs with better records.

The new rule did not affect any match-ups in 2005, but there were plenty of surprises to keep fans interested. The Chicago Bulls appeared in postseason play for the first time since Jordan's exit in 1998. Suspension-plagued Indiana finished the season 44-38 and took the defending champion Pistons to six games in the semi-finals before running out of gas. The Pacers' 79–88 defeat at home ended with a standing ovation for the retiring Reggie Miller, who spent his entire 18-year career in Indiana. And Vince Carter made it back to the playoffs after a three-year absence, thanks to a midseason trade that sent him to New Jersey.

In Miami, the addition of Shaq (22.9 points, 10.4 rebounds) and the improved play of Wade (24.1 points, 5.2 rebounds, 6.8 assists) led the Heat to an Eastern best 59 wins. Although O'Neal was hampered by a thigh contusion when the playoffs began, Miami still raced past New Jersey and Washington to take an 8-0 record into the Conference Finals. Detroit, 8-3 heading into the series, surprised the Heat on its home floor, winning the opener 90–81. Miami took Games 2 and 3, but lost Game 4, knotting the series at 2-2. The Heat held on to win Game 5 despite playing the fourth quarter without Wade, who strained his rib muscles in the third quarter. Dwyane did not play in Game 6, which was won by the Pistons in a 91–66 rout. Wade returned in Game 7, but was clearly hobbled by his injury. Detroit's defense set the tone, and the Pistons won 88–82, marking the first time since the Lakers' 2002 overtime victory at Sacramento that a team had won a Conference Final on the road.

In the West, the story of the year clearly belonged to the revamped Phoenix Suns, which improved from 29 wins in 2003-04 to a league-best 62-20 record in 2004-05. The Suns led the league with an offensive average of 110.4 ppg, nearly 7 points better than the second place Sacramento Kings (103.7). Despite critics' claims that a run-and-gun offensive would not suffice in the playoffs, Phoenix swept Memphis, then beat Dallas in six to advance to the Western Finals. Steve Nash (15.5 points, 11.5 assists) became the first point guard since Magic (1989-90) to win regular season MVP and only the fourth in NBA history.[20] Mike D'Antoni, who had taken over for Frank Johnson 21 games into the 2003-04 season, was named Coach of the Year.

Houston's new superstar combo of McGrady (25.7 points, 6.2 rebounds, 5.7 assists) and Yao (18.3 points, 8.4 rebounds) got the Rockets back to the playoffs, but Coach Van Gundy's defense lost out to the league's third best offensive team, Dallas (102.5), in an entertaining seven-game series. Another major surprise in the West was the rise of the Seattle Supersonics (52-30), led by All Star guard Ray Allen (23.9 points, 4.4 rebounds, 3.7 assists). Most critics had picked the Sonics to be among the year's worst teams, but Seattle's coach, former play-making guard Nate McMillan, got his club off to a 12-0 start and never looked back. The Sonics won the Northwest Division by three games over Carmelo (20.8 points, 5.7 rebounds, 2.5 assists) and his surprising Denver Nuggets (49-33), who were spurred on to a late season rally under the leadership of former Sonics coach, George Karl.[21] In postseason play, the Sonics beat the rebuilding Sacramento Kings 4-1 to advance to the semi-finals for the first time since 1997-98.

In an amazing turn of events, neither of the previous year's finalists, the Lakers and Timberwolves, qualified for the playoffs—the first time such an anomaly had occurred. The Lakers had been expected to falter without O'Neal, and the retirement of Malone and the loss of new coach Rudy Tomjanovich to health concerns less than halfway through the season did not aid their cause. Minnesota's collapse was far more shocking. Garnett was coming off an MVP year, and the Wolves had not made any major personnel changes. Unfortunately, team chemistry eroded amidst concerns regarding contract extensions and playing time. Flip Saunders, who had coached the team since its inception in 1995-96, was sacrificed midseason, but the Wolves were unable to regroup under interim coach and club GM Kevin McHale.

Meanwhile in San Antonio (59-23), the stoic, steadfast Tim Duncan led the Southwest Division champion Spurs past Denver and Seattle to earn yet another trip to the Conference Finals. The series was billed as a duel between the West's top offensive and defensive clubs, but never reached its full potential. The Suns were missing a key player in starting two-guard Joe Johnson (17.1 points, 5.1 rebounds, 3.5 assists), out with a fracture of the orbital bone around his left eye. Johnson attempted a return in Game 3, wearing a clear plastic face mask for protection, but his valiant effort (15 points, 3 assists, 2 rebounds) was not enough to stop the Suns from falling behind 0-3. The Spurs took the series in five.

And just like that, network television's worst-case scenario had come to pass: The NBA Finals would showcase the East's best defensive team against the West's best defensive team in a title series already known for its anemic scoring. "ABC seems certain to end up with the second-lowest Finals ever," wrote Michael Heistand in *USA Today*, "and might even set a new all-time low." And this headline from J. A. Adande of the *LA Times*: "Pistons, Spurs Will Play Right Way, but They Won't Be Must-See TV."[22] Hardly the kind of hype the league hoped to generate. To make matters worse, the first four games were blowouts. The Spurs won Games 1 and 2 by an average of 18 points, and Detroit returned the favor in the Palace, taking its first two home games by an average of 24. The media was quick to note the finals had never produced three consecutive games decided by 15 or more points, let alone four. And viewers were quick to note they had better things to do—or watch. Ratings for the first three games stood at 7.1, down 32 percent from the Pistons–Lakers series at the same point in the 2004 series.[23]

On the upside, the games were not as low-scoring as feared, at least for the winners. In its two victories, the Spurs scored 84 and 97 points. Detroit fared even better, posting totals of 96 and 102. And then along came Game 5, a surprisingly tight affair that resulted in a 96–95 Spurs win in *overtime*. The well-played contest very likely kept the series from breaking the Nets–Spurs rating debacle in 2003. The Pistons went on to win Game 6, 95-86, assuring there would be a winner-take-all Game 7 in the Finals for the first time since 1994.

Detroit looked poised to repeat as champions on the Spurs home court until former Olympian opponents Duncan and Ginobili ignited a spurt that tied the game at 57 heading into the fourth quarter. Duncan was everywhere from that point on, hitting shots, making passes, and collecting rebounds on his way to a 25-point, 11-rebound game. Ginobili saved his best for last, scoring 11 of his 23 points in the final 10 minutes on a variety of cuts and slashing drives to the hoop. Robert Horry chipped in 15 off the bench. Hamilton topped the Pistons with 15. Duncan, who had been criticized for having a subpar series (20 points, 14 rebounds) won his third Finals MVP.

The finale drew the highest Nielsen of the series at 11.9, bringing the rating for the 2005 Finals to 8.2. That translated into an average of 12.5 million viewers, down nearly 30 percent from the Detroit–L.A. series the previous year, but not the catastrophe pundits had predicted. It *was* a far cry from the 1980s, when the Finals—usually featuring Magic, Bird, or both—averaged a hefty 13.9. But that had been in cable's infancy and before the Internet. Viewers' habits have changed drastically since then. The World Series averaged a 22.4 during the 1980s, compared to only 13.5 in 2001-2004. And as popular as Tiger Woods has become, his late rally in the U.S. Open captured a 5.6—36 percent *less* than Game 5 of the Pistons–Spurs series.

As with any business, money is the bottom line, and on that end the NBA appears quite healthy. Television rights for 2004-05 totaled $766 million, compared with $558 for Major League Baseball.[24] Advertising revenue generated another $585 million.[25] The NBA averaged 17,454 fans per game in 2004-05, a new record and the best since 1995-96. There were 81 sellouts during the playoffs, eclipsing the previous high of 69. Total attendance for regular season and playoff games was 22,935,057, topping the previous year's record-setting season by more than a million.[26] Many of those fans purchased video games, team merchandise and apparel on their way out the door. All told, the NBA currently reaps some $3 *billion* in annual revenue.[27]

Of course the league's financial stability remains dependent on its image, an issue the new six-year collective bargaining agreement does much to address. Most notable is the concession by the players' union to accept a minimum age limit—something it had sharply opposed for years. The league was hoping for an age restriction of 20, but compromised on 19. The rule effectively ends the practice of high schoolers jumping directly to the NBA. Beginning in 2006, players must wait a minimum of one year after their high school class has graduated to qualify for the NBA draft. International players must be 19 by the end of the calendar year in which they become draft eligible. The statute is expected to drastically cut down, if not end, the practice of NBA scouts hanging out in high school gyms, long one of Stern's pet peeves. The contract also calls for more frequent drug testing. Under the old CBA, players were subjected to one test prior to the start of training camp; the new agreement calls for four tests conducted randomly throughout the season. Scrutiny regarding the increased abuse of steroids in professional sports are also addressed. Suspensions for using the drug increase from 5 games to 10 for a first offense; second offenders will be banished for 25 games; three-time users will lose a full year, and a fourth will result in a lifetime ban from the league.

"We will be a light in the darkness of misbehaving sports fans and players," Stern said of his league's attempted reconstruction. "We will demonstrate to players and fans alike that sports should be our proudest moment rather than one in which we are ashamed."[28]

Only time will tell if the commissioner's determination will lead the league back to its glory days of Bird, Magic, and Jordan, but clearly a pathway toward achieving that lofty goal has been established. Owners, players, and fans must now join ranks and complete the journey together. The game of basketball is, after all, a team sport.

Addendum

One of the most refreshing qualities of sports is its ability to defy predictability. For 44 years, pundits have argued Wilt Chamberlain's 100-point game on March 2, 1962, was an anomaly, a feat that could never be duplicated, especially in the modern era; the game has changed, defenses have become too tough, players too physical. To date, history has proven them right. Some great individual performances have made it into the record books, but aside from Wilt, only three other players managed to crack the 70-point mark as the 2005-06 season began. David Thompson netted 73 against the Pistons on April 9, 1978, Elgin Baylor had 71 against New York on November 15, 1960, and David Robinson logged 70 against the Clippers on April 24, 1994. Michael Jordan's best output was 69 against Cleveland in an overtime game on March 28, 1990.

A new scoring champion? On January 22, 2006, Kobe Bryant torched the Toronto Raptors for 81 points — the second best single-player total in NBA history. Earlier in the month, he became only the third player to score 45 or more points in four consecutive games, posting totals of 45, 48, 50, and 45. Chamberlain remains at number one with 100 points, but critics are no longer calling that record invincible (Steve Lipofsky Basketballphoto.com).

In early 2006, however, whispers have begun to circulate; perhaps Wilt's mark is not set in stone after all. On January 22, 2006, a sold-out Staples Center rocked with thunderous chants of "MVP" as Kobe Bryant connected on 28 of 46 field goal attempts, including 7 for 13 from behind the arc, and 18 of 20 free throws, for a grand total of 81 points in 42 minutes of play. That averages out to 1.9 points per minute. The outburst came at the expense of the Toronto Raptors, who held a 71–53 lead three minutes into the third quarter. Bryant went on to score 55 points in the second half—14 more than the entire Raptors *team*—leading the Lakers to a 122–104 win. Talk of his performance spread quickly throughout the sports world, pushing the all-important NFL conference championship game to the number two story of the day.

Kobe's milestone came on the heels of a 62-point outburst against Dallas on December 20, 2005, in which he single-handedly outscored the Mavericks through three quarters (Kobe 62, Mavericks 61). With that game well in hand, he sat out the entire fourth quarter. Might he have cracked 100 that night? He racked up 30 in the third quarter alone, leaving fans and critics to wonder what if.

For the month of January 2006, Bryant averaged 43.4 points in 13 games. As of this writing, he is averaging 34.9 points, 5.4 rebounds, and 4.5 assists through 52 games. If that holds, it will be the highest scoring average since 1987-88, when Michael Jordan netted a league-best 35. After spending a couple of years in the public doghouse, it would appear that Bryant, now in his 10th season but still only 27, has reemerged as a legitimate challenger for the Airness throne. Whether he will beat out LeBron James remains to be seen, but he is currently the odds-on favorite of several notable critics. "It was, dare it be said, Jordanesque," veteran sports journalist Mark Heisler wrote in the January 24 issue of the *Los Angeles Times*. "There have been fanciful comparisons of Jordan and Bryant for years, but, assuming Kobe doesn't do one of his 180s, it's finally legitimate." ESPN's Marc Stein called it "simply the greatest individual performance ever," in his January 23 article, which he boldly titled, "Sorry Wilt: You're no Kobe."

Will 2006 be the year Wilt's record falls? Stay tuned.

APPENDIX A:
EARLY PROFESSIONAL
BASKETBALL LEAGUES

Noteworthy

1. National Basket Ball League
   1898-99 to 1903-04

2. Philadelphia Basket Ball League
   1902-03 to 1908-09

3. Central Basket Ball League
   1906-07 to 1911-12

4. Eastern League
   1909-10 to 1917-18, 1919-20 to 1922-23

5. Hudson River League
   1909-10 to 1911-12

6. New York State League
   1911-12 to 1922-23

7. Pennsylvania State League
   1914-15 to 1917-18, 1919-20 to 1920-21

8. Interstate Basket Ball League
   1915-16 to 1916-17, 1919-20

9. Metropolitan Basket Ball League
   1922 to 1927-28

10. American Basket Ball League
    1925-26 to 1930-31

11. Eastern League
    1925-26, 1928-29 to 1935-36

12. Metropolitan Basketball League
    1932 to 1932-33

13. American Basketball League
    1933-34 to 1952-53

14. Midwest Basketball Conference
    1935-36 to 1936-37

Transitory

1. New England Basket Ball League
   1903-04

2. Western Massachusetts Basket Ball
   League
   1903-04

3. New England Basket Ball Association
   1904-05

4. Western Pennsylvania Basket Ball
   League
   1903-04, 1912-13, 1914-15

5. Connecticut State Basket Ball League
   1917-18, 1920-21

6. National Basketball League
   1926-27

7. National Basketball League
   1929-30

8. National Basketball League
   1932-33

9. Professional Basketball League of
   America
   1947-48

10. National Professional Basketball
    League
    1950-51

APPENDIX B:
PROFESSIONAL BASKETBALL
COMMISSIONERS

National Basketball League (NBL)

Hubert Johnson	(1937–unknown)
Ward Lamert	(1945–48)
Doxie Moore	(1948–49)

American Basketball Association (ABA)

George Mikan	(1967–1969)
James Gardner	(1969)
Jack Dolph	(1969–1972)
Robert Carlson	(1972–1973)
Michael Storen	(1973–1974)
Theodore Munchak	(1974–1975)
Dave DeBusschere	(1975–1976)

National Basketball Association (NBA)

Maurice Podoloff*	(1946–1963)
Walter Kennedy	(1963–1975)
Lawrence O'Brien	(1975–1984)
David Stern	(1984–present)

Includes service as President of the BAA prior to the 1949 merger.

APPENDIX C:
MISCELLANEOUS NBA
STATISTICS AND AWARDS

NBA Champions

Season	Team	Season	Team
1946-47	Philadelphia Warriors	1974-75	Golden State Warriors
1947-48	Baltimore Bullets	1975-76	Boston Celtics
1948-49	Minneapolis Lakers	1976-77	Portland Trail Blazers
1949-50	Minneapolis Lakers	1977-78	Washington Bullets
1950-51	Rochester Royals	1978-79	Seattle Supersonics
1951-52	Minneapolis Lakers	1979-80	Los Angeles Lakers
1952-53	Minneapolis Lakers	1980-81	Boston Celtics
1953-54	Minneapolis Lakers	1981-82	Los Angeles Lakers
1954-55	Syracuse Nationals	1982-83	Philadelphia 76ers
1955-56	Philadelphia Warriors	1983-84	Boston Celtics
1956-57	Boston Celtics	1984-85	Los Angeles Lakers
1957-58	St. Louis Hawks	1985-86	Boston Celtics
1958-59	Boston Celtics	1986-87	Los Angeles Lakers
1959-60	Boston Celtics	1987-88	Los Angeles Lakers
1960-61	Boston Celtics	1988-89	Detroit Pistons
1961-62	Boston Celtics	1989-90	Detroit Pistons
1962-63	Boston Celtics	1990-91	Chicago Bulls
1963-64	Boston Celtics	1991-92	Chicago Bulls
1964-65	Boston Celtics	1992-93	Chicago Bulls
1965-66	Boston Celtics	1993-94	Houston Rockets
1966-67	Philadelphia 76ers	1994-95	Houston Rockets
1967-68	Boston Celtics	1995-96	Chicago Bulls
1968-69	Boston Celtics	1996-97	Chicago Bulls
1969-70	New York Knicks	1997-98	Chicago Bulls
1970-71	Milwaukee Bucks	1998-99	San Antonio Spurs
1971-72	Los Angeles Lakers	1999-00	Los Angeles Lakers
1972-73	New York Knicks	2000-01	Los Angeles Lakers
1973-74	Boston Celtics	2001-02	Los Angeles Lakers

Season	Team		Season	Team
2002-03	San Antonio Spurs		2004-05	San Antonio Spurs
2003-04	Detroit Pistons			

NBA Regular Season MVPs

Season	Player/Team	ppg Average
1955-56	Bob Pettit (St. Louis)	25.7
1956-57	Bob Cousy (Boston)	20.6
1957-58	Bill Russell (Boston)	16.6
1958-59	Bob Pettit (St. Louis)	29.2
1959-60	Wilt Chamberlain (Philadelphia)	37.6
1960-61	Bill Russell (Boston)	16.9
1961-62	Bill Russell (Boston)	18.9
1962-63	Bill Russell (Boston)	16.8
1963-64	Oscar Robertson (Cincinnati)	31.4
1964-65	Bill Russell (Boston)	14.1
1965-66	Wilt Chamberlain (Philadelphia)	33.5
1966-67	Wilt Chamberlain (Philadelphia)	24.1
1967-68	Wilt Chamberlain (Philadelphia)	24.3
1968-69	Wes Unseld (Baltimore)	13.8
1969-70	Willis Reed (New York)	21.7
1970-71	Kareem Abdul-Jabbar (Milwaukee)	31.7
1971-72	Kareem Abdul-Jabbar (Milwaukee)	34.8
1972-73	Dave Cowens (Boston)	20.5
1973-74	Kareem Abdul-Jabbar (Milwaukee)	27.0
1974-75	Bob McAdoo (Buffalo)	34.5
1975-76	Kareem Abdul-Jabbar (Los Angeles)	27.7
1976-77	Kareem Abdul-Jabbar (Los Angeles)	26.2
1977-78	Bill Walton (Portland)	18.9
1978-79	Moses Malone (Houston)	24.8
1979-80	Kareem Abdul-Jabbar (Los Angeles)	24.8
1980-81	Julius Erving (Philadelphia)	24.6
1981-82	Moses Malone (Houston)	31.1
1982-83	Moses Malone (Philadelphia)	24.5
1983-84	Larry Bird (Boston)	24.2
1984-85	Larry Bird (Boston)	28.7
1985-86	Larry Bird (Boston)	25.8
1986-87	Magic Johnson (Los Angeles)	23.9
1987-88	Michael Jordan (Chicago)	35.0
1988-89	Magic Johnson (Los Angeles)	22.5
1989-90	Magic Johnson (Los Angeles)	22.3
1990-91	Michael Jordan (Chicago)	31.5
1991-92	Michael Jordan (Chicago)	30.1
1992-93	Charles Barkley (Phoenix)	25.6
1993-94	Hakeem Olajuwon (Houston)	27.3
1994-95	David Robinson (San Antonio)	27.6
1995-96	Michael Jordan (Chicago)	30.4
1996-97	Karl Malone (Utah)	27.4
1997-98	Michael Jordan (Chicago)	28.7

Season	Player/Team	ppg Average
1998-99	Karl Malone (Utah)	23.8
1999-00	Shaquille O'Neal (Los Angeles)	29.7
2000-01	Allen Iverson (Philadelphia)	31.1
2001-02	Tim Duncan (San Antonio)	25.5
2002-03	Tim Duncan (San Antonio)	23.3
2003-04	Kevin Garnett (Minnesota)	24.2
2004-05	Steve Nash (Phoenix)	15.5

NBA Finals MVPs

Season	Player/Team	Season	Player/Team
1968-69	Jerry West (Los Angeles)	1985-86	Larry Bird (Boston)
1969-70	Willis Reed (New York)	1986-87	Magic Johnson (Los Angeles)
1970-71	Kareem Abdul-Jabbar (Milwaukee)	1987-88	James Worthy (Los Angeles)
		1988-89	Joe Dumars (Detroit)
1971-72	Wilt Chamberlain (Los Angeles)	1989-90	Isiah Thomas (Detroit)
		1990-91	Michael Jordan (Chicago)
1972-73	Willis Reed (New York)	1991-92	Michael Jordan (Chicago)
1973-74	John Havlicek (Boston)	1992-93	Michael Jordan (Chicago)
1974-75	Rick Barry (Golden State)	1993-94	Hakeem Olajuwon (Houston)
1975-76	Jo Jo White (Boston)	1994-95	Hakeem Olajuwon (Houston)
1976-77	Bill Walton (Portland)	1995-96	Michael Jordan (Chicago)
1977-78	Wes Unseld (Washington)	1996-97	Michael Jordan (Chicago)
1978-79	Dennis Johnson (Seattle)	1997-98	Michael Jordan (Chicago)
1979-80	Magic Johnson (Los Angeles)	1998-99	Tim Duncan (San Antonio)
1980-81	Cedric Maxwell (Boston)	1999-00	Shaquille O'Neal (Los Angeles)
1981-82	Magic Johnson (Los Angeles)	2000-01	Shaquille O'Neal (Los Angeles)
1982-83	Moses Malone (Philadelphia)	2001-02	Shaquille O'Neal (Los Angeles)
1983-84	Larry Bird (Boston)	2002-03	Tim Duncan (San Antonio)
1984-85	Kareem Abdul-Jabbar (Los Angeles)	2003-04	Chauncey Billups (Detroit)
		2004-05	Tim Duncan (San Antonio)

All Star Game MVPs

Season	Player/Team	Season	Player/Team
1950-51	Ed Macauley (Boston)	1962-63	Bill Russell (Boston)
1951-52	Paul Arizin (Philadelphia)	1963-64	Oscar Robertson (Cincinnati)
1952-53	George Mikan (Los Angeles)	1964-65	Jerry Lucas (Cincinnati)
1953-54	Bob Cousy (Boston)	1965-66	Adrian Smith (Cincinnati)
1954-55	Bill Sharman (Boston)	1966-67	Rick Barry (San Francisco)
1955-56	Bob Pettit (Milwaukee)	1967-68	Hal Greer (Philadelphia)
1956-57	Bob Cousy (Boston)	1968-69	Oscar Robertson (Cincinnati)
1957-58	Bob Pettit (St. Louis)	1969-70	Willis Reed (New York)
1958-59 (tie)	Elgin Baylor (Minneapolis) and Bob Pettit (St. Louis)	1970-71	Lenny Wilkens (Seattle)
		1971-72	Jerry West (Los Angeles)
1959-60	Wilt Chamberlain (Philadelphia)	1972-73	Dave Cowens (Boston)
		1973-74	Bob Lanier (Detroit)
1960-61	Oscar Robertson (Cincinnati)	1974-75	Walt Frazier (New York)
1961-62	Bob Pettit (St. Louis)	1975-76	Dave Bing (Washington)

1976-77	Julius Erving (Philadelphia)
1977-78	Randy Smith (Buffalo)
1978-79	David Thompson (Denver)
1979-80	George Gervin (San Antonio)
1980-81	Nate Archibald (Boston)
1981-82	Larry Bird (Boston)
1982-83	Julius Erving (Philadelphia)
1983-84	Isiah Thomas (Detroit)
1984-85	Ralph Sampson (Houston)
1985-86	Isiah Thomas (Detroit)
1986-87	Tom Chambers (Seattle)
1987-88	Michael Jordan (Chicago)
1988-89	Karl Malone (Utah)
1989-90	Magic Johnson (Los Angeles)
1990-91	Charles Barkley (Philadelphia)
1991-92	Magic Johnson (Los Angeles)
1992-93	Karl Malone (Utah) and
(tie)	John Stockton (Utah)

Season	Player/Team
1993-94	Scottie Pippen (Chicago)
1994-95	Mitch Richmond (Sacramento)
1995-96	Michael Jordan (Chicago)
1996-97	Glen Rice (Charlotte)
1997-98	Michael Jordan (Chicago)
1998-99	No game (lockout season)
1999-00	Tim Duncan (San Antonio)
(tie)	and Shaquille O'Neal (Los Angeles)
2000-01	Allen Iverson (Philadelphia)
2001-02	Kobe Bryant (Los Angeles)
2002-03	Kevin Garnett (Minnesota)
2003-04	Shaquille O'Neal (Los Angeles)
2004-05	Allen Iverson (Philadelphia)

Top 10 Average Points Per Game Scoring Leaders

Michael Jordan	30.12	Shaquille O'Neal	26.74
Wilt Chamberlain	30.07	Bob Pettit	26.36
Allen Iverson	27.44	George Gervin	26.18
Elgin Baylor	27.36	Oscar Robertson	25.68
Jerry West	27.03	Karl Malone	25.02

Top 10 Average Assists Per Game Leaders

Magic Johnson	11.19	Kevin Johnson	9.13
John Stockton	10.51	Norm Nixon	8.32
Oscar Robertson	9.51	Stephon Marbury	8.27
Jason Kidd	9.27	Tim Hardaway	8.18
Isiah Thomas	9.26	Kevin Porter	8.06

Top 10 Average Rebounds Per Game Leaders

Wilt Chamberlain	22.89	Wes Unseld	13.99
Bill Russell	22.45	Walt Bellamy	13.65
Bob Pettit	16.22	Dave Cowens	13.63
Jerry Lucas	15.61	Elgin Baylor	13.55
Nate Thurmond	15.00	George Mikan	13.40

Coach of the Year

Season	Coach/Team	Season	Coach/Team
1962-63	Harry Gallatin (St. Louis)	1969-70	Red Holzman (New York)
1963-64	Alex Hannum (San Francisco)	1970-71	Dick Motta (Chicago)
1964-65	Red Auerbach (Boston)	1971-72	Bill Sharman (Los Angeles)
1965-66	Dolph Schayes (Philadelphia)	1972-73	Tom Heinsohn (Boston)
1966-67	Johnny Kerr (Chicago)	1973-74	Ray Scott (Detroit)
1967-68	Richie Guerin (St. Louis)	1974-75	Phil Johnson (Kansas City)
1968-69	Gene Shue (Baltimore)	1975-76	Bill Fitch (Cleveland)

Season	*Coach/Team*	*Season*	*Coach/Team*
1976-77	Tom Nissalke (Houston)	1991-92	Don Nelson (Golden State)
1977-78	Hubie Brown (Atlanta)	1992-93	Pat Riley (New York)
1978-79	Cotton Fitzsimmons (Kansas City)	1993-94	Lenny Wilkens (Atlanta)
		1994-95	Del Harris (Los Angeles Lakers)
1979-80	Bill Fitch (Boston)		
1980-81	Jack McKinney (Indiana)	1995-96	Phil Jackson (Chicago)
1981-82	Gene Shue (Washington)	1996-97	Pat Riley (Miami)
1982-83	Don Nelson (Milwaukee)	1997-98	Larry Bird (Indiana)
1983-84	Frank Layden (Utah)	1998-99	Mike Dunleavy (Portland)
1984-85	Don Nelson (Milwaukee)	1999-00	Doc Rivers (Orlando)
1985-86	Mike Fratello (Atlanta)	2000-01	Larry Brown (Philadelphia)
1986-87	Mike Schuler (Portland)	2001-02	Rick Carlisle (Detroit)
1987-88	Doug Moe (Denver)	2002-03	Gregg Popovich (San Antonio)
1988-89	Cotton Fitzsimmons (Phoenix)		
		2003-04	Hubie Brown (Memphis)
1989-90	Pat Riley (Los Angeles Lakers)	2004-05	Mike D'Antoni (Phoenix)
1990-91	Don Chaney (Houston)		

Appendix D:
Miscellaneous ABA
Statistics and Awards

ABA Champions

Season	Team	Season	Team
1967-68	Pittsburgh Pipers	1972-73	Indiana Pacers
1968-69	Oakland Oaks	1973-74	New York Nets
1969-70	Indiana Pacers	1974-75	Kentucky Colonels
1970-71	Utah Stars	1975-76	New York Nets
1971-72	Indiana Pacers		

ABA Regular Season MVPs

Season	Player/Team	ppg Average
1967-68	Connie Hawkins (Pittsburgh)	26.8
1968-69	Mel Daniels (Indiana)	24.0
1969-70	Spencer Haywood (Denver)	21.7
1970-71	Mel Daniels (Indiana)	21.0
1971-72	Artis Gilmore (Kentucky)	23.8
1972-73	Billy Cunningham (Carolina)	24.1
1973-74	Julius Erving (New York)	27.4
1974-75	Julius Erving (New York) and	27.9
	George McGinnis (Indiana)	
	(co–MVPs)	29.8
1975-76	Julius Erving	29.3

Playoff MVPs

Season	Player/Team	Season	Player/Team
1967-68	Connie Hawkins (Pittsburgh)	1972-73	Billy Cunningham (Carolina)
1968-69	Mel Daniels (Indiana)	1973-74	Julius Erving (New York)
1969-70	Spencer Haywood (Denver)	1974-75	Artis Gilmore (Kentucky)
1970-71	Mel Daniels (Indiana)	1975-76	Julius Erving (New York)
1971-72	Artis Gilmore (Kentucky)		

All Star Game MVPs

Season	Player/Team	Season	Player/Team
1967-68	Larry Brown (New Orleans)	1972-73	Warren Jabali (Denver)
1968-69	John Beasley (Dallas)	1973-74	Artis Gilmore (Kentucky)
1969-70	Spencer Haywood (Denver)	1974-75	Freddie Lewis (St. Louis)
1970-71	Mel Daniels (Indiana)	1975-76	David Thompson (Denver)
1971-72	Dan Issel (Kentucky)		

Top 10 Average Points Per Game Scoring Leaders

Julius Erving	28.7	Larry Jones	21.2
Dan Issel	25.6	Bob Verga	21.2
George McGinnis	24.8	Ralph Simpson	20.4
Artis Gilmore	22.3	George Thompson	20.1
George Gervin	22.3	Darel Carrier	20.0

Top 10 Average Assists Per Game Leaders

Larry Brown	6.67	Jimmy Jones	5.10
Bill Melchionni	6.06	Chuck Williams	4.84
Mack Calvin	5.75	Julius Erving	4.80
Louie Dampier	5.55	Freddie Lewis	4.20
Warren Jabali	5.34	Fatty Taylor	4.06

Top 10 Average Rebounds Per Game Leaders

Artis Gilmore	17.07	Julius Keye	11.01
Mel Daniels	15.12	Goose Ligon	10.88
Julius Erving	12.10	Dan Issel	10.85
Ira Harge	11.60	Red Robbins	10.50
Billy Paultz	11.10	Gerald Govan	10.45

Coach of the Year

Season	Coach/Team	Season	Coach/Team
1967-68	Vince Cazzetta (Pittsburgh)	1972-73	Larry Brown (Carolina)
1968-69	Alex Hannum (Oakland)	1973-74	Babe McCarthy (Kentucky)
1969-70	Bill Sharman (Los Angeles)	(tie)	and Joe Mullaney (Utah)
(tie)	Joe Belmont (Denver)	1974-75	Larry Brown (Denver)
1970-71	Al Bianchi (Virginia)	1975-76	Larry Brown (Denver)
1971-72	Tom Nissalke (Dallas)		

CHAPTER NOTES

Chapter 1

1. Bernice Larson Webb, *The Basketball Man: James Naismith* (Lawrence: University Press of Kansas, 1973), p. 22.
2. Ibid., p. 26.
3. Ibid., p. 38.
4. Ibid., p. 40.
5. Ibid., p. 45.
6. James Naismith, *Basketball: Its Origin and Development*, revised edition (Lincoln: University of Nebraska Press, 1996), p. 27.
7. Ibid, pp. 44–45.
8. Naismith made no mention of the incident in his book, *Basketball: Its Origins and Development*. However, 50 years passed between the time he invented the game and the book's original publication in 1941, so it is certainly conceivable that he had either forgotten about it by that point or deemed it unimportant.
9. *The Basketball Man*, p. 62.

Chapter 2

1. Fredrick McKissack, *Black Hoops: The History of African Americans in Basketball* (New York: Scholastic, 1999), pp. 6–7.
2. Naismith, *Basketball: Its Origins and Development*, p. 56.
3. Ibid.
4. Larson Webb, *The Basketball Man*, p. 67.
5. Naismith, *Basketball: Its Origins and Development*, p. 57.
6. Ibid., p. 60.
7. McKissack, *Black Hoops: The History of African Americans in Basketball*, pp. 6–7.
8. Naismith took over as head of the physical education department at the Denver YMCA, where he worked for the next three years while attending Gross Medical College in Denver. He graduated with a medical degree in 1898.

Chapter 3

1. John Blackwell, "1900: Basketball's First Dynasty," *Trentonian* (http://capitalcentury.com/1900.html).
2. McKissack, *Black Hoops: The History of African Americans in Basketball*, p. 12.
3. Robert W. Peterson, *Cages to Jump Shots: Pro Basketballs Early Years* (New York: Oxford University Press, 1990), p. 43.
4. Gene Brown (ed.), *The Complete Book of Basketball: A New York Times Scrapbook History* (New York: Arno Press and Bobbs-Merrill, 1980), p. 3.
5. McKissack, *Black Hoops: The History of African Americans in Basketball*, p. 13.
6. Peterson, *Cages to Jump Shots: Pro Basketballs Early Years*, p. 30.
7. Ibid., p. 53.
8. Naismith, *Basketball: Its Origins and Development*, p. 64.

Chapter 4

1. This cultural movement, which had its roots in Harlem, would later be known as the Harlem Renaissance.
2. Nelson George, *Elevating the Game: Black Men and Basketball* (New York: HarperCollins, 1992), p. 27.
3. Blacks were barred from the NFL in 1933. Interracial teams returned to pro football in 1946 when the new All American Football Conference began play.
4. Ron Thomas, *They Cleared the Lane: The NBA's Black Pioneers* (Lincoln: University of Nebraska Press, 2002), p. 5.
5. Ibid.
6. Ibid., p. 245.
7. Alexander Wolff, *Sports Illustrated: 100 Years of Hoops* (New Jersey: Crescent Books, 1995), p. 155.

8. McKissack, *Black Hoops: The History of African Americans in Basketball*, p. 58.

9. Peterson, *Cages to Jumpshots: Pro Basketball's Early Years*, pp. 77–78.

10. Wolff, *Sports Illustrated: 100 Years of Hoops*, p. 156.

Chapter 5

1. The ABL resurfaced in 1933 as an Eastern regional league and continued to operate through the 1945-46 season.

2. NY Renaissance Biography, the official Web site of the Basketball Hall of Fame (http://www.hoophall.com/halloffamers/NY%20Renaissance.htm).

3. Jay T. Smith, "Rewriting History: The Birth of the Globetrotters," Network Chicago Web site (http://www.wttw.com/chicagostories/harlemglobe.html).

4. Peterson, *Cages to Jumpshots: Pro Basketball's Early Years*, p. 105.

5. Smith, "Rewriting History: The Birth of the Globetrotters."

6. The Harlem Globetrotters, the official Web site of the Basketball Hall of Fame (http://www.hoophall.com/halloffamers/harlem_globetrotters.htm).

7. George, *Elevating the Game*, pp. 52–53.

8. Ibid.

9. Smith, "Rewriting History: The Birth of the Globetrotters."

10. Peterson, *Cages to Jumpshots: Pro Basketball's Early Years*, p. 112.

Chapter 6

1. Peterson, *Cages to Jumpshots: Pro Basketball's Early Years*, p. 125.

2. Webb, *The Basketball Man*, p. 293.

3. Stuart Naismith (with Douglas Stark), "Papa Jimmy," the official Web site of the Basketball Hall of Fame (http://www.hoophall.com/history/papa_jimmy.htm).

4. Ron Chimelis, "Naismith Untold," the official Web site of the Basketball Hall of Fame (http://www.hoophall.com/history/naismith_untold.htm).

5. "The Pioneer Years: Paving the Way," the official Web site of the Basketball Hall of Fame (http://www.hoophall.com/exhibits/freedom_pioneers.htm).

6. Paul Berger, "The First Season: 50 Years ago Serious Pro Basketball Was Born. Or at Least They Tried to Be Serious," *American Heritage*, May–June 1997, v48 n3 p. 94(8).

7. Brown (ed.), *The Complete Book of Basketball: A New York Times Scrapbook History*, p. 114.

8. Neil D. Isaccs, *Vintage NBA: The Pioneer Era 1946–1956* (Indianapolis: Masters Press, 1996), p. 109.

9. Ibid.

10. Berger, "The First Season."

11. Peterson, *Cages to Jumpshots: Pro Basketball's Early Years*, p. 148.

12. "Basketball Association of America 1946-47 Season Bests," the official Web site of the Basketball Hall of Fame (www.hoophall.com/history/baa_season_bests.htm).

13. Brown (ed.), *The Complete Book of Basketball: A New York Times Scrapbook History*, p. 116.

Chapter 7

1. Isaacs, *Vintage NBA: The Pioneer Era 1946–1956*, p. 67.

2. Susan Rayl, "Renaissance Man," the Official Web site of the Basketball Hall of Fame (www.hoophall.com/features/renaissance_man_gates.htm).

3. Isaacs, *Vintage NBA: The Pioneer Era 1946–1956*, p. 116.

4. Ibid., p. 171.

5. Peterson, *Cages to Jumpshots: Pro Basketball's Early Years*, p. 166.

6. Ibid, p. 171.

7. Thomas, *They Cleared the Lane*, p. 100.

8. McKissack, *Black Hoops: The History of African Americans in Basketball*, p. 94.

9. Thomas, *They Cleared the Lane*, p. 49.

10. Ibid., p. 58.

11. Clifton Brown, *True Trail Blazers*, www.nba.com/history.

12. Ibid.

13. Ronald Tillery, "Lloyd Was First to Clear Lane for Black Players in the NBA," Scripps Howard News Service, March 2, 2003.

14. Thomas, *They Cleared the Lane*, p. 59.

15. Brown, *True Trail Blazers*.

16. U.S. Census Bureau.

17. Peterson, *Cages to Jumpshots: Pro Basketball's Early Years*, p. 173.

18. NBA.com/history/allstar/recap.

19. NBA.com/history/rebounds.

Chapter 8

1. Brown (ed.), *The Complete Book of Basketball: A New York Times Scrapbook History*, p. 37.

2. Ibid., p. 41.

3. Terry Pluto, *Tall Tales* (New York: Simon & Schuster, 1992), p. 26.

4. Peterson, *Cages to Jumpshots: Pro Basketball's Early Years*, p. 180.

5. Committee on the Judiciary House of Representatives, Organized Professional Team Sports.

6. Pluto, *Tall Tales*, p. 26.

7. www.NBA.com/history.

8. Committee on the Judiciary House of Representatives, Organized Professional Team Sports.

9. Peterson, *Cages to Jumpshots: Pro Basketball's Early Years*, p. 181.

10. Pluto, *Tall Tales*, p. 21.

11. DuMont ceased broadcast operations in 1956.

12. Pluto, *Tall Tales*, p. 177.

13. Committee on the Judiciary House of Representatives, Organized Professional Team Sports.

14. Peterson, *Cages to Jumpshots: Pro Basketball's Early Years*, p. 176.

15. Isaacs, *Vintage NBA: The Pioneer Era 1946–56*, p. 224.

16. Pluto, *Tall Tales*, p. 296.

17. Isaacs, *Vintage NBA: The Pioneer Era 1946–56*, p. 224.

18. www.nba.com/history/players/mikan_bio.html.

19. www.nba.com/history/24secondclock.html.

20. John Kekis, "Time Has Come for Shot-Clock Inventor," Associated Press, May 25, 2000.

21. Pluto, *Tall Tales*, p. 29.

22. Kekis, "Time Has Come for Shot-Clock Inventor."

23. Committee on the Judiciary House of Representatives, Organized Professional Team Sports.

24. Ibid.

Chapter 9

1. Dunking was considered taboo by coaches and thus rarely performed during actual game play.

2. Lisette Hilton, "Auerbach's Celtics Played as a Team," ESPN.com.

3. Pluto, *Tall Tales*, p. 298.

4. www.nba.com/history.

5. Pluto, *Tall Tales*, p. 106.

6. www.bostonceltics.com/history.

7. Five years would pass before he gave up his dream of playing Major League Baseball.

8. Pluto, *Tall Tales*, p. 111.

9. Ibid., p. 128.

10. The numbers remain somewhat in dispute, as Cousy's performance occurred during a double-overtime game.

11. Pluto, *Tall Tales*, p. 144.

Chapter 10

1. Thomas, *They Cleared the Lane: The NBA's Black Pioneers*, p. 198.

2. Ibid.

3. Pluto, *Tall Tales*, p. 171.

4. Ibid.

5. NBA.com/history/players/Baylor_bio.html.

6. Pluto, *Tall Tales*, p. 172.

7. Association for Professional Basketball Research.

8. Jerry West (with Bill Libby), *Mr. Clutch: The Jerry West Story* (Englewood Cliffs, New Jersey: Prentice Hall, Inc., 1971), p. 41.

9. Ibid., p. 57.

10. Ibid., pp. 76–77.

11. www.nba.com/history/players/robertson_bio.html.

12. John Hareas (contributing writer), *NBA's Greatest*, Anja Schmidt, ed. (New York: DK Publishing and NBA Properties, 2003)p. 129.

13. Pluto, *Tall Tales*, p. 194.

14. Ibid., p. 203.

Chapter 11

1. Brown (ed.), *The Complete Book of Basketball: A New York Times Scrapbook History*, p. 144.

2. Pluto, *Tall Tales*, p. 268.

3. Ibid., p. 266.

4. Ibid., p. 264.

5. *Pittsburgh Courier*, April 30, 1966.

6. www.nba.com/history/finals/19671968.html.

Chapter 12

1. http://www.nfl.com/history/chronology/1961–1970.

2. Brown (ed.), *The Complete Book of Basketball: A New York Times Scrapbook History*, p. 157.

3. Terry Pluto, *Loose Balls: The Short Wild Life of the American Basketball Association* (New York: Simon & Schuster, 1990), pp. 48–49.

4. Brown (ed.), *The Complete Book of Basketball: A New York Times Scrapbook History*, p. 159.

5. Pluto, *Loose Balls*, p. 45.

6. Ibid., p. 65.

7. Ibid., p. 87.

8. Ibid., p. 99.

9. West, *Mr. Clutch*, p. 215.

10. http://espn.go.com/classic/s/addhawkinsconnie.html.

11. http://www.nba.com/history/players/hawkins_bio.html.

12. Pluto, *Loose Balls*, p. 128–29.

13. Pluto, *Tall Tales*, p. 258.

14. Brown (ed.), *The Complete Book of Basketball: A New York Times Scrapbook History*, p. 164.

15. Haywood spent his first year of eligibility playing for Trinidad State, a junior college in Colorado.

16. Pluto, *Loose Balls*, p. 184.

17. Although the Oaks-turned-Capitols had moved to Washington, D.C., they remained in the Western Division for the 1969-70 season.

18. www.basketballreference.com/awards/all star.htm.

19. Monroe was the second overall pick in the 1967 draft, a rarity for a guard.

20. Pluto, *Loose Balls*, p. 127.

21. Association for Professional Basketball Research.

22. Pluto, *Loose Balls*, p. 96.

23. Brown (ed.), *The Complete Book of Basketball: A New York Times Scrapbook History*, p. 170.

24. http://users.pullman.com/rodfort/PH SportsEcon/Common/OtherData/NBASalaries/NBASalLeagueAverage.xls.

Chapter 13

1. The ABA invested the money and insured all accounts with Prudential. Many players today continue to receive their deferred payments.

2. Pluto, *Loose Balls*, p. 116.

3. http://www.basketballreference.com/teams/teamyear.htm?tm=MIL&lg=N&yr=1970.

4. http://www.remembertheaba.com/ABA AllStarGames/AllStar.html.

5. Wilkens had been traded from the Hawks to Seattle in 1968.

6. Brown (ed.), *The Complete Book of Basketball: A New York Times Scrapbook History*, p. 172.

7. Pluto, *Loose Balls*, p. 288.

8. Ibid., p. 32.

9. Brown (ed.), *The Complete Book of Basketball: A New York Times Scrapbook History*, p. 177.

10. http://umassathletics.collegesports.com/trads/numbers.html.

11. Brown (ed.), *The Complete Book of Basketball: A New York Times Scrapbook History*, p. 177.

12. Schmidt (ed.), *NBA's Greatest*, p. 27.

13. http://www.basketballreference.com/leaders/leadersbyseason.htm?stat=ppg&lg=a&yr=1971.

14. Abdul-Jabbar translates into "noble, powerful, servant."

15. Brown (ed.), *The Complete Book of Basketball: A New York Times Scrapbook History*, p. 171.

16. Ibid., p. 82.

Chapter 14

1. http://members.aol.com/bradleyrd/atten dance.html.

2. http://www.remembertheaba.com/ABA

AllStarGames/AllStar.html.

3. http://espn.go.com/classic/s/Classic_1972 _usa_ussr_gold_medal_hoop.html.

4. http://www.redbirds.org/PDF/MBB Prospectus.pdf.

5. Pluto, *Loose Balls*, p. 287.

6. Ibid.

7. Cunningham had signed with Cougars while still under contract to the 76ers, but played out his option year with Philly before jumping leagues for the 1972-73 season.

8. Brown (ed.), *The Complete Book of Basketball: A New York Times Scrapbook History*, p. 178.

9. Pluto, *Loose Balls*, p. 234.

10. Ibid., p. 233.

11. The Squires' Willie Sojourner was also included in the deal.

12. Pluto, *Loose Balls*, p. 234.

13. http://www.hoophall.com/halloffamers/Chamberlain.htm.

14. Pluto, *Loose Balls*, p. 318.

15. Ibid., p. 319.

16. Association for Professional Basketball Research.

17. Pluto, *Loose Balls*, p. 273.

Chapter 15

1. http://www.insidehoops.com/nba-tv-con tracts.shtml.

2. Pluto, *Loose Balls*, p. 32.

3. Wolff, *Sports Illustrated: 100 Years of Hoops*, p. 111.

4. Brown (ed.), *The Complete Book of Basketball: A New York Times Scrapbook History*, p. 186.

5. Association for Professional Basketball Research.

6. Paul Silas replaced Oscar Robertson as head of the Players' Association in 1975, but Robertson's name remained on the antitrust suit for its duration.

7. Michael Murphy, "For Pure Entertainment, Basketball Was a Slam Dunk," http://www.remembertheaba.com/ABAArticles/MurphyArticleABA.html.

8. Ibid.

9. http://www.remembertheaba.com/ABA YearlyGameLogs/7576Part3.html.

10. Pluto, *Loose Balls*, p. 420.

11. Ibid., p. 400.

12. Ibid., p. 398.

13. Powers later admitted he had ignored Silas because he hadn't wanted the game to be decided on a technicality.

14. http://www.nba.com/history/finals/1975 1976.html.

Chapter 16

1. Pluto, *Loose Balls*, p. 429.
2. Brown later used the cash to purchase the Boston Celtics.
3. Darren Rovell, "Spirit of ABA Deal Lives on for Silna Brothers," January 22, 2002, espn.com.
4. http://www.basketballreference.com/players/playerpage.htm?ilkid=WALTOBI01.
5. The Celtics were down 0–2 to the Lakers in the 1969 Finals, but needed 7 games to pull out the win.
6. Brown (ed.), *The Complete Book of Basketball: A New York Times Scrapbook History*, p. 194.
7. www.twbookmark.com/books/46/0316279722/chapter_excerpt15933.html.
8. Ibid.
9. Brown (ed.), *The Complete Book of Basketball: A New York Times Scrapbook History*, p. 197.
10. Curry Kirkpatrick, "Shattered and Shaken," *Sports Illustrated*, January 2, 1978.
11. www.sacbee.com/content/sports/basketball/kings/story/1535910p-1612430c.html.
12. Kirkpatrick, "Shattered and Shaken."
13. www.insidehoops.com/nba-tv-contracts.html.

Chapter 17

1. www.brainyquote.com/quotes/authors/l/larry_bird.html.
2. www.sportsstats.com/bball/national/players/NPOYS/Larry_Bird.
3. www.hoophall.com/halloffamers/bird.htm.
4. Records include all tournament play prior to championship game.
5. Wolff, *100 Years of Hoops*, p. 128.
6. www.nba.com/history/players/johnsonm_bio.html.
7. www.sportsstats.com/bball/national/players/NPOYS/Larry_Bird; www.sportsstats.com/bball/national/players/1970/Magic_Johnson.
8. Brown (ed.), *The Complete Book of Basketball: A New York Times Scrapbook History*, p.108.
9. www.usatoday.com/sports/college/mensbasketball/tourney04/2004-03-14-spirit-of-79_x.htm.
10. Joey Johnston, "Spartans' Effort More than Magic," http://tampabayonline.net/final4/kelser.htm.
11. Walton sued the Blazers over the injury; the case was later settled out of court.
12. The record stood until 1996–97, when the Spurs posted a 36-game improvement over the previous season.

13. www.nba.com/history/finals/19791980.html.
14. John Papanek, "Arms and the Man," *Sports Illustrated*, May 26, 1980.
15. Ibid.
16. http://tsn.sportingnews.com/archives/nbafinals/1980.html.

Chapter 18

1. NBC: Nielsen Media Research.
2. www.usatoday.com/sports/nba/02playoffs/2002-06-11-ratings.htm.
3. www.wikipedia.org/wiki/USA_Network.
4. www.nba.com/history/finals/19801981.html.
5. Bob Ryan, "The Two and Only," *Sports Illustrated*, December 14, 1992.
6. Laura Bird, "Magic Johnson Slams Converse Ad Philosophy," *Wall Street Journal*, July 23, 1992.
7. Riley was on the Lakers 1972 championship team.
8. www.insidehoops.com/nba-tv-contracts.html.
9. Ibid.
10. http://members.aol.com/bradleyrd/apbr-faq.html.
11. http://members.aol.com/bradleyrd/attendance.html.
12. http://www.askmen.com/men/business_politics/50b_david_stern.html.
13. http://members.aol.com/apbrhoops/labor.html.
14. The Lakers acquired the top pick via a trade with Cleveland.
15. http://www.sixersonline.net/history/champs1983.htm.
16. http://inicia.es/de/allstar/1984.htm.
17. Marc Spears, "Thomas Stole the Show and Grabbed MVP Honor," *Denver Post*, December 26, 2004.
18. Mark Stern, "Q and A with the Commish," ESPN.com, January 22, 2004.
19. Ibid.
20. http://www.nba.com/history/thompson_bio.html.
21. Alan Paul, "John Lucas: Second Chance Points," SLAM.com, January 10, 2005.
22. Ryan, "The Two and Only."
23. www.sportsillustrated.cnn.com/2003/basketball/nba/09/04/bc.bkp.lgns.halloffame.r/index.html.
24. www.nba.com/history/finals/19831984.html.
25. Ryan, "The Two and Only."
26. www.nba.com/history/finals/19831984.html.
27. Ryan, "The Two and Only."
28. Roland Lazenby, *The Lakers: A Basketball*

Journey (New York: St. Martin's Press, 1993), p. 244.

29. http://big.chez.tiscali.fr/webuns/finals/1984.htm.

30. http://tsn.sportingnews.com/archives/nbafinals/1984.html.

31. http://big.chez.tiscali.fr/webuns/finals/1984.htm.

32. www.nba.com/history/finals/19831984.html.

33. Ibid.

34. http://tsn.sportingnews.com/archives/nbafinals/1984.html.

Chapter 19

1. http://cgi.superstation.com/about_us/milestone.htm.

2. Michael has one younger sister, Roslyn, an older sister, Delois, and two older brothers, Larry and James.

3. http://www.usoc.org/26_604.htm.

4. Since the camp began in 1966, more than 320 of its attendees have gone on to play at least one NBA game.

5. http://www.five-starbasketball.com/about.htm.

6. http://tarheelblue.collegesports.com/sports/m-baskbl/archive/unc-m-baskbl-history/greatest.html.

7. Ibid.

8. The Pan American Games, created by the International Olympic Committee in 1951, are held in the summer during the year preceding the Olympics.

9. http://www.usabasketball.com/history/mpag_1983.html.

10. http://www.usabasketball.com/history/moly_1984.html.

11. Terry Boers, "Here Comes Mr. Jordan," *Hoop Magazine*, January 1985.

12. Ibid.

13. http://www.nba.com/history/allstar/slamdunk_year_by_year.html#1985.

14. http://tsn.sportingnews.com/archives/nbafinals/1985.html.

15. Lazenby, *The Lakers: A Basketball Journey*, p. 253.

16. http://tsn.sportingnews.com/archives/nbafinals/1985.html.

17. Ibid.

18. Ibid.

19. http://webuns.chez.tiscali.fr/finals/1985.htm.

20. Lazenby, *The Lakers: A Basketball Journey*, p. 255.

21. http://www.hfmgv.org/exhibits/pic/2000/00.may.html.

22. Ibid.

23. http://members.aol.com/bradleyrd/apbr-faq.html.

24. Ibid.

25. Association for Professional Basketball Research.

26. Frederick C. Klein, "Fun and Folly in the National Basketball Asylum," *Wall Street Journal*, October 28, 1982.

27. "NBA Attendance, Revenues Up in Marked Recovery," *Wall Street Journal*, June 8, 1984.

28. Lazenby, *The Lakers: A Basketball Journey*, p. 256.

29. http://www.nba.com/jordan/mj8586.html.

30. Bird became only the third player to win three consecutive MVPs, joining Bill Russell and Wilt Chamberlain.

31. http://webuns.chez.tiscali.fr/finals/1986.htm.

32. http://www.nba.com/history/finals/19851986.html.

33. http://www.skybook.com/nbafinals_1986.asp.

34. http://www.nba.com/history/finals/19851986.html.

Chapter 20

1. Association for Professional Basketball Research.

2. Brett Ballantini, "The Middle of a Magic Era," *Basketball Digest*, January/February 2004.

3. Sam Goldaper, "King of the Court," *New York Times*, November 11, 1986.

4. Jordan's average remains the sixth best in NBA history. Four of the other five positions are held by Chamberlain.

5. Roy Johnson, "Lakers Outrun Hobbled Celtics," *New York Times*, June 7, 1987.

6. Ira Berkow, "They Went Whichaway?" *New York Times*, June 4, 1987.

7. Roy Johnson, "Johnson Right Hook Is a Real Knockout," *New York Times*, June 10, 1987.

8. Sam Goldaper, "Celtics Rout Lakers and Trail 3–2," *New York Times*, June 12, 1987.

9. Roy Johnson, "Celtics Can Smile Despite Sad Ending," *New York Times*, June 15, 1987.

10. Ira Berkow, "The Coloring of Bird," *New York Times*, June 2, 1987.

11. Roger Lowenstein, "Many Athletes Have a Tough Time Playing in the Endorsement Game," *Wall Street Journal*, August 29, 1986.

12. Ibid.

13. Phil Patton, "The Selling of Michael Jordan," *New York Times*, November 9, 1986.

14. Roy Johnson, "McAdoo Is Enjoying Success in Europe," *New York Times*, October 24, 1987.

15. Alexander Wolff, "The Hoop Life," *Sports Illustrated*, September 9, 2002.

16. Association for Professional Basketball Research.

17. Sam Goldaper, "Pistons Knock Out Celtics to Reach the Final Round," *New York Times*, June 4, 1988.

18. Peter Alfano, "Celtics Miss Their Shots and the Finals," *New York Times*, June 4, 1988.

19. Thomas's 25-point quarter remains an NBA Finals record.

20. William C. Rhoden, "N.B.A Playoffs; After the Victory, Los Angeles Loses Its Usual Cool," *New York Times*, June 23, 1988.

21. Sam Goldaper, "N.B.A. Playoffs; Lakers Hold Off Pesky Pistons to Regain Their Title," *New York Times*, June 22, 1988.

22. William C. Rhoden, "N.B.A. Playoffs; Pistons Top Lakers to Lead Series 1-0," *New York Times*, June 8, 1988.

23. Terry Lefton, "Stern's Turnaround Jumpstart," *Brandweek*, November 1, 1999.

24. Mark Vancil, "Michael Jordan: Phenomenon," *Hoop*, December 1991.

25. Ibid.

26. Peter Alfano, "Basketball Team Faces Tall Order," *New York Times*, August 2, 1988.

27. Robinson had been selected with the overall number one pick in 1987, but due to a prior commitment to the military, would not join the Spurs until 1989.

Chapter 21

1. http://p69.webcindario.com/modules.php?name=Content&pa=showpage&pid=28.

2. Jones was fired by Auerbach after the team's playoff loss to Detroit.

3. Robert Thomas, "NBA Optimistic on Finances," *New York Times*, June 7, 1988.

4. Ibid.

5. Michael Maren, "Rebound! David Stern's Magic and Entrepreneurial Skills," *Success*, June 1990.

6. William C. Rhoden, "Bulls Keep Marching Along," *New York Times*, May 22, 1989.

7. William C. Rhoden, "Thomas Scores 33 and Pistons Even a Series," *New York Times*, May 24, 1989.

8. Sam Goldaper, "Pistons Earn First Title By Sweeping Lakers," *New York Times*, June 14, 1989.

9. Ibid.

10. Jackson averaged 6.7 points and 4.3 rebounds in his 12-year NBA career.

11. George Vecsey, "Big Fella Goes Back A Few Years," *New York Times*, June 15, 1989.

12. "The Franchise Retires," *New York Times*, June 19, 1989.

13. Harlan Schreiber, "A History of Foreign Players in the NBA," *Hoopsanalyst*, January 26, 2004.

14. Joining Divac for the '89-90 season were before-mentioned Alexander Volkov and Drazen Petrovic, along with Zarko Paspalj (Spurs) and Sarunas Marciulionis (Warriors). Paspalj played in only 28 NBA games.

Chapter 22

1. Technically, Bird's career-low averages of 19.3 points and 6.2 rebounds came in 1998–99, but he played only six games before opting for surgery to remove bone spurs in his feet.

2. Joe Lapointe, "More Weary Than Tough, Pistons Succumb to Hawks," *New York Times*, April 28, 1991.

3. Ira Berkow, "The Pistons Were a Disgrace," *New York Times*, May 29, 1991.

4. Clifton Brown, "Bulls Brush Aside Pistons for Eastern Title," *New York Times*, May 28, 1991.

5. Harvey Araton, "No Kisses, Just Great Players in Final," *New York Times*, June 2, 1991.

6. Clifton Brown, "Jordan Heroics Fall Just Short as Lakers Win," *New York Times*, June 3, 1991.

7. Ira Berkow, "Johnson Heaps Praise on Bulls and Jordan," *New York Times*, June 13, 1991.

8. http://www.nba.com/history/finals/1990 1991.html.

9. Magic had won both MVPs in 1987, but finished 10th in scoring.

10. Clifton Brown, "Magic's Act Could Disappear after Finals," *New York Times*, June 12, 1991.

Chapter 23

1. http://www.insidehoops.com/nba-tv-contracts.html.

2. Association for Professional Basketball Research.

3. The committee included University of Kentucky's athletic director C. M. Newton, NBA GMs Wayne Embry of the Cavaliers, the Pacers' Donnie Walsh, Jan Volk of the Celtics, the Spurs' Bob Bass, former Olympian Quin Buckner, Seton Hall coach P. J. Carlesimo, Hall of Famer Billy Cunningham, Coaches Mike Krzyzewski of Duke and George Raveling from USC, the executive director of the NBA's player association Charles Grantham, and Rod Thorn, a vice president of the NBA.

4. Richard W. Stevenson, "Basketball Star Retires on Advice of His Doctors," *New York Times*, November 8, 1991.

5. *Sacramento Observer*, November 13, 1991, p. G-1.

6. Ira Berkow, "All Stars to Give Magic a Nervous Embrace," *New York Times*, February 7, 1992.

7. Ibid.

8. http://www.basketballreference.com/awards/allstarbox.htm?yr=1991&lg=N.

9. Clifton Brown, "For One Stirring Afternoon, Magic Johnson Dazzles Again," *New York Times*, February 10, 1992.

10. Michael Martinex, "Stage Has Been Set for Drexler's Rise," *New York Times*, June 1, 1992.

11. Clifton Brown, "Two Likely Opponents Add Double Intrigue," *New York Times*, May 31, 1992.

12. Jordan's 46-point game was a Finals career high.

13. Thomas George, "Cavalier Youth Serves Up a Blowout of Aging Celtics," *New York Times*, May 18, 1992.

14. Michael Martinex, "U.S. Basketball 'Cannon Fodder' is Worthy of Praise," *New York Times*, June 22, 1992.

15. Michael Martinex, "A Familiar Smile is Back on the Court," *New York Times*, June 23, 1992.

16. Harvey Araton, "U.S. Men Make the Shots and Snapshots," *New York Times*, June 29, 1992.

17. http://www.usabasketball.com/history/mtoa_1992.html.

18. Harvey Araton, "U.S. Must Consider Another Playmaker," *New York Times*, July 1, 1992.

19. Dave Kindred, "A Shoo-in," *Sporting News*, August 10, 1992.

20. Tom Callahan, "The Lopsided Dream," *U.S. News & World Report*, August 10, 1992, v113, n6, p. 37.

21. Mark Heisler, "Barcelona '92Olympics/Day 15: They Enjoyed the Inevitable Basketball," *Los Angeles Times*, August 9, 1992.

22. Tom Dungee, "Golden Dreams and Nightmares in Barcelona," *Los Angeles Sentinel*, August 13, 1992.

23. Mark Heisler, "Barcelona '92Olympics/Day 15: They Enjoyed the Inevitable Basketball," *Los Angeles Times*, August 9, 1992.

24. *Forbes*, Jul 20, 1992, v150 n2, p. 92.

25. Steve McClellan and Rich Brown, "NBC Claims Silver in Olympic Effort," *Broadcasting*, August 10, 1992, v122 n33, p. 6.

26. http://legalminds.lp.findlaw.com/list/cyberjournal/msg00111.html.

27. Dave Kindred, "A Shoo-in," *Sporting News*, August 10, 1992.

28. Pico Iyer, "The Win-Win Games," *Time*, August 10, 1992, v140 n6, p. 50.

29. Mike Downey, "A Team That Lived Up to Its Legend," *Los Angeles Times*, August 9, 1992.

30. Michael Bradley, "It's in the Bag ... for Now," *Sport*, August 1992, v83 n8, p. 56.

Chapter 24

1. Thomas Bonk, "Celtic Larry Bird Retires," *Los Angeles Times*, August 19, 1992.

2. Joseph Pereira, "Larry Bird Retires After Stellar Career With Boston Celtics," *Wall Street Journal*, August 19, 1992.

3. Ibid.

4. Ibid.

5. Earvin "Magic" Johnson (with William Novak), *My Life* (New York: Random House, 1992), xiii.

6. Philip J. Hilts, "Magic Johnson Quits Panel on AIDS," *New York Times*, September 26, 1992.

7. Ibid.

8. Ibid.

9. Harvey Araton, "Johnson's Return to League Isn't Welcomed by Some," *New York Times*, November 1, 1992.

10. Ibid.

11. Ibid.

12. Ira Berkow, "Magic's Collision Course," *New York Times*, November 3, 1992. 13. Harvey Araton, "NBA Finds it Can't Outleap Reality," *New York Times*, November 3, 1992.

14. Editorial page, *New York Times*, November 3, 1992.

15. Tom Friend, "Barkely Shines But Bulls Still Win," *New York Times*, June 12, 1993.

16. Magic won three Finals MVPs, but not in consecutive order.

17. Clifton Brown, "The Bulls Belong to Past and Future," *New York Times*, June 22, 1993.

18. *Los Angeles Times*, June 16, 1998.

19. Harvey Araton, "Petrovic Carried Torch for European Players," *New York Times*, June 10, 1993.

20. Richard Sandomir, "The Economics of a Sports Cliché," *New York Times*, June 22, 1993.

21. Ironically, Pat Riley, who had coached the Lakers during their failed three-peat quest, had registered the trademark phrase in 1989, earning him an undisclosed percentage of the NBA's take for 1993 Bulls merchandise.

22. Sandomir, "The Economics of a Sports Cliché."

23. Harvey Araton, "Petrovic Carried Torch for European Players," *New York Times*, June 10, 1993.

24. Robert McG. Thomas Jr., "Jordan Thanks the Public, but Scolds the Media for Speculation," *New York Times*, August 20, 1993.

25. Mike Downey, "Without 'Anything Else to Prove,' Jordan Retires Sports," *Los Angeles Times*, October 7, 1993.

26. Ibid.

27. Weekly Compilation of Presidential Documents, October 11, 1993, 29, 40; Research Library Core, p. 2017.

28. The catchphrase "Be Like Mike" originated from an early '90s Gatorade ad campaign featuring Jordan.

29. Mark Heisley, "If Anything, an Insanity Cap Seems to Be in Order," *Los Angeles Times*, October 31, 1993.

30. Ibid.

31. Ibid.

32. Bill Barnard, "NBA Season without Big Names But with Big Bucks," *Los Angeles Times*, October 31, 1993.

33. Ibid.

34. "Barkley and Green Lead Suns in Munich," *Los Angeles Times*, October 24, 1993.

35. http://www.canoe.ca/NBAPlayoffs99/june20_nba.html.

Chapter 25

1. Richard Sandomir, "Players Seeking Antitrust Reversal," *New York Times*, September 23, 1994.

2. Association for Professional Basketball Research.

3. The Toronto Huskies played in the BAA during the 1946-47 season, prior to the merger that created the NBA.

4. http://www.nba.com/jordan/mj9394.html.

5. Mike Wise, "Jordan Hasn't Lost Stuff in Basketball," *New York Times*, September 10, 1994.

6. Ira Berkow, "The Jordan Show Is Returning to the Air Today," *New York Times*, March 19, 1995.

7. Ira Berkow, "The World Watches Jordan Hold Court," *New York Times*, March 20, 1995.

8. Richard Sandomir, "NBC's Ratings Soar Higher Than Jordan," *New York Times*, March 21, 1995.

9. http://webuns.chez.tiscali.fr/finals/1995.htm.

10. Hill and Jason Kidd were voted co–Rookies of the Year, the first time two players had shared the award since 1970–71.

11. Richard Sandomir, "For Houston's Dignified Superstar, It's a While New Game," *New York Times*, June 15, 1995.

12. Ibid.

13. Murray Chass, "N.B.A Locks Out Players in First Work Stoppage," *New York Times*, July 1, 1995.

14. Murray Chass, "N.B.A. Players Support Union By a Landslide," *New York Times*, September 13, 1995.

15. "Owners Approve Labor Deal," *New York Times*, September 16, 1995.

16. Tom Friend, "After 4 Years, His Return Begins Tonight," *Los Angeles Times*, January 29, 1996.

17. Harvey Araton, "Did the Fears Vanish, Like Magic?" *New York Times*, February 4, 1996.

18. http://www.basketballreference.com/teams/boxscore.htm?yr=1995&b=19960130&tm=LAL.

19. Tom Friend, "Johnson Still Has the Touch," *New York Times*, February 1, 1996.

20. "Johnson Gives TNT a Lift," *New York Times*, February 6, 1996.

21. Tom Friend, "More Decisions Loom For Lakers' Johnson," *New York Times*, May 2, 1996.

22. "Bulls Score in TV Ratings," *New York Times*, June 18, 1996.

23. Malcolm Moran, "The Decline and Fall of the American Empire (Coming Soon)," *New York Times*, August 5, 1996.

24. Basketballreference.com.

25. The number included three seasons (1946-47 to 1948-49) spent operating as the Basketball Association of America (BAA).

Chapter 26

1. Clifton Brown, "It's Time to Bid for (Not So) Free Agents," *New York Times*, July 7, 1996.

2. The collective bargaining agreement required that players exchanged must be of equal salary value.

3. Malcolm Moran, "Lakers Get O'Neal in 7-Year Contract," *New York Times*, July 19, 1996.

4. "Sports People; Pro Basketball; Seattle Signs McIlvaine," *New York Times*, July 23, 1996.

5. Selena Roberts, "N.B.A. Giving Birth to 9-Figure Contract," *New York Times*, July 15, 1996.

6. Mike Wise, "Injuries Take Sparkle of All-Star Luster," *New York Times*, February 8, 1997.

7. Harvey Araton, "Jordan's Only Competition Is Past and Future," *New York Times*, June 15, 1998.

8. http://www.wnba.com/playoffs2003/history_1997.html.

9. www.wnba.com/about_us/historyof_wnba.html.

10. Mike Wise, "Wolves May Be Limited By Garnett's Contract," *New York Times*, October 3, 1997.

11. Jason Diamos, "The Mets Agree to Make Piazza Baseball's Richest Player," *New York Times*, October 25, 1998.

12. Stern signed a five-year, $30 million contract extension in February 1996.

13. "Stern in the $30 Million Dollar Man," *New York Times*, February 12, 1996.

14. Mike Wise, "N.B.A. Suspends Player Who Attacked His Coach," *New York Times*, December 5, 1997.

15. Only Abdul-Jabbar had more MVPs (six).

16. Mike Wise, "It's Their Ball, and N.B.A. Owners Call for Lockout," *New York Times*, June 30, 1998.

17. Mike Wise, "Labor Standoff Knocks Out N.B.A.'s Exhibition Season," *New York Times*, October 6, 1998.

18. Mike Wise, "He Has Lost the Desire to Play at 35," *New York Times*, January 14, 1999.

19. Harvey Araton, "Star System is Declining in the N.B.A.," *New York Times*, July 3, 1998.

20. Cleveland won one playoff game during Kemp's three years with the team. He was traded to Portland prior to the start of the 2000-01 season.

21. Association for Professional Basketball Research.

22. http://users.pullman.com/rodfort/PH SportsEcon/Common/OtherData/NBATicket Price/NBATicket98-9.xls.

23. http://users.pullman.com/rodfort/PH SportsEcon/Common/OtherData/mlbfancosti ndex/MLBFCI99.xls.

24. http://users.pullman.com/rodfort/PH SportsEcon/Common/OtherData/nflfancosti ndex/NFLFCI99.xls.

25. http://users.pullman.com/rodfort/PH SportsEcon/Common/OtherData/nhlfancosti ndex/NHLFCI98-99.xls.

26. www.usatoday.com/sports/nba/02play offs/2002-06-11-ratings.htm.

27. Association for Professional Basketball Research.

28. Richard Sandomir, "Shoe Industry Questioning Star Power," *New York Times*, July 7, 1998.

Chapter 27

1. http://webuns.chez.tiscali.fr/all_star_game/1998.htm.

2. Sandomir, "Shoe Industry Questioning Star Power."

3. Ibid.

4. The contest was not held in 1998 due to a lack of interest among players. No All Star festivities or game was played in 1999 because of the shortened season.

5. Richard Sandormir, "Carter under Glass, and Over the Top, on NBC," *New York Times*, February 29, 2000.

6. http://www.basketballreference.com/teams/boxscore.htm?yr=1999&b=20000227&tm=TOR.

7. Sandormir, "Carter under Glass, and Over the Top, on NBC," *New York Times*, February 29, 2000.

8. Liz Robbins, "Carter & Co. Recharge Spirits," *New York Times*, April 25, 2000.

9. Mike Wise, "Carter Hype Raises Concerns About His Growth," *New York Times*, February 27, 2000.

10. www2.indystar.com/library/factfiles/peo ple/m/miller_reggie/reggie.html.

11. Bird became disenchanted with coaching and resigned after a successful three years to pursue other interests.

12. Chris Broussard, "Gill Poised to Leave the Nets and Join the Lakers," *New York Times*, August 4, 2000.

13. www.usabasketball.com/history.

Chapter 28

1. www.espn.go.com/classic/biography/s/Woods_Tiger.html.

2. Ibid.

3. Lisa DiCarlo, "Six Degrees of Tiger Woods," *Forbes*, March 18, 2004.

4. Bill Vlasic and Mark Trudy, "Is Tiger Buick's Fountain of Youth?" *Detroit News*, February 10, 2000.

5. Tom Kertes, "Greed Is Grinding the Game Down," *Basketball Digest*, March/April 2004.

6. Ibid.

7. Steve Wilstein, "Youth Movement Catches up to NBA," Associated Press, February 21, 2005.

8. Ibid.

9. Association for Professional Basketball Research.

10. "The NBA Selects Digitas as Strategic Partner to Develop Integrated Web Presence," *Business Wire*, July 19, 2000.

11. Ira Berkow, "Heart of a Champion Still Beats for Jordan," *New York Times*, February 11, 2002.

12. "Michael Jordan Returns to the NBA for 'The Love of the Game,'" *Jet*, October 15, 2001.

13. The others were Tyson Chandler (#2, Clippers), Eddy Curry (#4, Bulls), and DeSagana Diop (#8, Cavaliers).

14. Staci D. Kramer, "Jordan Pumps up TBS," *Cable World*, November 12, 2001.

15. Chris Broussard, "Jordan Returns to the Garden But His Magic Doesn't Follow," *New York Times*, October 31, 2001.

16. The team's previous best record of 55 wins was set in 1963–64, when it played as the Cincinnati Royals.

17. Sean Deveney, "Lakers drained and pained but championship trained," *The Sporting News*, June 10, 2002.

18. "Kings-Lakers game draws high TV ratings," *Sacramento Business Journal*, June 3, 2002.

19. "Finals ratings lowest in 20 Years," *Los Angeles Times*, June 14, 2002.

20. *SportsIllustrated.com*, June 6, 2002.

Chapter 29

1. http://www.allstarz.org/yaming/bio.htm.

2. Ibid.

3. http://www.nba.com/draft2002/quotes_020626.html#yao.

4. Chris Broussard, "Foreign All-Stars Lead an Anticipated Invasion," *New York Times*, February 9, 2002.

5. Ten years later, Scottie Pippen was the only small forward to appear in the top 20.

6. The first infraction resulted in a resetting of the shot clock and the ball out of bounds. Subsequent violations gave the offensive team a free throw and the ball out of bounds.

7. Dave D'Alessandro, "No-Zone Rule Separates Pros from the College Boys—Offense Play," *Sporting News*, April 16, 2001.

8. Brett Ballantini, "Rule Changes? Bring 'Em On," *Basketball Digest*, Summer 2001.

9. Jerry Mittleman, "Has NBA Shooting Really Gone South?" *InsideHoops.com*, December 15, 2003.

10. "Michael Jordan heads into his final retirement amid fans' cheers," *Jet*, May 5, 2002.

11. George Kimball, "Off the Air waves," *Boston Herald*, April 4, 2003.

12. Erik Brady, "Wizards show Jordan the door," *USA Today*, May 7, 2003.

13. Ibid.

14. www.nba.com/jordan/hubieonjordan.html.

15. http://www.nba.com/history/players/stockton_bio.html.

16. http://tsn.sportingnews.com/archives/nbafinals/2003.html.

17. Ibid.

18. Michael Heistand, "ABC's ratings for the NBA Finals among lowest in history," *USA Today*, June 16, 2005.

19. www.allstarz.org/yaoming/bio.htm.

20. Rick Horrow, "NBA at Finals Time: Sustaining Three Business Goals," *SportsLine.com*, June 3, 2003.

Chapter 30

1. Taylor Bell, "When it Comes to LeBron, You Can Believe the Hype," *Chicago Sun Times*, April 4, 2003.

2. Following Sprewell's suspension in 1998, he signed on with the Knicks, where he played five strong seasons without a major incident.

3. http://www.usatoday.com/sports/scores104/104124/20040503NBA--DETROIT---0.htm.

4. Bryant spent much of the season traveling back and forth from Denver, where he was being tried for sexual assault. The case was eventually dropped by the prosecution.

5. Dana Gauruder, "Piston Notes," *Daily Oakland Press*, May 31, 2004.

Chapter 31

1. Pete Alfano, "NBA'S Anemic Efforts," *Fort Worth Star-Telegram*, June 13, 2004.

2. "Pistons Drive Off with NBA Title," Associated Press, June 16, 2004.

3. Bill Bradley, "Continued Teamwork means Pistons will be in the hunt to repeat," *The Detroit News*, November 3, 2004.

4. Fox retired without ever reporting to Boston. Payton rebuffed the trade initially but went on to have a solid year under coach Doc Rivers, averaging 11.3 points, 6.1 assists, and 3 rebounds.

5. http://www.dfw.net/~patricia/misc/salaries93.txt.

6. http://www.hoopshype.com/salaries.htm.

7. www.usabasketball.com/history/moly_2004.html.

8. Alan Crosby, "Dream Team Jeered Off Court," *London Independent*, August 28, 2004.

9. http://www.fiba.com/subsites/FIBAosg2004/game_stats_OSG04_M202.htm.

10. Ibid.

11. Michael Hunt, "U.S. Cast in Bronze," *Milwaukee Journal Sentinel*, August 29, 2004.

12. Bill Plaschke, "An Issue of Character," *Sporting News*, December 1977.

13. Tom Kertes, "Greed Is Grinding the Game Down," *Basketball Digest*, March/April 2004.

14. Larry Lage, "Black Eye for NBA," Associated Press via *The Fresno Bee*, November 20, 2004.

15. Sean Deveney, "The Artest Mess," *Sporting News*, November 29, 2004.

16. Ibid.

17. Artest had been benched for two games the previous week, stemming from an incident where he reportedly requested a month off from his duties with the Pacers to promote an R&B album for his production company. In 2002–03, he missed 12 games due to suspensions.

18. Associated Press, November 21, 2004.

19. Bill Walton, "Making Sense of Senseless Acts," *ESPN Insider*, November 23, 2004.

20. The others were Oscar Robertson (1963–64) and Bob Cousy (1956–57).

21. The Nuggets brought in George Karl to coach the team midway through the season. Karl led the team to a 32-8 record and went 1-4 in the playoffs, losing to the Spurs in the first round.

22. J.A. Adande, "Pistons, Spurs Will Play Right Way, but They Won't Be Must-See TV," *LA Times*, June 9, 2005.

23. Mark Heistand, "ABC's rating for NBA Finals among lowest in history," *USA Today*, June 16, 2005.

24. Mark Heisler, "Things Might Not Be as Bad as They Seem," *LA Times*, June 26, 2005.

25. Rick Harrow, "Fastbreak toward the NBA Finals: Playoff Business," CBS Sportsline.com, June 3, 2005.

26. "NBA Finals Delivers Record Attendance," *Business Wire*, June 27, 2005.

27. Rick Harrow. "Fastbreak toward the NBA Finals: Playoff Business." CBS Sportsline.com, June 3, 2005.

28. James Brown, David Stern interview, *Sporting News*, January 28, 2005.

BIBLIOGRAPHY

Books

Barkley, Charles (with Michael Wilbon). *I May Be Wrong But I Doubt It*. New York: Random House, 2002.

Benagh, Jim. *Basketball: Startling Stories behind the Records*. New York: Sterling Publishing, 1992.

Bird, Larry (with Bob Ryan). *Drive: The Story of My Life*. New York, Doubleday, 1989.

Bradley, Bill. *Life on the Run*. New York: Vintage Books, 1995.

Brown, Gene (ed). *The Complete Book of Basketball: A New York Times Scrapbook*. New York: Arno Press and Bobbs-Merrill, 1980.

George, Nelson. *Elevating the Game: Black Men in Basketball*. New York: Harper-Collins, 1992.

Isaacs, Neil D. *Vintage NBA: The Pioneer Era 1946–1956*. Indianapolis: Masters Press, 1996.

Jackson, Phil. *The Last Season: A Team in Search of Its Soul*. New York: Penguin Press, 2004.

Johnson, Earvin "Magic" (with William Novak). *My Life*. New York: Random House, 1992.

Karl, George (with Don Yaeger). *This Game's the Best*. New York: St. Martin's Press, 1997.

Lazenby, Roland. *The Lakers: A Basketball Journey*. New York: St. Martin's Press, 1993.

McKissack, Fredrick. *Black Hoops: The History of African Americans in Basketball*. New York: Scholastic, 1999.

Naismith, James. *Basketball: Its Origins and Development*, 10th edition. New York: Bison Books, 1996.

Peterson, Robert W. *Cages to Jump Shots: Pro Basketball's Early Years*. New York: Oxford University Press, 1990.

Pluto, Terry. *Loose Balls: The Short, Wild Life of the American Basketball Association*. New York: Simon & Schuster, 1990.

Pluto, Terry. *Tall Tales*. New York: Simon & Schuster, 1992.

Riley, Pat. *Showtime: Inside the Lakers' Breakthrough Season*. New York: Warner Books, 1988.

Schmidt, Anja (ed.) *NBA's Greatest*. New York: DK Publishing and NBA Properties, 2003.

Thomas, Ron. *They Cleared the Lane: The NBA's Black Pioneers.* Lincoln: University of Nebraska Press, 2002.

Webb, Bernice Larson. *The Basketball Man: James Naismith.* Lawrence: University of Kansas Press, 1973.

West, Jerry (with Bill Libby). *Mr. Clutch: The Jerry West Story,* fifth printing. Englewood Cliffs, New Jersey: Prentice Hall, 1971.

Wolff, Alexander. *Sports Illustrated: 100 Years of Hoops.* New Jersey: Crescent Books, 1995.

Web Sites

Association for Professional Basketball Research (www.members.aol.com/bradley rd/apbr.html)

Basketball Hall of Fame (www.hooplhall.com)

databaseBasketball.com (formerly BasketballReference.com)

ESPN.com

findarticles.com

hickoksports.com

hoopshype.com

insidehoops.com

Naismith Museum and Hall of Fame (www.naismithmuseum.com)

NBA.com

NBA.com/history

Remember the ABA (remembertheaba.com)

Sporting News (www.sportingnews.com)

Sports Illustrated (www.sportsillustrated.cnn.com)

USA Basketball (www.usabasketball.com)

U.S. Dept. of Labor, Bureau of Labor Statistics (www.bls.gov)

Archived Newspapers

New York Times
Los Angeles Times
Wall Street Journal

Magazine and Newspaper Articles

Adande, J.A. "Pistons, Spurs Will Play Right Way, but They Won't Be Must-See TV." *Los Angeles Times,* June 9, 2005.

Alfano, Peter. "Basketball Team Faces Tall Order." *New York Times,* August 2, 1988.

_____. "Celtics Miss Their Shots and the Finals." *New York Times,* June 4, 1988.

_____. "Did the Fears Vanish, Like Magic?" *New York Times,* February 4, 1996.

_____. "Johnson's Return to League Isn't Welcomed By Some." *New York Times,* November 1, 1992.

_____. "Jordan's Only Competition Is Past and Future." *New York Times,* June 15, 1997.

_____. "NBA Finds It Can't Outleap Reality." *New York Times,* November 3, 1992.

_____. "NBA'S Anemic Efforts." *Fort Worth Star-Telegram,* June 13, 2004.

Araton, Harvey. "No Kisses, Just Great Players in Final." *New York Times,* June 2, 1991.

_____. "Petrovic Carried Torch for European Players." *New York Times,* June 10, 1993.

_____. "Star System Is Declining in the N.B.A." *New York Times*, July 3, 1998.

_____. "U.S. Men Make the Shots and Snapshots." *New York Times*, June 29, 1992.

_____. "U.S. Must Consider Another Playmaker." *New York Times*, July 1, 1992.

Ballantini, Brett. "The Middle of a Magic Era." *Basketball Digest*, January/February 2004.

_____. "Rule Changes? Bring 'Em On." *Basketball Digest*, Summer 2001.

"Barkley and Green Lead Suns in Munich." *Los Angeles Times*, October 24, 1993.

Barnard, Bill. "NBA Season without Big Names But with Big Bucks." *Los Angeles Times*, October 31, 1993.

Bell, Taylor. "When It Comes to LeBron, You Can Believe the Hype." *Chicago Sun Times*, April 4, 2003.

Berger, Paul. "The First Season: 50 Years ago Serious Pro Basketball Was Born. Or at Least They Tried to Be Serious," *American Heritage*, May–June 1997, v48 n3, p. 94(8).

Berkow, Ira. "All Stars to Give Magic a Nervous Embrace." *New York Times*, February 7, 1992.

_____. "The Coloring of Bird." *New York Times*, June 2, 1987.

_____. "Heart of a Champion Still Beats for Jordan." *New York Times*, February 11, 2002.

_____. "Johnson Heaps Praise on Bulls and Jordan." *New York Times*, June 13, 1991.

_____. "The Jordan Show Is Returning to the Air Today." *New York Times*, March 19, 1995.

_____. "Magic's Collision Course." *New York Times*, November 3, 1992.

_____. "The Pistons Were a Disgrace." *New York Times*, May 29, 1991.

_____. "They Went Whichaway?" *New York Times*, June 4, 1987.

_____. "The World Watches Jordan Hold Court." *New York Times*, March 20, 1995.

Bird, Laura. "Magic Johnson Slams Converse Ad Philosophy." *Wall Street Journal*, July 23, 1992.

Boers, Terry. "Here Comes Mr. Jordan." *Hoop*, January 1985.

Bonk, Thomas. "Celtic Larry Bird Retires." *Los Angeles Times*, August 9, 1992.

Bradley, Bill. "Continued teamwork means Pistons will be in the hunt to repeat." *The Detroit News*, November 3, 2004.

Bradley, Michael. "It's in the Bag ... for Now." *Sport*, August 1992, v83 n8, p. 56.

Brady, Erik. "Wizards show Jordan the door." *USA Today*, May 7, 2003.

Broussard, Chris. "Foreign All-Stars Lead an Anticipated Invasion." *New York Times*, February 9, 2002.

_____. "Gill Poised to Leave the Nets and Join the Lakers." *New York Times*, August 4, 2000.

_____. "Jordan Returns to the Garden But His Magic Doesn't Follow." *New York Times*, October 31, 2001.

Brown, Clifton. "The Bulls Belong to Past and Future." *New York Times*, June 22, 1993.

_____. "Bulls Brush Aside Pistons for Eastern Title." *New York Times*, May 28, 1991.

_____. "For One Stirring Afternoon, Magic Johnson Dazzles Again." *New York Times*, February 10, 1992.

_____. "It's Time to Bid for (Not So) Free Agents." *New York Times*, July 7, 1996.

_____. "Jordan Heroics Fall Just Short as Lakers Win." *New York Times*, June 3, 1991.

_____. "Magic's Act Could Disappear after Finals." *New York Times*, June 12, 1991.

_____. "Two Likely Opponents Add Double Intrigue." *New York Times*, May 31, 1992.

Brown, James. David Stern interview. *Sporting News*, January 28, 2005.
"Bulls Score in TV Ratings." *New York Times*, June 18, 1996.
Callahan, Tom. "The Lopsided Dream." *U.S. News & World Report*, August 10, 1992.
Chass, Murray. "N.B.A. Locks Out Players in First Work Stoppage." *New York Times*, July 1, 1995.
_____. "N.B.A. Players Support Union By a Landslide." *New York Times*, September 13, 1995.
Crosby, Alan. "Dream Team Jeered Off Court." *London Independent*, August 28, 2004.
D'Alessandro, Dave. "No-Zone Rule Separates Pros from the College Boys — Offense Play." *Sporting News*, April 16, 2001.
Deveney, Sean. "The Artest Mess." *Sporting News*, November 29, 2004.
_____. "Lakers Drained and Pained but Championship Trained." *The Sporting News*, June 10, 2002.
Diamos, Jason. "The Mets Agree to Make Piazza Baseball's Richest Player." *New York Times*, October 25, 1998.
DiCarlo, Lisa. "Six Degrees of Tiger Woods." *Forbes*, March 18, 2004.
Downey, Mike. "A Team That Lived Up to Its Legend." *Los Angeles Times*, August 9, 1992.
_____. "Without 'Anything Else to Prove,' Jordan Retires Sports." *Los Angeles Times*, October 7, 1993.
Dungee, Tom. "Golden Dreams and Nightmares in Barcelona." *Los Angeles Sentinel*, August 13, 1992.
"Finals Ratings lowest in 20 years." *Los Angeles Times*, June 14, 2002.
"The Franchise Retires." *New York Times*, June 19, 1989.
Friend, Tom. "After 4 Years, His Return Begins Tonight." *Los Angeles Times*, January 29, 1996.
_____. "Barkley Shines But Bulls Still Win." *New York Times*, June 12, 1993.
_____. "Johnson Still Has the Touch." *New York Times*, February 1, 1996.
_____. "More Decisions Loom for Lakers' Johnson." *New York Times*, May 2, 1996.
Gauruder, Dana. "Piston Notes." *Daily Oakland Press*, May 31, 2004.
George, Thomas. "Cavalier Youth Serves Up a Blowout of Aging Celtics." *New York Times*, May 18, 1992.
Goldaper, Sam. "Celtics Rout Lakers and Trail 3-2." *New York Times*, June 12, 1987.
_____. "King of the Court." *New York Times*, November 11, 1986.
_____. "N.B.A. Playoffs; Lakers Hold Off Pesky Pistons to Regain Their Title." *New York Times*, June 22, 1988.
_____. "Pistons Earn First Title by Sweeping Lakers." *New York Times*, June 14, 1989.
_____. "Pistons Knock Out Celtics to Reach the Final Round." *New York Times*, June 4, 1988.
Harrow, Rick. "Fastbreak toward the NBA Finals: Playoff Business." CBS Sportsline.com, June 3, 2005.
Heisler, Mark. "Barcelona '92 Olympics/Day 15: They Enjoyed the Inevitable Basketball." *Los Angeles Times*, August 9, 1992.
_____. "If Anything, an Insanity Cap Seems to Be in Order." *Los Angeles Times*, October 31, 1993.
_____. "Things Might Not Be as Bad as They Seem." *Los Angeles Times*, June 26, 2005.

Heistand, Michael. "ABC's Ratings for NBA Finals Among Lowest in History." *USA Today*, June 16, 2005.

Hilts, Philip J. "Magic Johnson Quits Panel on AIDS." *New York Times*, September 26, 1992.

Horrow, Rick. "NBA at Finals Time: Sustaining Three Business Goals." SportsLine. com, June 3, 2003.

Hunt, Michael. "U.S. Cast in Bronze." *Milwaukee Journal Sentinel*, August 29, 2004.

Iyer, Pico. "The Win-Win Games." *Time*, August 10, 1992.

Johnson, Roy. "Celtics Can Smile Despite Sad Ending." *New York Times*, June 15, 1987.

_____. "Johnson Right Hook Is a Real Knockout." *New York Times*, June 10, 1987.

_____. "Lakers Outrun Hobbled Celtics." *New York Times*, June 7, 1987.

_____. "McAdoo Is Enjoying Success in Europe." *New York Times*, October 24, 1987.

"Johnson Gives TNT a Lift." *New York Times*, February 6, 1996.

Kekis, John. "Time Has Come for Shot-Clock Inventor." Associated Press, May 25, 2000.

Kertes, Tom. "Greed Is Grinding the Game Down." *Basketball Digest*, March/April 2004.

Kimball, George. "Off the Air waves." *Boston Herald*, April 4, 2003.

Kindred, Dave. "A Shoo-in." *Sporting News*, August 10, 1992.

"Kings-Lakers game draws high TV ratings." *Sacramento Business Journal*, June 3, 2002.

Kirkpatrick, Curry. "Shattered and Shaken." *Sports Illustrated*, January 2, 1978.

Kramer, Staci D. "Jordan Pumps up TBS." *Cable World*, November 12, 2001.

Lage, Larry. "Black Eye for NBA." Associated Press, via *The Fresno Bee*, November 20, 2004.

Lapointe, Joe. "More Wears Than Tough, Pistons Succumb to Hawks." *New York Times*, April 28, 1991.

Lefton, Terry. "Stern's Turnaround Jumpstart." *Brandweek*, November 1, 1999.

Lowenstein, Roger. "Many Athletes Have a Tough Time Playing in the Endorsement Game." *Wall Street Journal*, August 29, 1986.

Maren, Michael. "Rebound! David Stern's Magic and Entrepreneurial Skills." *Success*, June 1990.

Martinex, Michael. "A Familiar Smile Is Back on the Court." *New York Times*, June 23, 1992.

_____. "Stage Has Been Set for Drexler's Rise." *New York Times*, June 1, 1992.

_____. "U.S. Basketball 'Cannon Fodder' Is Worthy of Praise." *New York Times*, June 22, 1992.

McClellan, Steve, and Rich Brown. "NBC Claims Silver in Olympic Effort." *Broadcasting*, August 10, 1992, v122 n33, p. 6.

"Michael Jordan Heads into His Final Retirement Amid Fans' Cheers." *Jet*, May 5, 2002.

"Michael Jordan Returns to the NBA for 'The Love of the Game.'" *Jet*, October 15, 2001.

Mittleman, Jerry. "Has NBA Shooting Really Gone South?" InsideHoops.com, December 15, 2003.

Moran, Malcolm. "The Decline and Fall of the American Empire (Coming Soon)." *New York Times*, August 5, 1996.

_____. "Lakers Get O'Neal in 7-Year Contract." *New York Times*, July 19, 1996.

"NBA Finals Delivers Record Attendance." *Business Wire*, June 27, 2005.

"The NBA Selects Digitas as Strategic Partner to Develop Integrated Web Presence." *Business Wire*, July 19, 2000.

"Owners Approve Labor Deal." *New York Times*, September 16, 1995.

Papanek, John. "Arms and the Man." *Sports Illustrated*, May 26, 1980.

Patton, Phil. "The Selling of Michael Jordan." *New York Times*, November 9, 1986.

Paul, Alan. "John Lucas: Second Chance Points." SLAM.com, January 10, 2005.

Pereira, Joseph. "Larry Bird Retires After Stellar Career with Boston Celtics." *Wall Street Journal*, August 19, 1992.

"Pistons Drive off with NBA Title." Associated Press, June 16, 2004.

Plaschke, Bill. "An Issue of Character." *Sporting News*, December 1977.

Rhoden, William C. "Bulls Keep Marching Along." *New York Times*, May 22, 1989.

_____. "N.B.A. Playoffs; After the Victory, Los Angeles Loses Its Usual Cool." *New York Times*, June 23, 1988.

_____. "N.B.A. Playoffs; Pistons Top Lakers to Lead Series 1-0." *New York Times*, June 8, 1988

_____. "Thomas Scores 33 and Pistons Even a Series." *New York Times*, May 24, 1989.

Robbins, Liz. "Carter & Co. Recharge Spirits." *New York Times*, April 25, 2000.

Roberta, Selena. "N.B.A. Giving Birth to 9-Figure Contract." *New York Times*, July 15, 1996.

Rovell, Darren. "Spirit of ABA Deal Lives on for Silna Brothers." ESPN.com, January 22, 2002.

Ryan, Bob. "The Two and Only." *Sports Illustrated*, December 14, 1992.

Sandomir, Richard. "Carter Under Glass, and Over the Top, on NBC." *New York Times*, February 29, 2000.

_____. "The Economics of a Sports Cliché." *New York Times*, June 22, 1993.

_____. "For Houston's Dignified Superstar, It's a Whole New Game." *New York Times*, June 15, 1995.

_____. "NBC's Ratings Soar Higher Than Jordan." *New York Times*, March 21, 1995.

_____. "Players Seeking Antitrust Reversal." *New York Times*, September 23, 1994.

_____. "Shoe Industry Questioning Star Power." *New York Times*, July 7, 1998.

Schreiber, Harlan. "A History of Foreign Players in the NBA." *Hoopsanalyst*, January 26, 2004.

Spears, Marc. "Thomas Stole the Show and Grabbed MVP Honor." *Denver Post*, December 26, 2004.

"Sports People; Pro Basketball; Seattle Signs McIlvaine." *New York Times*, July 23, 1996.

Stern, Mark. "Q and A with the Commish." ESPN.com, January 22, 2004.

"Stern is the $30 Million Man." *New York Times*, February 12, 1996.

Stevenson, Richard W. "Basketball Star Retires on Advice of His Doctors." *New York Times*, November 8, 1991.

Thomas, Robert. "NBA Optimistic on Finances." *New York Times*, June 7, 1988.

Thomas, Robert McG., Jr. "Jordan Thanks the Public, but Scolds the News Media for Speculation." *New York Times*, August 20, 1993.

Tillery, Ron. "Lloyd Was First to Clear Lane for Black Players in the NBA." *Scripps Howard News Service*, March 2, 2003.

Vancil, Mark. "Michael Jordan: Phenomenon." *Hoop*, December 1991.

Vecsey, George. "Big Fella Goes Back a Few Years." *New York Times*, June 15, 1989.

Vlasic, Bill, and Mark Trudy. "Is Tiger Buick's Fountain of Youth?" *Detroit News*, February 10, 2000.

Walton, Bill. "Making Sense of Senseless Acts." *ESPN Insider*, November 23, 2004.

Wilstein, Steve. "Youth Movement Catches up to NBA." Associated Press, February 21, 2005.

Wise, Mike. "Carter Hype Raises Concerns About His Growth." *New York Times*, February 27, 2000.

_____. "He Has Lost the Desire to Play at 35." *New York Times*, January 14, 1999.

_____. "Injuries Take Sparkle of All-Star Luster." *New York Times*, February 8, 1997.

_____. "It's Their Ball, and N.B.A. Owners Call for Lockout." *New York Times*, June 30, 1998.

_____. "Jordan Hasn't Lost Stuff in Basketball." *New York Times*, March 19, 1995.

_____. "Labor Standoff Knocks Out N.B.A.'s Exhibition Season." *New York Times*, October 6, 1998.

_____. "N.B.A. Suspends Player Who Attached His Coach." *New York Times*, December 5, 1997.

_____. "Wolves May Be Limited By Garnett's Contract." *New York Times*, October 3, 1997.

Wolff, Alexander. "The Hoop Life." *Sports Illustrated*, September 9, 2002.

INDEX